INDIAN COUNTRY

INDIAN COUNTRY
A History of Native People in America

Karen D. Harvey
University of Denver

Lisa D. Harjo
Choctaw Nation of Oklahoma

Fulcrum Publishing
Golden, Colorado

Cover design by Alyssa Pumphrey

Illustrations by Rose Botone, Caddo/Kiowa; Mody B. Harjo, Seminole; Leslie Skinner, Lakota; Lisa Slicer, Mohawk; Frank Salcido Comes Charging, Dené–Navajo; and Chris Wright.

Library of Congress Cataloging-in-Publication Data

Harvey, Karen D.
      Indian country : a history of Native people in America / Karen D. Harvey, Lisa D. Harjo. — 1st Fulcrum trade pbk. ed.
          p.   cm.
      Originally published: Golden, Colo. : North American Press, c1994.
      Includes bibliographical references and index.
      ISBN 1-55591-428-4 (pbk.)
      1. Indians of North America—History. 2. Indians of North America—History—Study and teaching. I. Harjo, Lisa D. II. Title.
E77.H315   1998
970.004'97—dc21   98-18357
                                                  CIP

Printed in the United States of America

0 9 8 7 6 5 4 3 2

Fulcrum Publishing
350 Indiana Street, Suite 350
Golden, Colorado 80401-5093
(800) 992-2908 • (303) 277-1623
e-mail: fulcrum@fulcrum-books.com
website: www.fulcrum-books.com

PERMISSIONS

The quotation on page xv from *Land of the Spotted Eagle* by Luther Standing Bear is reprinted with permission of the University of Nebraska Press.

The quotation on page 5 from *Lame Deer Seeker of Visions* pp. 103–5, by J. Lame Deer and R. Erdoes, is reprinted by permission of Simon & Schuster, Inc. Copyright © 1972 by John Fire/Lame Deer and Richard Erdoes.

The quotation on page 7 from *Lame Deer Seeker of Visions* p. 243, by J. Lame Deer and R. Erdoes, is reprinted by permission of Simon & Schuster, Inc. Copyright © 1972 by John Fire/Lame Deer and Richard Erdoes.

The quotation on page 12 from *Atlas of the North American Indian* p. 129, by Carl Waldman is reprinted with permission from Facts on File, New York. Copyright © 1985 by Carl Waldman.

The Account of an American Ceremony on pages 19–20 originated by Eulala Pegram is reprinted with permission of the National Council for the Social Studies.

The quotation on page 21 from *Three Strands of the Braid: A Guide for Enablers of Learning*, p. 27, by Paula Underwood, is reprinted with permission of A Tribe of Two Press.

The quotation on pages 23 and 25 from *Native American Stories*, pp. 5–9, by Joseph Bruchac, is reprinted with permission of Fulcrum Publishing, Golden, Colorado.

The quotation on page 26 from *Across an Arctic Bridge*, p. 29, by J. D. Jennings, © National Geographic Society, is reprinted with permission of the National Geographic Society.

The quotations on page 31 from *The Choctaw Before Removal* by W. Brescia are reprinted with permission of the University Press of Mississippi.

The quotation on page 32 from "Basic Call to Consciousness," from *Akwesasne Notes* is reprinted with permission of *Akwesasne Notes*.

The quotation on page 33 from *Secrets from the Past* is reprinted by permission, National Geographic Society. Copyright 1979 Books for World Explorers, *Secrets from the Past*.

The quotation on page 52 by Wilma Mankiller, from *The Meaning of Life: Reflections in Words and Pictures on Why We Are Here* by David Friend and the Editors of Life is reprinted with permission of Time Life Books and Wilma Mankiller.

The quotation on page 63 is reprinted from *The Smithsonian Book of North American Indians Before the Coming of the Europeans*, Philip Kopper (Washington DC: Smithsonian Books, 1968) page 21, by permission of the publisher.

The quotation on page 67 by Tim Giago from *The Christian Science Monitor* is reprinted with permission of the author.

The quotation on page 73 from the *Denver Post*, October 12, 1991 by Glenn Morris and Russell Means is reprinted with the permission of Glenn Morris and Russell Means of the American Indian Movement of Colorado.

The quotation on pages 77–78, "Columbus Day," by J. Durham from *Books Without Bias: Through Indian Eyes* is reprinted with permission of West End Press.

The quotation on page 80 from *The Indian Heritage of America* by A. M. Josephy, Jr. is reprinted with permission of Alfred A. Knopf.

The quotation on page 81 from *The Indian Heritage of America* by A. M. Josephy, Jr. is reprinted with permission of Alfred A. Knopf.

The quotation by Bartholomew de Las Casas on page 86 from *The Indian Heritage of America* by A. M. Josephy, Jr. is reprinted with permission of Alfred A. Knopf.

The quotation on page 89 by J. H. Suina from "Pueblo Secrecy Result of Intrusions," from *New Mexico Magazine* reprinted with permission of the author.

The quotation on page 89 from *Many Winters* by Nancy Wood is reprinted with permission of Doubleday & Company, Inc.

The poem on pages 93–94 by Paula Spencer as printed in *Kui Tatk* is reprinted with permission of the author.

For Lisa's parents, Perry and Ione,
for Karen's family of friends at Rough Rock,
and for all kids and their parents, friends, and teachers.

Contents

Introduction

So, through the very agencies that reach the mass of people, that purport to instruct, educate, and perpetuate true history—books, schools, and libraries all over the land—there have been graven false ideas in the hearts and minds of the people. Even the boys and girls throughout the country, whose sources of information are inadequate, have the thought that the Indian is a curious creature, something to be amused at, and as not having contributed worth-while things to the culture of this country. This in spite of the fact that history for this continent did not begin with the landing of the Pilgrims, and that many notable cultural events had taken place before the coming of the European; that some of the truest and greatest patriots have been American Indians, and that such names as Red Jacket, Tecumseh, and Crazy Horse would brighten the pages of any history, while the name of Sequoyah not only lights the pages of American history, but the history of achievement of all mankind.

The mothers and fathers of this land do their children an injustice by not seeing that their offspring are taught the true history of this continent and its people; that the Indian fed and nourished the weary travelers from the seas and made it possible for them to remain to enjoy life and freedom; that they were not warlike demons, but that their philosophy was one of kindness; that some of their governmental principles were unequaled for equity; that some of their crafts are even today unsurpassed; and that this country has native contributions in song, stories, music, pageantry, dance, poetry, and oratory worthy of perpetuation. True, some noteworthy scholars have done diligent work along the lines of preservation, but their works have not yet found popular recognition. True, that valuable data have been com-

piled and can be found in reference libraries, but these statistical works lack the human touch, and the Indian of the cheap magazine and the movie still remain as the best type of the First American. So it is the parents and the grade teachers of this land who now fulfill the duty of demanding that true histories be placed in the hands of the young. (Luther Standing Bear, 1978, pp. 228–29).

These eloquent and persuasive words of a prominent Native American, Luther Standing Bear, dramatically present the urgent need for a resource for teachers who would like to teach Native American students and the youth of all our diverse cultures about the true history and culture of Native people in this land.

Although Luther Standing Bear first wrote these provoking words in 1933, our curriculum and view of our Native people have changed very little. Even though there has been a recurring concern for the integration of multicultural concepts and content into curriculum and instructional materials and a renewed concern over "revisionist" history, the challenge to place true histories in the hands of the young has not been met. Negative stereotypes of our indigenous people still prevail; history is still presented from an Euro-American perspective; and the damaging effects of a biased history continue to impact all children and especially Native children. Indian youth have been robbed of their history and their heroes. And all of America's children have been robbed of the history, legends, literature, music, and art of Native American people.

Consequently, the traditional lessons that include unquestioned acceptance of violent conquest and degrading prejudice (the lessons that should never have been taught) continue to teach powerful lessons to our children, thus providing dubious direction for all our children and perpetuating a negative self-concept for Indian youth.

A complete history of Native Americans in the United States cannot be presented in a book of this size. However, the following pages will present to teachers an alternative perspective on familiar events in American history—that of American Indians.

A first step in this direction was brought into the consciousness of the American public with the movie, *Dances with Wolves*. Probably somewhat biased or overstated in its content, the movie portrayed the Indians as the "good guys" and the American cavalry as the "bad guys." What perhaps is most significant about this award-winning movie, was that it introduced, at the personal "gut level", the concept of historical bias. Many decent American citizens were taught and have come to believe that Native people were cruel and savage warriors—whooping, scalping, burning, and destroying the lives of valiant pioneers. Somehow,

they had learned that it was our manifest destiny to conquer the new continent and to "civilize," educate, and convert to Christianity the strange people who inhabited it. They weren't taught about Indian humanity, Indian families, and Native lifeways and values. They didn't learn that history is reported through the personal, cultural, and political lenses of those who report events, study records, collect data, and write textbooks and historical novels. They haven't understood that the conqueror or the dominant culture writes the history of any nation, including ours.

This history of Native people in America will begin before Christopher Columbus encountered the new world and will end with exploring how Indian people live today in our contemporary society. Contrary to what most small children believe, Indian people are not dead and residing in museums; they are alive and struggling to revive their traditional cultural ways in a rapidly changing, multicultural society. Their contemporary lives and problems are common in many ways to those of many other Americans: however, they are a displaced, often impoverished, and too frequently powerless people with a unique historical relationship to American government.

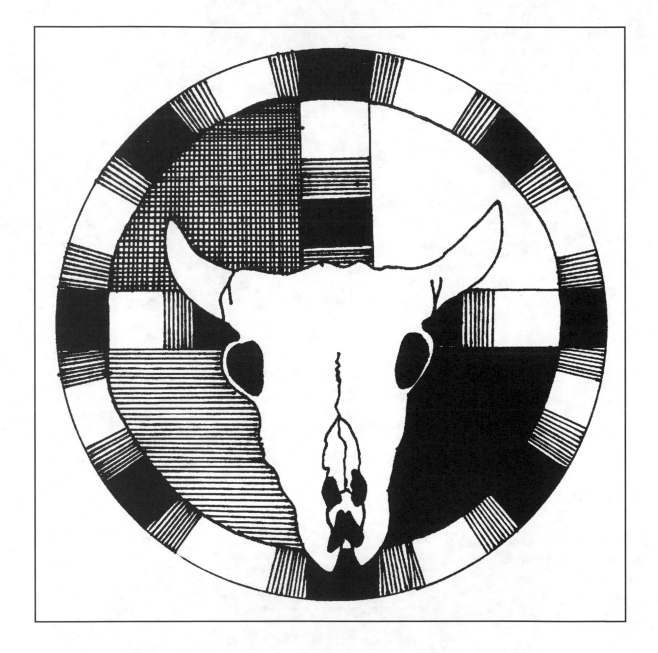

CHAPTER 1

About This Book

My brother the star,
My mother the earth,
My father the sun,
My sister the moon,
To my life give beauty,
To my body give strength,
To my corn give goodness,
To my house give peace,
To my spirit give truth,
To my elders give wisdom.
—*Source unknown*

Somehow this Indian prayer presents the right words to introduce a book—it echoes our universal needs for food, shelter, and a way of life that develops in peace, truth, and wisdom. It recognizes our enduring connection to the earth and the universe; it acknowledges that we are a part of something bigger and beyond understanding. And it asks for wisdom for those elders who lead us and make far-reaching decisions to guide our future.

Parents, caretakers, and teachers can be thought of as elders for they have adult knowledge and experience, and they guide our young people. Wisdom is acquired by delving, questioning, pondering, studying, and striving toward truth and goodness. The responsibility of elders is profound and enduring; they help children learn what they need to know; they help

to establish and maintain moral and ethical behavior; and they help fashion and mold each and every child's conception of the world, of what it is and what it can be, and of his or her place in the family and the universe.

This book will engage you in another view of American history through the stories of Native people, a story that has been previously untold (or told from another perspective). Readers are asked to engage in their own search for truth and wisdom by walking in another's moccasins. The goal is clear—American children must hear the history of Native American people. It is the responsibility of wise elders to protect the right of young people to look at many truths.

Two prominent Indian activists, Glenn Morris and Russell Means, make the following statement:

Unlike the Western tradition, which presumes some absolute concept of objective truth, and, consequently, one "factual" depiction of history, the indigenous view recognizes that there exist many truths in the world and many legitimate recollections of any given historical event, depending on one's perspective and experiences (Morris and Means, 1991, p. 7B).

It is time for all children to learn about events in American history from another perspective.

To make this book usable and adaptable to standard curriculum, its organizing structure will be based on the prevailing and familiar chronological approach to teaching American history and will have a strong emphasis on geography, anthropology, and political science. However, this book is not written just for history and social studies educators. Recognizing that while all children study American history throughout their school years, they learn about Indian people in many other places in the curriculum than their social studies or history classes. They learn through stories, celebration of traditional holidays, through the popular media, and through art, music, and food. Even nursery school and kindergarten children celebrate Thanksgiving (often in silly and superficial ways) and learn about the pilgrims and Indians. Most children also have missed opportunities for learning about Indian people.

One way to strengthen the accurate and sensitive teaching about Native people and their importance in the history of the United States is for teachers from the earliest grades to be better informed. This book will not only add to teachers' more complete understanding of Native people in America's history, it will suggest sound and practical teaching strategies.

We will follow a familiar chronological approach beginning with an initial overview of the European encounter and the early years of white penetration into North America. This basic chronological approach will extend into a central focus on the following five distinct periods of U.S. government policy toward American Indians:

1. *Separation,* during which the prime objective was to remove Indians from the land that whites desired and draw boundaries between the two peoples.

2. *Coercive assimilation,* during which whites sought to replace Indian ways with their own ways and to help them become self-sufficient farmers and artisans, under conditions dictated by whites.

3. *Tribal restoration, Phase One,* during which whites made an about-face and encouraged Indians to maintain their corporate tribal existence, if they chose to do so.

4. *Termination,* during which the objective was to break off all relationships of protection and assistance with the federal government.

5. *Tribal restoration, Phase Two,* during which tribal corporate adaptation to American society was again encouraged and cultural choice was reaffirmed (Spicer, 1982, pp. 176–203).

The long second period of cultural assimilation and the short fourth period of termination are related and must be understood as governmental policies that were intended to eliminate Indian communities, culture, political organization, and distinctive Indian ways. Indian people and culture were to die out—cease to exist—disappear into the melting pot.

By organizing the chronology of the book in this way, the understanding that public policy is a reflection of prevailing values, beliefs, and generally agreed upon goals of the citizenry and its chosen leaders will be reinforced. The intention is to lead the reader to the awareness that public policy validates, enforces, and perpetuates those identified beliefs and values and moves the nation toward these goals.

Vine Deloria, a prominent Indian scholar, adds understanding to the decision to organize the book around these five periods of American government policy with the following statement:

There is admittedly, considerably more to contemporary Indian life than legal and political notions, and it may be that unforeseen cultural changes may create a new climate in which policy considerations can be seen differently. But history tells us that cultural changes of any magnitude follow structural and institutional changes in the manner in which Indians live. The profound cultural changes Indians have experienced in the past century were partially derived from changes in the role and status of tribal governments caused by actions of the United States (1985, p. 14).

Geography is important to students' understanding of the development and history of indigenous cultures. In the

1. Arctic
2. Subarctic
3. Northwest Coast
4. Plateau
5. Plains
6. Northeast
7. Southeast
8. Southwest
9. Great Basin
10. California
11. Mesoamerica*
12. Circum-Caribbean*

*Areas outside of the geographical boundaries of the United States.
(Viola, 1990, pp. 18–19, and Waldman, 1988, p. x)

Figure 1.1—Cultural Areas of Native American People

study of Native American cultures, scholars have identified major culture areas (Figure 1.1). These culture areas, with only minor variations are designated as: (1) Arctic, (2) Subarctic, (3) Northwest Coast, (4) Plateau, (5) Plains, (6) Northeast, (7) Southeast, (8) Southwest, (9) Great Basin, (10) California, (11) Mesoamerica, and (12) Circum-Caribbean. The last two areas are not located within the United States but are a part of the history of European conquest of the Americas.

Although rich ancient cultures, such as the Aztec, Maya, Olmec, and Toltec, existed in the past in the Mesoamerican and Circum-Caribbean areas and their influence is an important part of the contemporary world, this book will not deal significantly with these culture areas as part of American history. Of course, the Taino and Arawak of the Caribbean are central to learning about the Columbian encounter, which is important to discuss. Their history is the beginning of the European conquest of Native people and the legacy of Columbus.

Too frequently, American history (from any perspective) is presented as a litany of dates, people, places, laws, and battles, draining the drama, the life, and the humanity from the story of the past. History is not dull—it is the story of people as they lived and worked to make their lives decent, honorable, meaningful, and better. It is the story of men, women, and children, tragedy and triumph, valor

and treachery, and despair, love and hope. It is the story of heroes and heroines and of everyday people just living and tending to their work, homes, and children. History should engage us in a wonderful, evolving story—a meandering story with multiple beginnings, middles, endings, and new beginnings.

To give this history the richness of human existence, case studies, stories, and Indian voice will be used along with other strategies to assist the reader in recognizing which ideas are important and how they relate to each other and major concepts and social science generalizations. To develop further knowledge of the diversity of tribal groups and how their environment and its natural resources impacted their lives, the following four major tribes or groups of tribes will be used in the case studies.

1. The Six Nations of the Iroquois Confederacy (Ir-uh-kwoy) (Northeast)
   - Mohawk (MO-hawk)
   - Oneida (O-NI-duh)
   - Onondaga (Au-nun-DAG-uh)
   - Cayuga (Ki-YOU-guh)
   - Seneca (Sen-uh-kuh)
   - Tuscarora (Tusk-uh-ROAR-uh)

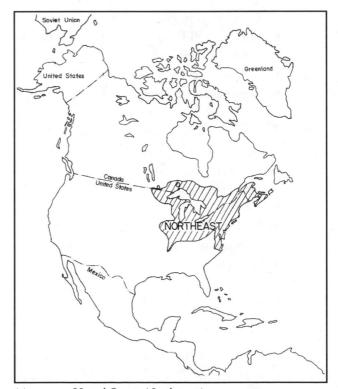

Map 1.1—United States, Northeast Area.

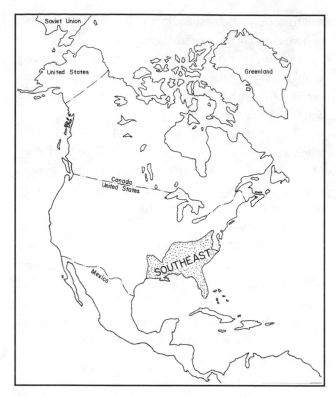

Map 1.2—*United States, Southeast Area.*

2. The Five Civilized Tribes (Southeast)
   - Cherokee (CHAIR-uh-key)
   - Chickasaw (CHICK-uh-saw)
   - Creek (CREEK) descendants of Temple Mound Builders
   - Choctaw (CHOK-taw)
   - Seminole (SEM-in-ole)

3. The Sioux (SUE) (Plains)
   There were four branches of Sioux, with different bands in each. The first and largest branch was the Teton Sioux, with the following bands:
   - Oglala
   - Brule (Sicangu)
   - Hunkpapa
   - Miniconjou
   - Oohenonpa
   - Itazipco (Sans Arcs)
   - Sihasapa

   A second branch was the Santee Sioux, with the following bands:
   - Sisseton

   - Wahpeton
   - Wahpekute
   - Mdewkanton

A third branch was the Yankton Sioux, with only one band, the Yankton.

A fourth branch was the Yanktonai Sioux, with the following bands:
- Yanktonai
- Hunkpatina
- Assiniboine—the Assiniboine later separated from their relatives.

Of all four branches, the Tetons use the Lakota version of the tribal name; the Santees say Dakota; and the Yanktons and the Yanktonais use Nakota. In the Siouan language, the name Dakota or Lakota or Nakota means "allies" (Waldman, 1988, p. 223).

4. The Desert People (Southwest)
   Many tribes live in the Southwest area, however, only two groups will be followed in the text.

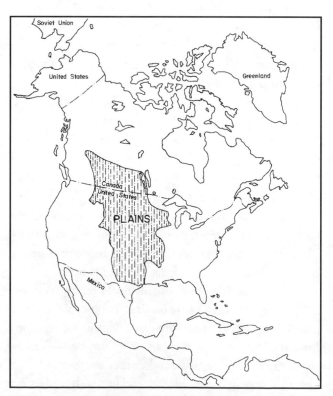

Map 1.3—*United States, Plains Area.*

- The Navajo (NAH-vuh-ho)
  The Navajos are currently the largest tribe in North America and have the most reservation lands, now sixteen million acres, including the Navajo Reservation, which is mostly in Arizona, with part in New Mexico and Utah, and the much smaller Canoncita and Ramah reservations in New Mexico (Waldman, 1988, p. 157).

- The Pueblo (PWEB-lo)
  The word "pueblo" means village in Spanish and stands for a certain kind of Indian village with a particular kind of architecture, as well as for the Indians who lived there. There were approximately nineteen different Pueblo peoples living in the Southwest culture area including the well known Zuni (Zoo-nee) people. The Hopi (HO-pee) people are within the Pueblo family but are often considered separately because of some fundamental differences.

Why only four areas? There are several practical reasons for using only four of the ten major culture

Map 1.4—United States, Southwest Area.

areas. One is to gain a sense of both continuity and change within specific and very diverse tribes or tribal groups. One recorded event in the story of a people is a snapshot in time and snapshots illustrate only a small part of a more important story. Tracing significant events through the lives of a people will help to provide a deeper understanding of and develop a more fundamental respect for their lives than the retelling of one event or story of one person. Another reason, important to the authors, is the recognition of the sacred nature of the number four in Indian spirituality—the four sacred mountains of the Navajo, the four sacred directions, the four sacred colors and so on throughout traditional Native beliefs. We honor the sacred ways.

Four is the number that is most wakan, most sacred. Four stands for Tatuye Topa—the four quarters of the earth. ... Four, the sacred number, also stands for the four winds, whose symbol is the cross. ... The Great Mystery Medicine Bag contained four times our things. ... The bundle contained four kinds of skins from the birds, four kinds of fur from the animals, four kinds of plants, four kinds of rocks and stones. ... Four things make the universe; earth, air, water, fire.

We Sioux speak of the four virtues a man should possess; bravery, generosity, endurance, wisdom. For a woman these are bravery, generosity, truthfulness, and the bearing of children.

We Sioux do everything by fours. We take four puffs when we smoke the peace pipe. Those of us who believe in the Native American Church take four times four spoons of peyote during a night of prayer. We pour water four times over the hot rocks in the sweat lodge. For four nights we seek a vision during a hanblechia.

... We set up four colored flags for all our ceremonies, which reminds me of the symbolism and powers of the colors. ... Red, white, black, yellow—these are the true colors. They give us the four directions; you might also say a trail toward our prayers (Lame Deer and Erdoes, 1976, pp. 103–105).

Cognizant of the learning styles of all students and the power of metaphor, analogy, pictures, and charts, throughout the book you will find biographies, literature, art, and graphic organizers to provide assistance to those who learn in visual ways. Graphic organizers

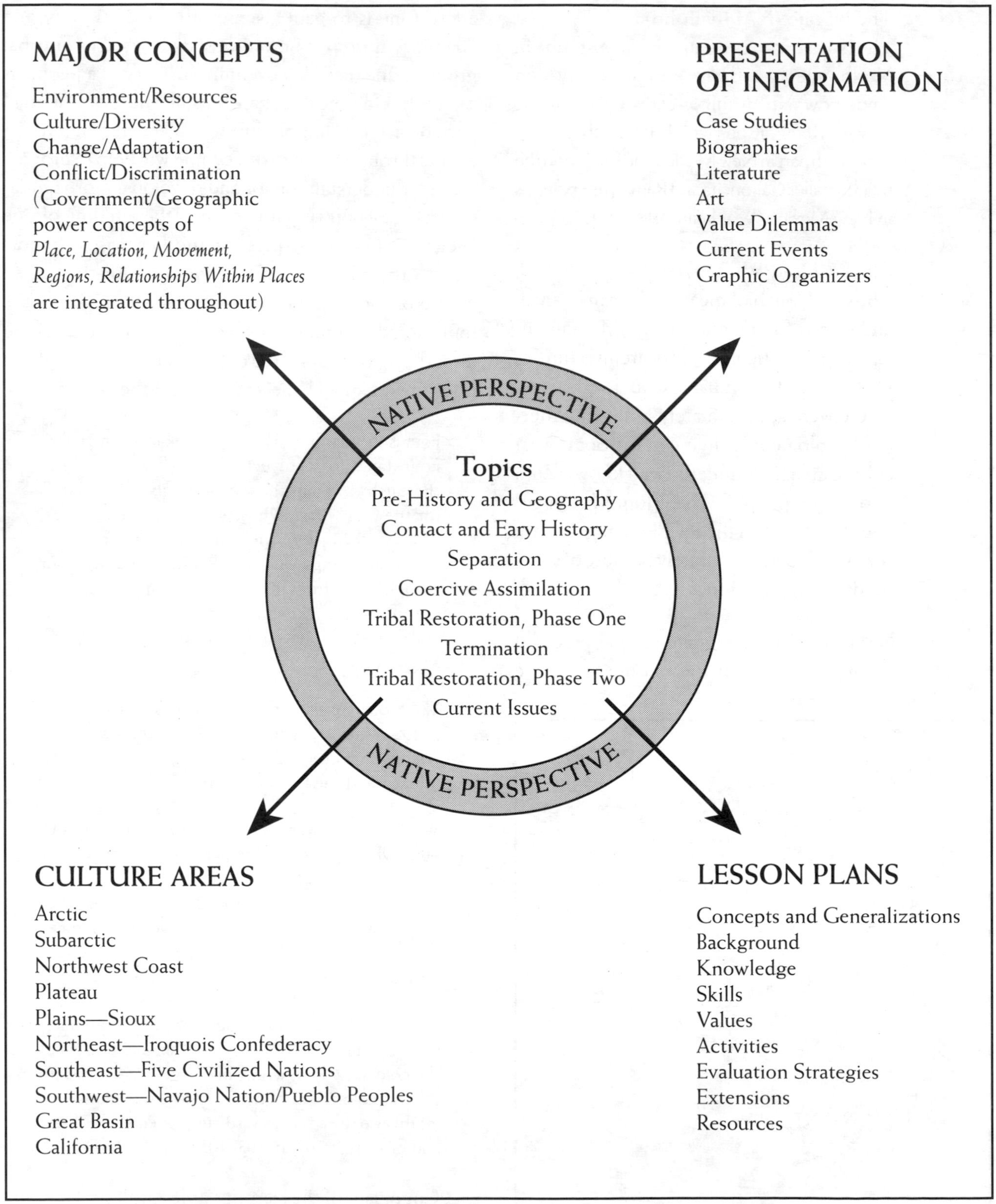

MAJOR CONCEPTS

Environment/Resources
Culture/Diversity
Change/Adaptation
Conflict/Discrimination
(Government/Geographic
power concepts of
*Place, Location, Movement,
Regions, Relationships Within Places*
are integrated throughout)

PRESENTATION OF INFORMATION

Case Studies
Biographies
Literature
Art
Value Dilemmas
Current Events
Graphic Organizers

NATIVE PERSPECTIVE

Topics

Pre-History and Geography
Contact and Eary History
Separation
Coercive Assimilation
Tribal Restoration, Phase One
Termination
Tribal Restoration, Phase Two
Current Issues

NATIVE PERSPECTIVE

CULTURE AREAS

Arctic
Subarctic
Northwest Coast
Plateau
Plains—Sioux
Northeast—Iroquois Confederacy
Southeast—Five Civilized Nations
Southwest—Navajo Nation/Pueblo Peoples
Great Basin
California

LESSON PLANS

Concepts and Generalizations
Background
Knowledge
Skills
Values
Activities
Evaluation Strategies
Extensions
Resources

Figure 1.2—Organizing Concepts

are such things as maps, charts, outlines, and other visual devices that summarize content and help students understand relationships between various parts of the presented material. The figures that have been used in this chapter are examples of graphic organizers as is Figure 1.2 which graphically presents how the book is organized. We also suggest stories be read aloud, shared as part of a rich oral history and providing yet another way for young people to learn.

Because history, as we know it, is not inevitable or confined to the past, current events and value dilemmas will be used. As citizens, we are making Native history each day. Further, important sociopolitical decisions are rarely easy. Embedded in each decision are personal and social values as well as the perspectives of multiple constituencies. Decisions often have a sense of urgency or immediacy, yet we are reminded by elders of the Iroquois that we must protect the safety and well-being of seven generations.

And finally, the content of each chapter will be summarized, in some way, for children in a form that can easily be duplicated for classroom use.

The White Buffalo Woman then turned to the children, because they have an understanding beyond their years and, among Indians, the right to be treated with the same respect which is shown to grownups. She told the little children that what the grown men and women did was for them. That the children were the greatest possession of the nation, that they represented the coming generations, the life of the people, the circle without end. "Remember this and grow up, and then teach your children," she told them (Lame Deer and Erdoes, 1976, p. 243).

Summary

This is the story of the Native peoples of North America—Indian Country. From time immemorial, from the beginning, they have lived on this sacred land and cared for it. They have struggled to maintain their individual cultures and the balance of the earth. We ask you to question old stereotypes, challenge biased history, and begin to walk through history in the moccasins of the people.

"We shall tell you of our struggles," they said.
"We are all the People of this land.
We were created out of the forces
of earth and sky, the stars and water.
We must make sure that the balance of the earth be kept.
There is no other way.
We must struggle for our lives.
We must take great care with each other.
We must share our concern with each other.
Nothing is separate from us.
We are all one body of People.
We must struggle to share our human lives with each other.
We must fight against those forces
which will take our humanity from us.
We must ensure that life continues.
We must be responsible to that life.
With that humanity and the strength
which comes from our shared responsibility
for this life, the People shall continue."

—Simon J. Ortiz
The People Shall Continue

Ortiz, S.J. (1988). *The People Shall Continue* (revised). San Francisco, CA: Children's Book Press.

CHAPTER 2

About Reading, Writing, Understanding, and Teaching History

If you and I were sitting in a circle of people on the prairie, and if I were then to place a painted drum or an eagle feather in the middle of this circle, each of us would perceive these objects differently. Our vision of them would vary according to our individual positions in the circle, each of which would be unique.

Our personal perceptions of these objects would also depend upon much more than just the different positions from which we looked upon them. For example, one or more of us might suffer from color blindness, or from weak eyesight. Either of these two physical differences would influence our perceptions of the objects.

There are levels upon levels of perspective we must consider when we try to understand our individual perceptions of things, or when we try to relate our own perceptions to those of our brothers and sisters. Every single one of our previous experiences in life will affect in some way the mental perspective from which we see the world around us.

If the thing I were to place within our circle should be an abstraction, such as an idea, a feeling, or a philosophy, our perceptions of it would then be even more complicated than if the object had been a tangible thing. And further, the number of different perceptions of it would become greater and greater as more and more people were added to our circle. The perception of any object, either tangible or abstract, is ultimately made a thousand times more complicated whenever it is viewed within the circle of an entire People as a whole. The understanding of this truth is the first lesson of the Medicine Wheel, and it is a vital part of Sun Dance Teaching.

Hyemeyohsts Storm, 1972, p. 4

The Reality of History

For far too many people history has come to mean long-ago battles, presidents, kings, dictators, and heroes and little "factlets" of the past. In teaching history, we have forgotten to introduce the challenge of the quest for knowledge, the excitement of inquiry, and the intrigue of an unfinished story. We have not led our youth to the stories of the past and the people who lived their lives as heroes, heroines, citizens, soldiers, politicians, leaders, and followers. We have not introduced them to the fascination of historical inquiry and the search for the missing pieces of our understanding.

Although the next section delineates some of the common problems of history, it is important to state clearly one of the major purposes of this book. We are telling a new story which is intended to help adults engage young people in the reality of history. With all its problems and flaws, history, nonetheless, includes the complex and intriguing stories of our past and the excitement and the intellectual challenge of dedicated inquiry leading to a greater understanding of both the past and the present.

This book, by presenting alternative perspectives, will add to greater understanding of history as disciplined inquiry and hopefully will engage students in the told and untold stories of the past and the emerging stories of today.

SOME PROBLEMS OF HISTORY
Limitations on the Historian

Although it is easy to be seduced by "facts," in reality history is complex and disorderly. When studying, teaching, or writing about history it is imperative to deal with the problems of history. Seemingly simple historical facts that have resided in our national consciousness for long periods of time, such as the "discovery" of America by Christopher Columbus or the immigration of Native people from Asia over the Bering Strait to North America and South America, become extraordinarily confusing when confronted in their complexity. Historians have delineated some of the more common problems of history which must be considered by children as well as the adults who teach them (Commager and Muessig, 1980).

The following cautions raised by Commager and Muessig should influence any presentation of the history of a people, place, period of time, or nation. History is distorted and biased—it can't be otherwise.

Availability of Historical Material

History is distorted by the limitations of the material that is available to us. Many materials of historical record come to us by chance—they reflect but a mere fraction of what may have actually happened or what may eventually be available. Consider the rare discovery of a pioneer diary, picture, or letter, incomplete figures portrayed in ancient rock art, bits of bone and pottery shards in a new digging site, and the vagaries of archaeology. How do we know if historical fragments like these, which have been recorded or discovered by chance, are an important part of the story of a people or event or a person's work or representative of a period of history? Do we even know what is accurate or authentic? We have come upon historical materials by chance and we build historical stories upon these materials.

European records are more readily available while the records of non-European societies are frequently lost, not available to scholars, or nonexistent. It is easy to assume that history is comprised of those records that are available to us and that those records are the whole of the past. Consequently, our knowledge of history, which is based entirely on the materials that are available to the historian, is fragmentary, incomplete, or lopsided, and has a decidedly European emphasis. Much of what we want or need for a true historical record is unavailable to us.

Emphasis on Written Material

History, as we know it, has been constructed largely from written records. Thus, there is a further bias in favor of the literary, history-conscious people and nations. In regard to the history of Native people, who in the past relied on the oral transmission of history and tradition, it is readily apparent that much history has been lost and that, in the early days, a great deal was recorded not by Native people, but by literate Europeans. It is this written European version of history that has come down to us and is widely accepted as true history. Consequently, the emphasis on written material has an important impact on the history of Native peoples as we know it and as it has been presented in our schools. Even much of the oral history has been obliterated. After European contact, the European diseases that nearly decimated Indian tribes also nearly destroyed the rich oral history of Native people. Many tribes were totally wiped out and in others disease was particularly cruel to the elders who were the repositories of much of the oral tradition. A great deal of oral history was lost forever when these elders died.

Enchantment with the Dramatic

What attracts the historian (and the average person) is the dramatic, the spectacular, the bizarre, and the catastrophic. One need only to read the daily newspaper or watch television news to verify this phenomenon. Is the dramatic the reality? Everyday life is rarely chronicled for the historian to review. It is understandable that the everyday life of Native people is not as well known as the lives of their leaders, famous battles, and unfamiliar ceremonies.

Spell of the Familiar

History has been conveniently divided into patterns for study. Patterns such as chronological, regional, national, and monarchial or presidential patterns, as convenient and familiar as they are, must be recognized as artificial patterns created by people, not history. History is not nearly so tidy. In fact, it is tempting to force what we know about the past into these familiar patterns. Carl Waldman gives an example of this phenomenon and how it has distorted the history of Native people:

> Once again, the various lists of wars are an oversimplification. They have been handed down historically with an implicit white bias, since more often than not their time frames have been established from army campaigns. From the Indian point of view, the Wars for the West can perhaps be best organized by tribes and by individuals. For Indian peoples, the struggle did not start and stop with particular battles, army campaigns, or treaties. For most, the war became a way of life once the settlers and soldiers began arriving, and it wasn't just a war against armies but also against hunger—as squatters usurped the land and hunger practically exterminated the buffalo for its hide—and against the whites' diseases (Waldman, 1985, p. 129). Copyright (c) by Carl Waldman. From *Atlas of the North American Indian*, reprinted with permission from Facts on File, New York.

This book also follows a familiar, but artificial, pattern—periods of governmental policy. By doing so, the study of Native people in America is more organized and perhaps easier to understand. It should be recognized

however, that this pattern was not discernible to the people living at that time. It is a product of hindsight, analysis, convenience, and perhaps of bias.

Present-Mindedness

The perspective of present-mindedness is one of the most seductive patterns. Present-mindedness has been defined as the "instinctive habit of looking at the past through our own eyes, judging it by our own standards, recreating it in our own words, or reading back into the language of the past our own meanings, assuming that whatever happened, happened in some 'past' and forgetting that every past was once a present." The past was as real to those who lived in it as the present is to us—and the outcome is not known, nor is the pattern clear. People in the past, like people in the present, live each day at a time, in the best way they know. We do not know how our own future is going to turn out nor did the people of the past.

Doctrine of Inevitability

Hindsight tends to distort history by making it seem inevitable. It is fine to acknowledge that "as far as we know, the course of history is not predestined." For example, it was not inevitable that the buffalo disappeared from the prairie, it was not inevitable that Indian people lost their ancestral land, nor is it inevitable that the problems that Indian people face today are nearly overwhelming.

This understanding compels us to try to understand the past and the present so that we might form or shape a preferable future. It is also a reminder how important it is to teach children about their own personal power and their social and political responsibility. History is made through daily decisions.

THE TROUBLE WITH FACTS
Too Few Facts

How little we actually know about prehistoric people! What is known is pieced together by expert conjecture, imagination, and deduction. We don't know now—nor will we ever know—how Indian people came to be here. We don't know enough about the mound builders, nor the Anasazi, nor the reasons why the Native language groups throughout North America are so diverse and scattered, nor where Crazy Horse was buried. We don't have enough facts.

Too Many Facts

Anyone who has tried to cope with the information explosion is aware how much information is available now and how much is being produced—faster than we can gather, assimilate, and analyze it. For example, the White House Conference on Indian Education convened in January 1992 to consider how to improve education for Indian children and attempted to synthesize myriads of factual information to determine why the academic achievement of Indian youth was lower than that of any other group in the United States. The facts regarding the achievement of Indian students were abundant and irrefutable—true understanding of this mass of data was limited however. Although information abounds, it is often difficult to use it in meaningful ways.

Factual Accuracy Is Unattainable

We can never know with certainty many things of historical interest and importance. We cannot know the population of North America when Columbus arrived or exactly how many people died in long ago battles. How were Native people psychologically affected by the tragedy of Indian removal or the trauma of Indian boarding schools, or how were stories changed as they were passed from generation to generation? What meaning or significance is lost or amended in the process of translation from one language to another? What is the meaning of the Great Serpent Mound? Why is alcohol a major problem for Indian people? Can we assume that the printed word, even in a government document, is true? What is information and what is "disinformation"? How do we determine motive or intention? Those who demand a "true" history will remain forever frustrated.

Facts Are Subjective

Consider again the people sitting in a circle on the prairie. The painted drum or eagle feather in the center of the circle is viewed differently by each person in the circle. An event is perceived uniquely by the people involved. Spaniards and Italians celebrate Columbus's discovery; Native people mourn Columbus's invasion. Even the written document that seems factual can reflect what the writer believes or what he or she wants others to believe. To complicate the issue of factual accuracy even more, think about how words and particularly abstract concepts, can convey a variety of meanings or are open to various personal and subjective interpretations. What does "medicine" mean to you? What are the rights of a sovereign dependent nation? Does the term "Indian Country" have the same meaning to Anglo-Europeans as it does to Native people?

INTERPRETATION AND BIAS

"Consciously or unconsciously, all historians are biased; they are creatures of their time, their race, their faith, their class, their country—creatures, and even prisoners." Some writers, acknowledging this situation, present their bias to the reader. In other cases, the reader is left to discern bias and attempt to understand the frame of reference of the writer. In any case, bias exists in any history. In fortunate circumstances, this bias can make history seem personal and passionate. In less fortunate circumstances, biased history is presented as truth and thus limits the intellectual curiosity that must be a part of history. Again, in all cases, we must question the concept of a "true" history—even when we are trying to present it.

JUDGMENT IN HISTORY

While it is readily acknowledged that the concept of bias permeates history, another important concept must be introduced. Is there a place for judgment in history? Should the historian merely observe and record with scientific detachment or should she make judgments of good, bad, right, wrong, moral, or immoral? Accepting that there are certain universal and timeless moral imperatives and that there are acts that are morally indefensible such as genocide, rape, and cruelty, historians must indeed make judgments. These judgments are not bound by culture, gender, time, or place—they are judgments of moral consciousness that transcend these narrow boundaries.

It is not only possible but imperative to judge the Sand Creek Massacre of 1864 morally *wrong*. Colonel John Chivington led a force of about seven hundred men, many of them drinking heavily, into an Indian camp under Chief Black Kettle (Cheyenne) who had raised both an American and a white flag over his tipi. Chivington had a policy to take no prisoners and as many as two hundred Indians, more than half of them women and children died. This was a massacre. To label it with any other term would lead us away from the valuable lessons of the past.

Luther Standing Bear has urged that true history be placed in the hands of young people. He wanted the stories of true Indian heroes and true Indian people to be told. Truth is impossible; but the presentation of history from alternative perspectives, from other parts of the circle is possible. Now it is time for the eagle feather and the drum, the heartbeat of the people, to be in the center of this circle—Native American perspectives on American history and its heroes will be heard.

Finally, the rich history of American Indian people cannot be allowed to be an unchallenged or lifeless history of the past! If teachers are going to teach about the history of Native people in America in a different way, they must 1) extend their knowledge of contemporary Native people, 2) teach about contemporary social and moral issues, and 3) teach Native history at every grade level and throughout the curriculum. The following ideas are offered as beginning points for professional thought and development.

Extending Knowledge of Contemporary Native People

People who live in urban areas or near reservations are certain to have available to them Native people and organizations who are willing to serve as appropriate resources. In addition, there are other ways for teachers and parents to hear the voices of Indian Country and to better understand an Indian world view. Those who wish to extend their knowledge can:

• Study: develop authoritative information about Native people by taking classes offered by colleges, universities, museums, and historical societies.

• Read: obtain a variety of perspectives on any given tribe, incident, policy, or period of time. Make every effort to read works by Native authors, including novels, in order to hear Indian voice. Native newspapers are appropriate resources on contemporary culture and issues (see Appendix L).

• Consult: seek the views and opinions of Native American elders, historians, artists, and tribal members to obtain their perspective.

• Participate: enjoy cultural events such as pow-wows, rodeos, and art shows in your community, whenever possible.

Teaching About Contemporary Social and Moral Issues

Native people are not dead and residing in museums—Indian history is being made today. To rely on textbooks is to teach about Indians as historical relics and ignore the issues that concern Indian people today. We must take care not to imply that Indians are part of a once great, but now dying, culture. Native people are alive and actively engaged in political, economic, and social issues. Do they allow nuclear waste to be deposited on ancestral lands? How do they educate their children to live productively in a rapidly changing technological society? How do they maintain or restore their traditional languages and culture? How do they deal with poverty? How do they use their valuable resources? How do they remain healthy? How do they deal with the insensitivity and racism inherent in the images of Indian people presented in popular books, songs, films, and television? By learning about contemporary Indian people and issues, we teach about history in the making.

Teaching Native History at Every Grade Level and Throughout the Curriculum

History is usually taught under the broader social science area designated as social studies. However, to teach about Indian people only in social studies classes is limiting. Indians are a unique part of the diverse peoples of this nation and they have made contributions in many fields. Consequently, we should refer to or teach about them in all areas of the curriculum including reading, language arts, literature, art, music, and science. Our indigenous people deserve a special place in the history of our country as well as recognition in all areas of the curriculum that they are a vital and valuable part of our present and future. We should note also that Indian values and lifeways are also represented in such outside-of-school activities as scouting; these too are opportunities for learning.

LESSON PLAN: PERSPECTIVES AND PERCEPTION

Grade Level: Primary/intermediate/middle school

Basic Concepts: Perspective and historical bias

Organizing Generalization: The same situation, action, and/or event can be reported or described differently by different people. Each person is likely to believe that his or her account is the "truthful" or objective account.

Objectives:

Knowledge

Students will:

1. Give an example of how people can describe a particular event or object differently.
2. Give at least one reason why people believe certain accounts of particular situations, events, or actions are "truthful" or objective.
3. Describe a situation or object from several perspectives.

Skills

Students will:

1. Analyze an object from several perspectives.
2. Extrapolate from a simulated situation to everyday situations where it is important to understand that alternative perspectives are possible.

Values

Students will:

1. Recognize that objectivity and the "true" story are hard to achieve.
2. Respect the validity of the viewpoints of others.

Activities:

There are several approaches to this lesson—either approach will achieve the desired objectives.

1. Seat students in a large circle in which you have placed an object or objects. A circle of stones, with a fire and several objects such as a drum and rattle in the center works well, but if that is impossible, the activity can still be used with other objects. Take care with the objects that you use—there should be some details that can only be noticed or described by students in certain parts of the circle. If possible, plan also for such details as a small bird that can be suspended inconspicuously above the fire and a figure of a small animal (a button to represent a bug will work). If using a make-believe fire, for example, use some sage or cedar incense to give additional sensory input.
2. Using a large chart to record responses, ask students to describe the center of the circle. For example:
   a. Did anyone notice how many stones there were in the circle? How many logs on the fire?
   b. What else did you see? Did anyone see the bird and the mouse (bug)?
   c. Did you smell anything?
   d. How did I light the fire?
   e. How long did it take to begin to burn?
   f. Describe the drum? How tall is it? How is it decorated?
   g. Shut your eyes—how many people are sitting around the fire? Are there more boys than girls? More girls than boys? Is anyone wearing a blue shirt (sweater)?

3. Another approach might be to talk first about the circle of people and the fire within the circle. Then read a story to students from your place within the circle. After the story, ask them to return to their seats and draw a picture of the circle, including the object(s) in the center. A wonderful story to read would be *Who Speaks for Wolf* by Paula Spencer. The Teacher's Guide for this book talks of the central fire—a concept that is explained later in this chapter.

4. Students' responses to the questions or their pictures should indicate different perspectives. Some students won't notice details, some won't be able to estimate time and size; all within the circle will have a different point of view.

5. Discuss what is the "right" description. Point out that each person within the circle has a different point of view—that each is right in his or her own way. Yet, each has missed something. You may also point out that the bird above and the tiny mouse or bug would have a different picture or description. (You might even ask the children to draw or describe the circle from the bird's or bug's place.)

Extensions:

1. Cut several pictures of children or families from other cultures from such magazines as *National Geographic*, include pictures of American children of differing racial and ethnic backgrounds, including Native Americans. Ask students to list adjectives that describe these people. They are likely to use terms such as weird, strange, and ugly to describe those who differ significantly from them. Discuss how we tend to use derogatory terms to describe people who are not like us and who we don't understand.

2. Reread *Who Speaks for Wolf* focusing on the concepts of perspective and alternatives. Decisions have consequences and those consequences can be considered from many perspectives. A good question to keep in mind would be, "Can we look at a problem or situation from another point of view?" These concepts are developmentally difficult (or impossible) for very young children. This is a good story to read, and reread, and reread. Don't press for your interpretation.

It is not in the manner of the People to explain. Rather, it is in the manner of the People to provide additional information and allow each individual to reach his/her own tentative conclusions (Spencer, 1984) p.3.

Evaluation: Stage an event—a scuffle, argument, or surprising incident—to occur unexpectedly in the classroom. Ask children to describe what happened. The children's accounts are likely to be significantly different, even though they observed the same incident. Children should be able to reflect the understanding that any story or recorded event is presented from a particular perspective and that there are other perspectives that can be considered as true also.

Materials/Resources:

1. Materials for a real or simulated campfire and a few appropriate objects to place near the fire.
2. Spencer, P. *Who Speaks for Wolf?* San Anselmo, CA: Tribe of Two Press, 1983.
3. Spencer, P. *Three Strands in the Braid: A Guide for Enablers of Learning.* San Anselmo, CA: Tribe of Two Press, 1984.

LESSON PLAN: HISTORICAL DISTORTION

Grade Level: Middle School

Basic Concepts: Culture, diversity, and ethnocentrism

Organizing Generalization: Situations, actions, and events are interpreted and reported through the cultural perspective of the observer.

Culture Area: Southwest

Time Period: Contemporary

Background: In order for students to understand some of the problems inherent in historical accounts, it is important for them to understand that any situation, action, or event is reported through the cultural perspective of the recorder. Interpretation of events then can often provide distorted interpretation. Judgments made from cultural, national, or personal perspectives are often invalid and can lead to serious misunderstanding about historical events and between cultures.

Objectives:

Knowledge
Students will:
1. Demonstrate basic understanding of the generalization by giving a concrete example.
2. Identify at least three problems of historical distortion when cultural perspectives are not considered when interpreting the behaviors of another cultural group.

Skills
Students will:
1. Hypothesize the values of a historian that are demonstrated in his/her report of a given event.
2. Distinguish between a descriptive and an interpretative account of an event.

Values
Students will:
1. Understand that history as well as current events are understood from a personal, cultural, and historical perspective.
2. Begin to seek other perspectives on cultures, events, and people before rendering a value judgment.

Activities:
1. Divide the class into teams of three, giving each team a copy of the Account of an American Ceremony (see p. 19–20) and a worksheet.
2. One member of each team will read the account aloud to team members. After a discussion of the account, team members will complete the worksheet.
3. After sharing some of the worksheet responses of each group the class will discuss the following question:
    What, if any, is the value of this exercise?
4. Each student will submit an "I learned ... " statement.

Extensions:

1. Collect newspaper articles such as the following that represent an alternative perspective on a commonly understood event. Students could write the news articles from yet another point of view or discuss what factors are likely to cause distortion in reported events.

   Representative Ben Nighthorse Campbell, Democrat–Colorado, the only American Indian in Congress, said Native Americans equate the celebration of Columbus Day and the colonization of America with Nazi Germany's Holocaust. "I don't go around pouring (simulated) blood on statues," said Campbell, a Northern Cheyenne, referring to militant anti-Columbus Day demonstrations. "But a majority (of Indians) see no reason to celebrate Columbus Day—other than that they weren't all killed" (Denver Post, October 15, 1991).

2. Some students might want to discuss how typical teen behavior appears to teachers and parents, and how it might be misunderstood.

Evaluation: The "I learned" statements will indicate if students have an understanding of the generalization.

ACCOUNT OF AN AMERICAN CEREMONY

One important ceremony in the American culture involves a seasonal ceremony featuring two religious factions.

The religious contests are held during the colder months in specially constructed ceremonial grounds surrounded by seats for people who, while not practitioners of the religion, seem to not be merely observers either. It is not clear what stake they have in the proceedings, unless it is to support, encourage, or possibly to record or learn a religion lesson from the participants of the ceremony. It appears not to be a historical pageant, for the outcome of the contest varies.

The participants themselves are dressed from head to foot in ceremonial garb especially designed to protect them during the ceremony. All of the representatives are male and are dressed alike except for color. The participants represent two distinct sects with the symbols that represent their deity or sect on their headgear.

Several other men are dressed in black and white clothing without protection. Their function in the ceremony seems to be that of high priests, since a shrill noise from them has the power to halt the ceremony while they make dramatic gestures that seem to be part of the ritual and have meaning to the participants and the observers. On occasion, humans dressed as animals dance about the arena, somewhat similar to kachinas. Usually there are several other male and female participants dressed in the same colors, but performing the function of exciting the observers, rather than participating directly in the ceremony.

The ceremonial arena itself has been decorated with religious markings and writings that seem to designate the significance of certain parts of the field.

The two areas at each end of the arena appear to be the holiest locations and the object of the contest seems to be to reach this holy sanctuary, since the response from the participants and the spectators is the most energetic when one of these areas has been entered, especially when the religious representative possesses an odd-shaped oblong object that is pointed at each end. This object seems to hold great religious significance to both sides and their supporters in the surrounding seats. The possession of this sacred object appears to be one of the objectives of the contest.

While the participants in each contest change from time to time, the activities of the ceremony involve lining up facing each other and, at some mysterious signal, each representative in the arena struggles with or tries to escape his opposite, or will sometimes try to catch and harm the possessor of the oblong icon. Each group meets together occasionally on the field to pray, but it is unclear whether these prayers are for strength, victory, or just courage for the next encounter.

Brute strength and running speed seem to be highly prized abilities in this religious sect. It appears to be a very common religion in America.

(The originator of *A Cultural Account of an American Ceremony* is Eulala Pegram, member of the Creek Tribe, who is a teacher in Colorado Springs, Colorado. This activity was first used, in a slightly different version, in *Teaching About Native Americans* (1990) which was published by the National Council for the Social Studies.)

WORKSHEET/DISCUSSION QUESTIONS

This is an historical account or record of a ceremonial event. The writer is describing what he or she has observed in objective terms.

1. What is being described?

2. What is factually correct about this description? How do you know?

3. What is wrong with this description? How do you know?

4. Has the writer ever talked to anyone who knows about this event?

5. Does this account tell very much about the culture of the participants?
   If so, what?

6. Does it tell very much about the culture of the writer? If so, what?

CENTRAL FIRE

Central Fire is anything that draws people together, casting light that enables otherwise impossible perceptions for anyone who opens their eyes. It is not that this is a chosen symbol to which much meaning is attached. Rather, it is the other way around. It has been the nature of all two-leggeds to gather around a fire, sharing its light and warmth, for so long that if you conceptualize anything that draws people together and enables new perceptions as a Central Fire, you use different parts of your brain for such thinking and enable a new and greater integration with all previous understanding, both within the individual and within the group.

So Grandfather's words are a Central Fire between him and the Boy of Eight Winters, drawing them together and casting a light enabling new perceptions to each if they will only open their eyes. The Boy shows by his questions that he is learning. Grandfather shows by his smile that he sees something in the boy's face he has and yet has not seen before, seeing with the reflected light of his own words.

It is inaccurate to say that all this symbolism is attached to a symbol. Rather, symbols are chosen because of their inherent meaning to the People. One walks through the symbol toward greater understanding. ... It is three-, not two-, dimensional.

The words are the wood one uses to lay the fire. The rhythm of the chant is the tinder. Listening is the spark which may or may not kindle the flame of understanding. Smoke is the residue of understanding, the implication of possible future fire, a sign to distant others that understanding is here.

Picture images, interacting with nonverbal concepts, allow more integrated understanding, draw the elements of individual thinking toward its own Central Fire.

So, in *Who Speaks for Wolf*, the text is the Central Fire, the wood and the kindling provided by the author, the spark by the reader, and the flame of understanding. ...

"Now, what favor have I done you with this explanation? Beauty is here, you say, but what beauty? The beauty is the understanding. The understanding is mine. In showing you my understanding, I have discouraged your own. Value gained for value lost?"

Spencer, Paula (1991) *Three Strands in the Braid: A Guide for Enablers of Learning*. San Anselmo, CA: Tribe of Two Press.

SUMMARY
SOME PROBLEMS OF HISTORY

The problem with studying about history is that history has so many problems! Strange as it may seem, there is no "true" history. The historical events that we have learned and assumed are "true" are merely the best efforts of historians to get as close to the truth as possible. However, their efforts are tentative reports of men and women who reflect the viewpoints of a particular time, race, religion, and country. And they work with incomplete information!

Pretend for a moment that each member of your class is a historian. As a group you must explain the American observance of Christmas in 1992 to people living in 2992. What was the meaning of Christmas? How was it observed? Why was it a holiday? Who celebrated Christmas? Will the people in your class have different points of view? Would your parents describe Christmas differently?

If you were living in 2992 you might have only fragmentary evidence of Christmas in 1992—such as the diary of a shop owner from what used to be known as Florida, a replica of a tree made of some sort of synthetic fiber, and several statues of an overweight male (probably a god or idol of some kind). How would you piece together a record of Christmas in 1992? Would your classmates reach the same conclusions? Who would be right?

Think of history as a giant jigsaw puzzle that has many pieces missing. Archaeologists and historians continually work to uncover more pieces of the historical puzzle, to interpret and reinterpret the pieces that they have, and to develop greater understanding of the world and its people.

In the meantime, we must understand that American history is distorted and biased—it can't be otherwise. Most frequently it has been told from a Euro-American perspective. Now we will hear the perspective of the Indian.

CHAPTER 3

In the Beginning

THE EARTH ON TURTLE'S BACK

Before this Earth existed, there was only water.

It stretched as far as one could see, and in that water there were birds and animals swimming around. Far above, in the clouds, there was a Skyland. In that Skyland there was a great and beautiful tree. It had four white roots which stretched to each of the sacred directions, and from its branches all kinds of fruits and flowers grew.

There was an ancient chief in the Skyland. His young wife was expecting a child, and one night she dreamed that she saw the Great Tree uprooted. The next morning she told her husband the story.

He nodded as she finished telling her dream. "My wife," he said, "I am sad that you had this dream. It is clearly a dream of great power and, as is our way, when one has such a powerful dream we must do all that we can to make it true. The Great Tree must be uprooted."

Then the ancient chief called the young men together and told them that they must pull up the tree. But the roots of the tree were so deep, so strong, that they could not budge it. At last the ancient chief himself came to the tree. He wrapped his arms around it, bent his knees and strained. At last, with one great effort, he uprooted the tree and placed it on its side. Where the tree's roots had gone deep into the Skyland there was now a big hole. The wife of the chief came close and leaned over to look down, grasping the tip of one of the Great Tree's branches to steady her. It seemed as if she saw something down there, far below, glittering like water. She leaned out further to look and, as she leaned, she lost her balance and fell into the hole. Her hand slipped off the tip of the branch, leaving her with only a handful of seeds as she fell, down, down, down, down.

Far below, in the waters, some of the birds and animals looked up.

The Navajo Emerge into this World.

"Someone is falling toward us from the sky," said one of the birds.

"We must do something to help her," said another. Then two Swans flew up. They caught the Woman From the Sky between their wide wings. Slowly, they began to bring her down toward the water, where the birds and animals were watching.

"She is not like us," said one of the animals. "Look, she doesn't have webbed feet. I don't think she can live in the water."

"What shall we do, then?" said another of the water animals.

"I know," said one of the water birds. I have heard that there is Earth far below the waters. If we dive down and bring up Earth, then she will have a place to stand."

So the birds and animals decided that someone would have to bring up Earth. One by one they tried.

The Duck dove down first, some say. He swam down and down, far beneath the surface, but could not reach the bottom and floated back up. Then the Beaver tried. He went even deeper, so deep that it was all dark, but he could not reach the bottom, either. The Loon tried, swimming with his strong wings. He was gone a long, long time, but he, too, failed to bring up Earth. Soon it seemed that all had tried and all had failed. Then a small voice spoke. "I will bring up Earth or die trying."

They looked to see who it was. It was the tiny Muskrat. She dove down and swam and swam. She was not as strong or as swift as the others, but she was determined. She went so deep that it was all dark, and still she swam deeper. She went so deep that her lungs felt ready to burst, but she swam deeper still. At last, just as she was becoming unconscious, she reached out one small paw and grasped at the bottom, barely touching it before she floated up, almost dead.

When the other animals saw her break the surface they thought she had failed. Then they saw her right paw was held tightly shut.

"She has the Earth," they said, "Now where can we put it?"

"Place it on my back," said a deep voice. It was the Great Turtle, who had come up from the depths.

They brought the Muskrat over to the Great Turtle and placed her paw against his back. To this day there are marks at the back of the turtle's shell which were made by Muskrat's paw. The tiny bit of Earth fell on the back of the Turtle. Almost immediately, it began to grow larger and larger and larger until it became the whole world.

The two Swans brought the Sky Woman down. She stepped onto the new Earth and opened her hand, letting the seeds fall onto the bare soil. From those seeds the trees and the grass sprang up. Life on Earth had begun.

Bruchac, J. (1991), 5-9.

This is a sample of the rich oral tradition that exists today among the American Indians concerning their emergence on this continent. However, there are at least two ways of explaining the origin or beginnings of the modern American Indian. One way is rooted in the rich tradition and spirituality of each tribe. Traditionally, each tribe tells their own emergence story which is a spiritual story and it tells where the "People" came into being and how to survive in this world. The other way, the way of the archaeologist, is more familiar and it is the story that commonly is told in our textbooks. Scientifically, archaeologists and anthropologists have come to believe that the American Indian crossed from Asia to Alaska via the Bering Strait in successive migrations.

Perhaps Alfonso Ortiz (1991) puts these two divergent theories in proper order, at least for many Indian people, when he states:

> But a Tewa is not so interested in the world of archaeologists ... A Tewa is interested in our own story of our origin, for it holds all that we need to know about our people, and how one should live as a human. The story defines our society. It tells me who I am , where I came from ...

Now, let's examine creation and the first Americans from both perspectives. Time is a continuum. The story of human past is a story of countless generations of animals and people. It is the history of their adaptation for continuous survival which has preceded contemporary people and provided a legacy for them. History is the time that came before us that is recorded in written form; prehistory is the story of human life before the written record. Prehistory is woven from oral tradition and the physical remains of human beings and their lives. Archaeologists also use ethnological studies of both modern and historic Indians to give a glimpse of how prehistoric Indians might have lived. The scientific story is told by the archaeologist; the origin story is passed along by traditional storytellers and the elders.

Both history and prehistory present problems for those who want to understand the past. We have discussed the problems of written history as recorded and interpreted by a variety of individuals with differing perspectives. Their stories of history reflect their own unique personal, political, and cultural perspectives.

Prehistory shares the problems of history but also has its own problems. Fundamental to these problems is its speculative nature—there are no written records. It is the process of piecing together bits of physical evidence such as bones of man or animal, fire coals, pottery, and other refuse from the distant past into a picture of early life. And many of the pieces are missing.

Scientific techniques such as stratigraphy, radiocarbon, dendrochronology and other means of scientifically examining and testing artifacts to determine dates of origin are not precise—however, new technology continues to render them more or nearly so. Sites with their physical evidence are wholly buried, finding them is not easy—thus the element of chance is present. As a consequence, researchers draw different and sometimes conflicting conclusions as a result of their research on prehistoric Indian peoples.

> The story I tell is of the American Indian before the writing of his history began. It is a story no scribe ever carved in stone, no wise old chieftain ever told to a circle of eager young faces. Archaeologists have had to tease it from the stubborn earth at a thousand places where its paragraphs and chapters lay hidden beneath the sediment of ages (Jennings, 1989, p. 29).

There are rigorous tests that are commonly used by scientists to determine whether or not a particular claim of prehistory is accepted. In regard to Paleo-Indian sites, a find must:

1. Lie sealed under unbroken layers of later sediment.
2. Yield diagnostic artifacts such as Clovis or Folsom points.
3. Be in close association with now extinct mammals like the mammoth.
4. Since 1950, yield radiocarbon dates older than 10,000 years ago (Jennings, 1989, p. 30).

In the scientific community, archaeologists study prehistory, and one of the frequently used tools of their research involves digging up the middens, or trash piles, of ancient civilizations. Artifacts are retrieved, classified, categorized, and analyzed to construct a "picture" of what life might have been like in ages past.

Archaeologists also use other known information about prehistory regarding geology, weather patterns, plants, animals, and insects. Physical evidence of ancient Native life is somewhat limited due to the lifestyle of the ancient Americans. During this long ago period of time on the North American continent wood, hide, and stone were used in daily life for thousands of years. These materials participated in Indian life. This is consistent with the life philosophy of the first Americans of living in harmony with nature; being a part of the natural life cycle. Unfortunately, however, for the archaeologist who wants to learn about these ancient lifeways, these natural materials do not always leave a permanent record of the life that existed. Dry caves in the southwest result in excellent preservation for perishable items. Wood, leather, textiles, even human hair and skin, are preserved.

Evidence has been found by archaeologists which has led to the establishment of periods of civilization or stages of development (evolution) of human beings in North and South America. These structures help to organize the study of the past and make it easier to understand. The following periods are not totally separate; they overlap each other. They have been established as if they were a puzzle, pieced together with all the information that was available at the time they were established. Not all the pieces are available to us. As years pass and new finds emerge, new theories are developed. A look at the periods, the evidence used, and the cultures that represent these periods confirms that prehistory is indeed difficult and there is still very little that is truly "known" about ancient America.

LITHIC PERIOD 50,000–5,000 B.C.

The Lithic Period can be divided into three stages: (1) the Pre-Projectile-Point stage, (2) the Paleo-Indian stage, and (3) the Protoarchaic stage. The three categories are usually referred to as simply the Paleo-Indian tradition.

Paleo-Indian Tradition

The Pre-Projectile-Point Period extends from approximately 50,000–25,000 B.C. It includes the development and use of projectile points by hunters. This period was characterized by the name Pre-Projectile because stone points on spears were not used as yet.

The site at Old Crow Flats in the Yukon Territory yielded a caribou bone tool which has been estimated to be twenty-seven thousand years old. Stones that appeared to have been chipped by human hands and which were found in the Orogrande cave in southern New Mexico date back to 38,000 B.C. These finds constitute some of the oldest evidence of the existence of humans that has been found in North America. Since stones were not as yet crafted for use as spear tips, the artifacts of the age include roughly crafted bone and stone instruments for scraping and pounding. It is believed that hunters used fire to harden the wooden spear tips used in hunting. The people of this time survived by following the large woolly mammoths.

Tentative dates become confusing. Most archaeologists believe that Native people are immigrants from Asia (thus leading to the concept that all American citizens are immigrants). The land bridge known in archaeology and cited in history books as Beringia was formed between twelve thousand to twenty thousand years ago by ice glaciers that drew up the waters of the earth revealing otherwise submerged land. It is generally believed that in successive movements, the people we now call Native Americans or American Indians crossed over this land bridge as it rose out of the water. The people were not conscious immigrants, they were simply following their major source of sustenance— the large woolly mammoths they needed in order to live. To live on the frigid Arctic tundra, the people needed to survive subzero temperatures for months on end, construct durable shelters, fabricate clothes of hides and fur, build fires at will, and hunt in groups.

This land bridge, Beringia, was created during the Pliestocene Age, a descriptive term for the stage of the land development that corresponds to the Pre-Projectile Period. During the Pliestocene Age, the earth was covered with ice four times. The tentative evidence that seems to support this conclusion are the distinctly different language groups and technological development in different areas of the North American continent. However, according to some scientists, the earth did not warm up for southern expansion until as late as fourteen thousand years ago. This contradicts the evidence dated as far back as 38,000–20,000 B.C. and demonstrates that differing opinions exist in the scientific community regarding the dates of the emergence

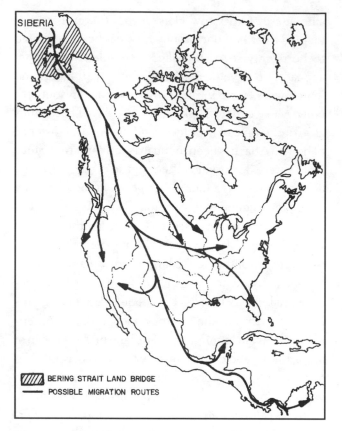

Map 3.1—*Beringia.*

mastodon bones. This type of arrow or spear point has not been found on the Asian continent, suggesting that this technology evolved in North America. Evidence has been found across the continent documenting the life of the people who lived at this time and demonstrating that they lived in various parts of the continent with differing technology. The Clovis point is characteristic of what is called the Llano culture.

The Folsom point became dominant about 8000 B.C. and characterizes the Folsom culture. The Plano point was active from about 7500–4500 B.C. and is used to name the Plano culture. These people hunted primarily extinct forms of bison. The Plano Indians are considered to be a bridge to the Archaic Period because they demonstrated a more varied economy than that of big game hunting of the Llano (Clovis), or Folsom people.

Other archaeological evidence of human life during the Paleo-Indian Period includes fragments of human bone dating back as far as 14,000–11,000 B.C. found in more than eleven layers of artifacts in a rock shelter near what today is Pittsburgh, Pennsylvania, and a turtle shell

of human beings on the North American continent and how they got here.

The Paleo-Indians are considered to be the first inhabitants of the Americas, yet they were probably not the very first arrivals. As we have noted, there are other claims of sites and artifacts that are older and would support the existence of humans in North America before this period.

Around 10,000 B.C. hunters began to fashion stones and flint into spear tips for hunting. Paleo-Indian phases are determined by the type of spear point, which characterized particular cultures. These include the Clovis point, the Folsom point, and the Plano point. Artifacts of this period have been found among bones of the animals that they were hunting. The Clovis point, named for the location in Clovis, New Mexico, where it was first discovered by archaeologists, was used by hunters from around 9500–8000 B.C. During this period the people were fierce hunters who had learned how to fashion tools to help them in their work. Clovis points have been found mostly in mammoth and

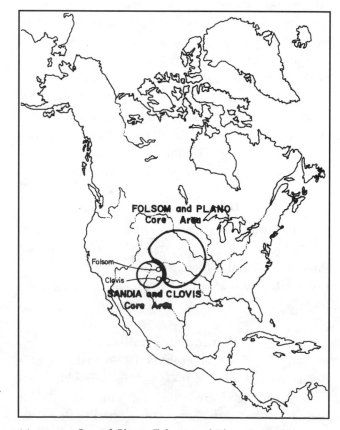

Map 3.2—*Sites of Clovis, Folsom, and Plano Point Cultures.*

was found in Little Salt Springs, Florida, dating back to around 10,000 B.C. The turtle had in it a wooden stake that yielded a radiocarbon date of 10,000 B.C.

ARCHAIC PERIOD 8000 B.C.
(OR 5000)–1000 B.C.

At the end of the Paleo-Indian tradition, there was a significant environmental change. As the climate became drier and warmer, the Pleistocene animals died off and were replaced by smaller game. To adapt to this changing environment, the Archaic Indians (foraging Indians) began to use a broader spectrum of resources, concentrating more on foraging and gathering and less on hunting. This is an important example of how early people adapted to a changing environment.

Thus, the Archaic Period is distinguished by gatherers of nuts, berries, seeds, and shellfish; hunters with spears; and the beginning use of pottery. This period lasted from about 8000–1000 B.C. and was characterized by migratory living. The warming of the earth and the environment yielded many new foods for the people and made their lives easier, changing their lifeways. Bone, wood, antler, stone, hide, and plant fiber were used to make tools and utensils such as spears, mauls, hammers, grinding stones, pipes, storage pots, cooking baskets, and other containers. Heated stones were used in baskets of boiling water for cooking along with roasting. The Cochise culture thrived during this time in modern-day Arizona and New Mexico. Their lives were tied to Lake Cochise and as the waters began to disappear their lives changed. They began to depend more on their own agricultural abilities. They gathered up all edible wild plants such as yucca, prickly pear, and piñon, nurturing these wild species. Evidence found in Bat Cave, New Mexico, reveals that they had domesticated corn as early as 3300 B.C. The original ears were very small, growing only to a length of three to four inches with diameter of one to one and one-half inches.

FORMATIVE PERIOD 1500 B.C.
(OR 1000)–1000 (OR 1500) A.D.

Life during this period on the continent centered on the raising of corn, gourds, and squash. In more northern territories, Native people hunted with the bow and arrow. The use of textile and pottery was common as well as basketry. Evidence reveals that cities of thirty thousand to forty thousand people grew up with complex societies and beliefs. This period extended from 1500 B.C.–1000 A.D. Civilizations of this period had mastered living in large, sedentary groups and agriculture that would support the population. Two very well-developed civilizations of this formative stage were the Mound Builders of the East and the Anasazi of the Southwest.

The Anasazi, named in Navajo meaning "Enemies of Our Ancient Ones," lived in the southwestern part of the United States. The early Anasazi lived in pit houses and cliff dwellings. By 700 A.D., they used creative irrigation techniques to support their corn and squash diet. According to their belief, the *kiva*, a religious structure and community building, had a *sipapu*, which is a small hole in the floor to provide access to the lower world from where humans had come. At this time they began to domesticate plants and animals and were able to stay in one place for a longer period of time. They soon learned to grow beans and weave baskets. They fired pots in the coals of the fire and used a bed of mulch to give new color and texture to their pottery.

They began to live in larger and larger above ground villages, some with populations as large as five thousand. Many pueblos had more than four hundred rooms and housed fifty to one hundred families. By 1200 A.D. the Anasazi had developed a flourishing economy and life that included sophisticated agriculture, architecture, engineering, trade, and social organization. Walls, bowls, and other serving dishes and utensils were decorated with painted designs. Their lifestyle was intertwined with the climate. Some villages were occupied only one hundred years. When the rains changed the people moved. Beginning about 1160 A.D. a prolonged drought set in the southwest and by 1300 A.D., the Anasazi disappeared. It is believed that they went south and east looking for land and climate that better suited their needs.

The Anasazi were descendants of the people who first used the Clovis point to hunt their game. They also followed the Folsom culture that thrived on the hunt of bison. The great movement of people during this time lead to the development of many tribal groups and languages among the Pueblo. They are survived by the modern-day Pueblos, including the Tewa, Hopi, Laguna, and San Ildefonso.

The Mound Builders (Adena and Hopewell Cultures) lived in the eastern part of the United States from about 1000 B.C.–700 A.D. and the Temple Mound Builders (Mississippian Culture) lived in the southeast from 700 A.D. to postcontact times. Evidence of their civilizations can be found in mounds that are scattered across the land between the Great Lakes and the Gulf of Mexico. Life at the Etowah Mound in northern Georgia in 1200 A.D. would find the sound of children laughing and dogs barking filling the air. Hunters would be returning from the woods carrying white tailed deer and wild turkeys. Acorns and corn were ground for flour and the smell of roasting venison drifted through the thatched roofs. The village grew to as many as three thousand people with complex social customs and ceremonial practices. Excavation of the mound at Etowah yielded marble statues, sheets of copper embossed with images of mythical birds, engraved shell ornaments, and over two hundred burials.

The people of Etowah lived in extended families and practiced clan systems that were identified on the tombs of the dead found in the mound. They include the Wind, Bear, Bird, and Panther clans. The original mound cities were constructed around several central large mounds. The tallest and most important mound was usually the Temple Mound. Here priests conducted religious ceremonies and burials. Mounds were built entirely by hand using baskets to shovel the earth. The mounds were surrounded by the fields where the crops were raised to feed the people.

By the time that European explorers reached the sites, the evidence of the Temple Mound Builders was hidden underground. The people who originally inhabited the mounds disappeared and little is known of them other than what has been learned from later archaeological excavations.

One of the Mississippian cultures that did survive for a time and which did interact with the Europeans was the Natchez Indians along the lower Mississippi. The French who came into this area and who ultimately destroyed them did record many of their lifeways firsthand.

TRADITIONAL ORIGIN BELIEFS

The Choctaw, Creek, Chickasaw, and Seminole are the descendants of the Temple Mound Builders.

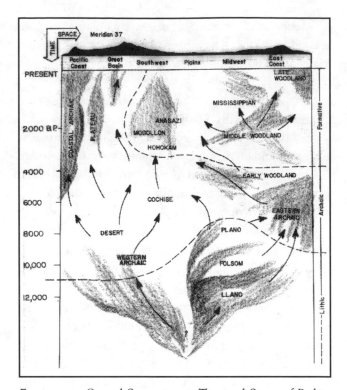

Figure 3.1—General Succession, in Time and Space, of Prehistoric Cultures in North America. Adapted from Jennings, J. D. Prehistory of North America, 2nd edition. New York: McGraw-Hill, 1984, p. 371.

Their stories of origin tell of the original people coming out of the mounds. Life in the mound cities was characterized by a close relationship to the earth. Their lives were bound by the seasons. In the spring, they planted. In the fall, they harvested. They held Green Corn Dances to give thanks and renew for a new year. The Choctaw, Seminole, Creek, and Chickasaw still hold Green Corn Dances for yearly renewal of the People. Just as the origin stories are handed down generation after generation, ancient ceremonies and beliefs are also passed on to the young of today.

The earlier passage written in modern times by Alfonso Ortiz, a Tewa from the Southwest, tells of a universal relationship that people have to their own emergence story. While the stories told by various Indian nations differ, they are their points of connection to the world. These stories have been handed down generation after generation, from old to young. Methods of recording the stories were used to help the story tellers keep the story intact through the generations. The Navajo often used string figures to help record and tell the story. The Sioux used pictures on hides known as winter counts, and the Iroquois used strings of shell beads sometimes called wampum belts. The stories begin at varying points in what is now known as either prehistory or history. Many nation's emergence stories describe physical places, mountains, mounds, and holes that play a part in the emergence or the way of life meant for the people. Some stories follow the nation through previous worlds, such as the Navajo, while others, such as the Choctaw, hinge on a time and place just before this one.

CHOCTAW ORIGIN STORIES (SOUTHEAST)

The Choctaw Nation currently resides in Oklahoma and Mississippi, organized as bands. All bands originally came from Mississippi. William Brescia, Jr., a member of the Mississippi Band of Choctaws, in his research regarding the emergence story of the Choctaw, discovered that there are several emergence stories among the Choctaw of Mississippi. They all center around the Nanih Waiya Mound, located in modern-day central Mississippi on the west side of Nanih Waiya Creek in the southern part of Winston County near the Neshoba County line. Nanih Waiya translates literally as *nanih* meaning "hill" and *waiya* meaning "slanted or bent." Some distance from the mound is a cave or hole in the ground, which is featured in the stories. Two of these emergence stories follow to demonstrate the similarity between and yet differences in origin stories of the tribal group. Remember that these stories have been handed down generation after generation for thousands of years.

The first story is known as a migration story. The people in this story buried the bones of their loved ones that had died along the way, for they had carried the bones of all who perished with them the entire journey, a journey that may have lasted years. The second story tells of the first of their race who came from the ground. Other stories tell of people coming from the bosom of a magnificent sea. The people believe that even as they emerged from the sea there were so many of them that they covered the sloping, sandy shore. Still other creation stories arc not uncommon among the Choctaw.

All of these origin stories are based on the relationship of the Choctaw to the Nanih Waiya Mound.

Variations of the last story are told with tribes coming out in different successions, with the Choctaw always last.

Many years ago, the ancestors of our people lived in the northwest. In time their populations became so large that it was difficult to exist there. The prophets of the tribe announced that a land of fertile soil and abundant game lay in the southeast and that the people could live there in peace and prosperity forever.

Under the leadership of Chahta, our people set forth. At the end of each day's journey, a sacred pole was planted erect in front of the camp. The next morning the pole would be found to be leaning one way or another; in that direction the tribesmen were to travel for that day. One day when the tribe stopped on the west side of a creek, Chahta planted the pole; heavy rain began to fall. The next day, the staff which had burrowed itself deeper in the ground stood straight and tall for all to see. Chahta proclaimed that the long sought land of Nanih Waiya had been found. Here we would build our homes and a mound as the sacred burial spot for our ancestors (Brescia, 1985, p. 7).

The ancient Choctaw believed that in the beginning of things, people came out of the ground at a certain hill and lay about its sides like locusts until they were dried. Several tribes came out in succession. First were the Cherokee. They lay upon the hillside until they were dried and then they went away.

After four others had made their appearance successfully, the Chickasaw and the Choctaw came out together. They derived their names from two brothers who were leaders of their respective bands. They remained together for a long time and became very numerous. Afterwards, they started off like the others still keeping together; but the Chickasaw were in the advance. Every night, when the latter camped, they left a mark by which to guide the Choctaw. This went on for a considerable period. One day, however, the Chickasaw went out to smoke, and while he was smoking he set the woods on fire, so that the marks were destroyed and the Choctaw lost their way. A long time afterwards they discovered each other again but found that their languages had diverged a little. It is not known which was more like the original tongue (Brescia, 1985, p. 11).

IROQUOIS ORIGIN STORIES
(NORTHEAST)

The Haudenosaunee Confederacy was established in the years 1300–1400 A.D. in the northeast region of this continent. They banded together as a result of widespread warfare among nations living in the eastern portion of the land. They lived in a land that had a harsh climate, yet where food was abundant. Their history has become a collective history that guides them all. The following passage was shared with the rest of the world in the hope that there is still time to learn from the wisdom of the past.

The Haudenosaunee, or the Six Nations Iroquois Confederacy, has existed on this land since the beginning of human memory. Our culture is among the most ancient continuously existing cultures in the world. We still remember the earliest doings of human beings. We remember the original instructions of the Creators of Life on this place we call Etenoha—Mother Earth. We are the spiritual guardians of this place. We are the Ongwhehonwhe—the real people.

In the beginning, we were told that the human beings who walk about on the Earth have been provided with all the things necessary for life. We were instructed to carry a love for one another, and to show a great respect for all the beings of this Earth. We are shown that our life exists with the tree of life, that our well-being depends on the well-being of the Vegetable Life, that we are close relatives of the four-legged beings. In our ways, spiritual consciousness is the highest form of politics.

Ours is a Way of Life. We believe that all living things are spiritual beings. Spirits can be expressed as energy form manifested in matter—grass matter. The spirit of the grass is that unseen force which produces the species of grass, and it is manifest to us in the real form of real grass.

All things of the world are real, material things. The Creation is a true, material phenomenon, and the Creation manifest itself to us through reality. The spiritual universe, then, is manifest to Man as the Creation, the Creation which supports life. We believe that man is real, a part of the Creation, and that his duty is to support Life in conjunction with the other beings. That is why we call ourselves Ongshehonwhe—Real People. (*Akwesasne Notes*, 1986, pp. 71–72).

Teachers will want to read origin stories to children for these are the stories that bind the beliefs of a people from generation to generation. In 1936 Jesse Cornplanter (Seneca) began to tell a story of origin in this way: "You have asked me for the story or rather legend about the origin of the world and the Indian in Seneca version. I am going to tell you in my own way, based from what I have been told or heard from old men who used to visit our home when I was real small. It is as authentic as I can make it ... ." This is the way stories are shared and cultural beliefs perpetuated. An excellent source for stories to be shared with children can be found in Michael Caduto and Joseph Bruchac's books, *Keepers of the Earth* and *Keepers of the Animals*.

Both archaeology and Native American mythology indicate that American Indians were the first people on this land. Perhaps one way to reconcile the two varying stories of the origin of the people on this land can be found in the following statement, "Indian people have been here for so long, that it seems as though it was always so." Native American people believe that they have been here since time immemorial. Or perhaps many of us can simply agree with Ortiz when he says that our own stories of origin hold all that we need to know about our people.

LITTLE EAGLE BECOMES THE EAGLE MAN

Come, nephew, sit here near the temple mound with me. Let us find shade. The sun shining on the temple is very bright today. This day reminds me of summer days long ago when I was a boy.

In that time, my uncle was the leader of our town. Like all our leaders, he was called the Eagle Man. He knew when we should plant our corn and when we should harvest it. He led us into battle against enemies who tried to take our land. He protected us. He was a very wise Eagle Man.

When he stood on the temple mound at dawn, it was something wonderful to see. As he raised his arms, the bright feather cape he wore spread wide. It looked like a pair of great, powerful wings. His voice was joyful music as he greeted the rising sun.

Then, without warning, he died. It happened one day as the sun went down. A great cry arose from the priests who were with him. They wrapped his body in painted cloth. Then they carried him up the steep stairs of a large mound in our town.

They took him into the funeral temple at the top of the mound. There, they bathed him and painted his face. They rubbed his long black hair with bear fat to make it shine. The women wound his hair into coils and covered them with ornaments. The priests put a cape of feathers around his shoulders. How beautiful it was with its big collar of beads! Other men hung his shell necklace around his neck.

Through all this, I sat beside him. I held his headdress made of copper. A priest said to me, "Little Eagle, since you are the Eagle Man's nephew, you will be our new leader when you grow up." Then I put the headdress on the Eagle Man's head.

We put him in a long basket beside the stone statues of our ancestors in the funeral temple. I sat there for a long time and thought about all the Eagle Men who had lived before.

Later, our people tore down the funeral temple. We buried the Eagle Man at the base of the mound where the temple had stood. Then we made a new mound that completely covered up the old one. We built a new funeral temple on top.

Now I greet the sun each day at dawn. I wear the cape that looks like giant wings. Someday, nephew, when I go to join our ancestors, you will take my place and be the new Eagle Man.

Reprinted by permission, National Geographic Society. Copyright 1979 Books for World Explorers, *Secrets from the Past*, p. 80–81.

LESSON PLAN: LIVES OF ANCIENT PEOPLE

Grade Level: Any grade level

Basic Concepts: Artifacts and culture

Organizing Generalization: The ancient artifacts that are found by archaeologists represent the culture and the lives of the famous and ordinary people of other times. Archaeologists study these artifacts and living cultures to help them understand cultures of the past.

Culture Area: Two examples are used in this lesson: (1) the Anasazi culture of the Southwest and (2) the Mound Builders of the Etowah Mounds in the Southeast culture area. Other ancient sites or artifacts can be used in the same type of lesson.

Time Period: Prehistoric

Background: The short story of Little Eagle, which can be used here, is a fictionalized account of a young boy in Etowah. It is a good example of how scientists and storytellers build stories from their imagination and from fragments of long ago cultures. The other longer story that should be used is from a book about the Anasazi of the Southwest, *The Village of the Blue Stone* (Trimble, 1990). This book is an excellent resource for this lesson, re-creating one year in the life of an Anasazi community centuries ago. It also speaks of the work of the archaeologist.

Objectives:
Knowledge
Students will:
1. Recognize that the work of archaeologists makes it possible for us to piece together a story of the people who lived in a particular place or period of time.
2. Understand the lives of ancient people probably had many similarities with people today, including families, traditions, and the basic needs for food, clothing, and shelter.

Skills
Students will:
1. Write a creative story about a person or place after viewing a museum exhibit with artifacts about a particular culture or site.
2. Use their imaginations to breathe life into descriptions of ancient sites and artifacts, using the skills of historians and archaeologists.

Values
Students will:
1. Appreciate that people throughout time have many of the same needs and challenges.
2. Develop an appreciation of the work of scientists who study prehistoric times.

Activities:
1. The study of the mysteries of the past can become more interesting to young people if they can imagine the lives of the people. Introduce the story above or the book, raising the question as to whether or not it was true. Students should readily recognize that they are the products of imagination which was based on available, but fragmented, knowledge.

2. Students should have the opportunity to view real artifacts of their particular region through museums, films, videotapes, or books.
3. Stories could be written about the same exhibit or artifact(s) or students could select a particular exhibit to write about. Stories can be illustrated. Look for sensible connections between objects and imaginations.

Extension:
1. Museums frequently make elaborate dioramas around particular artifacts that help give them a meaningful context. Students may also enjoy making dioramas.
2. Archaeology simulations help students discover the world of the archaeologist and to understand the tentative nature of knowledge.

Evaluation: Evaluation should be based upon the ability to construct a reasonable and interesting story from particular artifacts

Materials/Resources:
Trimble, S. *The Village of Blue Stone.* New York: Macmillan, 1990. This is a particularly outstanding book and will make a valuable contribution to students understanding of the study of ancient peoples.

LESSON PLAN: ARCHAEOLOGICAL DIGS

Grade Level: Elementary and middle school

Basic Concepts: Culture, diversity, environment, and resources

Organizing Generalization: The artifacts of a culture help scientists develop a picture of the lives of ancient peoples. The conclusions that they make are tentative and subject to change with more information.

Culture Area: Southeast

Time Period: Past and Contemporary

Background: Archaeologists dig through the trash heaps, or middens, of ancient civilizations to find artifacts that will help them learn more about the people that inhabited the various cities, homes, and villages of the ancient people before written history. Students can begin to understand the work of archaeologists and how incomplete and tentative is information we currently have about the past. Since young people generally believe that science and the printed word are "factual," it is important to emphasize the process of hypothesizing that is employed in all scientific investigation.

Objectives:
Knowledge
Students will:
1. Demonstrate the basic steps in scientific theory, including gathering evidence to support or reject hypotheses.
2. Describe how archaeologists make hypotheses and come to tentative conclusions to build knowledge about ancient cultures.

Skills
Students will:
1. Use the methods of inquiry used by archaeologists.
2. Practice the skills of problem solving.

Values
Students will:
1. Understand how little is known about ancient people.
2. Appreciate the work of archaeologists.

Activities:
1. Discuss the difficulties inherent in learning about prehistoric times and the methods and tools of archaeologists. Introduce this following activity as a modern archaeological dig.
2. Bring enough bags of trash to the classroom so that each group of three students has one bag in which to dig. Construct each bag of trash carefully, creating a culture but ensuring that there are pieces of trash that are difficult to understand or that don't seem to fit the picture. Take care that the trash you have used is clean and safe. Items might include food wrappers, cans, discarded envelopes, theater tickets, newspapers or newsletters, magazines, receipts, and other items of household or business trash. Prepare in advance a "reality" statement for each bag of trash—who it actually came from or the family or people it represents.

3. Ask each group of students to complete the following worksheet.
4. Share the students' hypotheses and conclusions. Probe for the reasons that they made their decisions. Next, discuss the "reality" statements. Discuss differences and similarities and point out examples of good reasoning.
5. Discuss how students decided about the culture or person that produced the trash. Introduce or review the basic steps of the scientific process, relating them back to the process that the students just completed.
   a. Formulation of problem
   b. Formulation of hypotheses
   c. Collection of data
   d. Evaluation and analysis of data
   e. Test hypotheses
6. Make a large chart or bulletin board that summarizes why prehistory is tentative.

Extensions:
1. Research other digs in the continental United States and record the date of the dig, the location, the artifacts, and the historical dating methods used. Develop charts and maps of the information to indicate where physical evidence of civilization has been found.
2. Read the creation stories of the Indian people who were known to inhabit particular areas in ancient times. Review the stories to see if they relate to physical characteristics of the land, and/or other information that is available about the people.
3. Read origin stories from various local tribal groups, finding similarities and differences.
4. Involve students in one of the simulations listed below or construct a similar activity.

Evaluation: The class discussion will indicate whether or not the students understand the unreliability of the archaeological theories.

Materials/Resources:
1. Bags of trash and "reality" statements
2. Books about archaeology and prehistory in North America

DIG IT!!! WORKSHEET

What three things do you know about the people who discarded this trash?

1.

2.

3.

What three things are probably true about them?

1.

2.

3.

Some words that describe the people who discarded this trash (male, female, young, old, family, singles, children etc.).

What type of work do you think they do?

Do you think they are:
_____ Rich _____ Poor   _____ Middle class

What clues did you use to decide their level of wealth?

What hobbies did they have? Did they participate in any sports or recreation?

One statement that you can make about the values of the owners of this trash.

Describe their culture.

SUMMARY
IN THE BEGINNING

How did Indian people come to be here? Archaeologists will tell you of how the people crossed the Bering Straits and spread over North and South America. They will point to evolving archaeological evidence that supports their theory.

But Indian people have their own beliefs and are not very interested in the work of archaeologists. Although Indian tribes have differing stories of their beginning, they hold fast to their own traditional beliefs that tell of how they are of this earth that is sacred to them.

According to Alfonso Ortiz, a Tewa, the story of their origin holds all the Tewa need to know about their people and how they should live as human beings. The story defines their society. It tells them who they are, where they came from, the boundaries and order of their world; how suffering, evil, and death came into the world; and what is likely to happen when they die.

Although the stories of the various Indian nations differ, they are basic as to how they, as Indian people, live in the world. There are generally two different types of origin stories—those that tell of emerging from the earth and those that tell of an earth diver. They begin either in times now known as either prehistory or history.

Many of the stories describe physical places such as mountains, mounds, or holes that play a part in the emergence from the earth or the way of life meant for the people. These places are often sacred places for the people of a particular tribe or nation.

These ancient stories of the beginning have been handed down generation after generation, from the old to the young, and they still guide Indian people.

TIME LINE: 50,000 B.C.–1026 A.D.

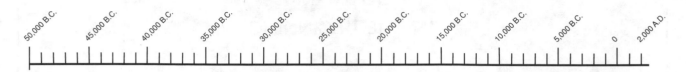

c. 50,000–11,000 B.C.
Groups of Paleo-Siberians cross the Bering Strait land bridge called Beringia and begin to disperse throughout North and South America

c. 50,000–5000 B.C.
Lithic or Paleo-Indian Period

c. 50,000–25,000 B.C.
Pre-Projectile stage

c. 15,000–8000 B.C.
Clovis or Llano Point culture

c. 8000–7000 B.C.
Folsom Point culture

c. 7500–4500 B.C.
Plano Point culture

c. 8000 (or 5000)–1000 B.C.
Archaic Period

c. 3000–1000 B.C.
Aleuts and Eskimos migrate from Siberia to new World

c. 1500 (or 1000) B.C.–1000 (or 1500) A.D.
Formative Period

c. 1000 B.C. –200 A.D.
Adena Mound Building culture in and around Ohio Valley

c. 300 B.C.–700 A.D.
Hopewell Mound Building culture in the East

c. 300 B.C.–1000 A.D.
Mogollon culture in Southwest

c. 100 B.C.–1500 A.D.
Hohokam culture in Southwest

c. 100 B.C.– 1300 A.D.
Anasazi culture in Southwest

c. 700–1700
Mississippian Mound Building culture in Southeast

c. 985–1014
Eric the Red and Leif Ericson establish settlements in Greenland and North America

c. 1025
Navajo bands migrate from the north into the Southwest

CHAPTER **4**

Mother Earth and Father Sky

The president in Washington sends word that he wishes to buy our land. But how can you buy or sell the sky? The land? The idea is strange to us. If we do not own the freshness of the air and the sparkle of the water, how can you buy them?

Every part of this earth is sacred to my people. Every shining pine needle, every sandy shore, every mist in the dark woods, every meadow, every humming insect. All are holy in the memory and experience of my people.

We know the sap which courses through the trees as we know the blood that courses through our veins. We are part of the earth and it is part of us. The perfumed flowers are our sisters. The bear, the deer, the great eagle, these are our brothers. The rocky crests, the juices in the meadow, the body heat of the pony, and man, all belong to the same family.

The shining water that moves in the streams and riverside is not just water, but the blood of our ancestors. If we sell you our land, you must remember that it is sacred. Each ghostly reflection in the clear waters of the lakes tells of events and memories in the life of my people. The water's murmur is the voice of my father's father.

The rivers are our brothers. They quench our thirst. They carry our canoes and feed our children. So you must give to the rivers the kindness you would give any brother.

If we sell you our land, remember that the air is precious to us, that the air shares its spirit with all the life it supports. The wind that gave our grandfather his first breath also receives his last sigh. The wind also gives our children the spirit of life. So if we sell you our land, you must keep it apart and sacred, as a place where man can go to taste the wind that is sweetened by the meadow flowers.

Will you teach your children what we have taught our children? That the earth is our mother? What befalls the earth befalls all the sons of the earth.

This we know: the earth does not belong to man, man belongs to the earth. All things

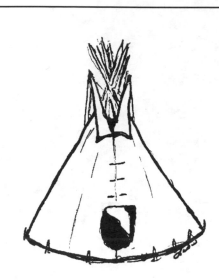

Tipi (Plains)

Longhouse (Northeast)

Hogan (Southwest)

Chickee (Southeast)

are connected like the blood that unites us all. Man did not weave the web of life, he is merely a strand in it. Whatever he does to the web, he does to himself.

One thing we know: our god is also your god. The earth is precious to him and to harm the earth is to heap contempt on its creator.

Your destiny is a mystery to us. What will happen when the buffalo are all slaughtered? The wild horses tamed? What will happen when the secret corners of the forest are heavy with the scent of many men and the view of the ripe hills is blotted by talking wires? Where will the thicket be? Gone! Where will the eagle be? Gone! And what is it to say good-bye to the swift pony and the hunt? The end of living and the beginning of survival.

When the last Red Man has vanished with his wilderness and his memory is only the shadow of a cloud moving across the prairie, will these shores and forests still be here? Will there be any of the spirit of my people left?

We love this earth as a newborn loves its mother's heartbeat. So, if we sell you our land, love it as we have loved it. Care for it as we have cared for it. Hold in your mind the memory of the land as it is when you receive it. Preserve the land for all children and love it, as God loves us all.

As we are part of the land, you too are part of the land. This earth is precious to us. It is also precious to you. One thing we know: there is only one God. No man, be he Red Man or White Man, can be apart. We are brothers after all.

(Speech of Chief Seattle as cited in Campbell, 1988, pp. 42–43)

The preceding passage was taken from a letter written in 1852 by Chief Seattle, of Salish stock and the chief of the Dwamish Nation, in response to an inquiry from the U.S. government regarding buying tribal lands for the arriving people of the United States. Chief Seattle's response is very eloquent considering the U.S. government at that time had at least a one-hundred-year history of removing American Indians from their land, most often using force, and resulting in the death of most, if not all, of the members of the nations forcibly moved. Yet Chief Seattle still tried to reason with the government of the United States with words. Chief Seattle believed in the words he wrote, and he and his people lived their lives with the same belief: that people are a part of the natural world and are needed to participate in the Great Mystery to maintain the world for the future. People need the land and the land needs the people.

Three years later, in 1855, after being forced to give up the lands of the Dwamish Nation in the Puget Sound of Washington, Chief Seattle addressed the governor of the state of Washington, Isaac Stevens, at the treaty signing:

> My people are few. They resemble the scattering trees of a storm-sweet plain ... . There was a time when our people covered the land as the waves of a wind-ruffled sea cover its shell-paved floor, but that time long since passed away with the greatness of tribes that are now but a mournful memory.... .

> To us the ashes of our ancestors are sacred and their resting place is hallowed ground. You wander far from the graves of your ancestors and seemingly without regret. Your religion was written on tables of stone by the iron finger of your God so that you could not forget. The Red Man could never comprehend nor remember it. Our religion is the traditions of our ancestors—the dreams of our old men, given them in the solemn hours of night by the Great Spirit; and the visions of our sachems, and is written in the hearts of our people.

> Your dead cease to love you and the land of their nativity as soon as they pass the portals of the tomb and wander away beyond the stars. They are soon forgotten and never return. Our dead never forget the beautiful world that gave them being ... .

> When the last Red Man shall have perished, and the memory of my tribe shall have become a myth among the white man, these shores will swarm with the invisible dead of my tribe, and when your children's' children think themselves alone in the field, the store, the shop or in the silence of the pathless woods, they will not be alone .... At night when the streets of your cities and villages are silent, and you think them deserted, they will throng with the returning hosts that once filled them and still love this beautiful land. The White Man will never be alone.

> Let him be just and deal kindly with my people, for the dead are not powerless.

> Dead—I say? There is no death. Only a change of worlds (McLuhan, 1987, p. 30).

American Indians of all nations lived for thousands of years in a manner that sustained the environment and the land, and, in turn, the land and its resources sustained the people. While there were hundreds of different nations with different languages and customs in North America before 1500 B.C., some patterns of development can be identified and related to the land areas where specific tribes lived.

American Indian people primarily used renewable natural resources to meet their daily needs for food, clothing, and shelter. These resources varied as the terrain and climate in regions of North America vary. Therefore, people who lived in the same climate with similar resources developed similar means of hunting, making shelters and clothing, and gathering, cooking, and storing food over a period of time.

There is an intimate relationship between Indians and the land. This relationship extends to all aspects of the physical and living world. Native people feel respect and responsibility for keeping it healthy, clean, and pure. Since the beginning of their existence, American Indians of all nations have held in common this respect for the earth. It has been manifest for thousands of years in the lifestyle of the people to always use only as need demanded while allowing for tomorrow.

The following quote from an old Wintu woman from northern California expresses the passion that Indian people have about their earth and the natural resources. It also talks of conservation and environmental issues from a very practical point of view. Native people knew that their very existence depended on the land, the weather and the available natural resources, and the natural balance and tension between them.

The White people never cared for land or deer or bear. When we Indians kill meat, we eat it all up. When we dig roots we make little holes. When we built houses, we make little holes. When we burn grass for grasshoppers, we don't ruin things. We shake down acorns and pinenuts. We don't chop down the trees. We only use dead wood. But the White people plow up the ground, pull down the trees, kill everything. The tree says, "Don't. I am sore. Don't hurt me." But they chop it down and cut it up. The spirit of the land hates them. They blast out trees and stir it up to its depths. They saw up the trees. That hurts them. The Indian never hurt anything, but the White people destroy all. They blast rocks and scatter them on the ground. The rock says, "Don't. You are hurting me." But the White people pay no attention. When the Indians use rocks, they take little round ones for their cooking.... How can the spirit of the earth like the White man? ... Everywhere the White man has touched it, it is sore (McLuhan, 1971, p. 15).

THE CULTURAL REGIONS

The land of North America is comprised of mountains, beaches, lowlands, prairies, hills, forests, deserts, glaciers, valleys, and everglades. The continent can be divided into ten regions to help understand the relationship of American Indians to their environment.

- Arctic
- Subarctic
- Northeast
- Southeast
- Plains
- Southwest
- Great Basin
- California
- Plateau
- Northwest Coast

It should be noted that these regions have no significance to the Indians nor to the Indian nations themselves. The boundaries are not finite or absolute nor do they have any relationship to language or specific culture. Migration over time has created change as well as parallel evolution. Religious beliefs and oral history have also contributed to the differences between nations within a region. Regardless of these limitations, the regions give us a way of organizing information and looking at an overall picture, providing a backdrop for the specific history and cultural development of each nation.

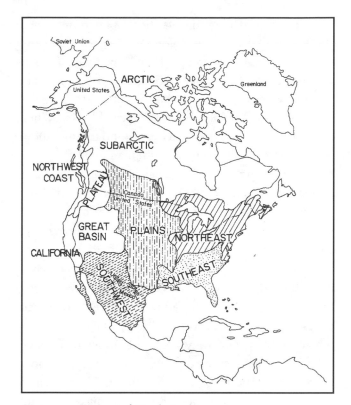

Map 4.1—Regions of North America.

The Arctic
Land and Climate

The rocky coast of the Arctic Region spans three oceans: the Pacific, the Arctic, and the Atlantic. The region covers over five thousand miles from the Aleutian Islands and Siberia to the coast of Greenland. The environment is harsh, with extreme cold, ice, and snow. In the north the land is covered with ice all winter, and the surface of the earth that is exposed during the summer never thaws. Therefore, no plants can root other than moss, lichens, and some scrub brush. As the ice melts it creates an abundance of tiny lakes and ponds, mud, and fog. Trees are almost nonexistent in most of the region with some forest land in Greenland and the southernmost portions of the region. The climate is harsh with extreme cold in the winter and only a brief summer. In this vast northern land the sun never sets for a period of time during the summer. For several days in the winter, there is no sun, as it remains below the horizon twenty-four hours a day.

Resources

Because of the harshness of the climate and land, the natural resources available to meet the survival needs of man and other animals, the people who inhabited this land since the beginning of time were, by necessity, creative, ingenious, and enduring. With no forests, there is no wood available. Often this makes driftwood, the only wood available, a valuable commodity. Homes are dug into the snow or out of ice blocks. When possible, homes are dug into the ground for insulation. The people lived primarily off mammals from the ocean including the walrus, seal, and whale, and land animals such as the caribou. The dog is a friend to the people of the North, helping them hunt on land and sea, carrying possessions and people, and protecting them from danger. The dog plays a major role in the lives of the people of the Arctic; together they survive.

The people survived this harsh land because they learned how to use their natural resources. They used hides for kayaks and clothing. They made candles of whale blubber, and they ate the blubber to insulate their bodies against the cold. Where there was copper along the northern coast of the Yukon, they used it to fashion tools. They even found time to make beautiful statues out of the walrus ivory.

In the southern parts of the region where there were forests, the people consumed a broader diet, lived in wooden and earth homes, and often traded with other Indians from the South. The land, which was less harsh, enabled them to develop a lifestyle that was different from the people of the far North.

Way of Life

The Arctic Region is occupied by Aleut in the southern part of the region and the Inuit people in the north. They are thought by some to have settled the area relatively late, around 3000 B.C. Other archaeological evidence supports the notion that the Arctic people had inhabited this barren, hostile land for thousands of years before this date. Regardless, the inhabitants of this land share similar lifestyles and the same language, known as the Eskimo-Aluet. The Inuit are often referred to as the Eskimo. Eskimo, however, is an Algonquin name meaning "raw meat eaters." The Inuit people themselves prefer the term Inuit which refers to "the People." The Inuit and Aleut people live where they can survive. They follow the land animals and the access routes to the sea mammals. They became the travelers of the north, often traversing six thousand miles from west to east in their migratory searches for game.

Because of their complete dependence upon the animals that sustained them, the people revered the animals as sacred. Ceremony and respect was a part of life. All of the animal hunted was used to protect or feed the Arctic people; nothing was left to spoil. They participated in the maintenance of the natural balance of life in the region and they perpetuated it.

The people of the Arctic are excellent carvers on both wood and ivory from which they made ceremonial objects and utilitarian tools. Today, the lives of the people remain similar in places where resources from the outside world do not reach, as they live in a world where natural resources dictate the way of life. Modern hunters who hunt and fish for sport or commercial reasons, however, have taken their toll on the available resources and the relationship between the animals and man. Accordingly, the natural balance has been changed, which may lead to the ultimate destruction of the land and people.

The Subarctic

Land and Climate

The Subarctic Region stretches across the entire North American continent from the Cook Inlet on the west coast to the island of Newfoundland on the east coast. It covers over two million square miles of the interior of Alaska and most of Canada. The land is covered with coniferous forests. The land is unusually consistent from coast to coast. There is an abundance of large rivers such as the Yukon, the Mackenzie, the Peace, and the Saskatchewan. Lakes include the Great Bear Lake, Lake Athabaska, Lake Nipigon, Lake Winnipeg, and Lake Winnipegosis. There are also small lakes, ponds, streams, and rivers. In the winter, the land is covered with snow. Winter is long, dark, and cold, with summers consisting of only thirty-five to fifty frost-free days. Even in summer, the soil may not warm above freezing due to continuous permafrost. This does not allow for a productive growing season for most cultivated crops.

Resources

The resources available to the people were very similar across the region because of the similarity of the forests—the Taiga in the south and the tundra in the north. Migrating herds of caribou travel through the mountains and valleys along with hare, deer, elk, musk oxen, Dall sheep, muskrat, porcupine, and squirrel. Black bears also wander the forests. The forests of pine, spruce, willow, and birch provide wood for shelters, canoes, and tools, materials for making baskets, and other edible and medicinal plants including berries and roots. Fish are abundant in the lakes and rivers and are a staple of life. Although there is an excess of snow in the winter, the natural resources provide for a variety of diets and living styles.

Way of Life

An obsidian spear point was found in the interior of Alaska that has been dated at 11,000 to 9000 B.C. The point was characteristic of Paleo-Indian hunters of the region. Since that time, and perhaps before, people have lived in the Subarctic Region of North America, battling the elements for survival while creating beautiful crafts and artwork. The lifestyles of the people varied to the extent that they had different resources available and different contact with other people. There are two main language families that are isolated by geography, with the people who speak Athapascan on the west of the Churchill River and the people who speak Algonquin to the east of the river. The Churchill River extends southwest from the Hudson Bay into the interior of Canada. Within each language-speaking group there are many different tribes with varying ways of life.

The economy was similar across nations. There were caribou and other forest animals including elk and deer, the animals that provided food, clothing, shelter, tools, and life. Because of the short growing season, the people were unable to cultivate crops and lived a somewhat migratory lifestyle following the animal herds. They lived mostly in conical-shaped, crude tipis; made their clothing out of hides and skins; used wood for making canoes, baskets, and cooking vessels; and existed on a diet of meat, berries, fish, and plants. People lived in small groups, depending on each other for survival in the harsh climate and land. Their social systems were not complex because of the nature of their nomadic way of life.

The people of this region arc well known for their birchbark baskets, pipes and ceremonial statues carved out of wood and stone, and quill work on leather.

The Northeast

Land and Climate

The Northeast Region extends from Maine on the Atlantic coast west to the Mississippi River Valley, then south from the Great Lakes to modern-day Tennessee. The land of this region varies with mountains, coasts, valleys, and rolling hills. Coniferous and deciduous forests abound and furnish the staples for the lives of the Native people and the forest animals. The climate of the region varies with cold, harsh winters and mild summers in the north and mild winters and hot, humid summers in the south. This region changed greatly after the Ice Age and the loss of glaciers. The melting revealed jagged rock formations, rushing rivers with great falls, lakes, and fertile land.

Resources

The people indigenous to this region had abundant resources available to them. They lived in forests that were coniferous in the north and deciduous in the south parts of the region. The wood was used to build longhouses, dugout canoes, baskets, and for fuel. The people ate the animals of the forest including rabbits, turkeys, deer, bear, and squirrel; gathered berries and other native plants; and cultivated sunflowers and squash. There is an abundance of lakes and rivers in this region as well as an ocean coastline. The people of this area became excellent fishermen and built canoes to travel on the waterways.

Way of Life

Since the people lived more sedentary lives, they developed complex social systems, including clans and societies. There is much more diversity among the Native people of this region than the Arctic and Subarctic regions. One well-known source, Carl Waldman (1985), designates the five following sub-areas to describe the variations.

1. The Nova Scotia, New England, Long Island, Hudson Valley, and Delaware Valley Algonquin-speaking tribes
2. The New York and Ontario Iroquoian-speaking tribes
3. The Great Lakes Algonquins
4. The Prairie Algonquins

5. The southern fringe tribes in the vicinity of the Chesapeake Bay and Cape Hatteras, both Algonquins and Iroquoians

Archeological sites in this region include the Serpent Effigy Mound in Ohio, which appears to be a snake with an egg in its mouth overlooking a stream from a one-hundred-foot cliff. Evidence has been unearthed in various parts of the region that places Paleo-Indians here twelve thousand years ago.

Fortified villages were established to protect the families from outside tribes and animals. They have been maintained through the years, with some relocation due to infertile fields or seasonal or climate changes. The people of this region lived mainly in longhouses which housed multiple families. The longhouses were also constructed for ceremonial and meeting purposes. Today they are still used for ceremonial purposes and large gatherings of the tribe.

The technology that allowed for the development of canoes and transportation on waterways lead to a lifestyle that included trading with other tribes that lived along the waterways. Thus, they were able to meet their needs for survival in a new way. For example, copper, found in ample supplies in the Lake Superior area, was made into tools, traded, and found as far away as the Rocky Mountains.

The people of the Northeast are known for their quillwork on leather, carved stone artifacts, and perhaps most of all for their "White Roots of Peace" and the Iroquios Confederacy. Many contemporary scholars credit the contributions that the Iroquois made to the development of the current U.S. Constitution and Bill of Rights. This was acknowledged by the U.S. Senate with the passage of a Senate Bill declaring 1992 the Year of the American Indian (see Appendix K, page 308).

The Southeast
Land and Climate
The Southeast Region includes the present states of Florida, Georgia, Alabama, Louisiana, Mississippi, South Carolina, and North Carolina and parts of West Virginia, Virginia, Kentucky, Arkansas, and Maryland. The region covers coastal areas, mountains, hills, marshes, everglades, and valleys. Most of the land is forested, yielding wood and wildlife for its inhabitants.

The cold winters and hot summers of the north are a much harsher climate than the southern climate, where hot, humid weather lingers most of the year. Because of the rich soil and the mild climate, people across the region were able to cultivate crops.

Resources
This region is located close enough to the equator that the weather is generally friendly and supportive of plant cultivation. Additionally, the mild climate requires less effort to meet the needs for clothing and shelter. Food is abundant without cultivation; however, cultivated crops allow for specialty foods and staples throughout the year. The most common dwellings in the region are the gable-thatched house or the wattle, daub, and chickee, made of thatched brush and straw with a raised floor. Family homes were built in communities that eventually became permanent. With permanent villages, the people improved their ability to store food and increased their population and security; this increased stability ultimately changed their lives.

Way of Life
Abundant resources to meet life's needs allowed time for the people to pursue tasks not associated with survival. Permanent villages were built and fortified. Bonds were made with neighboring people for peace and trade, and the civilizations grew to be very sophisticated. The Native people of this region spoke a variety of languages including Muskogean, Siouan, Iroquioian, and Caddoan, and well as many other dialects or isolated variations. They developed societies independent and different from each other while using similar resources.

Artifacts dating back to 1500 B.C. have been recovered from Louisiana, and remains of the mound builders culture abound throughout the southern states. In fact, some of the mound cultures were alive at the time of exploration by Hernando de Soto. The last of the mound people were killed either by disease from Europe or warfare with the French. The mounds were burial grounds for thriving civilizations that grew up in 1000 through 1500 A.D. The bodies were buried with jewelry and other carved objects that seem to denote stature in the community, personal power, or help for the departed one in the next world.

The people of the Southeast are known for their basketry, pottery, and weaving. Once they obtained trade goods from the Europeans, people of this region began sewing patchwork clothing and designed a type of European-style dress. The Five Civilized Tribes are known for their internal organization and their confederacy with each other for peace and prosperity.

The Plains

Land and Climate

The Plains Region stretches from the Mississippi River Valley to the Rocky Mountains, and from present-day Manitoba in the north to Texas in the south. The Plains are mostly grassland with low, rolling hills, receiving only ten to twenty inches of rainfall each year. Winters in the north are very cold with an abundance of snow. There are miles and miles of grazing land for the buffalo and other animals that find nourishment in the tall grasses. A change in the wind and drought could settle in and change the nurturing land into a wasteland. Willows and cottonwoods line the river valleys. Remarkable land formations such as the Black Hills, the Ozarks, and the Dakota Badlands interrupt a vast land of prairie.

Resources

The people of the Plains were originally Plano culture hunters. They followed the great bison until a time when they disappeared because of drought around 5000 to 2500 B.C. The rains returned about 2500 B.C. and allowed for the growth of herds of buffalo. The majority of the descendants of the Plano culture had become farmers in the river valleys and did not return to the area until the 1500s when the reintroduction of the horse made it possible for the people to follow the buffalo. The people of this region used the hide of the buffalo to make their shelters known as tipis. They also used hide to make moccasins, clothing, travois, pouches, and other items used for survival. The Plains people even used the bones of buffalo and birds that had been killed for food for needles and other small tools. The meat of the buffalo was eaten immediately or prepared for storage for the long winters. Turnips were dug, berries picked, and plants were collected for medicine and food. The willows were used to build sweat lodges and make baskets.

Way of Life

The people of this region through the years have been nomadic people, following the bison and depending on them for survival. They did not build permanent villages or large civilizations. They lived in small groups that were necessary for survival. Their homes were portable, as were all of their belongings. Their culture surrounded their source of life. They believed in the sacredness of life, that they played an important role in the circle of life, and that the eternal balance is maintained when all keep their sacred responsibilities. They held yearly renewal ceremonies, and gave thanks for their wealth and success in hunting.

The people of this region are known for their quillwork, their leather craft, and their ingenuity. Like the Inuit of the Arctic, the natives of the Plains region faced a barren landscape and yet survived and flourished for thousands of years.

The Southwest

Land and Climate

The Southwest Region extends from the southern tip of Colorado and Utah down through New Mexico and Arizona, and includes portions of southern Texas and northern Mexico. The weather of the region is arid with an average annual rainfall ranging from five to twenty inches per year. The seasons are characterized by hot, dry summers and temperate winters. The land in the region, however, varies greatly. There are the grand canyons and flat-topped mesas of the north, raging rivers like the Colorado and Rio Grande, mountains including the Sandias and the Mogollon Mountains of Mexico, and hostile deserts. Along the Gulf of Mexico there is a beautiful coastline. The vegetation of the region consists of plants that live with little water. This includes piñon, juniper, cactus, and mesquite.

Resources

Water is a precious resource of this region as it is very scarce. Therefore, the people of the desert had to learn to control the snow melt and save it for crops. They also had to learn how to direct water to flow to the crops. This was necessary for communities to develop. By 3300 B.C. the people of this region had domesticated corn, beans, squash, and cotton. Corn became a staple of the diet and a part of life and ceremony.

The people believed that a delicate balance with the natural elements must be maintained in order to preserve the water for the crops that sustained the life of the people. Homes in this region are made of adobe for insulation from the extreme heat in the summer and the cold of the winter. Some of the people of this region lived in cave houses known as cliff dwellings. Remains of cliff dwellings in this region date back to 700 to 1300 A.D. The people hunted the animals of the desert such as rabbits and small deer, making moccasins and other clothing from the hides. They made baskets from the willow and reeds that grew along the rivers and small streams, using them for storage, cooking, and trading. The people of this region are also well known for their pottery. They learned how to use the land of the desert and mesa to meet their needs.

Way of Life

People have inhabited this region for centuries. Evidence from archaeological excavations reveal chipped stone points that have been dated 9000 B.C. and before. These early arrivals, the Hohokam and their descendants, devised ways to grow and store corn and make adobe, baskets, and irrigations canals. Sometime after they disappeared, the Anasazi moved into the region. They also grew corn, beans, squash, and cotton. They developed basket-making into an art. Their complex civilization flourished until drought or some other unknown element drove them out of their homes. They are believed to be the ancestors of the Hopi and Zuni people. The Pueblo Nations of the Southwest, including the Hopi and Zuni, are agriculturists, achieving great success in the heart of the arid lands with their planting techniques and irrigation methods. Their homes and communities were permanent and fortified. Today the pueblos still stand amidst the modern architecture and are inhabited. The Pueblo people of today practice their traditional religion and continue to be successful with their crops.

Around 1400 A.D. the Navajo and the Apache entered the Southwest. They were nomadic people who learned survival skills from the Pueblo people. With the introduction of the sheep into the Southwest the Navajo became herders and maintained a somewhat nomadic lifestyle. They built the hogan for protection from the weather, often having a winter hogan and a summer hogan some distance apart, allowing for herding the sheep. The Navajos became proficient weavers and to this day are famous for their blankets and rugs. The Apaches remained nomadic and lived in the hills and mesas of the Southwest, hunting and gathering to meet their needs. They wove beautiful baskets for storage, cooking, and transporting, with some large enough to hide a full-grown man.

The Great Basin

Land and Climate

The Great Basin is located in the western United States, covering almost all of Utah and Nevada and parts of Colorado, Wyoming, Idaho, Oregon, and California. It is natural desert basin that is almost completely surrounded by mountains and plateaus. To the east stand the Wasatch and Rocky Mountains; to the west, the Sierra Nevada; to the southwest, the Colorado Plateau; and to the north, the Columbia Plateau. The rivers and streams flow into the middle with no outlets to the ocean. Mountains block rain clouds so the region has low precipitation and few trees and vast expanses of flatland cause a high rate of evaporation. At one time, after the end of the Ice Age, this land held an abundance of lakes which have now all dried up or have become very saline. The weather is very harsh with hot, dry summers and cold, dry winters. Not enough snow falls in winter to support life throughout the year.

Resources

Resources available to the inhabitants of this region are limited by land and climate. Sagebrush, piñon, and juniper are common bushes and trees. Cactus grow in the desert areas and small berry bushes and willows line the streams. The people dug roots, and gathered seeds, berries, snakes, lizards, insects, and rodents. They lived in homes made of sticks and mud, called wickiups. The population of the people in this region remained small due to the lack of adequate resources to meet their basic needs.

Way of Life

The people of this region lived a hard life, spending most of their time hunting for food, water, or shelter. Because of their nomadic nature, they lived in small groups and had very simple social customs. They mainly spoke the Uto-Aztecan language with the exception of the Washo Nation who spoke a dialect of Hokan. In Danger Cave near the Great Salt Lake, artifacts dating back ten thousand years reveal that the ancient people of the Great Basin had arrow shafts, traps, and woven game decoys such as ducks. They also found pieces of leather that had been moccasins and other items that lead the anthropologists to speculate that the people of the Great Basin have always been nomadic hunters and gatherers.

California
Land and Climate

This region covers the current state of California and extends south to Baja California in Mexico. Coastal mountains run from the north to the south, providing a natural barrier between the coastal portion of the region and the area that touches the surrounding regions. The climate in the California Region varies some with moderate rainfall and rich soil. Rugged coastline in the north with rocky mountains and cliffs contrast with the Mojave Desert in the south and the central basin known as the San Joaquin Valley. They do hold in common one element: They have beautiful and abundant flora and fauna. The woodlands and hills, mountains and deserts were rich with plants that support life. The climate promoted their growth and the natural balance ensured their survival.

Resources

The natural resources of this region are generous. The people of this region are known for fishing, hunting, and gathering. They are not known for cultivation of crops or large villages or confederacies. People lived in small family groups that were often isolated from others for long periods of time. The land provided for the people. There were coastal deer—a smaller variety than known in the Rocky Mountains, bears, mountain lions, rabbits, coyotes, wolves, and other smaller forest animals. There were fish in the streams and rivers as well as the ocean. The people made boats and canoes and ventured out to sea fishing and exploring. Red willow was used to weave and make baskets and clothing. Clay was molded into pottery, and wood was carved. The people had abundant resources for survival

without the time invested in cultivation. People of this region lived in dwellings made of bark, thatch or hides, known as wickiups, or wigwams. They were shelters for warm weather and were ample for the people of this region. Shells from the ocean were used in their jewelry and clothing and as needles.

Way of Life

A great variety of lifeways developed among the Native people of the California Region. This is due in part to the varied geography and resources and in part to the natural isolation of people and cultures. The abundance of natural resources made it possible for the region to support more people than any other without cultivation of crops. Evidence has been recovered that supports the idea that the original inhabitants of this land lived here over seven thousand years ago. Their culture developed naturally through the years. They became expert weavers and potters, and created works of art as well as utilitarian tools.

The Plateau
Land and Climate

The Plateau Region is located in eastern Washington, northern Idaho, western Montana, northeast and central Oregon, southeast British Columbia, and a tiny portion of California. The area is a large plateau with several rivers, including the Columbia and the Fraser. The rivers are the center for life in the region and provide for man and animal alike. The weather in the region is warm in the summer and cold with abundant snow in the winter. The region is bordered by mountains or forest on three sides and a desert on the other.

Resources

Natural resources of the region are less abundant than those of the Northwest region or the California region. People and animals cling to the rivers, the source of life in the dry plateau. Salmon ran in the rivers and provided the mainstay of life. Elk, deer, antelope, rabbit, and beaver walked the forests and rivers but were limited in number and availability. The Plateau people dug for roots and bulbs to supplement their diet. They dug houses in the ground known as pit houses which were covered by thatch and sod for protection from the elements.

Way of Life

The people of this region became expert fisher-men and learned to make a variety of tools in the process. They made hooks, line, gorge, trotline, dip net, gill net, seine, and funnel net, barbed spear and three-pronged leister, simple and toggled harpoon, noose—the list continues. They also learned to dry and store fish. More than two dozen distinct tribal groups inhabited the region. Two language stocks are dominant: Penutian in the south and Salish in the north. There are occasional Athapascan-speaking people and Algonquin-speaking bands from the north. People of this region are known for their beadwork, leatherwork, and drawing.

The Northwest Coast

Land and Climate

The Northwest Coast Region extends more than two thousand miles from the northern border of California to the southern border of Alaska, including a strip of Oregon, Washington, and British Columbia on the east. The region at its widest point is only 150 miles across. Almost the entire region is Pacific coastline, although a thin mountain chain runs the length of the region. The climate is temperate and moist, with the Japanese current warming the ocean. There is fog most days and rainfall is abundant, exceeding one hundred or more inches a year.

Resources

The region has abundant fish, game, and wild edible plants. The people lived mainly on the fish and game with the gathered plants. The climate allowed for the cultivation of crops of choice. There are many rivers running to the ocean which provide another source for fish. Deer, bear, mountain lion, beaver, and other small forest animals roam the coastal forests. There was plenty of wood for building, and the homes of the region were made of wood and known as plank houses.

Way of Life

The people of this region were hunters, fishers, and gatherers. They cultivated only tobacco and other plants of choice since their basic needs were met with natural resources. Salmon was the staple of life. If there was no other food available, there was enough salmon to feed the people. There were, however, many other animals and plants for food. The people made boats and canoes out of wood and navigated the ocean and rivers. They lived in small, extended family groups and achieved complex and affluent societies by the time of European contact. There were two major language families in the northwest, the Na-Dene spoken by the northern Natives and Penutian spoken by the people of the southern part of the region. People of this area are known for their carving on wood, creating masks and totem poles. They are also famous for the potlatch, a tradition in which the person being honored gives gifts to those who honor him. Great significance is given to the one who can give generously.

Summary

The Native people of North America lived for thousands of years, participating in a delicate balance between the land and its resources. Their lives were intertwined with the lives of the animals and the plants that shared their existence. They used creativity and ingenuity to meet the challenge of daily survival and created beautiful, efficient tools, homes, clothing, and lifestyles. The very way of life of the Native people conserved for the future and created a unique way of life for people of today to observe—particularly when the relationship of human beings to life and what they need to survive is almost broken, and we have become so urgently aware of the need to preserve the earth and environment.

Wilma Mankiller, a Cherokee woman of the 1990s and the current principal chief of the Cherokee Nation of Oklahoma, wrote the following tribute to the continuity of thought and belief of Native people in regard to their relationship with the earth.

> We human beings are only one small part of creation. Sometimes we act as if we were the whole rather than merely a
> other worlds besides th
> world and the animal wo
> parts of this creation. The
> in balance and harmony
> thing in creation. We must
> the interconnectedness o
> accept our individual role
> support of other life forms
> understand our own insignific
> things (Friend & The Editors o. _.ic, 1991).

LESSON PLAN: PREHISTORIC SHELTERS

Grade Level: Primary to intermediate

Basic Concepts: Environment and resources

Organizing Generalization: People use available resources to meet their basic needs for food, clothing, and shelter.

Culture Area: Northeast, Southeast, Southwest, Plains

Time Period: Prehistoric

Background: Children quite naturally assume that the lives of people, past or present, that differ from theirs are quaint or strange, when, in fact, they are marvelous and creative adaptations to the physical world. This lesson is designed to help children understand that the lifeways of any group of people are partially determined by the available natural resources needed for survival. Food, clothing, shelter, and religious and spiritual beliefs are developed in accordance with the physical environment and the available resources. People who live in similar environments and have access to the same natural resources may be different than other groups living in the same kind of environment and utilizing the same resources depending on how each of the cultures developed.

Objectives:
Knowledge
Students will:

1. Give examples of how people use available natural resources to meet their survival needs.
2. Describe how the availability of needed natural resources can determine the way of life of a people.
3. Identify at least four prehistoric shelters made by Natives of North America, name the resources used, and locate the original place of use on a map.

Skills
Students will:

1. Use reference materials for initial research about the natural resources available in the various regions of North America.
2. Hypothesize about how the people used the environment to meet their needs.
3. Match at least four prehistoric shelters to the regions where they were invented and discuss why they developed in that region.

Values
Students will:

1. Understand and respect the natural relationship between the environment and the lives of the inhabitants.
2. Appreciate the creativity and ingenuity of the American Indian.

Activities:

1. Initiate a discussion with the class about natural resources. List a few that are native to your local area, then introduce a large map of the United States. Ask students if they can name resources that are native to different parts of the country. If students need help, suggest that there are different resources along

the coast than there are in the mountains. Have students theorize about them and list their responses.

2. Introduce a map with the Southeast, Southwest, Northeast, and Plains regions outlined. Ask students to research the natural resources for each of the regions, or divide the class into four groups and have them research the resources cooperatively. Have students look for resources and natural limitations.

3. Immediately following the research and listing of the resources by region, ask the students to pretend that they lived a long time ago, before grocery stores, lumber yards, and department stores. How would they build a house? What would they eat? How would they make clothing? Have each student select one of the four regions and draw a picture of the homes they would build.

4. Introduce shelters designed by the Native people of the four regions (tipi, longhouse, hogan, and chickee). Show pictures, tell the names, discuss resources used, but do not assign to a region. Ask the students (or groups of students) to review each shelter and its materials and match them to the region on the blank map, and tell the class why they matched it as they did.

Extension:

1. Research how many of the prehistoric homes are still in use, how they are used, and how they have changed.

2. Report on how Indians live today, their shelters, food, clothing. Why have they changed? Will they continue to change? This research could easily be reported in a mural.

3. Make models of different types of Indian homes and place them in an appropriate diorama of the environment.

4. Use the reading *The Eagle Feather Award* (page 55) to illustrate how contemporary Native Americans demonstrate their respect for Mother Earth in their conservation efforts. Students can be encouraged to establish the Eagle Feather Award for individual, local, or school environmental projects. Older students can track environmental issues that impact Native people as reported in the press. In later chapters more attention will be given to the preservation of our land and its resources and the continuing struggle for Native people to conserve land and wisely use its resources, as well as make economic progress in a highly technological society.

Evaluation: The activity of matching the Indian prehistoric homes to their regions after doing the research will reveal if the students can identify the shelters and place them correctly. Class discussion will indicate if the students understand that the same relationship exists today between physical and natural resources and lifeways.

Materials/Resources:

1. Geography books for research on natural resources.
2. Blank map of North America.
3. Map of North America with regions outlined.
4. Drawings of shelters of the four regions.

Billard, J. (ed.). *The World of the American Indian*. Washington, D. C.: National Geographic Society, 1989.

Kopper, P. (ed.) *The Smithsonian Book of North American Indians Before the Coming of the Europeans*. Washington, D.C.: Smithsonian Books, 1986.

Other books and resources from the library on individual Indian nations, Indian art, and legends will also serve as good resources for the research.

A field trip to a museum of natural history or art will expose students to actual art objects that could be listed on the regional chart.

THE EAGLE FEATHER AWARD

The Eagle Feather is awarded by *Native Monthly Reader* to those tribes that have out tricked the trickster and are protecting Native land, Native people, and the future. These tribal people carry on the tradition of respect for the land.

Mohawk:

The Mohawks on the Akwesasne Reservation in upstate New York have been deluged with proposals for hazardous waste, sewage sludge, and medical waste incinerators. Chambers Development, a waste disposal company, wrote a letter to an Akwesasne chief in 1989, but the proposal was not pursued by the Mohawks.

Navajo:

The Navajo community of Dilkon, Arizona, rejected a hazardous waste incinerator proposed by Waste-Tech and Pegler-Welch Engineering in 1989. The Navajo people organized an environmental group CARE (Citizens Against Ruining Our Environment) to successfully oppose the project. The people of Dilkon also rejected a toxic waste dump proposed under the guise of a "recycling facility" by Pegler-Welch, Silicate Technology, and Hi-Tech Recycling. The company representatives never told the community that a toxic waste dump was a major part of the plan, claiming only that some recycling would be done on the site.

Sioux:

In a daring and forthright move, the Yankton Sioux Tribe in South Dakota, besieged with proposals from the waste industry, banned all such facilities on their land.

THE TRICKSTER WATCH
Excerpt from: *Native Monthly Reader* (1991–1992), 3 (1), p. 2.
Information from "The Toxic Threat to Indian Lands," a Greenpeace Report by Bradley Angel, June 1991.

LESSON PLAN: LIFEWAYS AND THE ENVIRONMENT

Grade Level: Grades 5–8

Basic Concepts: Culture, environment, and resources

Organizing Generalization: The lifeways of a people, including foods, clothing, shelter, legends, beliefs, music, and ceremony, are directly related to their environment and resources.

Culture Area: All regions

Time Period: Past and present

Background: Most people are aware that their way of life is related to the physical environment and the available natural resources. The relationship between art, music, legend, and ceremony to the natural resources and environment seems more obvious in the past that the present. Each American Indian tribe has art and stories that are representative of their region. For example, Eskimo and Aleut people of the North carve ivory, but the Pima and Apache people of the Southwest weave baskets. The Navajo people of the Southwest have a story in which they learn to construct a hogan from the animals of the Southwest, using materials native to the region. The Cherokee of the Southeast have a story in which they learn how to make pottery from a wasp that lives along the local creek bed. The art, story, and ceremony of people are unique and directly related to their natural resources.

Objectives:

Knowledge
Students will:

1. Give examples of art, story, or ceremony from tribes in each region that are related to their natural resources.
2. Explain how each tribe and region differs based on available natural resources.
3. Describe how the lifestyle of various people is related to environment.

Skills
Students will:

1. Use research skills.
2. Practice cooperative skills in gathering information.

Values
Students will:

1. Appreciate that differences in cultures are often because of the physical environment and natural resources.
2. Appreciate the ingenuity and beauty of different cultures.

Activities:

1. In a large group activity, list the regions of North America on a chalkboard and discuss climate, resources, and land formations for each. Encourage students to consider climate and land when listing natural resources. Then introduce several art objects (either real or pictures) created by Native Americans. Ask students to match these objects with the correct region, giving reasons for their choice.

2. Group students into research teams, one for each region. Allow groups to select a region then locate at least one art object (baskets, pottery, carvings, weaving, and so on) and one story or ceremony that is related to the natural environment of the region. Be able to explain the relationship to the class.
3. In a large group share the results of the research. Make a list of the items for each region. Have students consider whether this same phenomena is true for non-Indian groups. Discuss other groups and how their culture is related to natural resources. For example, people who live in cold climates with mountains ski, ice skate, and sled. While those who live on the coast go fishing, swimming, and boating in the ocean. Their lifeways have developed in relationship to these environmental variables.

Extension:
1. Find art, ceremony, or story that is related to the region in which they live.
2. Learn to do one or more of the crafts that is native to their region.
3. Make a display of folk crafts of a particular region such as cornhusk dolls and wood carvings. If possible, invite local craftspersons to the classroom to demonstrate their craft.

Evaluation: Participation in the research groups and class discussions should demonstrate understanding of how way of life of people is related to available natural resources and the characteristics of their local region.

SUMMARY
MOTHER EARTH AND FATHER SKY

"As we are part of the land, you too are part of the land. This earth is precious to us. It is also precious to you. … No man, be he Red Man or White Man, can be apart. We are brothers after all." These words are believed by many people to be the words of Chief Seattle. Indian people have lived their lives with this belief that people are a part of the natural world and are needed to participate in the Great Mystery to maintain the world for the future.

Not only are people a part of the world, but all things in the world have their place of honor and respect—the four-leggeds ones, winged ones, those that swim and crawl, the wind, the rocks, the trees, and the plants. All things of the earth are interdependent.

Indian people have a special relationship with the land. They feel respect and responsibility for keeping it healthy, clean, and alive. They respect all things on the earth, using them only as need demands, ensuring continuing life and well-being for the planet.

Land, people, and culture cannot be separated. In part, culture develops from the particular environment in which people live. The physical and natural resources of a particular area determine traditional Indian food, clothing, shelter, art, social and political relationships, and ceremonies. For example, traditional homes have developed in harmony with a particular environment—hogans, tipis, pueblos, wigwams, wickiups, and longhouses. This relationship is true for all aspects of traditional Native American life.

Scholars have divided the North American continent into ten regions to help understand the relationship of American Indians to their environment. These regions include:

- Arctic
- Subarctic
- Northeast
- Southeast
- Plains
- Southwest
- Great Plains
- California
- Plateau
- Northwest Coast

CHAPTER 5

Contact and the Legacy of Columbus

They ... brought us parrots and balls of cotton and spears and many other things, which they exchanged for the glass beads and hawks' bells. They willingly traded everything they owned .... They were well-built, with good bodies and handsome features .... They do not bear arms, and do not know them, for I showed them a sword, they took it by the edge and cut themselves out of ignorance. They have no iron. Their spears are made of cane .... They would make fine servants .... With fifty men we could subjugate them all and make them do whatever we want.

As soon as I arrived in the Indies, on the first Island which I found, I took some of the natives by force in order that they might learn and might give me information of whatever there is in these parts.

—From the diary of Christopher Columbus

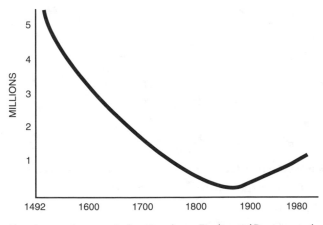

Figure 5.1—American Indian Population Decline and Recovery in the U.S. Area, 1492–1980. Population data from: Thornton, R. American Indian Holocaust and Survival. Norman: University of Oklahoma, 1987.

The discovery of America, and that of a passage to the East Indies by the Cape of Good Hope, are the two greatest and most important events recorded in the history of mankind.
—Adam Smith (Sale, 1990, prologue) p.3

Initially, it seems reasonable to acknowledge what is generally accepted to be true about Christopher Columbus and his four famous voyages to the new world. However, there isn't a citizen of the United States who hasn't learned about Columbus, his courage and bravery, his vessels, the Niña, Pinta, and Santa Maria, and his "discovery" of America. We actually know a great deal about Columbus and his voyages and, as educators, have taught about the encounter of 1492 as a vital part (usually the starting point) of American history.

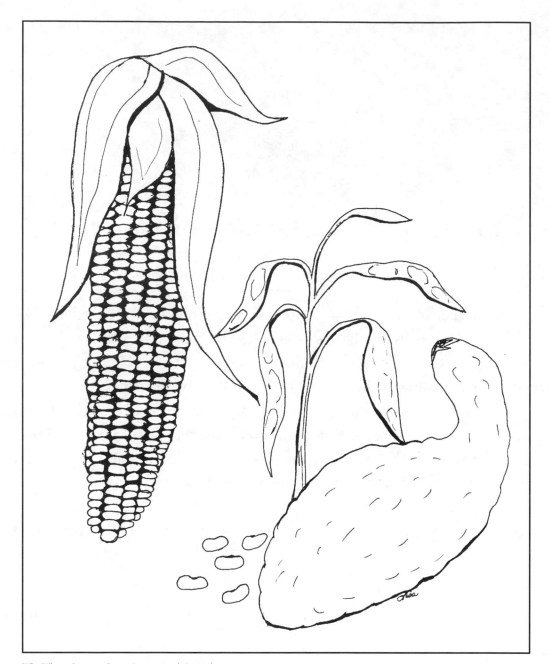

The Three Sisters: Corn, Beans, and Squash.

In recent years, this well-known and well-accepted story has changed profoundly and, most recently, people—particularly Native people—have questioned whether Columbus should be honored at all. Perhaps he should be presented less as an American hero than as the instigator of the destruction of sophisticated cultures and the holocaust of our indigenous peoples. The issue of the honor and reverence due to Columbus rests on fresh perspectives that have exposed the horrors of the conquest and revealed the legacy of the European encounter.

These new perspectives and the questions they have raised render our traditional approaches to teaching about Christopher Columbus somewhat trivial and nearly meaningless. Emphasis on what is known about Christopher

Columbus, the persistent man and the skilled mariner, and on the details of the voyages ignores the profound and enduring importance of the Columbian encounter. New research as well as heightened consciousness has exposed both the horrors of the past and the impact of the legacy. That the two old worlds would eventually discover each other is certain. However fascinating the story of this historical encounter may be, it is time to examine the reality of the conquest and the legacy of Columbus.

We know that others were here before Christopher Columbus. Then why is his voyage the one that stands out from the others and the one that is celebrated as one of the most important events in the history of mankind? Scholars have suggested the following reasons.

- It was an official, royal mission of Queen Isabella and King Ferdinand—not a mere fishing trip or a journey by those who had less than honorable motives, or a discovery by lost sailors. It was an officially funded and sanctioned voyage taken in the name of the Spanish royalty.

- The voyage was carefully documented through Columbus' own journals and the presence of others whose function was to provide independent verification of the authenticity of the voyages. Columbus also returned to Europe with tangible evidence of his discoveries, including human specimens.

- The voyage achieved not only a way across the ocean, but a way back. The intentional and careful records of the voyage allowed the feat to be repeated by others.

- The news of the voyage spread rapidly throughout Europe. If previous trips had succeeded in reaching new lands, the world was not informed.

- The voyage had purposes beyond fishing. The intent of the voyage was to initiate a process of trade, conquest, colonization, and exploitation and to establish Spain as a world power.

- Spain *needed* to expand to foreign shores because conditions in Europe were deplorable.

Kirkpatrick Sale (1990) states that "discovery" as such is irrelevant. "This exact moment rings down the corridors of time not because one foreigner comes to a tiny Bahamian island but because thus begins the European conquest of the world." It is with the understanding that the discovery cannot be understood as merely a brave journey into the unknown, nor only as the encounter of two old worlds, but also as the beginning of the European conquest of the world, that we will begin the story of Christopher Columbus and the legacy of his historic voyages with some understanding of Europe at the time of the historic voyages.

EUROPE IN 1492

Violence, disease, and famine characterized "the dark twilight" of Europe in the Middle Ages. Life was unbearably violent and fraught with disease, hunger, famine, and death. The hope of relief from this pervasive misery and suffering seemed to come from new ideas that had begun to take root in European consciousness. The following interrelated and revolutionary ideas are significant for in them we begin to see how the legacy of Columbus evolved and eventually affected Native peoples.

Humanism

This is the concept that implies that, as part of God's plan, human beings are elevated above all other species. It is the idea that allowed Europeans to subjugate plants, animals, and all other parts of nature that were believed not to be human. In Columbus' own journals, the belief is clearly articulated that Indian people were not human but mere savages, who could be subjugated like animals.

> ... the people here are simple in war-like matters, as your Highnesses will see by those seven which I caused to be taken and carried to Spain in order to learn our language, and return, unless your Highnesses should order them all to be brought to Castile, or to be kept as captives on some island. I could conquer the whole of them with fifty men and govern them as I pleased.
>
> Scott, W.R. The log of Christopher Columbus' first voyage to America in the year 1492 as copied out in brief by Bartholomew Las Casas. Hamden, CT: Linnett (1989).

This horror continued with unspeakable acts of atrocity as Columbus enslaved, tortured, raped, and worked to death the Native people that he encountered.

It is interesting that this new concept of humanism and "dignity of man" did not appear to include the indigenous people of the New World or Africa. These people were defined as "savage beasts" and "uncivilized"; they could be and were conquered, killed, or enslaved.

Rationalism

Rationalism designated science to be the new faith, logical, linear, and objective science. The rationalism of science replaced the idea that nature was sacred because God was present in all that He created with the belief that there was nothing sacred about nature. Aspects of nature were simply measurable combinations of chemical and mechanical properties, subject to scientific analysis, prediction, and manipulation. Nature could be used, conquered, and controlled by humans in the advance of science. Science also produced such incredible technologies as the printing press and firearms. In supporting scientific achievements, scientific attitudes were also encouraged. These attitudes manifested themselves in the urge to explore, to expand, to know and understand, and to improve.

Materialism

Materialism revealed itself in the love of objects, the cherishing of worldly goods. Material wealth assumed an importance that it had not had before. This need to acquire material goods, which was one of the stated reasons for the attempt to find a shorter way east, was a driving force in Columbus' adventures in the new world.

Capitalism

Materialism, a companion to humanism, rationalism, and materialism, created the essential conditions for the beginnings of capitalism. Lewis Mumford (Sale, 1990, p. 44) summarized this phenomenon in this way: "The whole moral change that took place under capitalism can be summed up in the fact that human purposes, human needs, and human limits no longer exercised a directive and restraining influence upon industry; people work, not to maintain life, but to increase money and power and to minister to the ego that found satisfaction in vast accumulations of money and power."

Nationalism

The beginnings of nationalism, or civic power, could then be seen in Europe. The rise of the nation-state was a driving force in the quest for national riches, recognition, power, and supremacy (Sale, 1990, pp. 38–45).

From this time and this world of 1492, Christopher Columbus set his sails for the east to discover and conquer a new world and to begin the process of spreading the culture of Europe around the globe.

INDIAN COUNTRY IN 1492

From the diligent work of archaeologists and the diaries and records of Columbus and the earliest explorers, we have a picture of Indian Country in 1492. Some scholars now refer to conditions in this period of time in the New World as paradise—at least an environmental and balanced paradise. Although the terrain of the country was much like it is today, as were the plants of the geographic regions, the range and abundance of the fish, animals, and birds were quite different. Increasing scientific discoveries are documenting through fossil pollen, seeds found in packrat and human middens, and bones and fossils that animals were found in quite amazing places—at least, amazing places to us. Jaguars roamed the Carolinas and buffalo grazed in Georgia and California. Agriculture flourished and the four sacred plants, corn (maize), squash, beans, and tobacco were cultivated with sophistication. There was a relative scarcity of domesticated animals, with the exception of dogs and turkeys.

Although scholars continue to debate, a reasonable estimation of the population of North America in 1492 is approximately five million. There is clear evidence that the indigenous people of North America and the Western Hemisphere were remarkably free of serious diseases before the Europeans and Africans arrived.

The Indians be of lusty and healthfull bodies, not experimentally knowing the Catalogue of those health-wasting diseases which are incident to other

Countries, as Feavers, Pleurisies, Callentures, Agues, Obstructions, Consumptions, Subsumigations, Convulsions, Apoplexies, Dropsies, Gouts, Stones, Toothaches, Pox, Measels, or the like, but spinne out the threed of their days to a faire length, numbering three-score, four-score, some a hundred yeares, before the worlds universall summoner cite them to the craving Grave (Thornton, 1987, p. 39).

At the time of the first voyage of Columbus, there existed at least two hundred to three hundred languages, and perhaps many more, in North America. Some estimates of distinct Indian languages once spoken in the Americas are as high as twenty-two hundred. More languages were spoken in California alone than are native to Western Europe! This diversity of languages meant that Native people from one tribal group, for example the Iroquois for the Northeastern cultural area, would have difficulty communicating with those from other tribal groups, such as the Pueblo in the Southwestern cultural area. Surprising to many people is the fact that these Native American languages were so diverse as to suggest they were not imported but rather they developed here from several primitive ancestral stocks. Linguists have great difficulty studying these language groups since all but the Mayan language were unwritten. It is interesting that regardless of the diversity of environments and languages, indigenous peoples of the New World called themselves the equivalent of "the people."

Social and political organization ranged from very simple to the complex. In broad terms, a general pattern existed in each of the cultural areas. Simple social organizations were a result of harsh climates and scarce natural resources. The people were primarily hunters and gatherers, and they banded together in small, cooperative groups to obtain what they needed to survive. The complex social organizations were a result of hospitable climates and rich, abundant resources. People in these areas were able to form large, stable communities with subsequent agricultural surpluses and natural resources to trade. They developed specialization, fine tools and crafts, and complex social systems with levels of social stratification. In some areas, with a wide range of environments, both the simple and complex social organizations existed. Note in Table 5.1 that the Navajo had just come upon the

scene in the Southwest in the 1400s, and at this time they had not developed the complexity that would come to characterize the Navajo Nation.

Scholars also remind us that war and slavery existed in the New World as did human slavery and sacrifice, and slashing and burning for agriculture. Paradise was not without human frailty.

Into such realms came the White invaders, self-assured in the extreme, bringing with them a technology that aided them in their determination to conquer the peoples they confronted; large, seaworthy vessels: firearms and other iron and steel weapons and armor; and horses, animals unknown to the natives. The newcomers sought material wealth ... and they set out to seize it any way they could.

Their inexorable drive to conquer, supported by guns, armor and mounts—and the unseen, unintended weapons of exotic diseases—made the newcomers irresistible, and the natives of the New World were vanquished and decimated. Many of those who survived had their bodies subjected to slavery and their souls to Christian conversion (Kopper, 1986, p. 21).

CHRISTOPHER COLUMBUS

... All this eventually meant a flood of silver, gold, land and sugar cane profits, as Spain became the most powerful country in Europe, with a far-flung, enduring empire. It also brought an appalling expansion of slavery. There was little in Columbus' background to make him feel glum about any of the above. He was very much a man of his time in his courage and in his faith that God wanted all this to happen, as well as in his passion for trade and his desire to exploit the physical world (Foote, 1991, p. 38).

Much has been written about Christopher Columbus—his youth, his family, and his four voyages. Investigation into the man himself suggests some characteristics that are generally absent from the usual reports for young people. His navigational skills and courage are often lauded, without a more serious look at other aspects of his personality and behavior.

To state that he was a man of his time infers that he had no reservations about exploiting land or enslaving people. His compelling need for material things allowed him to persevere unmercifully in his pursuit of gold and riches, to

Group	Language	Social/Political Organization	Geographic Area
The Six Nations of the Iroquois Confederacy	**Macro-Siouan**	Complex	Northeast
Mohawk	Iroquoian		
Oneida	Iroquoian		
Onondaga	Iroquoian		
Cayuga	Iroquoian		
Seneca	Iroquoian		
Tuscarora	Iroquoian		
The Five Civilized Tribes	**Macro-Siouan**	Complex	Southeast
Cherokee	Iroquoian		
	Macro-Algonquian		
Chickasaw	Muskogean		
Creek	Muskogean		
Choctaw	Muskogean		
Seminole	Muskogean		
The Sioux	**Macro-Siouan**	Eastern-Complex	Plains
Teton			
Santee		Western-Simple	
Yankton			
Yanktonai			
The Desert People			Southwest
Navajo	**Na-Dene**	Simple—the Navajo entered this area in the 1400s	
	Athapascan		
Pueblo	**Aztec-Tanoan**	Complex	
	Kiowa-Tanoan		
	Uto-Aztecan		
	Penutian (Zuni)		

Table 5.1—Overview of Four Native Groups in 1492

command the subjugation of a people, and to destroy ancient cultures and religions in his efforts to convert others to Christianity. He could countenance the rape of women, the death of children, and the torture of those who stood in his way. He was doggedly persistent and courageous in his drive to fulfill his destiny. It was his wish "to bypass no island without taking possession."

He was eager for personal riches and prestige, desiring the titles of viceroy and admiral of the Ocean Sea and ten percent of the wealth that would come to Spain as a result of a new route to Asia. In his later years he complained that he was owed more income even though he was a wealthy man. He was willing to lie and cheat his own men. He was not above withholding the truth or embellishing facts for his own reputation or gain, and he was a cruel and chaotic administrator who needed to be replaced. His persistence can be seen in some instances to be less noble than fanatic. Christopher Columbus set the pattern of conquest, cruelty, and control of people and the environment that shaped the encounter of the two old worlds.

As can be expected, the story of Christopher Columbus was in the past, as it is in the present, colored by the times and the perspectives of those who have studied him. The story has been told through European eyes. In fairness to Columbus, the encounter was inevitable. Further, if not Columbus, another "discoverer" was likely to have been European, grounded in the same prevailing values. Words that are so repugnant today—colonialism, racism, and exploitation—could also be framed in other words in another time as scientific discovery, change and adaptation, quest for new knowledge and expanding horizons. Nonetheless, it is not unreasonable to question the fact that Columbus has traditionally been held in honor.

THE LEGACY OF COLUMBUS

For the great community of the Americas, and for the rest of the world, the year 1492 holds deep historical and cultural consequence. From any point of view it must be recognized that the Spanish ships La Nina, La Pinta, and Santa Maria, captained by Christopher Columbus and others, were on the dawn of October 12 carrying the protagonists of an astonishing encounter of two worlds. From that moment, nothing would ever be the same (Sharp, 1991).

In an effort to understand the legacy of the Columbian encounter, the Smithsonian Institute developed a major exhibit for the National Museum of Natural History. This exhibit, Seeds of Change, is extraordinarily useful to help understand some of the massive global changes that occurred as a result of contact. These seeds changed the ethnic makeup of countries and continents, the world's flora and fauna, and the health, nutrition, and number of people who came to populate the two worlds.

Seeds of Change
Sugar

On Columbus' second voyage to the New World, he brought stalks of sugar cane to establish a sugar industry on Hispaniola. Sugar cane is a labor-intensive crop that demands extraordinary human effort. Spaniards first used Native people to work the sugar cane fields. However, diseases had such a negative effect on the Native population, that it soon became necessary for the Spaniards to import slaves from Africa. Thus began the importation and enslavement of millions of Africans into the New World. The harsh work required of African slaves and malnutrition diminished their birth rate, consequently the supply of slaves from Africa needed to be replenished constantly.

By the middle of the sixteenth century, the sugar industry was completely dependent on black slave labor. This relationship between the production of sugar and African slavery dominated Caribbean life for four centuries. On some islands, Puerto Rico, Barbados, Cuba, and the Dominican Republic, sugar remains the main export. The cultures of Native America, Africa, and Europe dominate the West Indies today.

The cultivation of sugar cane also was the first step in the major destruction of the natural forestation of the land. As the forests were cleared for the cultivation of sugar cane, the region was plagued by drought and erosion.

Corn (Maize)

As contemporary Americans, we can hardly imagine not eating corn or products made of corn such as corn oil or tortillas. However, Europeans were not quick to adopt it for their own eating, feeding it instead to animals. The new animal food increased production of meat, lard, eggs, milk, butter, and cheese, and substantially increased the European intake of protein and the quality of their nutrition. Corn did for the animal population what potatoes did for the human population.

Corn—truly an American Indian gift to Europe—was also welcomed in Africa. Corn grew more reliably than did the traditional African staples of millet and sorghum. Unfortunately, however, corn also became a major source of nourishment and subsistence for Africans on slave ships, enabling them to survive the horrible trip. Corn and cassava root together created the great population explosion that continues in Africa today.

Potato

The potato was first cultivated in the Andes and slowly became a staple of the European diet. Quite

New World	Old World
Corn	Horse
Potato	Cattle
Tomato	Pig
Peppers	Sheep
(bell and chili)	Chicken
Chocolate	Honeybee
Vanilla	Wheat (Asian)
Tobacco	Rice, barley,
Beans (lima, pole,	oats, soy
navy, kidney)	Sugar cane
Pumpkin	Onion
Cassava root	Lettuce
(manioc)	Okra
Avocado	Peach
Peanut, pecan,	Pear
cashew	Watermelon
Pineapple	Citrus fruit
Blueberry	Banana
Sunflower	Olive
Petunia	Lilac
Black-eyed Susan	Daffodil
Dahlia	Tulip
Marigold	Daisy
Quinine	Dandelion
Wild rice	Crab grass

DISEASES

Syphilis	Smallpox
	Measles, mumps
	Diphtheria
	Cholera
	Whooping cough

Old World	New World

Table 5.2—*What Came From Where (Adapted from Schwartz, 1991, p. 62)*

amazingly, the potato enabled a European population, continually threatened by famine, to grow a nutritious supply of food in inhospitable soil on a very limited amount of land. Europeans had been dependent on grains, which were easily damaged by unpredictable weather. Potatoes cultivated in the New World were of unlimited variety (approximately three thousand kinds at the time of the Spanish conquest) and suited to many uses and many kinds of growing conditions. A field of

potatoes produces more food with more reliability and less labor than the same field planted in any grain. Potatoes don't require extensive milling and processing, and they can be consumed immediately or stored in a cool place for nearly a year. They can be cooked in innumerable simple ways.

The potato created a revolution that had the effect of increasing the quality of nutrition and thus the number of children who were born and who survived. With an increasing potato production and subsequent increases in population, countries with cool damp climates such as Russia, Germany, Ireland, Poland, Scotland, England, Belgium, and Scandinavia were able to progress. In many ways the potato seemed to be a miracle, for it cured Europe of the frequent famines that decimated the people and controlled population growth for centuries.

Horse

The horse, reintroduced by the Europeans to the Americas, changed forever many Native ways of life. Imagine for a moment the picture of a proud Sioux warrior astride a horse; this picture is so familiar that it is the nearly universal stereotype of the Native American. The horse is considered as part of traditional Indian ways and figures prominently in contemporary Indian life.

Horses were not new to these continents, but they were extinct at the time of contact. In 1501 there were from twenty to thirty horses on Epsilon and in two years there were at least sixty or seventy. They did not adapt well to the tropical lands of the continents, but their population exploded when they reached the temperate grasslands of the mainland. At the end of the sixteenth century their population was beyond counting.

Horses enabled Native people to hunt and wage war in ways previously unavailable to them. Because they were more mobile when hunting food, their communities became far more settled and stable. It was no longer necessary to move homes and families from hunting grounds to hunting grounds. Horses made their work more efficient, allowing time for leisure, specialization, art, and probably contemplation. Horses also promoted ranching, plowing, trade, and better communication between people separated by great distances.

Disease

Diseases that were introduced by Europeans into the Americas became invisible partners in the ultimate conquest of Native Americans. The Western Hemisphere was free of specifically human infections. Europeans, on the other hand, had many epidemic infections in childhood. Those who survived these childhood diseases were strong and immune to further disease. The list of diseases introduced by the Europeans included smallpox, measles, whooping cough, bubonic plague, malaria, yellow fever, diphtheria, amoebic dysentery, influenza, and probably others as well. Onslaughts of these diseases swept through Native populations for generations and decimated the people and helped to destroy their cultures.

The words of Tim Giago, editor of the *Lakota Times* in Rapid City, South Dakota, are a fitting summary of this chapter for they remind the reader of the strength and power of Indian people that have endured for more than five hundred years.

For once, and the quincentennial of Columbus may be the year it could happen, white America can make an effort to see this nation through the eyes of the Indian people, and maybe then they will understand why Indians will never be assimilated into a melting pot that would destroy them as a people.

Although their land base has greatly diminished and some cultures have been destroyed or altered, the one thing that has remained, even though it had to go underground for a few hundred years in order to survive, is the spirituality of the Indian people. This spirituality lives on, and having never died, need not be reborn. Perhaps this is the legacy of the indigenous people since Christopher Columbus (Giago, 1992, p. 12).

LESSON PLAN: COLUMBUS DAY

Grade Level: Grades 5–8

Basic Concepts: National principles and values, and change

Organizing Generalization: National holidays reflect the significant events and values of the nation. They are designated to commemorate and to honor people, or groups of people, whose achievements have furthered national principles or who represent dearly held values. Examples of this generalization, include the commemoration of people or groups such as President's Day, Martin Luther King, Christmas, Veterans Day, Memorial Day, Labor Day, and Mother's Day. Important events would include Independence Day, Thanksgiving, and Easter. In a democracy people are empowered through the rights of freedom of speech and representative government to decide when to designate a national holiday and, presumably, when to eliminate or modify it. The most recent example would include the events surrounding the designation of Martin Luther King Day as a national holiday.

Culture Area: Meso-American and Circum-Caribbean Culture Areas

Time Period: Contact–1492

Background: The national holiday of Columbus Day honors Christopher Columbus for his "discovery" of America. For many indigenous people, this is a day to mourn the destruction of their cultures and people. Is Christopher Columbus a hero worthy of honor? Should the subsequent brutal conquest of indigenous people under the initial command of Columbus be commemorated as a national glory or national dishonor? Is the honoring of Columbus acceptable in a multicultural country still populated by the conquered? The activity described below could be used to initiate an inquiry unit about Columbus or as a culmination of a unit of study.

Objectives:

Knowledge
Students will:
1. Identify core American values.
2. List American "icons" that commemorate Columbus such as cities, statues, buildings, parks, and institutions.
3. Learn about the processes and procedures that establish a national holiday.

Skills
Students will:
1. Analyze whether or not Columbus Day is congruent with stated American values.
2. Determine at least two different perspectives on a current issue.
3. Use research skills including interviewing.

Values
Students will:
1. Clarify their own personal values and take a personal stand, as future citizens, on the two issues raised.
2. Recognize that Native people generally feel strongly about the honoring of Columbus, the man whom they believed initiated the conquest of their people.
3. Recognize the diversity of American thought.

4. Understand the responsibility of citizenship to be informed, to question current practices, and to be active in supporting change, when it is deemed appropriate.

Activities:
1. Make a list of American national holidays and brainstorm with students why they believe these days are commemorated. Elicit the concept that holidays reflect people or events that we honor as part of our national heritage.
2. Make copies of the following excerpt of an editorial by Russell Means and Glenn Morris, members of the American Indian Movement (AIM) for each student. Students will need help with some of the vocabulary.
3. Ask students to work as partners and to restate the two proposals outlined in the statement.
4. Working in the following four groups, students will make lists of statements/facts/reasons for taking particular position advocated by their group. For lists, the references should be stated.
   Group A—Columbus Day should be replaced by a multicultural celebration.
   Group B—Columbus Day should not be replaced by a multicultural celebration.
   Group C—Columbus icons should be removed.
   Group D—Columbus icons should be retained.
5. Depending on the age and ability of the students, the teacher should make appropriate research materials readily available. If possible students should interview both Native and non-Native people. Students should substantiate their position with reasoned arguments.
6. Determine how students will present their lists/points of view to classmates (posters, debate, mock television commercials).
7. After thorough discussion of the various perspectives, ask students to vote on the two issues and cite the reasons for their decisions.

Extensions:
1. Take a poll of the positions of other students in the school regarding these issues.
2. Design a multicultural holiday to replace Columbus Day.

Evaluation: Students will write letters to the editor of a local paper in support of the position that they select. Letters should be informed and well written, but not graded on the position taken.

Materials/Resources:
1. A variety of appropriate resources are cited throughout this chapter; texts can also be included.
2. It is imperative to locate Native people to interview or to invite to class to speak on the topics.

LESSON PLAN: THE INTRODUCTION OF NEW DISEASES

Grade Level: Intermediate and Middle School

Basic Concepts: Disease and change

Organizing Generalization: Diseases which were brought to the New World were one of the most significant factors which enabled Europeans to conquer the Native people, and contributed to the eradication of Native culture.

Culture Area: Meso-American and Circum-Caribbean Culture Areas and general

Time Period: Immediately following European contact

Background: Diseases which were brought to the New World by Columbus and other early explorers totally destroyed some Native tribes and significantly contributed to the erosion of traditional Native cultures. Disease spread like ripples in a pond before the invading Europeans and had destroyed or weakened many tribal groups before they actually encountered the whites. Battles were easy to win against people who were weakened by disease. Nearly as destructive as physical death, was the loss of traditions as Native people, noticing that the Europeans were not as seriously affected, began to lose faith in their traditional healers and ceremonies. They converted to the Christian god, in hopes that his intervention would halt the spread of the diseases that were impervious to their own ancestral gods. This lesson lends itself to interdisciplinary study with an additional scientific emphasis on how diseases are transmitted. Teachers may want to discuss AIDS as a contemporary parallel.

Objectives:
Knowledge
Students will:
1. Discuss at least one reason why it is believed that Native people were immune to European diseases.
2. List the effects of European diseases on Native peoples (see Table 5.3).

Skills
Students will:
1. Locate the major disease epidemics throughout the New World on a map.
2. Chart the drop in the population of Native people as a result of disease, recognizing that although approximately 10 percent of the decline was caused by Indian-White conflict, the average tribal loss of life because of infectious diseases was 25–50 percent.

Values
Students will:
1. Recognize that Native people were not conquered by a superior people or by their technology, but largely by their diseases.

Activities:
1. Refer to the graph that introduces this chapter. Ask students to discuss why they believe the decrease in population was so great. List their hypotheses. They might speculate about the comparative effects of war and disease. Discuss the following statement. "The worst of the suffering [of Native peoples] was caused not by swords or guns but by germs."

2. Introduce how it is believed that the slow entry into the North and South American continents across the Bering Strait served as a "cold filter" destroying some sources of diseases and leaving Indian peoples relatively free of disease. Diseases also need crowded, unsanitary conditions which were not present in the New World, nor were domesticated animals which had introduced a wide array of diseases to Europeans. Over time, Europeans had become immune to many diseases to which Native people had not been exposed.

3. Students should then read, "The Great Disease Migration" by Geoffrey Cowley or other resource material.

4. Students can make individual maps of the major epidemics among Indians (see Waldman, p. 166) or chart the dramatic decline in Indian population as a result of European diseases. These maps and charts will be useful references as students study Indian people or American history further.

5. As a class, or as individuals, students should be able to construct a chart similar to Table 5.2. The chart can be used instead as an organizer for students' in-depth study.

Extensions:
1. Research how syphilis spread throughout Europe.
2. Report on the Native herbal remedies that were brought to Europe to cure diseases including syphilis.
3. Analyze the similarities between the spread of the diseases in the sixteenth century and of AIDS today.
4. Study how disease affected slavery in the New World.

Evaluation: See activity #5 above.

Materials/Resources:
Cowley, G. (1991, Fall/Winter). The great disease migration. *Newsweek* (Special Edition), p. 54 – 56. This article is suitable for older students or can be rewritten for younger children.

Hawke, S. D. & Davis, J. E. (1991). *Seeds of change.* Palo Alto, CA: Addison-Wesley.

Viola, H. J. & Margolis, C. (Eds.). (1991). *Seeds of change: A Quincentennial commemoration.* Washington, DC: Smithsonian Institution Press.

Waldman, C. (1985). *Atlas of the North American Indian.* New York, NY: Facts on File. pp. 166–67. The map used here is particularly important.

Introduction of European Diseases

DEATH OF THE PEOPLE	DESTRUCTION OF THE CULTURES
Indian people were too sick to defend their land and died in battle	More older people died and oral traditions were lost
They were too sick to plant or harvest crops and died of starvation	More children died so fewer young people grew up to have their own children
They were too sick to care for children who died from lack of care	They lost faith in their gods and ceremonies
Millions of Indian people died directly from disease	They became Christian to be protected by the white god
	Marriage changed as old traditions were changed to insure survival
	Small groups of survivors banded together to form new groups
	Entire tribes were destroyed by disease.

Table 5.3—Introduction of European Diseases: Smallpox, Mumps, Measles, Whooping Cough, Cholera, Yellow fever

A Columbus Day Statement

To dignify Columbus and his legacy with parades, holidays and other celebrations is intolerable to us. As the original peoples of this land, we cannot, and will not, countenance social and political festivities that celebrate our genocide. We are embarking on a two-pronged campaign in the quincentenary year to confront the continuing racism against Indian people.

First, we are advocating that the divisive Columbus Day holiday should be replaced by a celebration that is much more inclusive and more accurately reflective of the cultural and racial richness of the Americas. Such a holiday will provide respect and acknowledgement to every group and individual of the importance and value of their heritage, and will allow a more honest and accurate portrayal of the evolution of the hemisphere. It will also provide an opportunity for greater understanding and respect as our societies move ahead into the next 500 years. Opponents of this suggestion react as though this proposal is an attack on an ancient, time-honored holiday, but Columbus Day has been a national holiday only since 1971—and in 1991, hopefully, we can correct the errors of the past, moving forward in an atmosphere of mutual respect and inclusiveness.

Second, and related to the first, is the advancement of an active, militant campaign to demand that federal, state and local authorities begin the removal of anti-Indian icons throughout the country. Beginning with Columbus, we are insisting on the removal of statues, street names, public parks, and any other public objects that seek to celebrate or honor devastators of Indian peoples. We will take an active role in the removal of anti-Indian monuments and icons, and we will take an active role of opposition to public displays, parades, and celebrations that champion Indian-haters. We encourage others, in every community in the land, to educate themselves and to take responsibility for the removal of the anti-Indian vestiges among them.

For people of goodwill, there is no better time for a reexamination of the past, and a rectification of the historical record for future generations, than the five hundredth anniversary of Columbus' arrival.

—Glenn Morris and Russell Means, Colorado
American Indian Movement
the *Denver Post*, October 12, 1991

BERKELEY SETS INDIGENOUS PEOPLES DAY

October 12, usually celebrated across the country as Columbus Day, now will be honored as Indigenous Peoples Day in the bay area city.

The whole of 1992, which marks the 500th anniversary of Columbus' first landing in the Americas, has been designated The Year of Indigenous People by Berkeley officials.

"Berkeley wants to celebrate the important place that indigenous people hold in this country," said Mayor Loni Hancock, who joined other city leaders yesterday in beginning a yearlong series of events to mark the change.

"(Our) activities will be dedicated to an accurate history, with focus on learning from the mistakes of the past, instead of repeating them." The city's declaration underscored the revisionist notion that Columbus wasn't the heroic man who discovered America, but was a European colonist whose arrival in the New World led to the deaths of millions of Indians.

Berkeley apparently is the first U.S. city to officially change the name and focus of the explorer's holiday.

The change, first approved by the city council last fall, will bring everything from reprinted city documents to a new emphasis in school curriculums.

—Adapted from the *Denver Post*—January 11, 1992

SUMMARY
CONTACT AND THE LEGACY OF COLUMBUS

"In fourteen hundred and ninety-two Columbus sailed the waters blue." The voyage of Columbus in 1492, the first of four voyages, resulted in the encounter of two old worlds—the eastern hemisphere met the western hemisphere and things would never again be the same. It is incorrect to say "discover" or "new world" for Native people have been here for millenia and were hardly new to these continents. Nor were they savage and uncivilized people.

At the time of the first voyage of Columbus, there existed at least two hundred to three hundred languages spoken in North America. Both simple and highly developed cultures existed throughout the continent. The people were healthy and remarkably free of serious diseases.

In the year of the five-hundredth anniversary of the landing of Columbus, great controversy arose. Indian people were indignant that the world would celebrate a man who brought disease, death, and destruction to the people who had developed these rich and diverse cultures throughout North and South America.

The encounter between these two worlds was inevitable. However, the legacy of Columbus has been bitter and destructive for Indian people. The diseases brought by the Europeans destroyed entire tribes and weakened others. The Europeans attempted to convert Indian people to Christianity; they enslaved them, and attempted to destroy their cultures and seize their lands.

Columbus was not a hero. The exchange of cultures, however, has forever changed the world. Indian gifts include corn and potatoes, democracy, and new medicines. The Europeans brought horses and new technologies such as glass and certain metals. We are still learning how Indian values can make our lives better.

The Arrival of Coronado

CHAPTER 6

The First Years: 1492–1620

COLUMBUS DAY

In school I was taught the names
Columbus, Cortez, and Pizarro and
A dozen other filthy murderers.
A bloodline all the way to General Miles,
Daniel Boone and General Eisenhower.

No one mentioned the names
Of even a few of the victims.
But don't you remember Chaske, whose spine
Was crushed so quickly by Mr. Pizarro's boot?
What words did he cry into the dust?

What was the familiar name
Of that young girl who danced so gracefully
That everyone in the village sang with her
Before Cortez' sword hacked off her arms
As she protested the burning of her sweetheart?

That young man's name was Many Deeds,
And he had been a leader of a band of fighters
Called the Redstick Hummingbirds, who slowed
The march of Cortez' army with only a few

Spears and stones which now lay still
In the mountains and remember.

Greenrock Woman was the name
Of that old lady who walked right up
And spat in Columbus' face. We
Must remember that, and remember
Laughing Otter the Taino who tried to stop
Columbus and was taken away as a slave.
We never saw him again.

In school I learned of heroic discoveries
Made by liars and crooks. The courage
Of millions of sweet and true people
Was not commemorated.

Let us then declare a holiday
For ourselves, and make a parade that begins
With Columbus' victims and continues
Even to our grandchildren who will be named
In their honor.

Because isn't it true that even the summer
Grass here in this land whispers those names,
And every creek has accepted the responsibility
Of singing those names? And nothing can stop
The wind from howling those names around
The corners of the school.

Why else would the birds sing
So much sweeter here than in other lands?

(Durham, 1989, pp. 46–47)

In this way, the story of the European invasion begins in the New World with the conquistadors of Columbus, Cortez, and Pizarro and their violent conquest and enslavement of the Native people of the Caribbean. The poem speaks of latter-day "heroes," General Nelson Miles and President Dwight D. Eisenhower, whose leadership continued the destruction of Native people and cultures, but it also brings to our attention the survival of Indian people. It is this story of death and destruction that we continue in this chapter. And although we will talk of inhumanity and infamy, there are also acts of bravery, people of honor and noble intention, and Native survival to be recognized.

In this chapter we will outline the beginnings of the invasion of Europeans into what is now the United States. This period of time between Columbus (1492) and Jamestown (1607) has been called our forgotten century, the century in which Spain, France, and England first began the contest for superiority in the New World. Rather than the usual recounting of the adventures of such Europeans as Francisco Coronado, Hernando De Soto, Sir Frances Drake, Sir Walter Raleigh, Jacques Cartier, and Samuel De Champlain, we will explore this time when the outcome of supremacy was not clear—when no one people was politically dominant. And, more importantly, we will examine the various ways Indian people met initial invasion and subsequent conflict, coped with colonization and conquest, and adapted to the rapid changes that were forced upon them (see Table 6.1). We will note emerging patterns of Indian/European interaction that portend of events to come.

Term	General Meaning
Assimilation	To absorb into another cultural tradition
Passive resistance	To appear to submit to, accommodate to, or assimilate into the invading culture, while actually resisting assimilation
Defensive resistance	To defend one's own family, land, or possessions against invasion or attack
Aggressive resistance	To initiate resistance to invasion as to attack
Retaliation	To inflict harm or injury in return for a wrong, to take revenge, or exact retribution
Accommodation	To adjust to some of the ways of the other invading culture, often as a concession in order to achieve more important or long range goals
Collaboration	To cooperate with the invading force occupying one's own country
Negotiation	To confer with those of the invading culture so as to arrive at a settlement of some matter
Biculturalism	To function successfully within the culture of the conquering culture as well as maintaining identity with one's own traditional culture—acceptance of the validity of both cultures

These ways of dealing with and reacting to European invasion are not hierarchical, nor separate and discrete, nor specific to particular tribal groups or periods of time. However, they are useful in developing a general understanding of how Native people handled the invasion, conquest, and colonization of their lands and the attempts to obliterate their cultures.

Table 6.1—Ways Native People Reacted to European Invasion

First, a word about language. Historical accounts of this period of time speak from the perspective of the European, and the words most frequently used are "explorer" and "exploration." For people whose motive was acquisition of knowledge and understanding or peaceful coexistence, not land, wealth, power, prestige, or cultural change, the words "explorer" and "exploration" are appropriate terms. From the perspective of the indigenous people of the land who primarily experienced European exploration as death, destruction, and the loss of their land and culture, the better term for the European intrusion is "invasion." We will use the term invasion to explain the spread of Europeans throughout the continent and invaders or adventurers to describe those Europeans who ventured into this new land. The following supports this position:

> The European conquest of the Americas has been termed one of the darkest chapters of human history, for the conquerors demanded and won authority over the lives, territories, religious beliefs, ways of life, and the means of existence of every native group with which they came in contact. No one will ever know how many Indians of how many tribes were enslaved, tortured, debauched, and killed. No one can ever reckon the dimensions of the human tragedy that cost, in addition to lives, the loss of homes, dignity, cultural institutions, standards of security, material and intellectual accomplishments, and liberty and freedom to millions upon millions of people. The stain is made all the darker by the realization that the conflict was forced upon those who suffered; the aggressors were the whites, the scenes of tragedy the very homelands of the victims (Josephy, 1985, p. 278).

The European invasion of America lasted from the end of the fifteenth century into the nineteenth century and was a part of worldwide expansionist efforts. Five European nations sent expeditions to the New World and claimed title to territory by right of discovery—Spain, France, England, the Netherlands, and Russia. Portugal established claims in South America, and there were Swedish claims along the Delaware Bay from 1638 to 1654. However, the first century was dominated by the Spanish who spread north from Mexico and along the eastern and western coasts of the United States and who commanded the forces of invasion and exploitation in the sixteenth century.

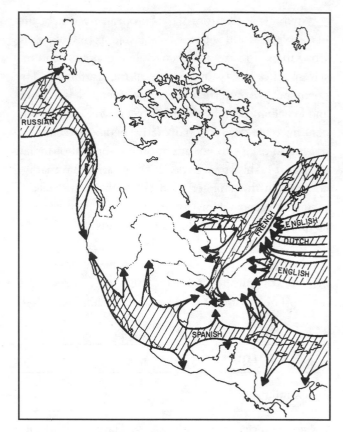

Map 6.1—General Paths of Early Penetration into North America by European Nations (Adapted from Waldman, 1985. p. 73).

Scholars point out that for the Indians, in both the east and the west, there was certainly no clear indication until the late 1700s that any one of these five newcomer European nations would be triumphant (Spicer, 1983).

In 1493, soon after Columbus' encounter with the New World, Pope Alexander VI divided the world outside of Europe between Spain and Portugal and gave Spain all of the western hemisphere except Brazil. In official policy, Spain gave priority to the conversion of the Native peoples to Catholicism and to the Spanish culture. The Spanish invaders and conquistadors were characterized not only by their zeal for conversion to Catholicism and their driving need to obliterate Native cultures, but by their lust, greed, and need to be served by a subjugated and, to their way of thinking, inferior people. A royal decree, the *requerimiento*, was required to be read by conquistadors to tribes informing the people of their duty to the Pope and the Spanish Crown and their right to freedom, if they submitted, and, if they refused, of the threat of war and enslavement.

In 1494, on his second voyage to the New World, Columbus established his first colony on Hispaniola. By 1515 there were seventeen Spanish towns on the island. An amazing transformation took place in approximately twenty years; the same people who had welcomed Columbus on his first voyage of discovery were now enslaved, working the mines and the crops of sugar cane, cotton, and grain. In a brief twenty years, the population of Native people on this one island diminished from approximately 250,000 to 14,000 and in a few more years the indigenous population would become nearly extinct. They died from military encounters, maltreatment, and European diseases. Rather than total extinction, eventually the survivors became mixed with the Spanish conquerors and with the black slaves who had been imported from Africa.

The Catholic missionaries, the military posts, and the civilian settlements of farmers, ranchers, miners, traders, and trappers all had a use for Indian people and policies such as the *encomienda* system were used to insure obliteration of Indian culture, Indian conversion to Catholicism, and cheap labor. The *encomienda* system was a grant made to a favored individual for the right to the land and labor of the Native people in a particular area. In return, the grantee was given responsibility for the physical and spiritual well-being of his charges. It was designed to put the Indians to constructive labor and to facilitate their conversion to Christianity. It was also to give the Indians some protection for the goals designated by the church and the crown. In practice, it became a tool for enslavement.

The goals of Columbus and explorers that followed him to subjugate the Indian people and to recreate them in their own image dominated Spanish ventures into new territories. The conquistadors conquered the Indians. The colonists colonized them. European diseases decimated them. Missionaries and reformers Christianized them. All efforts were designed to eradicate those beliefs, values, world views, and lifeways that defined Indian people and sustained their cultures. Never do we see major sustained efforts by the Spanish to live peacefully among the people or to establish a multicultural society in this new and spacious land. The story of the conquest of the lands that became the United States begins with the Spanish forays into the desert areas of the Southwest, into the Southeast, in the large expanse of land that was called La Florida, and along the western coast into what is now California.

The Spanish and the Pueblo People of the Southwest

The Spaniards who poured into the Americas in the wake of Columbus were bent on riches and glory. They were tough, rapacious plunderers, who used the aid of the Indians when they needed it, and then horrified the natives by their cruelty and lust (Josephy, 1985, pp. 286–287).

Spain's three major and best-known efforts in the New World include the expeditions of Francisco Vasquez de Coronado (the Southwest desert areas and into the Southern Plains), Hernando de Soto (La Florida), and Juan Rodriguez Cabrillo (California). Each of these ventures was significant to Native people and the history of Spanish influence is still readily apparent in California, Florida, and the desert Southwest.

In 1528, Panfilo de Narvaez along with four hundred colonists landed at Tampa Bay on the west coast of Florida. Their initial encounter with the Indians suggested that they were not welcome and some of the colonists turned back. However, de Narvaez continued inland with approximately three hundred men including armed horsemen. The Indians attacked the intruders and eventually the Spaniards killed their own horses, used their skins for boats, and put to sea and, hopefully, to safety. The Spaniards who survived finally landed in the vicinity of Galveston Island, Texas, where the Indians, unfamiliar with the way of the Spanish, fed and cared for them.

During the harsh winter months, the group was reduced to five survivors including Alvar Nuñez Cabeza de Vaca and an African slave named Estevanico, who became informal and trusted slaves to the Indians. Eventually, four of the survivors escaped; one of the five chose to remain with the Indians. Ultimately they headed west, where on their long and tortuous journey back to Mexico and the Spanish slave catchers who found them, they met people and heard enticing tales of rich cities to the north.

When they finally reached Mexico City in July 1536, their reports of wealthy and wondrous cities created a sensation. Hernando de Soto and young Francisco Vasquez de Coronado were selected to head explorations to find the legendary Seven Cities of Cibola—cities of gold. They were preceded by a reconnaissance team under Fray Marcos de Niza,

Estevanico, and an escort of friendly Mexican Indians. The first people encountered by the Spanish were the inheritors of the ancient Anasazi culture.

At this time there were approximately sixteen thousand people dwelling in perhaps eighty settlements along the Rio Grande Valley, each one politically autonomous. Pueblo communities were closely knit groups in which the individual was subordinated to the group for the welfare of all. There were no social classes or differences in wealth; everyone worked and shared as equals. They were generally good-natured and peaceful (the name Hopi means "peaceful ones"). While they would fight for their homes and freedom, they were not an aggressive people. Individualistic qualities such as competitiveness, aggressiveness, and ambition for leadership were looked upon as offensive.

Religion, as has been mentioned in previous chapters, was a daily experience, influencing all of life and serving as the force that united the people. Religious ceremonies were prescribed by tradition to achieve results that would benefit the entire Pueblo. It is believed that Pueblo men spent as much as half of their time engaged in religious activities.

The Pueblo people were primarily dependent on intensive agriculture, with corn as the central crop. Food was also obtained by hunting and gathering. Women owned the crops as well as the houses and furnishings in the matrilineal clan societies. They also did a large part of the construction, including the mud plastering on the houses, cooked, and made beautiful pottery and basketry. They were a monogamous people, but divorce was a simple affair of placing the husband's possessions outside the door of the home. It was into this peaceful world that the advance agents of Coronado's expedition intruded.

Estevanico's advance runners first arrived at Hawikuh, the westernmost Pueblo of the Zunis which is still inhabited by the Zuni people today. Far from shining cities of gold and material wealth, Hawikuh and the Pueblos of the area were multistoried buildings of adobe and their only riches were corn and turquoise. Estevanico was not welcomed by the Indians at Hawikuh and was ordered to turn back. Instead, he advanced to the Pueblo and was killed there. Fray Marcos returned to Mexico, filled with fear, but reporting to Coronado that he found a settlement larger than Mexico City in a land larger and better than all of those previously discovered. "Larger and better than Mexico or Peru!" The reports of Fray Marcos only whetted the appetites of the Spanish for the riches of the fabled northern cities.

Understandably, Coronado was eager to "discover" these rich, mysterious lands to the north that Fray Marcos described. His assembled expedition included armed men on horseback, foot soldiers, Indian allies in war paint, Fray Marcos and other Franciscans, and sheep, cattle, goats, and swine to drive along as food and to supply the projected settlement. The expedition left in February 1540 to explore the southwest in search of these fabled cities, the wealthy Seven Cities of Cibola. (The Spanish always referred to the "Seven Cities of Cibola," but only six are known to ethnologists.)

It is interesting to note that according to Angie Debo (1989, p. 24), Coronado was committed by the government and his own inclination to do no harm to the Indian he should find—except to invade and possess their country. He carried an ample supply of trinkets and trade goods for he would take nothing—except their liberty—without paying for it. Although in the beginning he offered peace (under his terms), hardship, death, and destruction would be his legacy to the Indian people of the Southwest.

Initially, remembering Fray Marcos, the Indians first met Coronado with hospitality, supplying them with provisions. As the Spanish continued northward, the Cibolans, aware of the Spanish, began to remove their women and children to safety in preparation of the battle to come. The Indian people intended to defend their land. Two or three hundred Cibolan warriors confronted Coronado at the Pueblo, and after a brief battle, the Pueblo was captured. The journey had been longer and more difficult than anticipated; supplies were short and the Spanish expedition suffered severely from hunger. The hungry Spanish entered Cibola with an uncharacteristic reaction—they overlooked the lack of silver and gold and were grateful for the abundant food.

The nearby Hopi Pueblos also mounted an initial defense against the Spanish, only to be swiftly conquered. It was in the Hopi towns that the Spanish learned of great rivers to the west (the Colorado) and to the east (the Rio Grande). With Hopi guides, the Spaniards first looked at the Grand Canyon of the Colorado River.

The people of Cicuye (Pecos Pueblo) had also heard of the explorers and sent a delegation to Hopi with gifts. Two chiefs of this delegation told of the plains to the north with buffalo too numerous to count and offered to guide Coronado there. One of the chiefs conducted the Spaniards back to his own town of Cicuye which was at that time the strongest of all the Pueblos. Here the visitors were again welcomed and given presents.

Here we see a form of collaboration. Two slaves from Cicuye then guided the Spaniards to the plains where they finally found the buffalo in great numbers. However, Coronado's interest in gold and riches made him vulnerable to false leads that promised great treasures as he, led by slave guides, then wandered to the grass huts of the Wichita Indians in Quivera on the plains of Kansas. Quivera was reputed to hold fabulous wealth in gold, silver, and fabrics. The trickery ended with the guides in iron collars and chains—and a great deal of hostility between the Indians and the Spanish.

The Indians continued to provide for the Spanish, but their hospitality and good will was becoming strained. The unpunished rape of an Indian woman caused even further rancor. In yet another incident, the Spanish set vicious dogs on the captive chiefs. And when the Indians' store of cloth was used, the Indians were stripped of the garments they were wearing in order to supply the Spanish. It wasn't long before the Indian people were plotting resistance. One of Coronado's men, Garcia Lopez de Cardenas, after storming one of the Pueblos, set up stakes, fastened Indian captives to them, and burned them alive. Coronado used this as an example of how the Spanish punished those who resisted them. An appalling number of Indians were killed eventually, and the women and children were captured and enslaved.

Ultimately, Coronado left Quivera and the Southwestern Pueblos. In April 1542 he started on the long trail back to Mexico. He left the Pueblo people with grievous losses and enduring hostility toward the Spanish. Coronado and his lieutenant Cardenas stood trial for the atrocities committed among the Indian people. Coronado was acquitted and Cardenas was fined and sentenced to a year of rigorous army service. After the return of Coronado, without gold, silver, or riches, the Southwest was abandoned until 1598.

For more than four decades the Pueblos were undisturbed. Then, in 1598, a large expedition of settlers, soldiers, and priests under Don Juan de Onate set out to establish control over the Pueblo country. Onate removed the Indians from their Pueblos on the Rio Grande and established a temporary capital for his new colony. Those Pueblos that resisted were destroyed and their inhabitants killed, tortured, or enslaved.

At Acoma Pueblo the Spaniards destroyed the Pueblo and massacred five hundred men and three hundred women and children. About five hundred women and children and eighty men were taken alive. All of the prisoners over twelve years of age were sentenced to twenty years of slavery; the men over twenty-one had one foot cut off as an additional penalty. All the girls under twelve were turned over to the friars to be distributed, and the boys were given to the Spanish victor, Vincente de Zaldivar. Some prisoners probably escaped. In another battle, eight or nine hundred Indians were slaughtered, three Pueblos were destroyed, and four hundred prisoners were taken.

The dreaded Spanish *encomienda* system, which enslaved the Indians, was imposed in the Pueblos. The Franciscan friars were established and Catholic churches were built to replace the established Native religions. By 1601, the once peaceful and prosperous Pueblos were a frightening scene of destruction. As the Indian population was decimated, it became more difficult to acquire adequate food and supplies and many of the Spanish returned to Mexico. Acoma Pueblo reestablished itself on the top of its mesa and in 1603 had achieved an uneasy peace.

A permanent Spanish capital was established at Santa Fe in 1610 by Onate's successor. Both Onate and Zaldivar were convicted and punished for their cruelty to the Indians but scholars point out that they could not have carried out their assignments without cruelty. The aristocratic Spanish expected to be fed, clothed, and served by the Indians—and there was no compassionate way to persuade them to do this.

An interesting course of action dominated the way that the Indians, once defeated in battle, dealt with the Spanish and that was through passive resistance. Though forced to become nominal Catholics, the peaceful Pueblo people clung secretly to their own customs and beliefs and continued to engage in their ceremonies in the underground kivas. Cruelty, conflict between civil and religious authorities, devastating droughts, and Apache raids worsened the plight of the Indian people, and they increasingly turned toward their own religion. They kept their thoughts secret and maintained a conspiracy of silence. Resisting change, they avoided contact with white people whenever possible and became determined to preserve their old culture.

This passive resistance was effective. The Spanish settlers and soldiers were not offended by what they saw or knew about and were willing to allow the Indians enough land to raise the food that they needed. "The organized and relentless reticence of the Indians prevented personal quarrels with the whites, and their obvious poverty offered no temptations to white thievery, so there was little friction" (Wissler, 1989, p. 240).

The stern rule of the Spanish led to the Pueblo Revolt of 1680 in which almost all of the eastern and western Pueblos united in resisting the common enemy. The Pueblo Revolt will be discussed more fully in the next chapter, but it is important to note that the peaceful Pueblo people were engaged for a long period of time in warding off Spanish dominion. Ultimately all the Pueblos were able to cling to their ancient beliefs and customs, despite the treatment of the Spaniards. Through both passive and active resistance and the deliberate policy of trying to exclude outside influences that might destroy their way of life, they have managed to retain many of their traditional cultural traits to the present day. The Pueblo people and their lifeways have survived.

The Spanish did introduce wood ovens, wheat, chilies, cantaloupe, horses, cattle, sheep, mules, and chickens to the Pueblos. They also taught the Indians blacksmithing, weaving wool, and woodworking. These were major modifications to traditional cultures.

The Spanish colonial pattern differed significantly from that of the French and the English in North America. In the Spanish colonies, the Spaniards became rulers of the Indians whose labor they employed to extract wealth from the land and produce commodities and a lavish lifestyle for the conquerors. This form of rule has been called "parasitic" in that it consumed everything and produced nothing. When the sources of wealth became scarce, other countries had become more industrialized, and Spain became a second-class power.

The English and the People of the Northeast

At this point, we will deviate briefly from our intent to use only the Iroquois of the Northeast to illustrate certain periods of time and patterns of interaction between the invading Europeans and the Native cultures. During this period, one rather romantic attempt of English colonization took place in North Carolina, and two major historic events took place along the eastern seaboard at Jamestown and Plymouth Rock. These events are worthy of mention.

In 1585, the first British settlement in North America was founded on Roanoke Island, North Carolina, headed by Richard Grenville and backed by his cousin, Sir Walter Raleigh. The settlement lasted only one year. Sir Walter Raleigh made a second attempt at a colony on Roanoke in 1586. The Roanoke colony failed when settlers disappeared. The mystery of the vanishing settlers remains unsolved. However, it is reasonable to conclude that the colonists may have taken refuge with Indians when their settlement failed.

It was during this attempt at colonization that the potato was brought back from the New World to England—an event that would have tremendous and enduring impact on the health and nutrition of the Europeans.

The English established their first permanent settlement in North America at Jamestown, Virginia, under John Smith in 1607. These settlers had extensive contact with the Tidewater tribes of the Powhatan confederacy. (We will discuss the importance of Creek and Iroquois confederacies in both the protection of Indian people and in the struggle for supremacy and survival in the following chapter.) John Smith's capture by the Indians gave rise to the romantic story of Pocahontas, the daughter of Chief Powhatan, who supposedly interceded on Smith's behalf and saved his life. As a romantic tale it leaves much to be desired for eventually Pocahontas was captured by the settlers. As a captive, she converted to Christianity. Eventually she married an Englishman, John Rolfe, and traveled to England to serve to demonstrate how the savages could be civilized. In our pictures of her, she looks much like a proper English woman. She died in England of a European disease in 1617. Her husband was killed in later battles with the Powhatans.

The approximately nine thousand Indians of the Powhatan confederacy were Algonquians. Each of nearly thirty tribes had its chief, but all were subject to Powhatan. The confederacy reigned up the Potomac River, west to the present site of Richmond, and south to the vicinity of the North Carolina border.

This period of time and the interaction of the English settlers with the Indians of the Powhatan confederacy is particularly interesting because it was interaction characterized by equality in that the English had not as yet achieved supremacy in the New World. However, the word equality must be used cautiously for interracial tensions and the assumption of the English that the Indians were "uncivilized" and "savage" were predominant. Unlike the Spanish who argued that Indians held legal title to their land, the English believed that the title of the land depended upon its use and that civilized people possessed a more legitimate claim to the land than the "savages." John Winthrop expressed this belief when he stated:

> that w[hi]ch lies common & hath never been replenished or subdued is free to any that will possess and improve it, for God hath give to the sonnes of man a double right to the earth, there is a naturall right & a Civill right (Viola, 1990, p. 73).

Other English colonists, such as Roger Williams, disassociated themselves from nearly all positions held by Winthrop and the Puritans. English policy would remain contradictory and confused throughout the colonial period.

Life was extremely harsh for the colonists and peace tentative; only 150 of the original 900 English colonists remained in Jamestown after the first three years. Of the seven thousand colonists sent there by the Virginia Company after 1607, only twelve hundred remained in 1624.

Initially, relationships between the colonists at Jamestown and the Indians of the Powhatan confederacy were reasonably peaceful. The Indians were attracted by the goods of the English—kettles, guns, beads, needles—that made their lives easier, and Powhatan recognized the benefits of peaceful trade with the colonists. The colonists needed food and, consequently, an uneasy peace prevailed. In the early years, the Indians of the Powhatan confederacy could have easily defeated the struggling Jamestown settlement.

Powhatan died in 1618 and relationships between the whites and Indians became steadily more strained. Soon war would break out and the Powhatan confederacy would be smashed.

Now, let us turn to our well-known Thanksgiving story. It begins for Indian people in 1615 when Squanto (or Tisquantum), a member of the Pawtuxet band of Wampanoags, was kidnapped and taken to Spain and sold into slavery. An Englishman took him to England where he learned English. In 1619 he returned to North America, finding his village totally gone as a result of European disease.

Squanto used his knowledge of English to assist the English settlers at Plymouth in living in a new and strange land. Our Thanksgiving stories tell of his help in planting corn and using fish for fertilizer and in saving the colonists from certain starvation. It is unlikely that the pilgrims would have survived without his assistance, and he is primarily responsible for our national holiday of Thanksgiving. In 1621, with Squanto acting as an interpreter, the pilgrims made a pact of peace and mutual assistance with Chief Massasoit of the Wampanoags, the first treaty between Indians and whites. Squanto died in 1622 of smallpox—one of the new diseases brought by the Europeans.

Squanto and Samoset, another well-known Indian in our history books, are good examples of a collaborative way of reacting to European invasion. This type of collaboration seems reasonable for those who initially do not perceive the settlers as conquerors. Later collaborative efforts are more directed to the achievement of mutual or self-serving goals.

Both England and France found that claiming possession of new lands in America was easy; making permanent settlements was not. The early attempts established a pattern in Indian–White relations. Initially, the Indians would share their food with the newcomers. When the supply ships were delayed, the settlers, having made feeble, ineffective, or no attempt to grow crops, would become demanding. The Indians, with their stores depleted, would refuse further aid. Then hostility would ensue (Debo, 1989, p. 33).

This is a kind of general pattern that is seen repeatedly as Europeans first encountered Native people. First, the Europeans received a welcome by the Indians, followed soon by their support, including food and supplies. Then, the Indians began to suffer abuse, which took a variety of forms, by European invaders. This abuse was then followed by retaliation by the Indian peoples.

Although the story of the Spanish, French, English, and Russian invaders, explorers, and conquerors is a story of subjugation, rape, pillage, slavery, torture, and death to great numbers of Native people and destruction of ancient lifeways, its cruelty and inhumanity were not unnoticed nor was it without outcries of sensitivity and conscience. And certainly it was not without its Native and occasionally non-Native heroes.

There are several people and policies of importance during this period that acknowledged and attempted to stem the decimation of Indian people and culture. The first is Bartholomew de Las Casas, a Catholic priest who accompanied Christopher Columbus and who went to Spain to intercede with King Ferdinand on behalf of Indian people. The conversion of Native people was officially declared to be the major purpose of Columbus' second voyage and six priests were sent to begin the task. Las Casas soon recognized that part of his religious duty must be to protect the indigenous people against the inhumane treatment they received from the Spaniards. He spent the rest of his life working on behalf of the Indian people. His writing, most notably, the works known as the Black Legend, were influential and although the acts of the conquistadors were not completely restrained, they were not as harsh as they might have been. The Black Legend was printed throughout Europe and there are those who believe that it is these words that initiated the prevailing prejudice held by many people today against Spaniards and those of Hispanic heritage.

> They [the Spaniards] came with their Horsemen well armed with Sword and Launce, making most cruel havocks and slaughters .... Overrunning Cities and Villages, where they spared no sex nor age; neither would their cruelty pity Women with childe, whose bellies they would rip up, taking out the Infant to hew it in pieces. They would often lay wagers who should with most dexterity either cleave or cut a man in the middle .... The children they would take by the feet and dash their innocent heads against the rocks, and when they were fallen into the water, with a strange and cruel derision they would call on them to swim .... They erected certain Gallowses ... upon every one of which they would hang thirteen persons, blasphemously affirming that they did it in honour of our Redeemer and his Apostles, and then putting fire under them, they burnt the poor wretches alive. Those whom their pity did think to spare, they would send away with their hands half cut off, and so hanging by the skin (Bartholomew de Las Casas as cited in Josephy, 1985, p. 287).

There were efforts made by the Church to ameliorate the treatment of Indians. In 1512, Pope Julius II issued a doctrine that the Indians were descended from Adam and Eve. Still they had to be Christianized and Hispanicized before they could be considered as less than inferior, pagan savages. The *encomienda* system was instituted to provide for conversion and "civilization" in return for nine months of labor each year. As previously noted, the system simply legalized enslavement. Those Indians who achieved "civilized" status were called *indios capaces*. Becoming "civilized" was perhaps an avenue to better treatment, but the cost was complete repudiation of what it meant to be Indian.

Pope Paul III in 1537 issued a papal bull that attempted to halt the resistance of natives to conversion by threatening excommunication to any whites who enslaved Indians or deprived them of their possessions. And in 1539, the lectures of Francisco de Vitoria in Spain advocated that Indians are free men and exempt from slavery. However, these pronouncements were made far from where they could be enforced, and they were generally ignored.

Herman Viola reminds us that there was a real basis for the stereotype of the noble red man and woman. Squanto, of course, is a good example of human helpfulness. And stories abound of shared feasts such as the Thanksgiving feast, acts of decency such as the intervention of Pocahantas in behalf of John Smith, marriages between Indians and whites such as that between Pocahantas and John Rolfe, and practical business and trading partnerships.

LESSON PLAN:
CONQUEST AND PASSIVE RESISTANCE—SOUTHWEST

Grade Level: Grades 5–8

Basic Concepts: Change/adaptation, passive resistance, cultural survival, and religious freedom

Organizing Generalization: When one nation conquers another, efforts are often made to impose the culture and lifeways of the dominant culture on the people of the conquered nation.

Culture Area: Southwest

Time Period: 1492–present

Background: One of the major goals of the Spanish, the conversion of Native people to Christianity, while forced upon and accepted by some, was resisted by others. Although the Spanish used extraordinary means to achieve that goal, many Indian people quietly, steadfastly, and secretly held to the traditional beliefs that had sustained them for centuries. In the Southwest today some Native people are Christian, yet traditional religions have survived and are practiced today. The privacy of the Pueblo Indians, developed as a means of dealing with the treatment of the Spanish, is still much a part of the Pueblo culture. In this book, we will follow this intolerance of Native religions through such important events as the development of the Ghost Dance, the battle of Wounded Knee, the passage of legislation to prohibit and then protect the rights of Native people to their traditional religious beliefs and practices, and, finally, to current issues regarding Native religions. Historically, the principle of religious freedom has not been extended to Native people, and this issue has continuing importance. The Hopi are an excellent example of the tenacity of Native people in retaining many of their ancient ways. This lesson can be restructured to emphasize different elements, depending on the age of the student.

Objectives:

Knowledge
Students will:
1. Define the term passive resistance.
2. Describe the methods of passive resistance used by Native people to preserve their traditional religious beliefs and practices.
3. Give at least one example of how Christian and Native religious practices are occasionally intertwined today.

Skills
Students will:
1. Practice predicting short-term and long-term outcomes.
2. Use written evidence to substantiate predictions.

Values
Students will:
1. Recognize the tenacity of traditional beliefs and the reluctance of many Native people to accept the beliefs of the dominant society.
2. Accept the validity of differing religious beliefs.

Activities:

1. After tracing the route of Coronado, and studying the values and goals of the Spanish adventurers, ask students to make a mural or individual drawings showing Coronado approaching the Pueblo people for the first time at the ancient Zuni site of Hawikuh. The first part of the brief article, *The Battle of Hawikuh*, can be read to set the scene of the impending battle.

2. Make the following chart on a handout for each pair or small group of students.

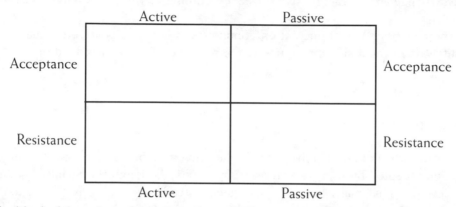

3. Using the blank chart, ask students to predict a possible response of the Native people to the Spanish attack. Then set aside the predictions and read in the text or other resources the actual outcome. Discuss the predictions. After conquest, would they continue to resist the Spanish actively?

4. Now lead students to a discussion as to how a people might react to conquest of the Spanish. Would they accept or resist Spanish ways? What were the goals of the Spanish? How might the Indian people resist without being killed? What would be important to them to save? Why?

5. Students can study the readings and define more specifically the term "passive resistance." The excellent article by Suina (1992, pp. 60–63) can be rewritten, if necessary, and read by students or read to them by the teacher. Help students to understand that the right to practice traditional religions was important to the survival of the people in the past and that the Pueblo people continue to protect their religion in the ways they learned from the conquest of the Spanish.

Extensions:

1. The history and folklore of New Mexico is particularly rich in Spanish, Indian, and Anglo traditions. Many Pueblo dances and ceremonies incorporate both Christian (Spanish) and Native traditions. Older students will enjoy research into New Mexico's contemporary expressions of this heritage.

2. Research the archaeological efforts at Hawikuh.

Evaluation: Students will define and give an example of how Indian people used passive resistance to protect their traditional religious beliefs and practices.

Materials/Resources:

Suina, J. H. "Pueblo Secrecy Result of Intrusions." *New Mexico,* (January 1992): 60–63.
Udall, S. L. "The Battle of Hawikuh." *Native Peoples* (Summer 1990): 25–29.
Weigle, M. and White, P. *The Lore of New Mexico.* Albuquerque: University of New Mexico, 1988.

READINGS

Historically, the reason why Pueblos withhold information derives from brutal encounters with early Europeans. The Spaniards viewed Pueblos as pagans, celebrating false idols, by Christian standards. They also saw the Pueblos as potential converts to the one true God through the Roman Catholic Church. Subverting the indigenous religion was the first step to replacing it with Christianity. Action against the Pueblo religion included collecting and burning religious paraphernalia before the public. Religious leaders were sought and whipped in front of their people to make examples of them. Such persecution resulted in more than just anger on the part of the Pueblos. It compelled them to value more deeply the core of their existence, their native religion.

Religious items, locations, ideas, activities, and leaders became well-guarded matters within the village. Secrecy became synonymous with preservation and was elevated to the status of a community-wide effort to save native religion. Eventually, much of what was considered religious was taken underground and guarded at all cost. The result was exactly the opposite of what the Spaniards had strived to achieve.
(Suina, 1992, pp. 60–63)

We have always had a religion. We have always believed in God and worshipped Him in our own way. It was not until the Spaniards came (in 1598) that we were told that God is a human being who lives up above the clouds somewhere. We were also told that there was a son of this god who came to live on the earth. He died in a horrible way to save us and that is why we were supposed to worship him.

At that time, these ideas were strange. To us, God was in rocks and trees and sky everywhere. We had the sun as our father and the earth as our mother; the moon and the stars were our brothers. We had never seen God as a human being before until the Spaniards came. Then the friars in their long brown robes went around with crossed sticks and prayers and water which they poured on our heads. They told us that we belong to their religion because they had just baptized us into it. Some of us mistook these friars for gods. Some of us resisted their religion because we were afraid of it. Some of us were beaten or put to death.

In the end we decided it did not make much difference what church there was on the outside. We have always had a church within ourselves. This is the one which counts. This is the one which will remain long after all of the outside churches have fallen down.
(Wood, 1974, p. 46)

SUMMARY
THE FIRST YEARS 1492–1620

The period 1492–1620 has been called our forgotten century, the time in which Spain, France, and England first began the contest for superiority in the "New World." This is a time when the outcome of European invasion was not clear—no European nation was dominant. Some Indian nations were as yet untouched (although European diseases spread rapidly, often preceding the white men).

You will be familiar with the names of the Europeans that began to explore this continent such as Francisco Coronado, Hernando De Soto, Sir Frances Drake, Sir Walter Raleigh, Jacques Cartier, and Samuel De Champlain. In the past, we have been taught that these men were heroes.

Now this is considered one of the darkest chapters of human history for these "explorers" were determined to take land, abolish traditional Indian religions and ways of life and destroy the ways that Indian people were able to provide for their well-being. It is said that the French wanted furs and trade, the British wanted land and power, and the Spanish wanted souls.

Bartholomew de las Casas, a Catholic priest who accompanied Columbus, was one of the first to speak out against the Spanish treatment of the Indians. His writing, known as the Black Legend, was influential throughout Europe and helped to lessen some of the cruelty of the Spanish.

One pattern of interaction that was seen repeatedly as Europeans first encountered Native people was initial welcome and hospitality. However, life was harsh for the first Europeans. When supply ships were delayed, the settlers, having made ineffective or no attempts to grow crops, would become demanding. The Indians, with their own supplies depleted, would refuse further aid. Then hostility would follow. Peaceful coexistence and mutual respect were rare.

TIME LINE: 1513–1621

1510 1520 1530 1540 1550 1560 1570 1580 1590 1600 1610 1620

1513
Juan Ponce de León (Spain) sailed from Puerto Rico to an island he named Florida.

1528–1536
Men of the Panfilo de Narvaez Expedition (Spain) including Alvar Nuñez Cabeza de Vaca and Estevan the Moor, trek though the Southeast into the Southwest.

1532–1534
Giovanni da Verrazano (France) explores the Atlantic Coast.

1534–1541
Jacques Cartier (France) explores the St. Lawrence River system in three voyages.

1539
Lectures of Francisco de Vitoria in Spain advocate that Indians are free men and exempt from slavery.

1539
Marcos de Niza and Estevan the Moor (Spain) explore the Southwest

1539–1543
Hernando de Soto (Spain) claims Florida for Spain and explores the Southeast.

1540–1542
Francisco Vasquez de Coronado (Spain) explores the Southwest in search of the Seven Cities of Cibola.

1542
Juan Rodriguez Cabrillo and Bartólome Ferrelo (Spain) explore the Pacific Coast.

c. 1560–1570
Iroquois League of Five Nations, including the Mohawk, Oneida, Onondaga, Cayuga, and Seneca tribes is formed by Deganawida, a Huron Iroquois prophet, and his Mohawk disciple Hiawatha.

1562–1564
Jean Ribault (France) establishes a short lived colony on Parris Island, South Carolina which was driven out by the Spanish.

1564–1565
René de Laudonnière (France) establishes a colony on the St. John's River in Florida until the Spanish drive them out. Among the French is the artist Jacques le Moyne, who creates the first-known European pictorial representations of Indians.

1565
Pedro Menendez de Aviles (Spain) found St. Augustine in Florida, the first permanent European settlement in North America.

1568
Jesuits organize a school in Havana for Indian children brought from Florida, which was the first missionary school for North American Indians.

1576–1578
Martin Frobisher (England) seeks the Northwest Passage to the Pacific.

1578–1579
Francis Drake (England) explores the California Coast.

1585–1586
Sir Walter Raleigh (England) backed the first British settlement, which lasted only one year, in North America on Roanoke Island, North Carolina.

1586–1590
Sir Walter Raleigh (England) established a second colony on Roanoke which failed when the settlers mysteriously disappeared.

c. 1586
Potato crop was brought back to England.

1598
Juan de Onate (Spain) founds colony in northern New Mexico, known today as San Juan Indian Pueblo.

1598–1599
Indians of Acoma Pueblo in New Mexico attack a group of visiting Spanish. One year later, a Spanish force under Juan de Onate retaliates and kills as many as eight hundred Indians.

c. 1600
Sheep brought into the Southwest by Spanish. Use of wool and loom introduced to Indians.

c. 1600–1770
Use of horse spreads from Mexico through the Southwest into the Great Plains.

1603–1615
Samuel de Champlain's (France) made numerous voyages in the Northeast.

1615
Champlain attacks Onondaga villages with Huron war party and turns Iroquois League against French.

1607
English establish their first permanent settlement in North America at Jamestown, Virginia, under John Smith.

1609
John Smith's capture by the Indians gives rise to the story of the intercession by Pocahontas, the daughter of Chief Powhatan, on Smith's behalf.

1609
Spanish found Santa Fe, New Mexico.

1609–1610
Henry Hudson (Holland) explores river now bearing his name.

1613
Pocahontas is captured by the settlers, converts to Christianity, marries John Rolfe, and travels to England, where she dies.

1614
United New Netherland Company begins developing the Dutch fur trade in North America.

1615
Squanto, a Wampanoag, is kidnapped and taken to England.

1620
Pilgrims (England) arrive in Plymouth. Squanto shows the Pilgrims how to plant corn and how to use fish as fertilizer.

1621
With Squanto acting as an interpreter, the Pilgrims make a pact of peace and mutual assistance with Chief Massasoit of the Wampanoags which was the first treaty between Indians and whites. The Pilgrims celebrate the first Thanksgiving.

The Great Tree of Peace

CHAPTER 7

The First Years Continued: 1621–1763

THE GREAT TREE OF PEACE

The Confederacy of Five (Iroquois) Nations began
with the Covenant—

The Covenant was the basis for the Law.
The Law was Peace.
Peace was a Way of Life.
characterized by Wisdom and Graciousness.
Wisdom sees Past, Present and Future at a glance.
Graciousness takes every individual understanding
into consideration as one part of the whole.
Understanding which is necessary for Peace.

These concepts are symbolized
by The Great Tree of Peace.
This Tree signifies the Law.
The Law is Peace among all Nations
which subscribe to the Constitution.
This Law undergirds the Constitution.

The branches of this Great Tree signify shelter,
giving each Individual
protection and security under the Law.

These branches are tended
by Those among the People who are Men.

The roots of this Great Tree
stretch to the Four Corners of the Earth—
signify the possible extension of this law
and this Peace
to any of Earth's children willing to accept them.

The White Roots of Peace are tended
by Those among the People who are Women.
Eagle—perched aloft—
sees Past, Present, and Future at a glance,
signifies watchfulness, wisdom, eternal vigilance.

Deganawida uprooted The Tree,
buried all weapons of war,
replacing The Tree to grow
and to shelter many Nations.
So be it.

Deganawida speaks through the People—
His hands are People's hands
His voice is the People's voice,
His wisdom is our wisdom.

—Turtle Woman Singing

(Spencer, 1987)

By the early 1600s, the Native nations of North America had begun to suffer greatly at the hands of the invaders from the East. During the first one hundred years of invasion, the nations were not well organized, nor did they have regular methods of communication with each other. As time went by and the nations from the East Coast gradually moved inward to the West, they exchanged tales of their experiences with the white men. Depending on where the Indians lived, they had dealings with one of three major countries, England, France, and Spain, or one of several other countries that had short-lived interest in land in North America. This exchange of information was the beginning of relationships between tribes that prepared the way for new ways of responding to the invasion.

In this chapter, we will discuss how Native people cooperated with each other in order to deal more effectively with the European invasion. This cooperation was manifested in loosely organized joint ventures, such as the Pueblo Revolt of 1680, and other well-known and effective cooperative efforts such as the confederacies of early times including the Powhatan Confederacy, the Creek Confederacy, and perhaps the best known of all, the Iroquois Confederacy. Confederacies were formed among Native nations for the purpose of protection and survival.

Particular strategies used by the confederacies varied depending on the circumstances and what they perceived to be in their best interests. For example, the Pueblo people joined together to mount the Pueblo Revolt of 1680 against the Spanish. They worked together as a group in a singular act of defiance of the Spanish rule. The Powhatan Confederacy, known as the Tidewater Tribes, was formed as a means of defense against the British. The Tidewater Tribes worked together for many years attempting to destroy the English settlements. The Iroquois initially joined forces to defend themselves against other tribes; then the initial six tribes conquered other Native nations to gain further strength and power. They later joined the English to further their own causes against the Huron and the French.

Some confederacies were large, while others were quite small. In some instances, the nations defended themselves when under attack while, in other cases, the nations attacked in revenge for a wrong against them.

Some nations appeared to succumb to the invaders while secretly maintaining their culture. Other tribes adopted the ways of the invaders to avoid destruction altogether. Each nation or group of nations experienced a very unique and individual destiny in their relationship with the Europeans because of their location, societal structure, resources, and size and stage of evolution.

The Powhatan Confederacy

Why will you take by force what you may obtain by love? Why will you destroy us who supply you with food? What can you get by war? ... We are unarmed, and willing to give you what you ask, if you come in a friendly manner ...

I am not so simple as not to know it is better to eat good meat, sleep comfortably, live quietly with my women and children, laugh and be merry with the English, and being their friend, trade for their copper and hatchets, than to run away from them ...

Take away your guns and swords, the cause of all our jealousy, or you may die in the same manner.

—Powhatan in a speech at Werowocomico, 1609
(Armstrong, 1984, p.1)

The Powhatan Confederacy occupied the region around Chesapeake Bay in modern-day Virginia. Powhatan, their "king," otherwise known as Wahunsonacock, believed that efforts toward negotiation with and accommodation to the English settlers and their ways would be rewarded. He lived his life clinging to the fragile peace that his philosophy created. However, after Powhatan's death in 1618, Opechancanough, his brother, became the leader of the Powhatan Confederacy which was also known as the Tidewater Confederacy. The Confederacy consisted of approximately thirty-two Algonquian-speaking tribes. During the four years that followed Powhatan's death there was a tenuous peace. The English continued to demand more land to grow the much needed tobacco for export to England. Opechancanough knew that he had to stop the encroachment of the English.

On the morning of March 22, 1622, Opechancanough and hundreds of warriors swept out of the forest and raided the colony's tobacco fields, killing every English settler in sight with casualties numbering around 340 men, women, and children. From this time on, the English colonists began the process of exterminating the Indians. Regular patrols of militia burned Tidewater villages and fields. When invited to meet for the purposes of establishing peace, the unsuspecting tribal representatives were poisoned by the colonists. Opechancanough plotted revenge. He battled until 1646, when he died at the hands of an angry guard after being caught by Governor William Berkeley during a raid on the colonists.

For thirty years a fragile peace existed between the colonists and the remaining Tidewater tribes. In 1675, fighting broke out again. This encounter was known as Bacon's Rebellion, for the man who led the group of vigilantes that decided to handle the Indian problem for themselves. Bacon died in 1676, probably of tuberculosis, and peace once again reigned in the Jamestown area.

The Tidewater Confederacy was a form of cooperation between tribes in the effort to save their lands from the English. In the beginning, the actions of Opechancanough and his warriors could be defined as methods of defensive resistance. They defended their homes and families against invasion and attack. By the time they began plotting revenge and planning attacks as retribution, they had initiated more aggressive methods of dealing with the settlers.

THE PEQUOT WAR

To the north of the Tidewater Tribes, the Pequot, Wampanoag, Narraganset, and Mohegan tribes were experiencing a similar fate. For some time after the founding of the Plymouth Colony, there was a state of peace between the Native people and the colonists. This fragile peace was held together by the power and charisma of a Wampanoag leader or *sachem*, Massasoit. As the numbers of colonists grew, the tension grew and conflict seemed inevitable. A lack of communication between tribes led to their isolated defensive maneuvers and their ultimate failure.

The Pequot Tribe was the first nation to lose patience with the colonists and their promises. They were surrounded on three sides by "enemies" with Dutch settlers to the north, English on the west, and the Narragansets to the east. This caused them to take a defensive posture. Tensions on all sides mounted and

as a reaction to two recent deaths of coastal traders at the hands of the Indians in 1636, Captain John Endecott and ninety men descended on Block Island, just off the coast of present-day Connecticut. They killed all of the adult males, mostly Narragansets, and then turned their fury on the mainland and the Pequots. The Pequots, knowing of the coming siege by the colonists, attacked the colonists during the winter of 1636–1637, before Captain Endecott could mount an attack.

Under the leadership of *sachem* Sassacus, the Pequots continued to defend their lives and their villages through the winter. The colonists gathered and organized their forces in the spring. They traveled to Narraganset country and enlisted their aid against the Pequots. The Miantinomo and Niantics also joined forces with the colonists. They attacked the Pequot village on May 25, 1637, at dawn, setting the wigwams aflame and waiting for the Pequots to flee. As they fled the burning village, the Narragansets and Mohegans cut them down. Those who stayed behind were burned to death. *Sachem* Sassacus escaped to Mohawk territory only to be beheaded by the Mohawks, anxious to prove their loyalty to the British. The remaining Pequot tribal members either joined neighboring tribes or were sold into slavery in the West Indies. A lack of communication between tribes and loyalty to each other against all odds contributed to the isolated efforts of each tribe to unsuccessfully defend themselves alone.

KING PHILIP'S WAR

Meanwhile, colonial missionaries were eager for new converts, creating the "praying Indians" among the Algonquians. Land was dwindling, resources were becoming scarce, and the number of colonists was growing. Metacom, also known by the English name, King Philip, was the son of Wampanoag *sachem* Massasoit. As a young boy growing up in these troubled times, he saw the peace that resulted from the efforts of his father to keep the Algonquian tribes together and maintain a sense of cooperation between the tribes and the colonists.

As Metacom grew older, he observed that the peace was harder to maintain. At the age of twenty-four, he saw his older brother die of poisoning at the hands of the colonists. When Metacom became the official *sachem* of his people, he too was arrested and brutally questioned. During his rule as *sachem* of his

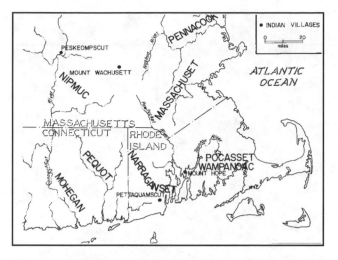

Map 7.1—Northeastern U.S.—Powhattan and Pequot Areas.

people, he worked to keep the land and resources for his tribe. Toward the late 1660s and early 1670s he saw that he could not stand alone against the growing number of colonists.

He then mounted an effort to form a confederacy among his neighboring tribes, ending years of tribal rivalries. But his efforts came too late and, in 1675, when war came to the region, the alliance had not been well enough established. The Wampanoags were left alone to fight the colonists and several other tribes who joined forces with the colonists. The Wampanoags were all but exterminated. Those who remained were sold as slaves or joined other tribes. A pattern had been set for Indian–white interactions, a pattern that would repeat itself time and time again.

The many wars on the Atlantic seaboard between the Native nations and the British and French were typical of the conflict that enveloped the seventeenth century and extended into the eighteenth century. The conflict in North America was an extension of the battle being waged in Europe between the French and the British. The battles in North America pitted tribe against tribe, each fighting on one side or another for what was offered by the European countries, such as firearms, blankets, and other trade goods. They accommodated France or England, while fighting against the other. King William's War (1689–1697), Queen Anne's War (1702–1703), King George's War (1744–1748), and the Great War for the Empire (1754–1763) are commonly known as the French and Indian Wars. The British were the victors over the French, but their rule

would be short lived as the new Americans would soon gain power over all others in North America. It was the Indian nations, however, who lost more than any other nation as the United States was born.

In contrast to the loosely knit and quickly formed coalitions of the Northeast were the Iroquois and the Creek Confederacies. These confederacies were well established with strong internal organization and internal and external communication systems when they came into direct contact with the Europeans. Due to this sophistication, they were able to stay together longer and mount stronger defenses. This strength also enabled them to maintain their language, culture and tradition with less adaptation into modern times than many other tribes. A closer look at the structure of these two confederacies will encourage a better understanding of their achievements.

THE IROQUOIS CONFEDERACY

Early life among the sovereign nations of New York was often hostile, with small fights and battles between nations. Then, a great visionary leader of the Mohawk Nation, known as Deganawida, established the Great Peace among the Mohawk, Oneida, Onondaga, Cayuga, and Seneca Nations. He accomplished this great task with the assistance of an Onondaga orator, Hiawatha. Most historians date the founding of the Great Peace around 1000 A.D., but the Iroquois insist that it was over a thousand years ago. The Great Peace, otherwise known as the Iroquois League or Confederacy, was based on the values of freedom, respect, brotherhood, and consensus. The Great Peace became six nations with the addition of the Tuscarora, who fled the Carolinas in 1722. The Tuscarora were considered a junior member of the League and were not given official status.

The Haudenosaunee, or The People of the Long house, each held position within the Great Peace. The Mohawks and the Senecas were known as the Older Brothers. They heard all issues first, and then made recommendations to the Younger Brothers, the Cayugas, and the Oneidas. When they disagreed, the Onondagas, or the Keepers of the Fire, would moderate and search for a way of compromise or understanding. Once discussion renewed and a decision made, the Keepers of the Fire were responsible for confirmation. As a last resort, when no other understanding could be reached, the Onondagas would extinguish the council fire and give all the nations the right to pursue independent action.

The Confederacy was governed by a Council of Fifty. These fifty seats were distributed with fourteen Onondagas, ten Cayugas, nine Mohawks, nine Senecas, and eight Oneidas. The Onondagas held the position of Council Head, because of the nature of their role in the Confederacy. They also occupied the roles of two counselors to the Council Head. An additional Onondaga held the position of Keeper of the Council Wampum. Meetings were held annually to decide on matters that were of mutual concern.

According to O'Brien (1989, p. 19), women could not hold seats on the Council of Fifty. They did, however, nominate the men who did sit on the council. The Clan mothers would observe the men, both young and old, looking for qualities such as generosity, loyalty, and tolerance—men who could hold their temper and talk a problem through to resolution. These were the type of men they nominated. When a young man was nominated and accepted into the council, the Clan mother who nominated him would often serve as a mentor until he could hold his own in the council.

The Solitary Pine Trees was another important group of men in the Great Peace. While they had no vote in the council, they had a right to speak at council meetings. This right they earned through bravery or merit. They acted as the voice for their respective communities relating their concerns, ideas, and questions to the council (O'Brien, 1989, p. 20).

Under the Great Peace, no civil leader could be a war leader. The enemy of one was the enemy of all. The council ruled on all matters not with a majority vote but with a unanimous vote. This was their strength. The goal of the Confederacy in the seventeenth Century was to subordinate other neighboring Indian nations and to resist the domination of the French. During this time, there were approximately thirty thousand Iroquois. The Mohawks numbered about five thousand, the Oneidas around three thousand, the Senecas around ten thousand, the Cayugas around three thousand, and the Onondagas around five thousand.

By the early 1600s the Iroquois Confederacy asserted its sovereignty in the northeastern woodlands of North America. They had a dual goal: first, to subordi-

Illustration 7.1—Wampum belt. Courtesy of Joel Monture.

nate the neighboring tribes in New England and both west and south from there, and second, to ward off the French. They established trade alliances with both the Dutch and English. The Dutch alliance was formed in 1630 with the Mohawks to enable the Dutch to reach further inland in their search for furs. The Dutch were soon to exhaust the supply on the eastern seaboard. For the Iroquois, this alliance also served the purpose of establishing a trade source, independent from the French, to arm and supply them. The relationship between the English and the Iroquois began with the Dutch. When the Dutch returned to Europe, the English assumed the Dutch lands and alliances.

A target for the Iroquois in their quest to control local tribes, trade, and land in the northeast was the Hurons who were friendly with the French. The French were an ever-increasing threat to the Confederacy. Their numbers grew, and their hunger for furs and land expanded. The French traded directly with the Hurons who once traded with the Iroquois. Years of tenuous relations ended, when, in 1649, the Mohawks and Senecas attacked the Hurons. The fighting left hundreds of Hurons dead. The Iroquois used their number and strength to overpower the Huron. Those who remained after two days of fighting were either adopted into the Iroquois nations or joined neighboring tribes. A few moved west and became known as the Wendats, or Wyandots.

The Iroquois continued to harass other neighboring tribes. They succeeded in dominating the Delawares, the Nanticokes, and several other small Algonquin groups. The Iroquois knew that they had strength in number as they dominated an increasing number of tribes. However, they did not find the same success in their battles with the French.

Beginning about 1666, the French attacked Mohawk, Onondaga, and Seneca villages, destroying food supplies and homes, and killing men, women, and children. The Iroquois fought back causing increased destruction. This lasted for nearly five years when a peace agreement was established between the French and the Iroquois that lasted until 1755 and the beginning of the French and Indian War. During the French and Indian War, the Iroquois and British joined forces to oust the French. This was accomplished in 1763. When the Iroquois joined forces with the British to fight against the French, they cooperated with an invading force to defeat what they perceived to be an even greater enemy.

By this time, the Iroquois Confederacy had begun to crumble from within. There was dissension as to whether they should side with the British against the French, and some tribes had become more enculturated by the British than others. The Mohawks, who built schools for themselves in 1712, had taken on many of the British customs, while the Seneca and Onondagas had remained less influenced. Christianity had also taken its toll on the Confederacy, with nearly all of the Mohawks baptized by 1760, and with two thirds of them moving to Canada. The Cayugas and Oneidas were also very Christianized. Factions developed and weakened the Confederacy. The years that followed would determine the destiny of the Iroquois Confederacy. Once strong and invincible, they were now weak and impotent. The future would hold a world of negotiation, collaboration, and continued defensive resistance.

THE CREEK (MUSKOGEE) CONFEDERACY

By the 1500s, the Creek Confederacy numbered over twenty thousand and occupied present-day Alabama, Georgia, and parts of neighboring states. Because of their policy of neutrality, they had little interaction with European nations until the early 1700s. The Confederacy grew by the absorption of other tribes into their number when they were forced to leave their own lands at the hands of the British or French. The Confederacy included many nations including the Yuchi, Shawnee, Yamassee, Natchez, and the Alabamas. Most of the Creek nations spoke one of the Muskogean languages, with the exception of the latest members.

The Confederacy was governed through consensus. Each town, or *talwa*, was autonomous. The *talwa* was the home for one hundred to two thousand people. The unity of the confederacy came from the strength of the Great Council. The Great Council was composed of the leaders of each of the *talwa* in the union. Annual meetings were held to debate and decide matters that impacted the entire group, admission of new groups, treaties, and wars. They were cause for celebration and had great social significance. Each *talwa* had its own council to decide matters of local concern. There were approximately one hundred *talwas* in the Creek or Muskogee Confederacy. Four of the *talwas* were known as the mother *talwa*: Tukabahchee, Koweta, Kasihta, and Abihka. They took the lead in political affairs, trade, commerce, and communication between *talwas*. Clans also played a major role in the organization of the *talwas* and the conducting of daily life (O'Brien, 1989, p. 21).

Among the *talwas* there was a division of responsibility. *Talwas* and clans were classified as either red or white. Red *talwas* and clans were generally associated with war-related matters, while the white *talwas* and clans were responsible for activities of peace. The clan system among the Muskogee nations is matriarchal and exogamous. This means that newborn children follow the clan of their mother and, when marrying, one must marry outside of his or her own clan. These customs could lead to a family that had members of all of the clans, promoting close ties and loyalty throughout the confederacy.

The duality of the clan and *talwa* system extended to the organization of affairs of each *talwa*. Each *talwa* had two leaders: a civil chief and a war chief. The civil chief, or *micco*, received all matters relating to peace and matters of custom and ceremony. The *micco* was usually chosen by the opposing group. For example, in red *talwas*, the White Clan members would choose the *micco* from the Red Clan. The *micco* was a person who had achieved great honor and the trust of the people. He ruled not by command or coercion, but through harmony and consensus. The war chief, or *tvstvnvke*, was chosen by the *micco* from among the members of the Red Clan. He advised the *micco* on matters of war, maintained public order, and arranged stick ball games between *talwas*.

The *micco* had also two other groups of advisors: the *henneha* and *este vcakvlke*. The *henneha*, or "second men," were the advisors on matters of public works including communal fields, new dwellings, and organizing work details. They had the honor of preparing the "black drink," an important beverage in ceremonies and stick ball games. The *este vcakvlke*, or "beloved old men," were the third group of advisors that the *micco* had to help guide him. These three groups formed the governing council of a *talwa*.

> … there is no coercive power. … Their Kings can do no more than persuade. All the power they have is no more than to call their old men and captains and to propound to them the measures they think proper. After they have done speaking, all the others have liberty to give their opinions also; and they reason together with great temper and modesty, till they have brought each other into some unanimous resolution.
>
> Then they call in the young men and recommend the putting in execution the resolution with their strongest and most lively eloquence. In speaking to their young men they generally address to the passions; in speaking to their old men they apply to reason only (James Oglethorpe, governor of Georgia, speaking of the Muskogees in 1764, from *American Indian Tribal Governments* by Sharon O'Brien, p. 22. Copyright © 1989 by the University of Oklahoma Press).

The Creek or Muskogee Confederacy was able to maintain its culture and traditions amidst a changing world because of "buffers" to the east, north, south, and west. The Choctaws were south and west of the Muskogees. They allowed themselves to get involved in the French aggression, became divided, and thus were not a threat to the Muskogees or French. The Chickasaw to the northwest served as a buffer as the advancing British and French north of Ohio, and the Cherokees, on the northeast, provided the greatest barrier to the Virginians and other Long Knives of the British. Border disputes were common, but these various tribes held the advancing Long Knives at bay and allowed the Muskogee people to continue to speak their language and live in the way that they had for hundreds of years. This means that the Creeks, or Muskogees, were less assimilated than many other Eastern nations by the 1700s. This strength in culture and traditions has been maintained into the twentieth century.

After 1733, however, the Georgians became the "foreign power" with which the Creeks had to contend. The Georgians did not recognize the Creeks' right to the land, and they fought unscrupulously and aggressively to gain control. They broke through where the Muskogee borders were weak and posed the first real threat to Creek neutrality. A series of battles marked this time for the Confederacy, but they were able to maintain cultural and linguistic independence and their own religion throughout the 1700s. By the end of the century, however, things would change.

THE PUEBLOS

The union of the various Pueblos in the fight to repel the Spanish from their lands in 1680 was a coalition for a singular purpose rather than a confederacy. The coalition was a strategy used in the effort to rid the region of the Spanish in one concentrated act. In the early 1600s, the Pueblos of the Southwest were under the control of the invading Spanish. The Spanish had imposed the *encomienda* system on the Pueblos, exacting tithes from the Pueblo people. They were forced to pay tithes to the church and to the civil leaders of the area. While these tithes were a burden to the Pueblos, the real change in the economy came as a result of the grazing of the Spanish cattle on the land. Overgrazing and soil erosion contributed to other factors increasing the probability of drought. This was to be devastating for the Pueblos.

We have spoken of the passive resistance of the Pueblo people toward the Spanish who brought Catholicism with them. The Pueblo, who believed in the natural order of life, practiced a rich ceremonial life to help maintain harmony. As a result of their deep need to preserve and maintain their spiritual selves, they appeared to submit to the Spanish while actually resisting in secret.

The Pueblo of the Southwest were patient and tolerant. The Spanish were very cruel, but the Pueblo people maintained their aloofness for their physical survival and the survival of their way of life. They adjusted to some of the ways of the Spanish in order to have the room for secret maintenance of their way of life. This was a form of accommodation. The kiva system of worship does not reveal the identity of the spiritual leaders, a practice which helped them stay alive during the Spanish reign and perform their religious functions (O'Brien, 1989).

When Coronado first came into the Southwest and found the Pueblos, it is estimated that there were about eighty Pueblos with some sixty thousand inhabitants. By the mid 1600s, the population of the remaining forty-three Pueblos had dropped to only forty thousand. This enormous reduction was caused by smallpox, by forced labor and the cruelty of the Spanish, and by Apache and Navajo raids.

By 1680, the Pueblo had been under the rule of the Spanish for over eighty years. The cruelty and harassment did not abate and the Pueblo finally revolted. The revolt is traced by some to Pope, a medicine man of the Opi society of the San Juan Pueblo. Publicly whipped five years earlier in Santa Fe, he traveled the Southwest talking to the various independent pueblos, convincing them to band together and fight against the Spanish. He led a coalition of all but two pueblos in the year 1680 as they fought the Spanish for control of their lives. After three weeks of rebellion, 375 colonists and 21 missionaries were dead and the remaining Spanish were on their way back south. This valiant, cooperative resistance was unusual for the peaceful and autonomous Pueblo people.

The Pueblo people washed off their Catholic baptisms in the river and returned to their own way of life. However, in many ways it was too late for years of grazing and soil erosion, combined with dry winters, diminished the Pueblo people's ability to provide for themselves. At the same time, the Apache and Navajo increased raids on the Pueblos. Even though they were finally free, they could not return to the life they had

before the coming of the Spanish.

Before proceeding to a new chapter in the history of Native people in America, the period in which the policy of the United States was to separate Indian people from their land in the East and remove the threat that they posed to the settlers who wanted their land, it is important to review some other events in other parts of the country.

THE LAKOTA

Up to this point, we have not mentioned the Sioux; their contact with the invading Europeans had been minor and without major conflict. However, the Pueblo Revolt of 1680 introduced the horse to the Plains Indians. Before the introduction of the horse to the Sioux, they lived in the present-day states of Wisconsin, Minnesota, North Dakota, South Dakota, Kansas, Nebraska, Iowa, Ohio, and Illinois. They rarely roamed west of the Missouri, except on seasonal buffalo hunts, providing for their basic needs by farming, gathering wild rice, and hunting small animals. By the late 1600s they began moving farther west.

The Lakota lived in family units that included several related families. This unit or group of families was known as the *tiyospaye*. Often these groups consisted of up to thirty tipis. The *tiyospaye* could pack up and leave on a moment's notice. They traveled on foot and used a travois, consisting of two long poles fastened at one end to a dog who pulled the poles. Baggage was tied between the two poles with leather nets and ties.

Because their lives were dependent on seasonal game and plants as well as farming, they lived a seminomadic life. The *tiyospaye* were loosely knit into bands that were members of the three main divisions of the Sioux Nation. Their lifestyle demanded that their leadership be based in the community and communities were not dependent on each other. Large meetings of the bands were held yearly to discuss issues that related to everyone. The band and the *tiyospaye* were lead by headsmen and governed and protected by societies. There are two main types of societies; *akicitas* and *nacas*. The *akicitas* are police societies and are "by invitation only." They maintained order during camp moves and hunts. The *nacas*, or civil societies, functioned as the tribal council (O'Brien, 1989, pp. 21–22).

With the advent of the horse to the Sioux way of life, they could follow the buffalo with ease and transport their belongings with less effort. The Sioux were excellent horse breeders who greatly admired the horse, which they called the Spirit Dog, Holy Dog, and Medicine Dog. It changed their way of life and the way that they related to other Plains Indians. The honor of counting coup and capturing large herds of horses gained through raiding other tribes encouraged continued skirmishes between Crows, Sioux, Kickapoo, and Comanche. Their loosely related style of organization was perfect for their lifestyle both before and after the introduction of the horse to their culture. It would also play a key role in the relationship that the Sioux would establish with the white settlers.

The Sioux did not face battle or confrontation from Spain, France, or England. By the time the westward expansion of settlers and soldiers impacted the land of the Plains Indian, the colonists had become settlers and citizens of the United States. The Plains Indians fought against the U.S. cavalry to defend their homes. The U.S. government made the mistake of thinking that any leader of one of the Sioux bands could speak for all of the Sioux. This caused much confusion and led to extended battles for land and freedom.

THE ARCTIC

And finally, we need to mention briefly the influence of the Russians who had come later to the land now known as the United States. Although the influence of the Russians is not as widely known, nor is Russian influence still as evident as the influence of the French, Spanish, and English, it is important to mention their forays into North America. In many ways, the Russians caused less havoc and disruption than the Spanish, French, or English. Simply, they came later and left earlier, and their major interest was fur trading, not colonization and settlement. However, the Russian explorers and tradesmen had the same disdain for Native people and the beliefs that guided their lives.

Nearly 125 years after the settlement of Jamestown, Czar Peter the Great sponsored two unsuccessful expeditions into the Arctic region. These expeditions were motivated by the abundance of furs and the wealth to be accrued by fur trading. By 1784, the Russians had established a year-round center of trading on Kodiak Island. These expeditions, as could be predicted, resulted in conflict with the Native people. Although, ultimately unsuccessful, the succeeding Siberian fur hunters made a serious negative impact on the people and on the fragile environment.

The aboriginal people of the Aleutian Islands were nearly obliterated by the Russians. At one time they numbered approximately twenty thousand. After a century of contact with the Russian fur hunters, they numbered only twenty-five hundred. In 1781, reform was initiated and the mass destruction was somewhat abated. The nurturing of positive relationships between the Russians and the Alaskan Native Aleuts and Inuits characterizes their relationship today. A little known phenomenon is the presence of Russian settlers in California as late as 1812. Their influence is seen in many unexpected ways in today's Californian Indian people, including people of mixed blood with heavy beards.

The following excerpt is from a pamphlet written by Benjamin Franklin after the massacre of friendly Conestoga Indians in 1764. It expresses well the treatment the Indians received at the hand of the Euro-American people during this period of time.

Narrative of the
Late Massacres in Lancaster County

There are some (I am ashamed to say it) who would extenuate the enormous wickedness of these actions by saying: "The inhabitants of the frontiers are exasperated with the murder of their relations in the present war." It is possible. But though this might justify their going out into the woods, to seek for their enemies and avenge upon them those murders, it can never justify turning into the heart of the country and murdering their friends. If an Indian injures me, does it follow that I may revenge that injury on all Indians? ...

It is well known that Indians are of different tribes, nations, and languages, as well as the white people. In Europe, if the French, who are white people, should injure the Dutch, are they (the Dutch) to revenge it on the English, because they, too, are white people ... I beg that I may not be misunderstood as framing apologies for all Indians ... I can only observe that the Six Nations, as a body, have kept faith with the English ever since we knew them, now near an hundred years; and that their governing body have notions of honour, whatever may be the case with the rum-debauched, trader-corrupted vagabonds and thieves on the Susquehanna and Ohio, at present in arms against us ...

What had poor Old Shehaes done? (He, so old he had been present at Penn's 1701 treaty, was cut to pieces in bed.) What could he or the other poor old men and women do? What had the little boys and girls done? What could children of a year old, babes at the breast, what could they do that they must be shot and hatcheted? And in their parents arms! This is done by no civilized nation in Europe. Do we come to America to learn and practice the manners of barbarians? But this, Barbarians as they are, they practice against their enemies only, not against their friends (Benjamin Franklin as cited in Armstrong, 1984, p. 24).

LESSON PLAN:
INVASION AND THE NORTHEASTERN TRIBES

Grade Level: Middle school

Basic Concepts: Adaptation and accommodation

Organizing Generalization: People develop a variety of different responses to conflict and change.

Culture Area: Northeast

Time Period: Early European Contact (1600s)

Background: When early colonists arrived in North America, they depended on the Indians for their survival. As time went by, the colonists wanted more land and they used force and a variety of other means against the Indians to obtain it. This forced the Indians to develop strategies for surviving. Indian leaders reacted in a variety of ways to adapt to or accommodate change.

Objectives:
Knowledge
Students will:
1. Name five tribes of the Northeast in the 1600s and their leaders (e.g., Mohawk, Seneca, Cayuga, Oneida, and Onondoga).
2. Give examples of the diverse responses to attack and invasion developed by these tribes and their leaders.
3. Discuss the results of the different strategies and their value in retrospect.
4. Review current events in Indian life today to determine whether there are current situations and strategies that American Indians are using to confront invasion of their lands and ways of life.

Skills
Students will:
1. Locate on a map the original lands of the identified tribes and their current location.
2. Chart the different strategies employed by the different tribes and their leaders.

Values
Students will:
1. Discuss the results of the different strategies and their value in retrospect and why.
2. Apply what they learned in the review of current events and the various responses to invasion and defend why one approach is "better" than another.

Activities:
1. Have books available from the resource list in this lesson plan for students to use in research on the tribes of the 1600s in the Northeast. Students can work in small groups to develop charts of the names of the tribes, their leaders, and their locations.
2. Chart on a map together, and on individual maps if possible, the location of the tribes then and now.
3. Initiate a class discussion about what the different tribes' responses were to invasion and how things have turned out for the tribes today.
4. Ask an American Indian to come to the class and discuss how their tribe responded to invasion.

Extensions:
1. Research other tribes history during the period from the 1600s to the 1800s specifically looking at their response to invasion of their land and way of life.
2. Collect newspapers for articles about current events that involve American Indians and treaty rights, especially regarding land and natural resource usage. Articles can be clipped and saved to support a discussion or paper on contemporary responses to invasion.

Evaluation: Students will be able to name five tribes of the Northeast Region and their leaders during the 1600s in a class discussion. They will also be able to locate these tribes on a map both in the 1600s and now, and give examples of the tribe's responses to invasion. Students should be able to express why the responses to invasion were appropriate or made sense to the tribes involved.

Materials/Resources:
Map of the Northeastern Region in 1600 and now. Include tribal homes and modern states.
Resource books on the French and Indian Wars, the tribes of New England, King Philip, and the Iroquois Confederacy.
Cwiklik, R. *King Philip and the War with the Colonists*. Englewood Cliffs, NJ: Silver Burdett, 1989.
Feest, C. F. *The Powhatan Tribes*. Englewood Cliffs, NJ: Chelsea House, 1990.
Josephy, A. Jr. *The Patriot Chiefs*. New York: Penguin, 1989.
Morris, R. B. *The Indian Wars*. Minneapolis: Lerner, 1985.
Ochoa, G. *The Fall of Quebec and the French and Indian War*. Englewood Cliffs, NJ: Silver Burdett, 1990.
Roman, J. *King Philip: Wampanoag Rebel*. New York: Chelsea House, 1992.

SUMMARY
THE FIRST YEARS CONTINUED: 1621–1763

The period of time extending roughly from 1621–1763 was a time when the Native inhabitants of North America faced the reality that the visitors from the East wanted their ancestral land, their home, and they would take it by force.

The people fought for their lives, their homes, their crops, and their families. When they could fight no more, they also escaped to the mountains and forests. A powerful strategy was the formation of various alliances to repel the invaders from their land. Another strategy was to treat the invaders as friends and try to live together with the white people from the East.

Powerful formal and informal Indian confederations were formed. The most well known of these confederacies were the Powhatan Confederacy, the Creek Confederacy, and the Iroquois Confederacy. The Great Peace, otherwise known as the Iroquois League or Confederacy, was originally comprised of the five nations of the Mohawk, Oneida, Onondaga, Cayuga, and Seneca, but became six nations with the addition of the Tuscarora.

The Great Peace was based on the values of freedom, respect, brotherhood, and consensus. The principles of the Iroquois Confederacy were a great influence on the founders of the new government—the United States of America.

Originally, the nations of the Iroquois Confederacy sought to control local tribes, trade, and land in the northeast. They also united against the French and became allied with the British during the French and Indian War.

The Pueblo Revolt of 1680 was another example of a cooperative effort to resist European invasion and conquest. This was a cooperative venture to achieve a singular purpose—to rid the Southwest of the Spanish. Although the Spanish were to return, the pueblos of the Southwest continue today to retain much of their land, languages, and cultures.

However, divided goals, missed timing, and a lack of understanding of the immense size and depth of the invasion contributed to the lack of success of the various strategies.

TIME LINE: 1622–1763

1620 1630 1640 1650 1660 1670 1680 1690 1700 1710 1720 1730 1740 1750 1760 1770

1622
Powhatan confederacy of thirty-two Tidewater Tribes, under the leadership of Opechancanough, attack settlers at Jamestown.

1624
Dutch settlers found a colony at Fort Orange in New Netherlands.

1626
Canarsee Indians sell Manhattan Island to Peter Minuit, governor of New Netherlands, for sixty guilders worth of trade goods. Later, the Dutch have to negotiate with the Manhattan Indians who actually hold the territory.

1627
Company of New France is chartered to colonize and develop fur trade with the Indians.

1629–1633
Spanish start missions among the Acoma, Hopi, and Zuni Tribes.

1636
Roger Williams founds Rhode Island, insisting that the settlers there purchase the land from the Indians, not expropriate it.

1633
General Court of Massachusetts colony begins land allotment to Indians and the central rather than local governmental handling of Indian affairs.

1638
Pequot War in New England claims the lives of more than six hundred men, women, and children.

1640–1685
Iroquois League of Nations wars with neighboring nations, Huron, Tobaccos, Neutrals, Eries, Mahicans, and Susquehannocks.

1644
Powhatan Confederacy attacks Jamestown settlers for the second time. Opechancanough dies in captivity.

1661
Spanish raid the sacred kivas of the Pueblo Indians in an effort to destroy the religion and culture.

1663
New France becomes a colony with a royal governor.

1664
In partnership with the Iroquois League of Nations, the English take New Netherland from the Dutch.

1675
The English increase their dealings with Indians and establish the first Secretary of Indian Affairs in Albany, New York.

1675–1676
King Philip wages war against the Wampanoags, Narragansets, and Nipmucs, and the New England colonies.

1680
Pueblo Indians stage a successful revolt against the Spanish rule and religions. In 1689 the Spanish return to the area.

1689–1697
King Williams' War was one of the first conflicts that comprised the French Indian Wars. Generally, Iroquois sided with the British and the Algonquin Nations fought with the French.

1703–04
Queen Anne's War between England and France in the Northeast and England and Spain in the South and other Native nations.

1722
Tuscarora Tribe becomes accepted and recognized as a member of the Iroquois Confederacy.

1723
Williamsburg, Virginia, becomes the home of the first permanent Indian School created by the British.

1730
Seven Cherokee Chiefs visit London, England and form an alliance with French King George II known as The Articles of Agreement.

1744–1748
King George's War between French and British divides the Indian tribes.

1750
Moor's Indian Charity School is founded in Connecticut. In 1769 it is moved to New Hampshire and becomes Dartmouth College, which has promoted the enrollment of Indian students to the present.

1751
Benjamin Franklin sites Iroquois League as a model for his Albany Plan of Union.

1755
British government appoints superintendents of Indian Affairs for northern and southern departments.

1755
Iroquois League persuaded to side with the British against the French by Indian Affairs superintendent.

1760
War on the frontier between the colonists and the Cherokee.

1761
Aleuts of Alaska revolt against the Russians.

1763
France cedes New France to England and Louisiana to the Spain as a result of the European Seven Year War.

The Cherokee Trail of Tears

CHAPTER 8

Separation: 1763–1839

Government soldiers rode before them, on each side of them, behind them. The Cherokee men walked and looked straight ahead and would not look down, nor at the soldiers. Their women and their children followed in their footsteps and would not look at the soldiers.

Far behind them, the empty wagons rattled and rumbled and served no use. The wagons could not steal the soul of the Cherokee. The land was stolen from him, his home; but the Cherokee would not let the wagons steal his soul.

As they passed the villages of the white man, people lined the trail to watch them pass. At first, they laughed at how foolish was the Cherokee to walk with the empty wagons rattling behind him. The Cherokee did not turn his head at their laughter, and soon there was no laughter.

And as the Cherokee walked farther from his mountains, he began to die. His soul did not die, nor did it weaken. It was the very young and the very old and the sick.

At first the soldiers let them stop to bury their dead; but then, more died—by the hundreds, by the thousands. More than a third of them were to die on the Trail. The soldiers said they could only bury their dead every three days; for the soldiers wished to hurry and be finished with the Cherokee. The soldiers said the wagons would carry the dead, but the Cherokee would not put his dead in the wagons. He carried them. Walking.

The little boy carried his dead baby sister, and slept by her at night on the ground. He lifted her in his arms in the morning, and carried her.

The husband carried his dead wife. The son carried his dead mother, his father. The mother carried her dead baby. They carried them in their arms. And walked. And they did not turn their heads to look at the soldiers, nor to look at the people who lined the sides of the Trail to watch them pass. Some of the people cried. But the Cherokee did not cry.

Not on the outside, for the Cherokee would not let them see his soul; as he would not ride in the wagons.

And so they called it the Trail of Tears for it sounds romantic and speaks of the sorrow of those who stood by the Trail. A death march is not romantic.

You cannot write poetry about the death-stiffened baby in his mother's arms, staring at the jolting sky with eyes that will not close; while his mother walks.

You cannot sing songs of the father laying down the burden of his wife's corpse, to lie by it through the night and to rise and carry it again in the morning—and tell his oldest son to carry the body of his youngest. And do not look … nor speak … nor cry … nor remember the mountains.

It would not be a beautiful song. And so they call it the Trail of Tears.

(Carter, 1976, pp. 41–42)

Now we enter a new period—from a time of confusion with Spanish, French, Dutch, and British forays into what had been solely Indian Country, to a time of British and then American dominance. The Revolutionary War was imminent in 1763. And a new country was about to emerge. So, we move from the time when this land was Indian Country because "they had been here so long, that it seemed as though it was always so" to a time when Indian Country became a legal term for the official governmental policies that separated Indian people from their ancestral lands and from the new American settlers.

According to Edward Spicer (1982, p. 178), the roots of the earliest U.S. policy toward Native people lay in the British colonial experience and was a result of the struggle for land between the English settlers and the Indians. At the close of the French and Indian War, this policy was embodied in the Proclamation of 1763. The proclamation established a line along the crest of the Appalachian Mountains that no English settlers could cross until representatives of the government negotiated treaties and land cessions with the Indians who lived there. This proclamation was an attempt to keep the settlers east of the Appalachian Divide and establish an Indian Country of protected lands to the west. Theoretically, this line assured the Indians that they would be secure on their lands until they were willing to sell them to the British. From 1763–1773, this north-south line was further defined through new treaties and Indian land cessions.

Two principles in this proclamation became the policies that were to guide U.S. actions toward Indian people for a significant period of time. The first principle was that Indian nations were political entities to be considered much like the territory-controlling nations of Europe. And they would be dealt with in a similar fashion through diplomacy, warfare, and treaty, and their lands would not be taken without their permission nor without compensation. The second principle was that conflict would be prevented if there were established, centrally controlled boundaries between the colonists and the Indians. These principles implied that the British possession of the lands east of the line were legitimate, the result of warfare, treaty, and purchase. Needless to say, this implication itself would be difficult for Indian people to accept.

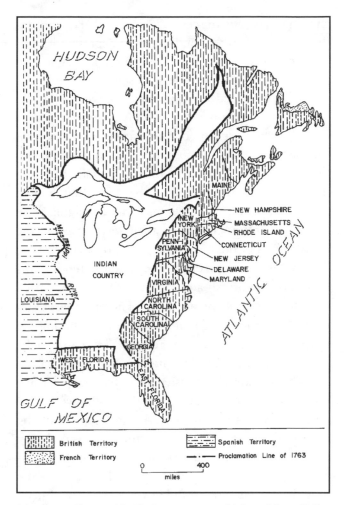

Map 8.1—Eastern North America 1763 (Adapted from Kelly, L. C. (1990) Federal Indian Policy. NY: Chelsea. p, 22)

The proclamation also meant that Indian relations would be regulated by the central English government in London through people who would be appointed specifically to coordinate Indian policy; the individual British colonies would no longer deal directly with the Indians. This policy, however, made by a government far across an ocean, had little effect on the resentful white settlers who were hungry for new land and who generally ignored the supposed boundary lines.

In 1775, the Continental Congress of the American Revolutionary Government organized a Committee on Indian Affairs, formulated an Indian policy and named commissioners for northern, middle, and southern departments. The northern department was responsible for the tribes in the north including the tribes of the Iroquois Confederacy; the southern department was responsible for the Indians to the south, including the Cherokee; and the central covered all of the Indians between the northern and southern departments.

The War of Independence, the war of American patriots against British rule, had several enduring aspects that impacted the relationship between the patriots and Native people. Many Native people did favor the British because most of their trade goods came from England and it was the colonists who were settling on their land. Even though the Indians actually had little influence in the outcome of the war, their limited participation left a legacy that was damaging. The American patriots extended their fervor against the British to all of the Indian people who sided with the British. In actual practice they often extended this hatred of the British and the Indians who supported them to any and all Indian people. Therefore, as a result of the war, there was a prevailing notion among the new Americans that Indian people, *all* Indian people, should be punished for joining forces with the British.

The war was also divisive for Indian people, causing even further damage. The Indians who were most involved with the British were the Iroquois of the Northeast. Some tribal groups within the Confederacy had become quite acculturated in the way they lived and they had adopted Christianity. These groups, the Oneida and Tuscaroras, did not side with the British, while the others did. In many ways, the war set one group of Native people against another. The powerful Iroquois Confederacy, strong for over two hundred years, became fragmented, disunited, and ultimately completely disintegrated.

Although the outrageous atrocities of war were committed by both whites and Indians, the focus on brutality was attributed to Native participants. The Indian style of warfare was considered "savage," encouraging destruction of all people regardless of age, gender, or circumstances. This perception, whether or not it was justified, also did enduring harm to Indian people. In fact, it became something of a rallying cry for the Americans justifying their later actions of inhumanity.

The War of Independence thus ended with several significant effects for Indian people. They were left with great hostility against them for their real or imagined efforts in the war and the unity of the great Iroquois Confederacy was shattered. And, of course, they also suffered great loss of lives, homes, crops, and land.

In 1778, the Continental Congress made its first treaty with Indian people—the Delawares. It is interesting to note that the Delaware tribe was offered the prospect of statehood. Needless to say, this never came to pass.

In the Treaty of Paris of 1783, which ended the American Revolution, there was no provision made for the tribes that had supported the British. Carl Waldman states:

> Officials of both sides apparently considered them as incidental to both the past and future of the white race in America .... The new nation and its Founding Fathers might at this time have been preoccupied with democracy, equality, liberty, and justice, but not with regard to the Indian (1985, p. 114).

After the war, Secretary of War Henry Knox was charged with the development of Indian policy. It was the Indian trade and intercourse acts that Congress passed between 1790 and 1796 that established the concept of "Indian Country" and congressional regulation of Indian–white affairs. These acts provided for the appointment of Indian agents and licensing of federal traders who could barter with the Indians for furs.

It is important to note that U.S. policy as it developed toward Indian people is a manifestation of significant lack of understanding of Indian people and misconceptions about their lifeways and value systems. It also is a manifestation of belief in superiority and the right of conquest. In 1803 Thomas Jefferson made the following statement:

> I consider the business of hunting as already become insufficient to furnish clothing and subsistence to the Indians. The promotion of agriculture, therefore, and household manufacture, are essential in their preservation, and I am disposed to aid and encourage it. This will enable them to live on much smaller portions of land ... while they are learning to do better on less land, our increasing numbers will be calling for more land, and thus a coincidence of interests between those who have such necessaries to spare, and want lands. ... Surely it will be better for them to be identified with us, and preserve the occupations of their lands, than be exposed to the many casualties that may endanger them while a separate people (Ford, 1892, p. 214).

The Northwest Ordinance of 1787 reaffirmed the policy of a separate Indian Country and a boundary line dividing whites from Indians. However, the settlers continued to push on to the Mississippi River. The Louisiana Purchase of 1803 added vast new lands and prompted the idea of moving Indian people further west and past the Mississippi. Although talk was of trading lands east of the Mississippi for lands west, all sorts of coercive methods were used to force Indian removal. This concept became policy in 1825 and Indian Territory was established with the Trade and Intercourse Act of 1834 and the Indian Removal Act of 1830. The Intercourse Act again specified an Indian Country and made it inaccessible to all whites except those who received special authorization. The Indian Removal Act made forcible removal legal.

When President Andrew Jackson signed the Indian Removal Act he initiated a decade of dishonor for the United States and defeat and displacement for the Indian tribes of the Southeast. In order to have more land, forcible removal of Indian people from their ancestral lands began. The Five Civilized Tribes (Cherokee, Creek, Choctaw, Chickasaw, and Seminole) were forcibly removed from their land to Indian Territory west of the Mississippi River into Arkansas and Oklahoma.

The peaceable Choctaws were the first to leave their homeland. The main body of the tribe were removed during the period 1830–1832. The Creeks came next, then the Cherokees, then the Chickasaws, and finally the Seminoles. The story of each removal is poignant and tragic, and it is made even more so when one considers the significance of the land—their mother—to Native people. Angie Debo quotes H. B. Cushman in illustrating this particular grief as it was experienced by the first tribe to leave, the Choctaw.

> The main body of the tribe was removed during 1830–33. Many died from the hardships of the migration and the settlement of a wild frontier— and from plain heartbreak. One observer noticed that many of them reached out and touched the trunks of the trees before they turned away on their journey. One gathering point was near a mission station, and the young son of a missionary never forgot the wailing of the women as they sat in groups with their children, their heads covered with blankets, their bodies swaying, and their cries rising and falling in unison, while the men stood

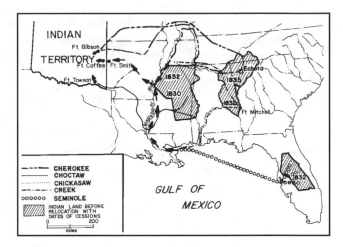

Map 8.2—*The Routes of Removal (Adapted from Waldman, 1985, p. 184).*

> silent and sad. This went on day and night until their departure (from *A History of the Indians of the United States*, by Angie Debo, p. 118. Copyright © 1970 by the University of Oklahoma Press).

The following story of the Cherokee Trail of Tears is a startling example of the U.S. government policy of separation, of greed and avarice, of betrayal and cruelty, and of courage and resilience. We urge the reader to remember that, although the Trail of Tears is better known than other removal efforts, it is only one of many removals and all left trails of tears.

Let's discuss why the Cherokee and the Choctaw, Creek, Chickasaw, and Seminole tribes were called the "Five Civilized Tribes," for this is part of the tragedy.

According to the invading Europeans, "to be civilized" meant to be more European. The more English (or Spanish, French, Dutch, or Russian) the Native people appeared and behaved, the more civilized they were. The tribes who lived in the fertile and abundant Southeast began early to adopt the ways of the white man. Unlike other tribal groups in the country, they were primarily farmers and many came to own small farms, a few owned large plantations, and some eventually adopted the practice of keeping black slaves. Over the years the Cherokee had intermarried with the Europeans to a significant degree. Scottish and Irish names such as Ross, Taylor, MacGregor, Lowrey, Smith, McCoy, and Montgomery were common. Further, they admired many of the gifts of the Europeans and wished to adopt parts of the white man's culture that seemed to hold promise for their own. For example, it is said that education was nearly as important to the Cherokee as was their religion. Traditional homes were replaced by cabins and women learned to weave and adopted new crafts. Eventually, the tribes became known as "civilized."

This effort to become more European, more civilized was not enough; soon it became clear that other, more significant, adaptations would have to be made. Land cessions and war threatened the existence of the Cherokee. The state of Georgia had adopted a policy to eliminate all Indians from their borders. Settlers were invading from northeast. As part of a deal in which Georgia ceded land to the federal government in what became the state of Mississippi to the federal government in 1802, the government had agreed to extinguish Indian title to all land in the state of Georgia. Further cessions pushed the Cherokees continually southward and westward. And war was another pressure on the tribe; the Cherokees were involved with the Americans against a faction of the Creeks who were involved with Tecumseh. It seemed as though they were fighting pressures from all sides.

During this time of pressure and turmoil, the Cherokee were quick to recognize that it would become increasingly necessary to be able to understand and deal effectively with the settlers if they were to retain their lands and survive as a people. This was a rational and deliberate effort, led by wise elders and young educated Cherokee men and women, to adopt American forms of political organization to the needs of the Cherokee to survive. This transformation, often called the Cherokee Renaissance, took place in a relatively short time and consisted of a series of major adaptations and innovations designed to deal effectively with the tremendous problems that they faced.

The innovations in their political and community organization were not accomplished through disruptive, revolutionary tactics but were thoughtful and planned. They first established the Light Horse Guards for the maintenance of law and order. At the same time, they abolished the ancient tradition of clan revenge which would have rendered the Light Horse Guards ineffective. A bicameral legislature was formed, consisting of a national committee and a traditional council, and a judicial system was established. Finally, in

1827, a National Constitutional Convention was convened to draw up a constitution. The constitution, which embodied these changes, was approved in 1828.

Education was a major part of this renaissance. Many Indian people had been cruelly deceived when they were unable to read official papers and tribal elders encouraged education by allowing Christian missionary efforts. There was little interest in the evangelical part of the missionary efforts; in fact, there were remarkably few Christian conversions. When church groups emphasized evangelical work and were slow to build and operate schools, the Cherokee put considerable pressure on them to provide the promised schools.

An unexpected and important event in this reorganization and renaissance occurred when Sequoyah, a full-blooded Cherokee with no formal schooling, through years of diligent effort and spurred by the "talking leaves" of the Europeans developed a syllabary of eighty-six signs for the Cherokee. An alphabet has a sign for every sound in the language; a syllabary has a sign for every syllable. This Cherokee syllabary was easy to learn and within a short time the Cherokee people were able to read and write in their own language. A Cherokee newspaper, the *Cherokee Phoenix*, was published and widely read. Elias Boudinot, a man well respected in Cherokee history, was the first editor of the *Phoenix*. It was this ability to read and write and the Cherokee newspaper that enabled the reforms to spread so swiftly.

Two major events were then to change irrevocably the lives of the Cherokee—just as they had achieved a political and social organization that was intended to be compatible with American people and government. First, gold was discovered in Georgia, and second, Andrew Jackson was elected president.

Some people believe that it was the gold and the belief that vast riches lay hidden in Cherokee Country that spurred removal efforts. However, the ongoing conflict between the settlers who wanted and needed land and the Indians who wanted to retain their ancestral lands was probably the most important factor. Also, the Cherokees had been allies of the British in the Revolutionary War.

It was Andrew Jackson who finally pushed the Indians off their land. The sequence of major events occurred in this way. The Cherokee people demonstrated their "civilized" behavior by taking their grievances to court, arguing that the federal government had granted them their land by treaty and therefore they should be protected from the gold miners, from the greedy settlers, and from the government of the state of Georgia. Georgia governor George Gilmer summed up the position of the state of Georgia regarding the land treaties with the Indians in this way: "Treaties were expedients by which ignorant, intractable, and savage people were induced without bloodshed to yield up what civilized people had a right to possess."

After a Cherokee lawsuit reached the U.S. Supreme Court, the court ruled in 1832 that the federal government must protect the Cherokee Nation from its invaders. However, only the president had the authority to send troops to assist the Cherokee, and Andrew Jackson refused to do so. It was then that he said, "The Court has made its decision now let them enforce it."

The stunned Cherokee had different responses to the impending removal. Chief John Ross wanted to fight removal through the courts. Another respected elder, Major Ridge, urged people to move to the West because he believed that President Jackson's position was unshakeable.

While the many cases were being argued in court, the state of Georgia organized a lottery to distribute Cherokee land. The winners of the lottery were given 160-acre farms or 40-acre mining sites, all to be taken as soon as the Indians were forced from their land.

Through their battles in the courts, the Cherokee people resisted removal until 1838. At this time the federal government acted on a treaty agreement, concluded two years earlier. This treaty gave away all Cherokee lands east of the Mississippi in exchange for new lands in the West and a cash settlement. The agreement was signed by only a very small minority of the Cherokee people—most of whom had been bribed by government officials. However, the federal government insisted that the treaty was valid.

The long nightmare for the Cherokee people began in 1838. General Winfield Scott led an army of seven thousand troops into Cherokee land. This was about one soldier for every two or three Cherokees. Without warning, the troops burst into Cherokee homes, dragging the people outside where they were driven to stockades. Those who moved too slowly or were reluctant to leave were prodded by the bayonets of soldiers.

> In a mountain cove, close by the Oconaluftee River, stood a small group of log cabins, where the blue smoke rose in the early morning of August, 1838. A Cherokee Indian child played with a stone marble in one of the yards, while his mother cooked fatback on the hearth fireplace inside. Unseen by the two, a small detachment of soldiers carefully began the encirclement of the cabins. At a signal from the sergeant in charge, six armed men appeared at the front doors. The mother, hearing the noisy soldiers, rushed to the front door and started to grab the child. She was too late. This began the final chapter of the Eastern Cherokee Nation. ... No day in all America's history is blacker nor no deed more shameful than the forced removal of a peaceful tribe of people who asked only to be let alone in peace and understanding (Underwood, 1961, p. 33).

The whites descended on Cherokee homes and lands like thieves, stuffing sacks with whatever they wanted or needed, including pots, pans, silverware, and musical instruments. Savage fights broke out over the loot. Some whites, aware that Indians often buried their dead with gold and silver jewelry, dug up graves and sifted through decaying bodies searching for precious metals. In 1838, a Baptist minister commented that, "It is the work of war in time of peace."

There are no words to describe the horrors of the Trail of Tears—a trail that killed about one out of four of those who began the journey. The trip across over one thousand miles took more than six months. The Cherokee died of exhaustion, heat, cold, thirst, hunger, brutality, and disease, and buried their friends and families in shallow graves all along the trail of forests, mountains, swamps, raging rivers and streams, and tortuous wilderness roads.

> Long time we travel on way to new land. People feel bad when they leave old nation. Womens cry and make sad wails. Children cry and many men cry, and all look sad when friends die, but they say nothing and just put heads down and keep on go towards West. Many days pass and people die very much. We bury close by trail (Stein, 1985, p. 29).

LESSON PLAN:
SPEECH OF OLD TASSEL: THE CHEROKEE TRAIL OF TEARS

Grade Level: Grades 5–8

Basic Concepts: Values, discrimination, and power

Organizing Generalization: When cultures have different values, one culture will often use power to force the other to relinquish their particular values and lifeways. The disregard for Native values and lifeways and the use of power in the interaction between the American government and settlers and the people of the Cherokee nation are evident. In spite of the Cherokee request for fairness, the Americans pressed for land and for their way of life.

Culture Area: Southeast

Time Period: The speech that will be used in this lesson plan was delivered in the 1780s; it is a precursor to the forced removal of the Cherokee from their homelands in 1838.

Background: Through the speech of Old Tassel, students will begin to identify the differences in Cherokee values and American values and see how power (both in numbers and technology) was used for American settlers to gain Cherokee land. This use of power was ultimately used in the removal of the Cherokee on the Trail of Tears.

Objectives:

Knowledge
Students will:
1. Identify both Cherokee values and American values that are presented in the speech.
2. Discuss what the term "civilization" means.
3. Identify how power was used in the American search for land.
4. Discuss how value conflicts can be resolved in ways other than conquest.

Skills
Students will:
1. Work cooperatively to interpret the speech of Old Tassel.
2. Use the skills of inference to predict the future of Cherokee lands.
3. Make a time line, which can be used in further study, that begins with this speech in 1780 and extends to 1840.

Values
Students will:
1. Appreciate that the Cherokee people desired peace and coexistence.
2. Recognize that when values are in conflict alternatives do exist for peaceful coexistence.

Activities:
1. Ask students to form groups of three to five to read this speech. It may be read initially by the teacher or rewritten for younger or less skillful readers. Each group should make a list of words the group members don't know. These words can be understood in the context in which they were used, as explained by the teacher or by dictionary definition.
2. Each group should complete the worksheet on page 120 before a class discussion. This activity should take a thoughtful period of time.

3. Arrange the students in a circle to discuss their answers.

4. Using individual student maps, students should draw the boundaries of:
   - the original Cherokee claims,
   - the Cherokee boundary at the close of the Revolution,
   - the Cherokee Boundary at the final cession, and
   - the present Cherokee Reservation (Qualla boundary).

   Ask students to speculate why and how the land of the Cherokee shrunk to such a small reservation in North Carolina. These maps can be saved for reference in the study of the Trail of Tears as can a timeline prepared to record events in the removal.

5. This lesson can be used to introduce the events leading to the Cherokee Trail of Tears or other acts of Indian removal.

Extensions:

1. Research the term "beloved man." Was there a "beloved woman"? Is this a term that is still in use? Would we speak of our president as a "beloved man"? Who might be considered a "beloved man" or "beloved woman" in today's society? What values should a "beloved person" demonstrate?

2. There are innumerable biographies of well-known Cherokee people during the time of removal. In preparation for the study of the Trail of Tears, students may be asked to read and present reports on some of these people including, Major Ridge, John Ross, Sequoyah, and Elias Boudinot.

Evaluation: Individually or in pairs, using Old Tassel's speech, students should write a brief paragraph that (1) summarizes what the Americans wanted from the Cherokee people and how they planned to achieve their goals, (2) specifies what the Cherokee people wanted from the Americans, and (3) predicts who will succeed and why. They should demonstrate an awareness that the Americans have power that the Cherokee do not. These points can also be made in a class discussion.

Materials/Resources:

1. Classroom maps or individual outline maps.
2. Old Tassel's speech.

CHEROKEE MEMORIAL PROPOSED

Chattanooga, TN (AP)—More than 150 years after the Cherokees trudged the Trail of Tears to Oklahoma, an ambitious memorial honoring their tragic journey is in the works.

Planners from several local, state, and federal agencies are trying to raise money for the proposed Meigs County Cherokee Memorial Park in southeast Tennessee. They want to build the park, including a genealogical research library, at the site of an old Cherokee agency about thirty miles north of Chattanooga.

The thirty-acre tract is also on the Trail of Tears, the route Cherokees traveled in 1839 after the government forced them to leave their homes in Georgia, North Carolina, and Tennessee.

Plans unveiled earlier this month call for a large memorial marker shaped like a Cherokee star that will includes the names of seven thousand Cherokees who were moved to Oklahoma.

News From Indian Country, (Mid-July 1992): 7.

Spoken at Treaty Negotiations in the 1780s by a Leading "Beloved Man" of the Cherokee— Called Old Tassel by the Whites

It is surprising that when we enter into treaties with our fathers, the white people, their whole cry is more land. Indeed it has seemed a formality with them to demand what they know we dare not refuse. But on the principles of fairness of which we have received assurance during the conduct of this treaty I must refuse your demand.

What did you do? You marched into our towns with a superior force. Your numbers far exceeded us, and we fled to the strongholds of our woods, there to secure our women and children. Our towns left to your mercy. You killed a few scattered and defenseless individuals, spread fire and desolation wherever you pleased, and returned to your own habitations.

If you term this a conquest, you have overlooked the most essential point. You should have fortified the junction of the Holston and Tennessee Rivers, and thereby conquered all the waters above. It is now too late for us to suffer from your mishap of generalship. Will you claim our lands by right of conquest? No! If you do, I will tell you that WE marched over them, even up to this very place; and some of our young warriors whom we have not had opportunity to recall are still in the woods and continue to keep your people in fear.

Much has been said of the want of what you term "civilization" among the Indians. Many proposals have been made to us to adopt your laws, your religions, your manners, and your customs. We do not see the propriety of such a reformation. We should be better pleased with beholding the good effect of these doctrines in your practices than with hearing you talk about them, or of reading your own papers to us on such subjects. You say, "Why do not the Indians till the ground and live as we do?" May we not ask with equal propriety, "Why do not the white people hunt and live as we do?"

We wish, however, to be at peace with you, and to do as we would be done by. We do not quarrel with you for the killing of an occasional buffalo or deer on our lands, but your people go much farther. They hunt to gain a livelihood. They kill all our game; but it is very criminal in our young men if they chance to kill a cow or a hog for their sustenance when they happen to be in your lands.

The Great Spirit has placed us in different situations. He has given you many advantages, but he has not created us to be your slaves. We are a separate people! He has stocked your lands with cows, our with buffalo; yours with hogs, our with bears; yours with sheep, our with deer. He has given you the advantage that your animals are tame, while ours are wild and demand not only a larger space for range, but art to hunt and kill them. They are, nevertheless, as much our property as other animals are yours, and ought not be taken from us without our consent, or for something of equal value.

From: J. P. Brown. This excerpt can be written in language more appropriate for younger or less skillful readers.

WORKSHEET
THE SPEECH OF THE CHEROKEE
"BELOVED MAN" OLD TASSEL—1780

With your partners, discuss the following questions and be prepared to participate in the class discussion.

1. What do the white people want? What is important to them?

2. How have they attempted to get what they want?

3. Are the Cherokee willing to give up their land easily? Explain your answer.

4. In your own words, describe what Old Tassel thinks of the American efforts to civilize the Indians.

5. In your own opinion, is it reasonable for Old Tassel to ask why the white people don't hunt and live as the Cherokee do?

6. What do the Cherokee people want? What is important to them? Think of least two possible answers.

7. Predict what you think is going to happen to Cherokee land.

LESSON PLAN:
TSALI: AN AMERICAN INDIAN HERO

Grade Level: Grades 3–6

Basic Concepts: Tradition, values, and courage

Organizing Generalization: Throughout history, there have been people who have exemplified the highest values and standards of their particular culture and who are held in particular reverence in that culture. These heroes and heroines serve as models for others and their acts are remembered in the stories, legends, and ceremonies of the group.

Culture Area: Southeast

Time Period: Cherokee Removal–1838

Background: The story of Tsali is a story of individual resistance and courage and it is also the story of the Eastern Cherokees. Although most of the Cherokee people were removed from their land in the Southeast and moved to Arkansas and Oklahoma, there was a group that remained in the Southeast. For a time they could not legally hold land and their land was held through white friends or was left alone because no one thought it was worth having. A white Indian trader, Colonel William Thomas, bought land for individual Indians and held it in his own name. Years later and after considerable negotiation with the U.S. government, the land became what is now known as the Cherokee Indian Reservation or the Qualla Boundary. Today Eastern Cherokees reside on this small reservation in North Carolina. This lesson could be used as an introduction to the study of Indian removal or as part of a study of traditional Cherokee people, as an example of an American hero.

Objectives:

Knowledge

Students will:

1. Differentiate between the Eastern and Oklahoma Cherokees.
2. Describe how the Eastern Cherokees came to be separated from those who were removed to Oklahoma.
3. List the qualities that made Tsali a hero to his people.

Skills:

Students will:

1. Draw a map of the original homeland of the Cherokee, locating the present-day reservation.
2. Compare Tsali with another contemporary Native American hero or heroine.

Values

Students will:

1. Appreciate the courage and bravery of Cherokee men and women like Tsali.
2. Recognize the importance of heros and heroines to any culture.

Activities:

1. Discuss with students how, during the Trail of Tears, some Indian people actively resisted the treatment afforded them by the U.S. Army and were actually able to stay in their homeland in the Southeast.

2. If possible, have pictures available of the Great Smoky Mountains and a map showing the territory that was originally Cherokee land and the Cherokee land that is currently in North Carolina. Excerpts from *The Education of Little Tree* (Carter, 1989) will help to describe the physical context of the mountains. In addition, students can make a map of the area.

3. Introduce the story of Tsali (see p. 123). Engage students in a discussion of the story. Why did Tsali want to fight back when his wife was prodded with a bayonet? Would you have made the same decision that he did? Why? Why not? Why did the army ask Cherokee men to form the firing squad? What did it mean for Tsali to refuse the blindfold? What did his last words mean to him? To you?

4. Ask students to list the qualities that made Tsali a hero to his people.

5. It might be useful to point out that we have traditional American heroes as well as famous words that have become a part of our heritage. ("Give me liberty or give me death." "Ask not what your country can do for you …") Why are these people heroes? Why do we remember their words?

6. Discuss why we may not be familiar with Native American heroes, why they are important to Indian people today, and why they too should be a part of our national history.

7. Make available to students books about other Native heroes such as Sequoyah, Geronimo, Chief Joseph, Tecumseh, and others.

Extensions:

1. Capable readers will enjoy reading *The Education of Little Tree*. This is a story about the Eastern Cherokees in North Carolina and is an exceptionally fine story about the descendents of Tsali and the others who successfully resisted removal.

2. Write to Cherokee Publications, P.O. Box 256, Cherokee, NC 28719, for additional information about the Eastern Cherokees.

3. Research how the Cherokee reservation in North Carolina legally came to be.

4. Read the birthday letter of Private John G. Burnett of the 2nd Regiment, 2nd Brigade, Mounted Infantry, Cherokee Removal in the Teachers' Guide that accompanies this book. This is the story of the removal of the Cherokee from the perspective of a U. S. soldier and of the white man who endeavored to help the Cherokee and was a small hero in this sense.

Evaluation: Students should be able to discuss the qualities that make someone a hero and the importance of heroes and heroines in our cultures and our collective history.

Materials/Resources:
Bedford, D. R. *Tsali*. San Francisco, CA: Indian Historian Press, 1972.
Carter, F. *The Education of Little Tree*. Albuquerque: University of New Mexico Press, 1976.

TSALI

Tsali was a leader of the Cherokee resistance against removal. In May 1838, soldiers came to his cabin to lead him and his family to the stockade to prepare for the long walk from their homeland to the West. On the trip to the stockade, his wife stumbled and an army officer jabbed at her with his bayonet. Tsali made a plan with his son, Ridges, and his brother-in-law, Lowney, to punish the soldier for this and to escape from the removal. In the scuffle with the soldiers that soon followed, one soldier was killed by his own gun and another escaped into the woods.

Tsali hid out that summer with his family in a cave in the Great Smoky Mountains. They were joined by other mountain Cherokees. General Winfield Scott knew it would be difficult to capture Tsali and the other Cherokees who were resisting removal by hiding in the mountains. So he sent a message to Tsali that if he would give himself up the army would no longer search for the others who were hiding in the hills.

Tsali agreed to the terms and gave himself up. He was tried by a military court and sentenced to death, along with Lowney, and his son, Ridges. They were executed by a firing squad.

As a final act of humiliating cruelty, the army forced some of the Cherokee prisoners to be the members of the firing squad—Cherokee prisoners were the ones who had to shoot and kill Tsali.

Tsali refused a blindfold, choosing instead to spend his final moments looking at the red soil of his beloved Cherokee Nation. It is said that his last words were, "It is sweet to die in one's own country."

Although some of the events of the story of Tsali are unproven, the descendants of Tsali and the other Cherokees who escaped from the forced Trail of Tears make up the Eastern Cherokees of North Carolina. Tsali has a special space in Cherokee history and is celebrated for his heroism and self-sacrifice in tribal festivals.

(From: Stein, 1985 and Waldman, 1990, p. 359)

SUMMARY
SEPARATION: 1763–1839

This was a time that the confusion created by the Spanish, French, Dutch, and British excursions into Indian Country became clear, and the British and then the Americans became dominant. This land was called Indian Country, and the term had special meaning because "they had been here so long, that it seemed as though it was always so." Now it had new meaning as a legal term for the official governmental policies that separated Indian people from their ancestral lands and from the new American settlers.

At the close of the French and Indian War the Proclamation of 1763 established a line that no English settlers could cross until representatives of the government negotiated treaties and land cessions with the Indians who lived there. This line was to assure the Indians that they would be secure on their lands until they were willing to sell them to the British. This policy had little effect for the settlers were hungry for new land.

Later, another act of congress, The Indian Removal Act of 1830, specified an Indian country and made it inaccessible to all whites and made forcible removal of Indian people from their land legal. This initiated a decade of dishonor for the United States and meant defeat and displacement for the Indian tribes of the Southeast.

Forcible removal of Indian people from their ancestral lands began. The Five Civilized Tribes (Cherokee, Creek, Choctaw, Chickasaw, and Seminole) were forcibly removed from their land to Indian Territory west of the Mississippi River.

Although the tragedy of the Cherokee Trail of Tears is better known than other removal efforts, it was only one of many removals. Listen to these words: "And so they called it the Trail of Tears for it sounds romantic and speaks of the sorrow of those who stood by the trail. A death march is not romantic."

TIME LINE: 1763–1839

1760   1770   1780   1790   1800   1810   1820   1830   1840

1763
Proclamation of King George III, prohibiting displacement of Indian people without both tribal and Crown consent, attempts to keep settlers east of the Appalachian Divide and establish an Indian Country of protected lands to the west.

1763–1773
The north-south line dividing Indian people from the settlers is further defined through new treaties and Indian land cessions.

1763–1764
Chief Pontiac rebels against the British in the Great Lakes region. Pontiac is assassinated in 1769.

1769
California is claimed for Spain and the first missions were established under Juanipero Serra.

1775–1783
The American Revolution takes place. The Declaration of Independence is signed in 1776.

1775
The Continental Congress of the American Revolutionary government formulates an Indian policy and appoints commissioners for northern, middle, and southern departments.

1778
The first U.S.–Indian treaty is negotiated between the United States and the Delaware Indians. The Delaware tribe is offered the prospect of statehood.

1778
The Iroquois, under Joseph Brant, and British regulars attack American settlers on the western New York and Pennsylvania frontiers.

1779
The American counteroffensive under General Sullivan and General Clinton breaks the power of the Iroquois League.

c. 1780
Using European materials, the Great Lakes Indians develop a ribbonwork style of dress. The craft spreads to the South and the West.

1781–1789
The Articles of Confederation define federal and state relationships, including the principle that the central government should regulate Indian affairs and trade.

1783
The Continental Congress issues a proclamation warning against squatting on Indian lands.

1784
The Congress orders the War Office to provide troops to assist the commissioners in their negotiations with the Indians.

1786
The Secretary of War is made responsible for Indian affairs.

1789
Congress establishes a Department of War and formally grants the Secretary of War authority over Indian affairs.

1787
The Northwest Ordinance calls for Indian rights, the establishment of reservations, and the sanctity of tribal lands.

1787–1789
The Constitution is given the power to regulate commerce with foreign nations, among the states, and with Indian tribes.

1790
Spain signs the Nootka Convention, ceding the Pacific Northwest to England and the United States.

1794
The Battle of Fallen Timbers takes place.

1799
The Russian American Fur Company is chartered under the traders Gregory Shelikov and Alexander Baranov.

1799
Handsome Lake, a Seneca chief, founds the Longhouse religion.

c. 1800
Silverwork becomes widespread among the Indians of the Northeast, eventually spreading to the Indians of the Southwest.

1802
Federal law prohibits the sale of liquor to Indian people.

1802
Congress appropriates funds to "civilize and educate" Indian people.

1803
The Louisiana Purchase by the United States from France, which had gained the territory back from Spain two years before, adds a large Indian population to the United States.

1804
The Louisiana Territory Act affirms the intent of the United States to move eastern Indians west of the Mississippi.

1803–1806
Meriwether Lewis and William Clark expeditions open the American West.

1806
The Office of Superintendent of Indian Trade is established in the War Department under the Secretary of War to administer federal Indian trading houses.

1809–1811
Tecumseh, a Shawnee chief, tries to unite tribes of the Old Northwest, South, and the Mississippi Valley against the United States.

1809–1821
Sequoyah creates a Cherokee alphabet to enable his people to read, write, and communicate more effectively.

1812–1815
The War of 1812 between the United States and England. Tecumseh, a brigadier general for the British, is killed in 1813.

1813–1814
The Creek War takes place in the Southeast. Andrew Jackson takes Creek lands in the Treaty of Fort Jackson.

1817–1818
Andrew Jackson invades Florida to punish the Seminole Indians.

1819
Spain cedes Florida to the United States.

1825
Separate Indian Country west of the Mississippi is first defined.

1827
The Cherokees adopt a constitution patterned on that of the United States, but it is nullified by the Georgia legislature.

1828–1835
Cherokee Phoenix, a weekly newspaper, is published which uses Sequoyah's syllabary.

1830
The Indian Removal Acts calls for relocation of eastern Indians to an Indian territory west of the Mississippi River. This is contested in court.

1832
The Supreme Court decides in favor of the Cherokees, but Andrew Jackson ignores the decision.

1831–1839
The Five Civilized Tribes of the Southeast are relocated to the Indian Territory.

1832
Bureau of Indian Affairs, organized as part of the War Department, is recognized by a law of Congress.

1834
Congress creates the U.S. Department of Indian Affairs within the War Department.

1834
The Trade and Intercourse Act redefines the Indian Territory and the Permanent Indian Frontier and gives the army the right to quarantine Indians.

1835
Texas declares itself a republic independent from Mexico.

1838–1839
The Cherokee "Trail of Tears" takes place.

Sioux Warrior

CHAPTER 9

Separation Continued: 1839–1887

FAREWELL TO BLACK HAWK

You have taken me prisoner, with all my warriors. I am much grieved; for I expected, if I did not defeat you, to hold out much longer, and give you more trouble before I surrendered. I tried hard to bring you into ambush, but your last general understood Indian fighting. I determined to rush upon you, and fight you face to face. I fought hard, but your guns were well aimed. The bullets flew like birds in the air, and whizzed by our ears like the wind through the trees in winter.

My warriors fell around me; it began to look dismal. I saw my evil day at hand. The sun rose dim on us in the morning, and at night it sank in a dark cloud, and looked like a ball of fire. That was the last sun that shone on Black Hawk. His heart is dead, and no longer beats quick in his bosom. He is now a prisoner to the white men; they will do with him as they wish. But he can stand torture, and is not afraid of death. He is no coward. Black Hawk is an Indian!

He has done nothing for which an Indian ought to be ashamed. He has fought for his countrymen, against the white men who came, year after year, to cheat them and take away their lands. You know the cause of our making war. It is known to all white men. They ought to be ashamed of it. The white men despise the Indians and drive them back from their homes. But the Indians are not deceitful. The white men speak bad of the Indian, and look at him spitefully. But the Indian does not tell lies. Indians do not steal. An Indian who is as bad as a white man could not live in our nation. He would be put to death and eaten by the wolves.

The white men are bad schoolmasters. They carry false looks and deal in false actions. They smile in the face of the poor Indian, to cheat him; they shake him by the hand to gain his confidence, to make him drunk, and to deceive him. We told them to let us alone, and keep away from us; but they followed on, and beset our paths, and they coiled themselves among us, like the snake. They poisoned us by their touch. We were not safe; we lived in danger. We were becoming like them, hypocrites and liars; all talkers and no workers.

We looked up to the Great Spirit. We went to our Father. We were encouraged. His great council gave us fair words and big promises; but we obtained no satisfaction. Things were growing worse. There were no deer in the forest. The opossum and the beaver were fled. The springs were drying up, and our people were without food to keep them from starving. We called a great council and built a big fire. The spirit of our fathers arose and spoke to us to avenge our wrongs or die. We set up the war whoop and dug up the tomahawk; our knives were ready, and the heart of Black Hawk swelled high in his bosom when he led his warriors to battle. He is satisfied. He will go to the world of the spirits contented. He has done his duty. His father will meet him there and commend him. Black Hawk is a true Indian. He feels for his wife, his children, his friends, but he does not care for himself. He cares for the nation and for the Indians. They will suffer. He laments their fate.

The white men do not scalp the head, they do worse—they poison the heart. It is not pure with them. His countrymen will not be scalped, but will in a few years be like the white men, so you cannot trust them; and there must be in the white settlements as many officers as men, to take care of them and keep them in order.

Farewell, my nation! Black Hawk tried to save you, and avenge your wrongs. He drank the blood of some of the whites. He has been taken prisoner, and his plans are stopped. He can do no more! He is near his end. His sun is setting and he will rise no more. Farewell to Black Hawk!

The final speech of Black Hawk spoken after his capture in August of 1832. (From *Indian Oratory: Famous Speeches by Noted Indian Chieftains* by W.C. Vanderwerth, pp. 77–79. Copyright © 1971 by the University of Oklahoma Press).

The spirit among the Indians, including Black Hawk, from the mid- to late 1800s was one of disillusion and defeat. The warriors were not without honor, for they had fought a good fight. The great leaders led their people in what seemed to be their last struggle to maintain their homes and traditional ways of life. But the numbers and strength of the Americans grew and grew and the Indians were outnumbered and overpowered. The weapons of the people from the East were deadly and as time passed, their cities became more established. Indians were beginning to realize that the white men would not go away. The Indians were being separated from their homes forever.

For a long period of time the Native people of the Plains were protected from the intruding settlers. The Plains were still considered a great desert, and the land was undesirable to the white settlers. However, the Louisiana Purchase of 1807 and the discovery of gold in California in 1848 and in Colorado in 1858 helped bring to an end Indian freedom in the Plains. Gold was again the impetus for removing Indian people from their land when gold was discovered in the Black Hills of South Dakota in 1874.

In times past, the Indians of the East had fought against men from several countries who were rivals amongst themselves. Now, the enemy had changed from the many European invaders to the American settlers who wanted to cross the Indian lands of the Plains on their way to gold in the west. And, as trails were established and the transcontinental railroad begun, the settlers grew in number. As they moved west, they pushed the Lakota and the other Indians of the Plains further and further west. For a time, the Civil War occupied the efforts of the army. But when the fighting was over, the army moved west to protect the settlers and to remove Indians from their lands.

The strong arm of the U.S. government flexed during the mid- to late 1800s in the process of creating more available land for the growing number of citizens who were moving West. Congress passed legislation creating reservations for tribal use, and the government sent the cavalry to round up the Indians, force them to sign the treaties giving up ownership of the land, and contain them on the newly established reservations.

A quick analysis of the reservations established in the first 150 years of the United States reveals that they were often established on useless land in very extreme climates, making it nearly impossible to sustain traditional lifeways. Additionally, in some areas they are located in close proximity, forcing differing nations to live together with few resources. Although the Plains Indians did not endure forced marches to new and foreign lands as did the Five Civilized Tribes, they nonetheless were separated from their ancestral lands and placed where their presence would not interfere with the westward expansion of the United States.

Tribes were conquered by the cavalry and then coerced into signing treaties which surrendered their homelands. Some treaties were not ratified by the required number of tribal members, and yet they were still honored by the U.S. government. By 1857 the government had acquired over 174 million acres through treaties with various Indian tribes. The Indians found themselves living on barren or uncultivated lands which were unfit for farming and had little wild game for food. The rations promised in the treaties were often undelivered and the Indians were made to work long hours in back-breaking labor for minimum wages. The notes of army doctors tell of food doled out to Indian people that was unsanitary and sour.

This story is repeated in the Southwest. Through the Treaty of Guadalupe Hidalgo in 1848, the Spanish Southwest and its many Indian tribes became part of the United States. Again, issues arose over land for settlers and Indian people were removed from their land. The Long Walk of the Navajo, like the Cherokee Trail of Tears, is a painful chronicle, unlike the Five Civilized Tribes and the Indians of the Plains, however, the Navajo ultimately returned to their own land.

By 1890 the death rate exceeded the birth rate and there were only an estimated 175,000 American Indians. With the admission of new Western territories and states, the traditional homelands of Indian people were reduced even further. Reservations were divided and reduced in total size. The saga of the resistance and retaliation of the Indian tribes is familiar, but often the real story is ignored. In this chapter we will review how the lives of the Plains and Navajo Indians changed as a result of the policy of separation.

THE WARRIORS OF THE PLAINS

The lives and lifestyles of the Indians who roamed the Great Plains in the mid-1800s had been greatly changed by the introduction of the horse and gun. With horses and guns, they could travel easier and hunt with greater success and cover more country with less effort. Their lives were enriched at least for a time. Two of these tribes were the Cheyenne, who came from Minnesota, and the Lakota (Sioux), who originated in the Great Lakes region. Up until early 1800, they maintained a sense of control over their lives and destiny. They were moved further west by the movement of the Eastern tribes as they lost their lands to the colonists. The Lakota and the Cheyenne had little direct contact with the white men and, therefore, were a century behind the Eastern Indians in their knowledge of the strength and cunning of the Europeans.

As time passed, the Cheyenne people became divided, with part of the tribe sharing the Powder River country with the Lakota and the other part going south of the Platte River in present-day Colorado and Kansas. Many of the Arapahos, longtime friends of the Cheyenne, also followed their lead, with some going north and the others south. The Lakota remained in the central plains and lived in their traditional seven bands under leadership of long time warriors and heroes of their people.

During the 1840s, there were a number of isolated conflicts between the Lakota and the U.S. Calvary. The Lakota and neighboring tribes were unhappy with the fear and violence that the settlers and the calvary had brought to the plains. Almost ten thousand Indians gathered together for the signing of the Treaty of Fort Laramie in 1851 in hopes that the terms of the treaty would be kept and the settlers and army would stop invading Indian lands. The treaty repeated the guarantee of other treaties that specified that no one would enter Indian land without Indian consent and that the Indians would stop raiding.

Three years passed in peace, but in 1854, when a settler complained that Indians had killed his cow, an army lieutenant named J. L. Grattan and a small group of soldiers launched an attack on a Lakota encampment. This became known as the Grattan Affair and initiated renewed hostilities through the next few years. Problems accelerated as the settlers crossed Indian land as they moved west on the Oregon Trail to the north and on the trail to the south between the Missouri and the Rocky Mountains. The Cheyennes who had moved south also found themselves living in the path of the settlers.

In June 1864, as part of the process of ridding the prairie of Indians and clearing the way for settlers, the governor of Colorado Territory, John Evans, sent out an announcement that all Arapaho and Cheyenne Indians should report to Fort Lyon where they would be safe. At the same time, he issued orders to search out and kill all Indians not at the Fort. Since it was impossible to get the word to all of the Indians quickly, it was weeks before some of them heard of the notice to go to Fort Lyon. The army began attacking Indians for no cause and after some time, the Cheyenne warriors began raiding out of revenge.

When Black Kettle heard of the message, he was six days from the fort and he feared for the children and elders. He sent word that they needed an escort for themselves and the white prisoners that they had with them. When Major Edward W. Wynkoop, the commander from Fort Lyon arrived, they journeyed to Fort Lyon, stopping at Denver along the way to meet with John Evans. When the meeting yielded no benefits for the Indians, they continued to Fort Lyon. Black Kettle and White Antelope, the leaders of the Cheyenne, felt that Major Wynkoop was someone they could trust, and they settled their people to camp on the Sand Creek about 35 miles from Fort Lyon. They made their intentions for peace known. The Arapaho, who traveled with the Cheyenne, felt even more safe than the Cheyenne and they camped next to the Fort.

John Evans heard of Major Wynkoop's popularity with the Indians, removed him from his command, and replaced him with Major Anthony, a well-known Indian-hater. Soon after Wynkoop's departure from the fort, Major Anthony abruptly sent the Arapahos away from the fort to hunt. Sensing his impatience, they left immediately. When out of sight, they divided into two groups. One group went to camp at Sand Creek with Black Kettle's band while the other group, under the leadership of Little Raven, went south out of distrust of the new soldier chief.

On November 27, Colonel John Chivington and six hundred men arrived at Fort Lyon from Denver. The next night Chivington and his men attacked Black Kettle and his Cheyenne people. They attacked families in their sleep; men, women, and children huddled under the American flag for safety, and others ran from their homes in chaos. It was reported by survivors that they saw White Antelope stand and face the soldiers, cry out in English for help and then sing his death song as he was shot down. "Nothing lives long. Only the earth and the mountains" (Brown, 1974, p. 66). One source quotes the number of Cheyenne left dead that night at one hundred men, women, and children, while other sources say up to five hundred Cheyenne were massacred. This event, known as the Sand Creek Massacre, solidified the resistance of the Indians of the Plains.

Between 1864 and 1868 fighting continued between the army and the Indians. The Plains region became a dangerous place to live. The Treaty of 1868, negotiated through the efforts of Red Cloud, recognized the Black Hills, or *Paha Sapa*, as a sacred place and part of the Sioux Reservation. It was a second treaty in fifteen years between the Indians of the Plains and the U.S. government that promised money and rations in exchange for vast tracts of land. The Treaty of 1868 recognized the western half of modern-day South Dakota as the Great Sioux Reservation and allowed entry only to the Sioux or those with their permission. Peace was tenuous from the start, and the coming of the train and buffalo hunters made the Lakota even more uneasy. The scarce buffalo was disappearing and the increased dependence on rations made the Indian people feel helpless.

When Lieutenant Colonel George Armstrong Custer, in direct violation of the 1868 treaty, entered the sacred Black Hills in 1874 to determine the extent of the gold, word spread back East and hundreds of settlers raced to the Great Sioux Reservation. The government tried to purchase the Black Hills from the Lakota with no success. A deadline was given for all Lakota to report to the reservations and army troops were sent to round up the various bands. Members of the Northern Cheyenne and Lakota under the leadership of Sitting Bull, Crazy Horse, and Gall gathered along the Little Bighorn River in modern-day southeastern Montana.

Three columns of calvary were sent to the Little Bighorn in search of the encampment. Plans were made to surround the Indian camp. The Seventh Calvary under the leadership of Lieutenant Colonel Custer arrived first and, under Custer's orders, split into three groups and attacked the encampment alone. Unknown to Custer was the fact that the camp of Indians was a group of twelve hundred to two thousand warriors ready for battle. The Battle of the Little Bighorn claimed the lives of Custer and most of his men. They had greatly underestimated the strength of the Indians camping along the river.

After this famous battle, the bands split up. With the loss of the buffalo herds and the land, the Indians had to find a new way to live or a new place to live. One by one, the bands were defeated and gave in to reservation life. Sitting Bull fled to Canada and remained free for some time only to end his life on a reservation in modern-day South Dakota. The newspapers of the eastern cities told of the massacre of Custer and his men, and there was a rally cry to kill Indians. The Indians wanted to "fight no more forever."

> Tell General Howard I know his heart. What he told me before I have in my heart. I am tired of fighting. Our chiefs are killed. Looking Glass is dead. It is the young men who say yes or no. He who led the young men is dead. It is cold and we have no blankets. The little children are freezing to death. My people, some of them have run away to the hills and have no blankets, no food; no one knows where they are— perhaps freezing to death. I want to have time to look for my children and see how many I can find. Maybe I shall find them among the dead. Hear me my chiefs. I am tired; my heart is sick and sad. From where the sun now stands, I will fight no more forever (Chief Joseph, Nez Perce, 1877, as presented in McLuhan, 1971, p. 120).

Recognizing that the peace with the white man meant the end of many old ways, Red Cloud, an Oglala Sioux Chief, spoke to his people and other Oglala chiefs. He counseled his people that they should put away the wisdom of their fathers and begin in the ways of the white man. In these new ways, they were counseled to lay up food and forget the hungry, and when they had enough, they should look for a neighbor of whom they could take advantage and seize all the neighbor had.

THE LONG WALK OF THE NAVAJO

During this same period of time, the Navajo people would experience suffering like they had never seen before. Until 1845, the Navajo of the Southwest had dealt mostly with the Spanish. Their relationship had continued for over a century and had included times of goodwill and conflict. With the Treaty of Guadalupe Hildalgo in 1845 and the cession of modern-day New Mexico and Arizona to the United States, the Mexicans living in the area became citizens of the United States. The Navajo did not become citizens, but they did gain a new opponent in the battle for land and survival, the United States.

The Navajos, under Manuelito, Barboncito, and other Navajo leaders, lived peaceably with the whites for some time. They lived in small bands and had no real tribal unity. Fort Defiance was built in a grassy valley at the mouth of Canyon Bonito. A treaty was negotiated with several of the bands that restricted Navajo raiding and limited the travel of non-Navajos through Navajo lands. The peace lasted until several isolated incidents on both sides prompted retaliation raids that led to major confrontation between Manuelito, Barboncito, and the other Navajo leaders and the U.S. Army.

In the spring of 1862, just after the Civil War, General James Carleton, with Kit Carson at his side, entered Navajo territory and camped alongside the Rio Grande. Within a short time he felt a growing desire for the Navajo homeland. He created a plan to move the Navajo to Bosque Redondo, some worthless land three hundred miles away, and open the way for others to move into the beautiful Navajo homeland. In the spring of 1863, he arranged a meeting with the leaders of the Navajo to offer them land at Bosque Redondo in exchange for their homeland. Barboncito and the other leaders replied that they would never leave their land.

By summer, General Carleton had sent Kit Carson to Fort Defiance. He renamed it Fort Canby after a previous enemy of the Navajo and commander of the fort. He began offering money for Navajo livestock and practiced the "scorched earth" policy of burning all crops and killing the livestock. As the Navajo people were driven from their homes, they fled to the mountains to shelter and survival. The winter was harsh and food was scarce. The only place left was Canyon de Chelly. This is where the Navajo grew their beloved peach trees.

January of 1864 came with six inches of snow on the ground and temperatures well below freezing. General Carleton ordered Carson to go to Canyon de Chelly and capture or kill all the remaining Navajo.

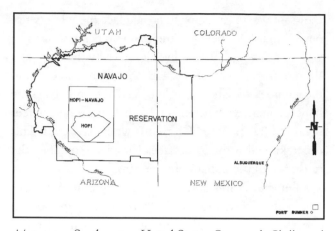

Map 9.1—Southwestern United States—Canyon de Chelly and Bosque Redondo with an Outline of the Navajo Reservation, as it is Today.

The canyon was taken from both ends and before long about sixty starving, freezing Navajos surrendered. Before Carson and the soldiers left the canyon, they burned more than five thousand peach trees. By early spring, nearly three thousand Navajo had turned themselves in to the two forts in Navajo country. During March, the Long Walk of the Navajo became a reality. Nearly 950 Navajo walked three hundred miles in snow and wind. At least 110 died en route during the two-month trek.

For some time, Manuelito and Barboncito still remained at large with their loyal followers. In September 1864 Barboncito was captured in Canyon de Chelly. There he joined others that had been forcibly separated from their homeland.

As time passed, the Navajos escaped from Bosque Redondo and returned to their home with tales of poor crops, little food, sickness, and cold. In February 1865 a few Navajo leaders were released from the Bosque to meet with Manuelito, the last holdout, to see if they could get him to surrender. He told them,

> My God and my mother live in the West, and I will not leave them .... Nor could I leave the Chuska Mountains. I was born there. I shall remain. I have nothing to lose but my life, and that they can come and take whenever they please, but I will not move. I have never done any wrong to the Americans or Mexicans. I have never robbed. If I am killed, innocent blood will be shed (Brown, 1974, p. 19).

In the best interests of his few weak, starving followers, he suggested that they give themselves up; only he and a few warriors remained.

Barboncito and several Navajos escaped from the Bosque Redondo that same year as did many others. The crops had failed and the Navajos were fed food that had been considered unfit for the soldiers. Because of the large numbers of runaways, orders were given to kill any Navajo found off of the reservation. When September came, both Manuelito and Barboncito surrendered with a handful of warriors at their side. All were wounded, starving, beaten men. Ironically, not three weeks after their surrender, General Carleton was removed from his post as commander of Bosque Redondo. The new superintendent, A. B. Norton, felt differently about the Navajos and found the conditions of the reservation deplorable. In his words, "The sooner it is abandoned and the Indians removed, the better ... ."

In 1868 the Navajos would be forced to sign yet another treaty. This one would allow them to return to their beloved homelands. This was one of the last treaties that would be made by the U.S. government with an Indian tribe. It contained provisions that included sheep allotments to every Navajo, attendance at schools with one teacher for every thirty Navajo children, and an agreement that the Navajos would stop raiding.

THE FIVE CIVILIZED TRIBES

Removal for the Five Civilized Tribes did not end with the journey to Oklahoma. By 1848 the removal of the Five Civilized Tribes to Oklahoma was nearly complete. Some fifteen thousand Creeks, Seminoles, Choctaws, Chickasaws, and Cherokees had died along the way. Members of each of the five tribes were split over the issue of removal. The main body of each nation remained in the East until the last possible moment. Once settled in the West, those among the five tribes who were advocates of removal, such as the Ridge family and Elias Boudinot of the Cherokee Nation, were assassinated.

Slowly the tribes began to rebuild after their removal, both politically and economically. Once the Native tongue became a written language, each council's laws were codified. The people continued farming as a way of life and, after a period of time, found themselves enjoying most of the same benefits of life as before removal. They had learned farming in their Georgia home. Their schools flourished and most of the people were literate in both English and their Native language. But the issue of land still remained. By 1860 the tribal councils of the Five Civilized Tribes once again found themselves locked in a battle with the federal government over the remaining land in Indian Territory.

When the Civil War broke out in 1861, many members of the Five Civilized Tribes joined the South, which promised the return of their lands. When the war was over and the North won, the Indians were punished for fighting for the South and half of the lands designated as Indian territory was removed from their jurisdiction. These lands became the new home for the Cheyenne, Arapahos, Kickapoos, Sacs and Foxes, and the Iowa.

By the late 1860s, the Five Civilized Tribes had adopted new constitutions and established new codes of laws. These laws reflected the recent past and they supported unity and teamwork. For example, in October 1867 the two factions that had grown within the Creek Nation (or Muscogee) signed an agreement that said, " ... they should unite and live as one nation. ... There was to be no North and South among the Muscogee People, but peace and friendship." The tribal leaders learned quickly that the Bureau of Indian Affairs, now under the Department of the Interior, could not be trusted to protect the Indians' interests. Therefore, the tribes kept a representa-

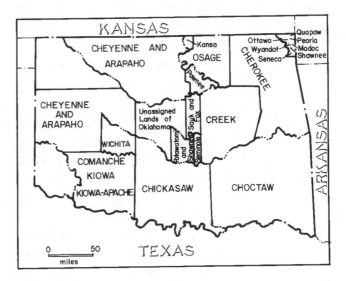

Map 9.2—Indian Territory after the Civil War.

tive in Washington to observe Congress and inform the tribes when action was being taken against them. They knew that they needed to work together. The Five Civilized Tribes worked under poor conditions to develop both economically and politically in a way that would be compatible with the federal government. This was another attempt at accommodation for the purpose of survival.

The overt process of forced separation of the Indians from their land came to a halt in the mid 1880s. The year 1871 marked the end of making treaties. Most tribes had signed treaties with the government and were living on reservations. The deplorable treatment of the Indians of various tribes was publicized and it became increasingly difficult for overt hostility against the Indians to continue. In 1870 President Ulysses Grant gave control of Indian agencies to twelve different Christian denominations instead of army officers. They played a major role in Indian agencies and also many of the schools until 1917, when Congress stopped payments to religious groups for work on reservations.

The use of education and religious coercion instead of outright fighting changed the method of assault on Native people, but it did not get rid of it. In fact, it was in many ways a far worse fate for Indian people. The Christians questioned and undermined the traditional ways of life of Indian people. In some cases, the reservations did not include all of the sacred places and the agents prohibited many Native ceremonies. Tribal members adopted the ways of the Christians, or at least made it appear that way, in order to maintain some freedom to practice their own religion. Small groups of individuals would make the trip into the mountains or to remote lakes and buttes to conduct ceremonies. Participation in sacred ceremonies was kept secret and those who continued the traditional ways feared discovery and the loss of their way of life. This was only the beginning of the prohibition of Native religion that the Indians would experience in the coming years.

Indian people of various nations operated their own schools as early as 1791. The Choctaw of Mississippi operated over two hundred schools and academies and sent many graduates to "white" colleges in the east. The Cherokee are also well known for their extensive schooling system. Literacy rates of Cherokees in both Cherokee and English during the nineteenth century are as high as ninety percent. The Senecas operated their own schools as well as the Chickasaws, the Seminoles, and Creeks. But by the late 1800s all of these schools were closed by the federal government and replaced by government (Bureau of Indian Affairs) and mission schools.

The new schools denied the Native languages of the various tribes and required student participation in Christian religious ceremonies. Children were stolen from their homes, their hair was cut, and they were taken far away to go to school. Congress took an increased interest in the education of the Indian as it became apparent that it was very important in the process of assimilation of the Indian.

With the involvement and support of the government, Richard Pratt founded the Carlisle Indian School in Pennsylvania in 1879 to assist in the process of assimilating the Natives into white culture. In Pratt's address to Congress, he said, "We accept the watchword, let us by patient effort kill the Indian in him and save the man" (O'Brien, 1989, p. 76). An emphasis was placed on boarding schools as they were more successful at assimilation since they forced children to leave home at a very young age. When the children returned home, they seldom could speak their language and were strangers to the ways of their people.

By 1887 there were more than fourteen thousand Indian students attending 227 schools. Of these schools, the Bureau of Indian Affairs operated the majority, with missionaries operating the rest. Some of the efforts to improve conditions on Indian reservations came through groups established at the time such as the Indian Protection Committee, the Indian Rights Association, the Women's National Indian Association, and the National Indian Defense Association. While their efforts were sincere, they only changed the face of the oppressor rather than destroyed it. Efforts to isolate Indians on reservations had failed. New strategies were needed to increase the amount of land available for settlers and eradicate the Indian problem. The method of assimilation had changed from violence to education and religious conversion. The issue of land still remained.

LESSON PLAN:
THE LONG WALK OF THE NAVAJO

Grade Level: Intermediate and middle school

Basic Concepts: Tradition, values, history, and culture

Organizing Generalization: Significant events of history affect the present. The Long Walk of the Navajo was so important in their history that present generations learn of this event in history, and it lives as a part of their contemporary lives and binds them to the generations that went before them. History is not forgotten but remains in the collective memory of the Navajo people.

Culture Area: Southwest

Time Period: The poetry to be used in this lesson tells of the Long Walk in 1864 and demonstrates how it is a part of the contemporary lives of Navajo people.

Background: This activity should be done after students have a good understanding of the Long Walk; it will assist them in understanding the significance of this event to the Navajo people of today. Future generations look to their ancestors for lessons to help them in their contemporary lives. This relationship is ignored by modern generations, unless they are taught about their past through stories and poems. The poetry of Luci Tapahonso, a Navajo, helps the reader understand this link between past and present in a simple but eloquent way. The poem also highlights the relatively recent product of the contact between two cultures.

Objectives:
Knowledge
Students will:
1. Give examples from the poem of how events of the past impact the present lives of the Navajo people.
2. Identify how Navajo culture is taught to new generations.
3. Discuss Navajo lifestyle before the Long Walk.
4. List three Navajo customs that originated at Fort Sumner.

Skills
Students will:
1. Locate Canyon de Chelly, Fort Sumner, the Chuska Mountains, the Rio Grande River, and the modern-day Navajo Reservation on a map.
2. Analyze the meaning of the poem, *1864*.

Values
Students will:
1. Appreciate both the positive and negative relationships of the past and the present.
2. Recognize the importance of perpetuating the history of the people.

Activities:
1. Gather the students together and read the poem, *1864* (see pp. 138–40). Take time to explain the following terms, Bilagaana, Redshirt, Dinetah, and Hweedli.

2. On a map of modern-day Arizona, Colorado, Utah, and New Mexico, plot the locations of Canyon de Chelly, the Chuska Mountains, the Rio Grande River, Bosque Redondo, and the modern-day Navajo Reservation. Students can draw their own individual maps, determining the distance from Canyon de Chelly to Fort Sumner. It would also be useful to determine the terrain and the temperature that would be encountered in a walk.

3. Ask students to break into small groups to discuss the meaning of the following phrases which are central to understanding the poem.
   - "He couldn't stay there any longer. The place that contained the pain and cries of his own relatives; the confused and battered spirits of his own existence."
   - "'We will be strong as long as we are together.'" I think that was what kept us alive. We believed in ourselves and the old stories that the holy people had given us. 'This is why,' she would tell us, 'this is why we are here because our grandparents prayed and grieved for us.'"

Extensions:

1. Work in small groups to create murals to depict the various scenes in the poem.
2. Conduct research on other American Indian tribes who experienced forced removal and compare their experiences. Examine the length of stay, long-term impact, living conditions, distance from home, and other appropriate topics.

Evaluation:

1. Students will be able to name at least three Navajo customs that originated at Fort Sumner.
2. Students will locate Canyon de Chelly, Fort Sumner, the Chuska Mountains, the Rio Grande River, and the modern-day Navajo Reservation on a map.
3. Students will participate in a class discussion that focuses on the lifestyle of the Navajo before and after the Long Walk, how culture is transmitted, and how the present Navajo lifestyle has been impacted by the past.

Materials/Resources:

1. A classroom map or atlas that would show the location of the Navajo Reservation and Fort Sumner.
2. *1864*, by Luci Tapahonso (pp. 138–40).
3. Resource books about the Navajo and the Southwest.

Arthur, C., Bingham, S., and Bingham J. *Between Sacred Mountains.* Tucson: Sun Tracks and the University of Arizona Press, 1982.

Gilpin, L. *The Enduring Navaho.* Austin: University of Texas, 1988.

Locke, R. F. *The Book of the Navajo* (5th edition). Los Angeles: Mankind, 1992.

Iverson, P. *The Navajos.* New York: Chelsea, 1990.

Tellens (Producer). *Navajo* (Video). Flagstaff: Museum of Northern Arizona, 1982.

1864

by Luci Tapahonso

In 1864,

8,354 Navajos were forced to walk from
Dinetah to Bosque Redondo in southern
New Mexico, a distance of 300 miles.
They were held for four years until
the United States government declared
the assimilation attempt a failure.
Over 2,500 died of smallpox, depression,
severe weather conditions, starvation,
and other illnesses. The survivors
returned in June of 1868.

While the younger daughter slept, she dreamed of mountains,
the wide blue sky above, and friends laughing.

We talked as the day wore on, the stories and highway
beneath became a steady hum. The center lines were a blurred guide.
As we neared the turn to Fort Sumner, I remembered this story:

A few winters ago, he worked as an electrician on a crew
installing power lines on the western plains of New Mexico.
He stayed in his pickup camper, which was connected to a
generator. The crew parked their trucks together
and built a fire in the center. The nights were cold
and there weren't any trees to break the wind.
It snowed off and on—a quiet, still blanket.

The land was like he had imagined from the old stories;
flat and dotted with shrubs. The arroyos and washes
cut through the soft dirt. They were unsuspectingly deep.

During the day, the work was hard and the men were exhausted.
In the evenings, some went into the nearby town to eat
and drink a few beers. He fixed a small meal for himself
and tried to relax.

Then at night, he heard cries and moans carried by the wind
and blowing snow. He heard the voices wavering and rising
in the darkness. He would turn over and pray, humming songs
he remembered from his childhood. The songs returned to him
as easily as if he had heard them that very afternoon.
He sang for himself, his family, and the people whose spirits
lingered on the plains, in the arroyos, and in
the old windswept plants. No one else heard the thin wailing.

After the third night, he unhooked his camper,
signed his timecard, and started the drive north to home.

He told the guys, "Sure, the money's good, but I miss my kids
and it sure gets lonely out here for a family man."
He couldn't stay there any longer. The place that contained
the pain and cries of his own relatives; the confused and
battered spirits of his own existence.

After we stopped for a Coke and chips, the storytelling resumed:

My aunt had always started the story saying, "You are here
because of what happened to your great-grandmother long ago."

They began rounding up the people in the fall. Some were
lured into surrendering by offers of food, clothes,
and livestock. So many of us were starving and suffering
that year because the bilagaanas kept attacking us.
Kit Carson and the Army had burned all the fields and
they killed our sheep right in front of us. We couldn't
believe it—I cover my face and cried. All my life,
we had sheep; they were like our family. It was then
I knew our own lives were in great danger. We were
all so afraid of that man, Redshirt, and his army.
Some people hid in the foothills of the Chuska Mountains
and in Canyon De Chelly. Our family talked it over and
we decided to go to this place. What would our lives be
without sheep, crops, and land? At least, we thought we
would be safe from gunfire and our family would not starve.

The journey began and the soldiers were all around us.
All of us walked, some carried babies. Little children
and the elderly stayed in the middle of the group. We walked
steadily each day stopping only when the soldiers wanted
to eat or rest. We talked among ourselves and cried quietly.
We didn't know how far it was or even where we were going.
All that was certain was that we were leaving Dinetah—our home.
As the days went by, we grew more tired and soon, the journey
was difficult for all of us—even the military. And it was
they who thought all this up.

We had such a long distance to cover.
Some old people fell behind and they wouldn't let us
go back to help them. It was the saddest thing to see—
my heart hurts so to remember that. Two women were near
the births of their babies and they had a hard time
keeping up with the rest. Some army men pulled them
behind some big rocks and we screamed out loud when we heard
the gunshots. The women didn't make a sound, but we cried out
loud for them and the babies. I felt then that I would not
live through all this.

When we crossed the Rio Grande, many people drowned.
We didn't know how to swim—there was hardly any water
deep enough to swim in at Dinetah. Some babies, children,
and some of the older men and women were swept away by
the river current. We must not ever forget their screams and
the last we saw of them—hands, a leg or their hair floating.

There were many who died on the way to Hweedli.
All the way, we told each other, "We will be strong as long
as we are together." I think that was what kept us alive.
We believed in ourselves and the old stories that
the holy people had given us.

"This is why," she would tell us, "this is why we are here
because our grandparents prayed and grieved for us."

The car hums steadily and my daughter is crying softly.
Tears stream down her face. She cannot speak.

Then I tell her that it was at Bosque Redondo,
they learned to use flour dough and now, fry bread
is considered to be the "traditional" Navajo bread.
It was there that they acquired an eternal appreciation
for strong coffee. The women learned to make long, tiered
calico skirts and fine velvet shirts for men.
The women decorated their dark velvet blouses with silver dimes,
nickels, and quarters. They had no use for money then.

It is always something to see—silver flashing in the sun
against dark velvet and black, black hair.

Note: "Dinetah" means "Navajo country" or "homeland of The People." Fort Sumner was also called "Bosque Redondo" due to its location. Kit Carson was called "Redshirt" by the Navajos. "Bilagaana" is the Navajo word for Anglos.

Fort Sumner

    • Tribes to be honored—Navajo and Mescalero Apache Indians who were forced from their homelands in the late 1860's and imprisoned at Bosque Redondo will be honored with a memorial at Fort Sumner. The state legislature (New Mexico) has allocated $23,000 to plan the memorial.

    Navajo Nation President Peterson Zah said the existing monument at Fort Sumner represents the U.S. military's point of view and should be expanded to include tribal perspective.

The Denver Post—March 1992

SUMMARY
SEPARATION CONTINUED: 1839–1887

The spirit among the Indians from the mid- to late 1800s was one of disillusion and defeat. The warriors were not without honor, for they had fought a good fight. The great leaders led their people in what seemed to be their last struggle to maintain their homes and traditional life. However, the Indian was beginning to realize that the white men would not go away. The Indian was being separated from his home forever.

Now the focus of the struggle had changed from the European invaders to the American settlers who wanted to cross Indian lands of the Plains on their way to gold in the West. Congress passed legislation creating reservations for tribal use and the government sent the cavalry to round up the Indians, force them to sign the treaties giving up their lands, and contain them on the newly established reservations.

Although the Plains Indians did not endure forced marches to new and foreign lands as did the Five Civilized Tribes, they were separated from their ancestral lands and placed where their presence would not interfere with the westward expansion of the United States.

By 1857 the government had acquired over 174 million acres through treaties with various Indian tribes. The reservations established in the first 150 years of the United States were on useless land in very extreme climates, making it nearly impossible to maintain traditional lifeways.

Indians found themselves living on barren or uncultivated lands that were unfit for farming and had little wild game for food. Rations promised in the treaties were often undelivered, and the food was frequently unsanitary and sour.

This story was repeated in the Southwest. The Long Walk of the Navajo was another march to unfit land—although the Navajo would return.

TIME LINE: 1844–1885

1840   1850   1860   1870   1880   1890

1844

The first issues of the *Cherokee Advocate* are published in Oklahoma, and federal soldiers confiscate the press.

1845–1848

The United States and Mexico go to war over the American annexation of Texas. With the Treaty of Guadalupe Hidalgo in 1848, the Spanish Southwest and its many Indian tribes become part of the United States.

1848–1849

Gold is discovered in California, starting the California Gold Rush and the destruction of California and Plains Indians.

1849

The Bureau of Indian Affairs is transferred from the War Department to the Department of the Interior.

1851

The Treaty of Fort Laramie is made between the U.S. government and the tribes of the Northern Plains.

1853

Gadsden Purchase enables the United States to acquire from Mexico the lands in New Mexico, Arizona, and California.

1853–1854

Liquidation of the northern portion of the Indian Territory creates the state of Kansas and the Nebraska territory.

1853–1856

The United States acquires 174 million acres of Indian lands through fifty-two treaties, all of which are subsequently broken by whites.

1854

The Commissioner of Indian Affairs calls for the end of the Indian removal policy.

1854

U.S. Cavalry officer, William Grattan, initiates a major conflict with the Sioux.

1858–1859

Gold is discovered in Colorado and another Gold Rush begins.

1861–1865

During the Civil War, to encourage support of the Indians, the South makes promises to the Indians concerning the return of their tribal lands. After the war, as punishment for their support of the Confederacy, the Five Civilized Tribes are forced to accept a treaty relinquishing the western half of the Indian Territory to twenty tribes from Kansas and Nebraska.

1862

The Homestead Act opens up Indian land in Kansas and Nebraska to homesteaders, who are deeded 160 acres plots after inhabiting them for five years.

1863–1866

The Navajo War in New Mexico and Arizona.

1864

The Navajo people are forced on the "Long Walk" to Bosque Redondo. Manuelito surrenders in 1866.

1864

Colonel John Chivington's Colorado Volunteers kill more than three hundred Indians in the Sand Creek Massacre.

1864

Indians are regarded as competent witnesses under federal law and allowed to testify in trials.

1865

The United States gives contracts to Protestant missionary societies to operate Indian schools.

1866

Railroad Enabling Act appropriates Indian lands for railway use.

1866–1868

War for the Bozeman Trail in Wyoming and Montana involves the Sioux, Cheyenne, and Arapaho Indians under Chief Red Cloud. A second Fort Laramie Treaty resolves the conflict in 1868.

1867

The United States purchases Alaska from Russia, adding Eskimos and Aleuts to its own population.

1867

Plains tribal leaders accept permanent lands within the Indian Territory in the Treaty of Medicine Lodge.

1867

A U.S. "Peace Commission" recommends that the current treaty process be abandoned. This commission and the Nez Perce Indians negotiate the last of 370 treaties between the federal government and the tribes.

1868

The Commissioner of Indian Affairs estimates that the Indian Wars in the West are costing the government 1 million dollars per Indian killed.

1868

Indians are denied the right to vote as a result of the 14th Amendment.

1868–1869

The Southern Plains War involves the Cheyennes, Sioux, Arapahos, Kiowas, and Comanches.

1869

President Grant's "Peace Policy" is inaugurated and lasts until 1874.

1869

Brigadier General Ely Parker (Seneca) becomes the first Indian Commissioner of Indian Affairs serving until 1871.

1869

Transcontinental railroad is completed when the Union Pacific and the Central Pacific join at Promontory Point, Utah.

c. 1870

The use of peyote begins to spread from the Mexican Indians to the Comanches, Kiowas, and other tribes.

1870

President Grant gives control of the Indian agencies to twelve different Christian denominations instead of to army officers.

1871

Congress passes a law forbidding further negotiations of treaties with Indian tribes. Indians are now subject to acts of Congress and executive orders.

1871

General Sheridan issues orders forbidding Western Indians to leave reservations without the permission of civilian agents.

1871

White hunters begin wholesale killing of buffalo.

1874

Gold is discovered in the Black Hills of South Dakota. The miners ignore the treaties that protected Indian lands.

1876–1877

The Sioux War for the Black Hills involves the Sioux, Cheyennes, and Arapahos, under chiefs Sitting Bull and Crazy Horse.

1876

The Battle of Little Bighorn.

1877

The Nez Perce under Chief Joseph in the Northwest take flight.

1878

Congress provides for Indian Police. In 1883 tribal units are authorized to administer justice in all but major crimes

1879

Richard Pratt found the Carlisle Indian School in Pennsylvania with the intent of assimilating Indians into white culture.

1881

Sitting Bull and his band of 187 surrender to officials at Fort Buford, North Dakota.

1881–1886

Apache Resistance under Geronimo in the Southwest. Geronimo surrenders in 1886.

1884

Congress acknowledges the rights of Eskimos to Alaskan territorial lands.

1885

The last great herd of buffalo is exterminated.

1885

The Major Crimes Act gives federal courts jurisdiction over Indian cases involving major crimes.

1886

Mohawk Indians in Quebec are trained in high-steel construction work on a bridge across the St. Lawrence River, beginning a tradition among the Iroquois.

CHAPTER 10

Coercive Assimilation: 1887–1910

I have shaken hands with a great many friends, but there are some things I want to know which no one seems able to explain. I cannot understand how the Government hands a man out to fight us, as it did General Miles, and then breaks his word. Such a Government has something wrong about it ... . I do not understand why nothing is done for my people. I have heard talk and talk, but nothing is done. Good words do not last long until they amount to something. Words do not pay for my dead people. They do not pay for my country, now overrun by white men. They do not protect my father's grave. They do not pay for my horses and cattle.

Good words do not give me back my children. Good words will not make good the promise of your war chief, General Miles. Good words will not give my people good health and stop them from dying. Good words will not get my people a home where they can live in peace and take care of themselves.

I am tired of talk that comes to nothing. It makes my heart sick when I remember all the good words and all the broken promises. There has been too much talking by men who had no right to talk. Too many misinterpretations have been made; too many misunderstandings have come up between the white man and the Indians.

If the white man wants to live in peace with the Indian he can live in peace. There need be no trouble. Treat all men alike. Give them all the same law. Give them all an even chance to live and grow. ... You might as well expect the rivers to run backward as that any man who was born free should be contented penned up and denied liberty to go where he pleases. If you tie a horse to a stake, do you expect he will grow fat? If you pen an Indian up on a small spot of earth and compel him to stay there, he will not be contented nor will he grow and prosper.

I have asked some of the Great White Chiefs where they get their authority to say to the Indian that he will stay in one place, while he sees white men going where they please. They cannot tell me.

I only ask of the government to be treated as all other men are treated. If I cannot go to my own home, let me have a home in a country where my people will not die so fast. ...

I know my race must change. We cannot hold our own with the white men as we are. We only ask an even chance to live as other men live. We ask to be recognized as men. We ask that the same law shall work alike on all men. If an Indian breaks the law, punish him by the law. If a white man breaks the law, punish him also.

Let me be a free man—free to travel, free to stop, free to work, free to trade where I choose, free to choose my own teachers, free to follow the religion of my fathers, free to think and talk and act for myself—and I will obey every law or submit to the penalty.

(Chief Joseph, Nez Perce, 1879, as presented in McLuhan, 1971, pp. 123–124).

"Let me be a free man—free to travel, free to stop, free to work, free to trade where I choose, free to choose my own teachers, free to follow the religion of my fathers, free to think and talk and act for myself." These words written by Chief Joseph in 1879 are a reasonable request and they ring true to American traditions and values. Yet this humble request was not to be. Chief Joseph must have read the signs that a new period of American history known as coercive assimilation was near at hand. During this period, the policy of the U.S. government was to force Native people to assimilate into the dominant American culture. Ostensibly, this goal of assimilation was the protection and preservation for the Indian. Francis Paul Prucha summarizes the reality of coercive assimilation policies and practices when he states:

> But beyond protection and preservation there was the ultimate goal of transformation: to induce the Indians all to become cultivators of the soil, to adopt the white man's language, customs, and religion, and finally to be self-supporting citizens of the commonwealth, a goal that all but a few believed was entirely practicable if only the proper means were applied. Agriculture, domestic and mechanical arts, English education, Christianity, and individual property (land allotted in severalty) were the elements of the civilization program that was to be the future of the Indians (Prucha, 1986, p. 110).

The last two decades of nineteenth-century American Indian policy were dominated by a group of earnest men and women who called themselves "the friends of the Indian." Their purpose was to solve the Indian problem, and, drawing upon their own vision of what was right, proper, and patriotic, this purpose was to be achieved through religion and "Americanization."

> They had great confidence in the righteousness of their cause, and they knew that God approved. Convinced of the superiority of the Christian civilization they enjoyed, they saw no need to inquire about positive values in the Indian culture, nor to ask the Indians what they would like. With an ethnocentrism of frightening intensity, they resolved to do away with Indianness and to preserve only the manhood of the individual Indian. There would then be no more Indian problem because there would be no more persons identifiable as

Indians. All would be immersed in the same civilization (Prucha, 1978, p. 1).

Other goals of assimilation were based on the accelerating need for more land and the emerging need to protect American settlers from the Indians of the West who were trying to protect and preserve their land, the buffalo, and their ways of life. Assimilation was the way to solve the "Indian problem," to legally acquire more land and to remove Native people from where they could harm white settlers.

In this chapter, we will discuss the General Allotment Act, a policy that attempted to change totally the lives of Indian people, and give several examples of how this policy was implemented in the Oklahoma Land Run, extended in the Curtis Act, and resisted in the Snake Uprising. The loss of Blue Lake, which so profoundly affected the Taos people of the Southwest, was executed in yet another manner during this period of time. In addition to allotment, two other major forces were also at work at this time to force the assimilation of Indian people: Christian missionaries and education. Allotment, religion, and education were the tools of coercive assimilation—the tools used to change the way of life of Native people, to transform their way of providing for themselves, to eradicate their languages, to abolish their traditional religious ceremonies and practices, and to school them in "civilized ways."

> In our intercourse with the Indians it must always be borne in mind that we are the most powerful party ... we assume that it is our duty to coerce them if necessary, into the adoption and practice of our habits and customs (Secretary of the Interior Columbus Delando, 1872 as cited in Spicer, 1982, p. 182).

GENERAL ALLOTMENT ACT (DAWES ACT)

The General Allotment Act, or Dawes Severalty Act of 1887, was a disaster for Indian people. The intent to create individual "civilized farmers" out of a people whose tradition was one of tribal community had multiple negative effects. Not only did they not become farmers, but, because of the provisions of the act and unscrupulous whites, the 155,632,312 acres of land that they held in 1881 was reduced to 48,000,000 by 1934 when the policy of allotment was reversed. Of the acres that remained, approximately half were desert or semi-desert areas on which it was nearly impossible to scratch out a living through agriculture or ranching.

Again, although clothed in humanitarian and protective terms, the reasoning behind the General Allotment Act was that of insensitivity and superiority. Carl Schurz, one of the foremost reformers of this time, made the following statement in 1881:

> I am profoundly convinced that a stubborn maintenance of the system of large Indian reservations must eventually result in the destruction of the red men, however faithfully the Government may endeavor to protect their rights. It is only a question of time. ... What we can and should do is, in general terms, to fit the Indians, as much as possible, for the habits and occupations of civilized life, by work and education; to individualize them in the possession and appreciation of property, by allotting to them lands in severalty, giving them a fee simple title individually to the parcels of land they cultivate, inalienable for a certain period, and to obtain their consent to a disposition of that part of their lands which they cannot use, for a fair compensation, in such a manner that they no longer stand in the way of the development of the country as an obstacle, but form part of it and are benefitted by it (Prucha, 1978, p. 14).

The act authorized the president to allot all tribal land in the United States, excepting the lands of the Five Civilized Tribes, the Osages, and a few others who held land under patented titles, to individuals. The standard share was 160 acres to each head of a family, with smaller parcels to unmarried men and minors. In 1891, as a result of strong Indian opposition to the "head of a family" concept, the act was amended to provide equal shares to all. Each person (including married women and children) received 80 acres of agricultural land and 160 acres of grazing land.

The allotments were to be held in trust status, inalienable and nontaxable for twenty-five years in order to protect the people from exploitation. Any transactions regarding the land during the trust period were null and void, and the president could extend the period of trust at his discretion. In addition, tribes would negotiate with the government for the sale of the land remaining after the allotments were made. The money paid to the Indians for the surplus lands was to be held by the government for the sole use of the tribes to whom the reservation belonged. However, these funds from surplus lands could be used by Congress for the education and civilization of the Indians involved.

With Indian lands divided in this way, in theory, the Indian people would have land and the settlers would have land. It was also anticipated that Indian people living among the whites in this way would adopt their ways quicker and assimilate sooner.

At the end of the trust period of twenty-five years, all allottees were to become citizens of the United States.

Amendments to the Allotment Act quickly followed. In 1891 Congress made leasing of allotted lands possible. Indians who, by reason of age or other disability, were personally unable to occupy and improve their allotments could lease their land. And, in 1894, the term "inability" was added to age and disability as a reason for leasing. In 1906 it was decided to delay the awarding of citizenship to permit removal of the trust restrictions from the allotments of "incompetent" Indians.

In fairness, there was some opposition to the allotment. A minority report of the House Indian Affairs committee stated: "The real aim of this bill is to get at the Indian lands and open them up to settlement ... . If this were done in the name of greed it would be bad enough, but to do it in the name of humanity, and under the cloak of an ardent desire to promote the Indian's welfare by making him like ourselves, whether he will or not, is infinitely worse." The National Indian Defense Association, founded in 1885, also opposed the act; but it was the only organization of all those that had been created to defend the Indian that did so (Debo, 1989a, p. 300).

CURTIS ACT

The Five Civilized Tribes had been excluded from the General Allotment Act, along with several other tribes. Pressure was great to incorporate these advanced and powerful groups into civilized, American citizenship. The first step in this process was the establishment of the Cherokee Commission in 1889. The work of the commissioners resulted in agreements in which the Plains tribes and others that had moved into Indian Territory relinquished more than 15 million acres in 160-acre allotments to each man, woman, and child on tribal rolls. As can be predicted, the surplus land was bought by the government for homesteading. As white settlers increased, counties were formed and incorporated into Oklahoma Territory. When surplus lands were officially opened to homesteaders in 1893, the great Oklahoma land run occurred with over one hundred thousand people rushing in to claim land in "Indian Territory."

The second step involved the extension of the federal judicial system over the region. In 1895 Congress created two new U.S. courts for the Indian Territory and, as a consequence, traditional Indian governments were weakened. The Curtis Act of 1898 abolished tribal laws and tribal courts. Thus, all people in Indian Territory, white or Indian, were under the authority of the United States.

At this time the Commission to the Five Civilized Tribes (Dawes Commission) was created. The Commission asserted that the tribal governments had perverted their trust regarding the allotted land and it was the duty of the United States to enforce the intent of the trust. There had been grievous incidents documented, such as a few tribal citizens, Indian by intermarriage, becoming the owners of the largest and best parts of the lands and "corruption of the grossest kind" in tribal governments. Fraud and deception were rampant. The commission moved toward the dissolution of the Five Civilized Tribes.

In 1897 the Dawes Commission negotiated an agreement with the Choctaws and Chickasaws, in 1898 with the Seminoles, in 1901 with the Creeks, and in 1902 with the Cherokees. The Choctaws and Chickasaws received 320 acres each, the Cherokees 110 acres, the Creeks 160 acres, and the Seminoles 120 acres. In total 19, 526,966 acres were surveyed and 15,794,400 acres were allotted to those on tribal rolls. The rest was designated for towns, schools, and public needs; coal and mineral lands were held for tribal benefit. There was little surplus land within the Five Civilized Tribes that was opened to whites.

In 1901, U.S. citizenship was granted to every Indian in the Indian Territory of Oklahoma.

RESISTANCE TO ALLOTMENT

In approximately 1895, twenty-four thousand Creek, Cherokee, Choctaw, and Chickasaw formed the Four Mothers Society. Although it is believed that the existence of the society was unknown to the federal government, it was active until 1906 and members paid their monthly dues (one dollar for men, twenty-five cents or more for the women, and five cents or more for children) at least until 1915. The society sent frequent delegations to Washington to work toward the restoration of the traditional ways. They also hired a white attorney to secure favorable legislation.

The Snake Uprising of 1901, led by Chitto Harjo or Crazy Snake (Creek) defended the old ways and became a threat to the more "progressive" Indians. Crazy Snake urged that the guarantees of the removal policies be enforced.

> He told me that as long as the sun shone and the sky is up yonder these agreements will be kept.... He said as long as the sun rises it shall last; as long as the waters run it shall last; as long as grass grows it shall last ... He said, "Just as long as you see light here, just as long as you see this light glimmering over us, shall these agreements be kept, and not until all these things cease and pass away shall our agreement pass away." That is what he said, and we believed it. ... We have kept every turn of that agreement. The grass is growing, the waters run, the sun shines, the light is with us, and the agreement is with us yet, for the God that is above us all witnessed that agreement (from *A History of the Indians of the United States* by Angie Debo, p. 55. Copyright © 1970 by the University of Oklahoma Press).

The followers of Crazy Snake harassed the white settlers and tried to intimidate those Indians who accepted allotment. Ultimately, the Snake Uprising had little effect, serving only to delay the inevitable. However, there remained various groups that continued to intimidate tribal members in an effort to prevent them from selecting or accepting allotments. There were also those who refused their allotments, even when oil was found on their land. Some groups even planned to accept their allotments, sell them to the white settlers, and purchase land in Mexico or South America where they could keep their traditions alive. Even though the grass was growing, the waters were running, and the sun was still shining, these attempts were futile.

The events that occurred during this period of coerced assimilation devastated once strong and proud

Indian nations. Stripped of their homelands (their mother), their sacred ceremonies, their ways of providing for themselves, their tribal and communal ways, and their governments, they became despondent, impoverished, and dysfunctional.

BLUE LAKE

There were other methods by which the government took land and attempted to diminish traditional ways. The people of Taos Pueblo fought for sixty-four years to regain their sacred Blue Lake and the surrounding wilderness. This land was not taken from them through the policies of allotment, but was appropriated by the U.S. government in 1906 to become a part of the Carson National Forest.

The battle was fought under the leadership of two powerful men, the Tribe's spiritual leader, the Cacique Juan de Jesus Romero and Gifford Pinchot, the first Chief of the Forest Service. Pinchot believed in a policy of "multiple use" of forested land, which meant using the land for recreation and grazing, and scientifically producing raw materials from the land. This policy conflicted with the Taos Indians' need for privacy in the practice of their ancient religion at Blue Lake. Pinchot had little to do with the long battle for Blue Lake, but his principles were one of the central issues in the battle. For the people of Taos, Blue Lake was considered the symbolic source of all life, the retreat of the souls of their ancestors after death, and the central symbol of their religion. They were fighting for ancestral lands and freedom of religion.

On one side of the debate, in support of Nixon and the Taos Tribe, was the unlikely coalition of Senate majority whip Robert Griffin, Ted Kennedy, Fred Harris, and Barry Goldwater. On the other, in grimly determined opposition, were Senators Clifford Hansen, Henry Jackson, Clinton Anderson, and Lee Metcalf. And high up in the Senate gallery sat four old Indians, intensely making medicine (Gordon-McCutchan, 1991, p. 4).

The long battle was won when, in 1970, President Richard Nixon signed H. R. 471 into law, restoring Blue Lake to the Taos people. It was also President Nixon who initiated the policy of self-determination in 1975. We will discuss self-determination in later chapters.

Illustration 10.1—*Taos Pueblo celebrates the return of Blue Lake to them. Courtesy of Marcia Keegan Photography, Santa Fe, New Mexico.*

GHOST DANCE

Suppression of Native religions had begun before the Allotment Act. Beginning in 1885 the government began to prohibit the Sun Dance, the most holy of Sioux traditions. During the Sun Dance ceremony, the skin of the dancers is pierced as sacrifice. This "self-mutilation" was prohibited by the government. Southwestern tribes were forbidden the use of mescal, a desert plant that produces dreams and visions. Then, in the far west, among the Paiute, a medicine man had a great vision.

> The whole world is coming,
> A nation is coming, a nation is coming,
> The Eagle has brought the message to the tribe.
> The father says so, the father says so.
> Over the whole earth they are coming.
> The buffalo are coming, the buffalo are coming,
> The Crow has brought the message to the tribe,
> The father says so, the father says so.
> (A Sioux Ghost Dance song
> in Armstrong, 1971, p. 129).

Reservation life for the Sioux had not brought acculturation or revitalization. The Sioux were devastated. Then from the west came news of this Paiute messiah, called Wovoka. The message of Wovoka was essentially Christian in its teachings and 'Indian' in its ritual. He asked the people to be peaceful, honest, and industrious and to perform the dance that God had taught him. Holding hands in a circle, the dancers were to dance to the left for four nights once every six weeks. Then the white people would be flung back across the ocean, the earth would be regenerated, the buffalo, deer, and horses would return, there would be no more illness, the dead would return from the stars, everyone would be young and healthy, and life would resume as it had been.

> Grandfather (the messiah) says, when your friends die you must not cry. You must not hurt anybody or do harm to anyone. You must not fight. Do right always. It will give you satisfaction in life.

> Do not tell the white people about this. Jesus is now upon the earth. He appears like a cloud. The dead are all alive again. I do not know when they will be here; may be this fall or in the spring. When the time comes there will be no more sickness and everyone will be young again. Do not refuse to work for the white and do not make any trouble with them until you leave them. When the earth shakes (at the coming) do not be afraid. It will not hurt you (Armstrong, 1971, pp. 128–129).

The Sioux sent a delegation to Wovoka to investigate the new religion. The suffering of the Sioux was so great that the Ghost Dance was readily modified and incorporated into a ceremony of significance. Ghost dances spread throughout the west and became popular among the Sioux people. The ghost shirts of the dancers were supposed to be impervious to the white man's bullets and protect the wearers. Trances were common and the dancers envisioned a new land, devoid of whites, and repopulated by the good things of the earth and Indian people.

Illustration 10.2—Example of Ghost Dance. Photo courtesy of Smithsonian Institution, Washington, D.C.

WOUNDED KNEE

Well-known leaders such as Sitting Bull on the Standing Rock Reservation, Big Foot and Hump at Cheyenne River, Red Cloud at Pine Ridge, and others became advocates of the new religion as it spread throughout the Plains. According to the family of Sitting Bull, he did not practice the Ghost Dance although it was done in his camp. And the whites, believing it was a war dance, became increasingly frightened of the fervor of the new dance. Government agents also began to be alarmed and attempted to suppress the Ghost Dance. In 1890 General Nelson Miles brought eight thousand soldiers to the Dakotas to stop the Ghost Dancing and arrest its leaders. In the ensuing efforts, Sitting Bull was killed along with other Indian supporters and members of the Indian police, and Hump surrendered without serious incident. Thirty-eight of the followers of Sitting Bull fled south from the reservation to the camp of Chief Big Foot.

Big Foot was ill and his people were tired; he surrendered to Major Samuel Whiteside of the 7th Cavalry, Custer's old regiment. The chief was placed in an ambulance, and the Indians were sent to the cavalry base camp at Wounded Knee Creek, which was under the command of Colonel George A. Forsyth. Forsyth had 470 soldiers—and there were 340 Indians, of which only 106 were warriors.

The warriors were ordered to disarm and to seat themselves in a circle. Big Foot was carried, coughing, to the center. While the Indians were guarded, the soldiers searched the tipis for weapons. After the tipi search the warriors were searched personally. One warrior, Black Coyote, had a Winchester rifle that he refused to surrender. Black Coyote was deaf and did not hear the warnings of the soldiers. A shot was fired, more than likely accidentally, and the massacre of Wounded Knee began.

Big Foot and at least 150 Indians, mostly women and children, were killed. Wounded Knee was the end of the Ghost Dance and the end of the Sioux Indians' last hope of bringing back their sacred world. The past was gone.

Historian Robert Utley has concluded "It is time that Wounded Knee be viewed for what it was, a regrettable, tragic accident of war that neither side intended, and that called forth behavior for which

Illustration 10.3—The body of Chief Big Foot at Wounded Knee. Photograph courtesy of Smithsonian Institution, Washington, D.C.

some individuals on both sides, in unemotional retrospect, may be judged culpable, but for which neither side as a whole may be properly condemned" (Prucha, 1986, p. 249). We will see later, however, that the Ghost Dance remains symbolic and the massacre of Wounded Knee is a vivid memory that stirs Indian people of the twentieth century and symbolizes their resolve for strength, unity, and survival.

> I did not know then how much was ended. When I look back now from this high hill of my old age, I can still see the butchered women and children lying heaped and scattered all long the crooked gulch as plain as when I saw them with eyes still young. And I can see that something else died there in the bloody mud, and was buried in the blizzard. A people's dream died there. It was a beautiful dream … the nation's hope is broken and scattered. There is no center any longer, and the sacred tree is dead (Black Elk in Brown, 1981, p. 419).

In the next chapter we will continue to explore other tactics of coercive assimilation, particularly the influence of religious groups and their efforts to educate the Indians.

LESSON PLAN: SITTING BULL

Grade Level: Adaptable to all grade levels.

Basic Concepts: Culture, conflict, leadership, and power

Organizing Generalizations: All cultures have men and women who exemplify the traditions and values of their people and who are honored and respected leaders. When cultures and circumstances differ, people view leaders in divergent ways and consequently honor different people.

Culture Area: Plains

Time Period: Period of Coercive Assimilation–Sitting Bull (born approximately 1831 and died 1890).

Background: During the time of the Plains wars and until shortly before the Massacre of Wounded Knee, Sitting Bull was one of the most famous and courageous leaders of the Sioux nation. He played a major part in the Battle of Little Bighorn and in the events that preceded the important and final massacre, Wounded Knee. His life and his leadership demonstrate many important concepts in the conflict between two cultures which culminated in the famous Wounded Knee massacre. The integrity and leadership of Sitting Bull provide a personal way to study this conflict between cultures and the study of his life is one way to honor this famous Indian leader.

Objectives:

Knowledge

Students will:

1. Recall the major events in the life of Sioux (Hunkpapa) chief, Sitting Bull.
2. Discuss the achievements and characteristics that made him a man worthy of respect and honor.
3. Recognize that all cultures, past and present, have heroes and leaders who guide and inspire their people.
4. Discuss several reasons why Sitting Bull was not considered a hero by many Americans who lived at that time.

Skills

Students will:

1. Make a web or timeline indicating the characteristics, achievements, and major events in the life of Sitting Bull.
2. Practice taking several perspectives on whether or not Sitting Bull was a heroic leader.

Values

Students will:

1. Appreciate Sitting Bull as a man who lead wisely and fought bravely for his people.
2. Understand that principled behavior often has its price.

Activities:

1. Provide students with some background information about the Sioux, their country, and their traditional ways of life. This can probably be done best visually with maps, videotapes, or films. Books about the traditional way of life can be made available. The study of the life of Sitting Bull should be a part of a larger unit of study. Pictures of famous chiefs are readily available.
2. Begin to explore with students the values that helped to define leadership in Indian cultures through discussion. The quotations on p. 155, Words of Sitting Bull, should be used to initiate discussion. List students' ideas on a chalkboard or chart. Bravery, generosity, wisdom, and spirituality should be emphasized either now or later.

3. If students have the background knowledge, they should discuss whether Lieutenant Colonel Custer was a hero or if Sitting Bull was a hero. How would you determine who is or is not a hero? This is a question that should be left unanswered until students have learned more about Sitting Bull and his life.

4. There are numerous ways students can obtain information about Sitting Bull—history books, biographies, encyclopedias, films, and videotapes. Divide students into groups to gather information from various sources to make a composite picture of him. In the upper grades, it would be useful to provide older materials that tend to portray Custer in a positive manner. Students should be encouraged to find information about Sitting Bull's personal characteristics, his achievements, and the milestones in his life.

5. Compile the information about these three aspects into a description or biography of Sitting Bull. One good way to do this would be to develop webs or timelines during the research.

6. Discuss these descriptions and why Sitting Bull was a leader to his people and how he is remembered with respect.

7. Ask older students to imagine themselves as settlers in the Northern Plains or as newspaper readers on the Eastern coast during the time of Sitting Bull. Why might their opinions of his leadership and bravery in battle be different? Some possible responses should include lack of accurate information available to them, conflict in personal interests and values, and lack of understanding of Native cultures.

8. It is important to conclude with the understanding that Native heroes defended their families, their land, their religion, and their way of life. They also exhibited extraordinary bravery in the face of certain defeat and humiliation.

Extensions:

1. Research one of the following chiefs:
   Hunkpapas—Gall, Crow King, and Rain-in-the-Face
   Ogalalas—Crazy Horse, American Horse, Flying Hawk, and Iron Tail
   Miniconjous—Lane Deer, Hump, and Kicking Bear
   Northern Cheyennes—Dull Knife, Little Wolf, Two Moons, Wooden Leg, and Yellow Hair

2. Adapting the Indian tradition of recording important events on a buffalo skin, decorate a simulated buffalo skin (wrinkled brown wrapping paper) with a pictorial description of the life of Sitting Bull.

3. Investigate local museums and reference materials for pictures or examples of Ghost Dancing Shirts. How were they made? How were they decorated? Were they worn by women?

4. Research how the traditional right of Americans to freedom of religion has affected Native peoples through time. The forbidding of the Sun Dance and the Ghost Dance are examples of the abrogation of this fundamental right. Does this interference belong just to the past? Is it present today for Native people?

5. Research the Battle of Little Bighorn and Lieutenant Colonel Custer, and the Battle of Wounded Knee which soon followed the death of Sitting Bull.

6. Read about Buffalo Bill Cody.

Evaluation: Students should be able to discuss the heroic and leadership qualities of Sitting Bull and how culture is a major factor in determining the characteristics valued in leaders and self-interest often determines whether or not someone is considered a person worthy of respect and honor.

Materials/Resources:

Black, S. *Sitting Bull*. Englewood Cliffs, NJ: Silver Burdett, 1989 (For older students).

Brown, D. *Wounded Knee: An Indian History of the American West* (adapted by Amy Ehrlich from *Bury My Heart at Wounded Knee*). New York: Holt, Rinehart & Winston, 1974.

Fleischer, J. *Sitting Bull: Warrior of the Sioux*. Mahwah. NJ: Troll, 1979 (For younger students).

Stein, R. C. *The Story of Wounded Knee*. Chicago: Childrens Press, 1983.

Waldman, C. *Who Was Who in Native American History*. New York: Facts on File, 1990.

Words of Sitting Bull

The famous Chief Sitting Bull (Sioux) fled to Canada after the Custer massacre. The following is his response when asked why he did not surrender and consent to live on a reservation.

Because I am a red man. If the Great Spirit had desired me to be a white man he would have made me so in the first place. He put in your heart certain wishes and plans, in my heart he put other and different desires. Each man is good in his sight. It is not necessary for eagles to be crows. Now we are poor but we are free. No white man controls our footsteps. If we must die we die defending our rights (Armstrong, 1971, p. 112).

* * *

These are his words before he was moved as a military prisoner to Fort Yates, then to the Standing Rock Reservation.

I do not wish to be shut up in a corral. It is bad for young men to be fed by an agent. It makes them lazy and drunken. All agency Indians I have seen were worthless. They are neither red warriors nor white farmers. They are neither wolf nor dog. But my followers are weary of cold and hunger. They wish to see their brothers and their old home, therefore I bow my head (Armstrong, 1984, p. 126).

* * *

Later, in 1889, Sitting Bull talked to a white teacher that he trusted at Standing Rock Reservation.

Our religion seems foolish to you, but so does yours to me. The Baptists and Methodists and Presbyterians and the Catholics all have a different God. Why cannot we have one of our own? Why does the agent seek to take away our religions? My race is dying. Our God will soon die with us. If this new religion is not true then what matters? I do not know what to believe? If I could dream like the others and visit the spirit world myself, then it would be easy to believe, but the trance does not come to me. It passes me by. I help others to see their dead, but I am not aided (Armstrong, 1984, p. 128).

SUMMARY
COERCIVE ASSIMILATION: 1887–1910

The policies of separation that were intended to eliminate the "Indian problem" were no longer as practical as the American settlers moved west. The next, equally tragic, period of federal Indian policy was the period of coercive assimilation. The goals of assimilation were said to be protection and preservation for the Indian. In reality, the goals were to eradicate traditional cultures and make the Indian people resemble white people. There would be no Indian problem because there would be no more people who could be identified as Indians.

Other goals of this period of forced assimilation were to free more land for the settlers and to protect them from the Indians of the West who were trying to protect and preserve their land, the buffalo, and their ways of life. English education, Christianity, agriculture, and individual property were the elements of the programs that were meant to "civilize" the Indian. The General Allotment Act of 1887 was a destructive policy that resulted in the loss of an enormous amount of Indian lands and was a disaster for Native peoples.

The act allowed the president to allot all tribal land in the United States, excluding the lands of the Five Civilized Tribes, the Osages, and a few others. Each head of a family received 160 acres; however, the act was later changed to provide equal shares to all. Each person including married women and children received 80 acres of agricultural land and 160 acres of grazing land.

The land was to be held in trust for twenty-five years to protect the people and the surplus lands could be sold to non-Indians. Land divided in this way would provide Indian people and settlers with land. This way the Indian people living among the whites would adopt their ways quicker and sooner. This policy stripped the people of their lands, their sacred ways, and their ways for providing for themselves— it was devastating.

TIME LINE: 1887–1910

1887

Congress passes the General Allotment Act (the Dawes Act) in which tribally held lands are given to individual Indians in parcels, opening up the surplus for whites. Indian people lose millions of acres of land as result of the General Allotment Act.

1889

Two million acres of Indian Territory are bought from the Indians and given to white settlers for the Oklahoma Land Run. This land run is somewhat symbolic of the lust of white settlers for Indian lands.

1890

The Ghost Dance Movement led by Wovoka (Paiute) gains in influence among Western Indians.

1890

In a major battle at Wounded Knee, U.S. troops massacre 350 Sioux Indians who were en route to a Ghost Dance celebration. The Battle of Wounded Knee has become symbolic to Indian people.

1890–1910

During these years the population of Native people falls to a low point of less than 250,000.

1891

Provision is made for the leasing by whites of allotted Indian lands.

1893

Indian Appropriations Act contains provision to eliminate Indian agents, transferring their responsibilities on reservations to superintendents of schools.

1895

Anti-allotment Cherokees, Creeks, Choctaws, and Chickasaws formed the Four Mothers Society.

1898

Curtis Act dissolves tribal governments, requires Indians of abolished Indian nations to submit to allotment, and institutes civil government for Indian Country, with the purpose of extending the effects of allotment policy to the Five Civilized Tribes.

1901

Chitto Harjo (Creek) led a rebellion in Oklahoma Territory known as the Snake Uprising to actively resist allotment.

1902

Reclamation Act encourages settlement of the West by whites through subsidies for water development.

1906

Burke Act amends the General Allotment Act, giving the Secretary of the Interior authority to remove restrictions on allotted Indian lands.

1906

Federal government seizes fifty thousand acres of wilderness land, the Blue Lake region in the mountains of New Mexico, sacred to Taos Pueblo Indians, and makes it part of a national park.

1907

Oklahoma Territory, including the Indian Territory is admitted as a state. The citizens of Oklahoma seek to have Indian lands on the market and subject to taxation.

1907

Seventy high-steel Iroquois construction workers were killed while working on the Quebec Bridge.

1909

Teddy Roosevelt issues executive orders transferring 2.5 million acres of timbered Indian reservation lands to national forests.

1910

The Bureau of Indian Affairs begins a regular Indian medical service.

CHAPTER 11

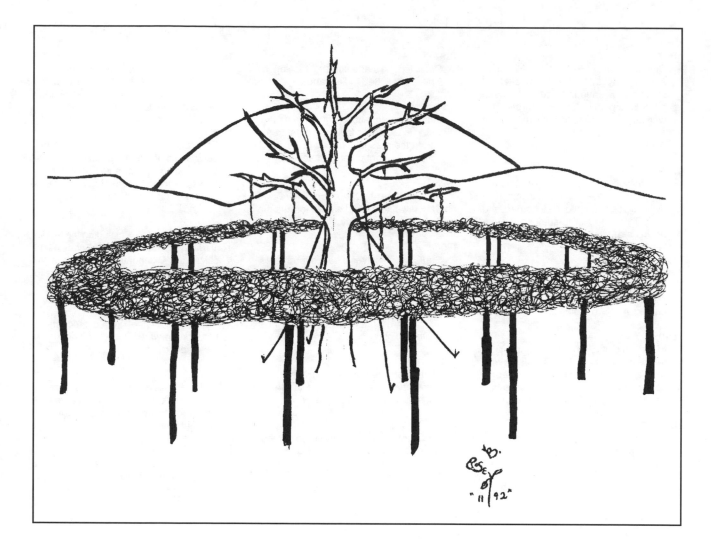

Coercive Assimilation Continued: 1910–1934

LOOKING AT THE SUN, THEY DANCE

Staring open-eyed at the blazing sun, the blinding rays burning deep into your skull, filling it with unbearable brightness ...

Blowing on an eagle-bone whistle clenched between your teeth until its shrill sound becomes the only sound in the world ...

Dancing, dancing, dancing from morning to night without food or water until you are close to dropping in a dead faint ...

Pulling, pulling away at a rawhide thong which is fastened to a skewer embedded deeply in your flesh, until your skin stretches and rips apart as you finally break free with blood streaming down your chest ... This is what some of us must endure during the sun dance.

Many people do not understand why we do this. They call the sun dance barbarous, savage, a bloody superstition. The way I look at it our body is the only thing which truly belongs to us. What we Indians give of our flesh, our bodies, we are giving of the only thing which is ours alone.

If we offer Wakan Tanka a horse, bags of tobacco, and food for the poor, we'd be making him a present of something he already owns. Everything in nature has been created by the Great Spirit, is part of Him. It is only our own flesh which is a real sacrifice—a real giving of ourselves. How can we give anything less?

For fifty long years they jailed us if we danced the sun dance, calling it a crime, an "Indian Offense." Freedom of religion doesn't always include us Indians.

The sun dance is our oldest and most solemn ceremony, the "granddaddy of them all," as my father used to say. It is so old that its beginnings are hidden as in a mist. It goes back to an age when our people had neither guns, horses nor steel—when there was just us and the animals, the earth, the grass and the sky. ...

Wi wanyang wacipi—the sun dance—is our greatest feast which brings all the people together. I told you of hanblechia, the vision quest, one man, alone by himself on an isolated hilltop, communicating with the mystery power. Well, the sun dance is all the people communicating with all the mystery powers. It is the hanblechia of the whole Sioux nation.

The sun dance is the most misunderstood of all our rites. Many white men think of it as an initiation into manhood, or a way to prove one's courage. But this is wrong. The sun dance is a prayer and a sacrifice.

(Lame Deer, 1976, pp. 187–88)

The turn of the century and the years that followed were a time when American Indian people throughout the United States saw their personal and group freedoms disappearing. The Sun Dance, the Ghost Dance and other traditional religious ceremonies were outlawed. Sacred religious places were taken away from tribes and were desecrated with mining, logging, and roads. Sacraments used in ceremonies and prayer were also banned. Indian policy was dominated by the "friends of the Indian." Their efforts, which focused on solving the Indian problem in the "right and proper" way, prepared the way for two of the most powerful modern tools of coercive assimilation—education and religion. These organized groups of well-meaning people believed their efforts were patriotic and righteous. For a time, their philosophy also satisfied those who were not considered "friends of the Indian" as it allowed for the continued taking of Indian land and rights in the name of "righteousness."

After the General Allotment Act and a century of treaty-making, the American Indians were contained on reservations. At the mercy of the Indian Affairs agent for rations, which sometimes included water as well as food and clothing, the Indian people were forced to adopt new ways of worship and communication. This chapter will take a closer look at these two forms of coercive assimilation and how they affected the lives of American Indians across the land.

RELIGION

For centuries, Indians lived in harmony with the natural elements in Indian Country. They lived their lives in a manner that supported all other life. In addition to a lifestyle that was fashioned to support the natural environment, many tribes held dances and ceremonies at certain places and times each year to help maintain the balance of the universe. Other tribes held dances to make offerings to the Creator, in return for their great success in hunting, harvest, or life itself. Native people journeyed to the mountains to pray in secluded sacred spots, to make their offerings to the Creator, and pray for tomorrow. They kept these traditions alive for thousands of years and, in turn, the earth had remained fertile and all things belonged and flourished.

Near the end of the nineteenth century when reservations were becoming standard throughout Indian Country, the United States government found that it was possible to regulate the activities of individuals and groups of Indians, and they began to deny the Indians the right to practice their Native religion. By 1884 the government had established regulations that banned the Sun Dance and other ceremonies, as well as medicine men. These policies are precisely stated in BIA Court of Indian Offenses regulations.

> The 'sun dance,' and all other similar dances and so-called religious ceremonies, shall be considered 'Indian offenses' and any Indian found guilty of being a participant in any one or more of these offenses shall … be punished by withholding from him his rations for a period of not exceeding ten days; and if found guilty of any subsequent offense under this rule, shall be punished by withholding his rations for a period not less than fifteen days nor more than thirty days, or by incarceration in the agency prison for a period not exceeding thirty days (Echo-Hawk, 1991, p. 8).

In the same document it further states:

> The usual practices of so-called "medicine men" shall be considered "Indian offenses"… [punishable by confinement] in the agency guardhouse for a term not less than ten days, or until such time as he shall produce evidence satisfactory to the court and approved by the agent, that he will forever abandon all practices styled Indian offense under his rule.

These regulations were in effect until 1934, when congressional legislation restored tribal government. As a result of these regulations and the abiding attitudes against "heathens" and "heathen worship," Big Foot and over 390 others lost their lives at Wounded Knee while dancing the Ghost Dance and many others died elsewhere while practicing their religious ceremonies.

Christianity was offered as an alternative to the traditional religion practiced by the various tribes. It came in the form of Jesuit missionaries and then Indian agents, teachers, and priests. The lives of the Indians on the reservations were saturated with representatives of the Christian faith. There seemed to be no escape. In order to maintain some connection to their traditional religious ceremonies and beliefs, the Indians of various tribes adapted the Christian holidays to their traditional ceremonies and they worshipped in both ways at the same time, or they hid their traditional ways and practiced Christianity openly.

An example of this adaptation that continues today are the Easter ceremonies at Guadalupe, a small town outside of Phoenix, Arizona. A great procession and religious activities are held each year that include Catholic and Native Yaqui religion. Deer Dancers mingle with those carrying the symbolic body of Christ in a procession through the streets. Examples of Native religion that have not adapted to the Christian religion are the Sun Dance currently practiced by the Lakota and other tribes of the Plains and the Stomp Dance of the Creek and Seminole Tribes of the Southeast. The Native people persevered and maintained their religion against all odds and great pressure.

As time passed, and more and more people moved into Indian Country, it became harder for the Indians to maintain their relationship with their sacred lands. Some of these sacred lands were taken with force and by treaty while others were illegally commandeered by presidents and the congress for national parks. When there were only a few people settling in the west, most Indians could still make their yearly pilgrimages to the sacred spots and pray for the balance and harmony of the earth and all of the elements. Greater number of settlers made access to these sacred places harder to secure for the Indians, as the settlers fenced and sectioned off the land.

When the Indians were unable to practice their religion and keep their commitments to their Creator, they became disillusioned and felt abandoned. An anonymous Blackfoot summarized the disillusionment in the following way:

> … We fast and pray, that we may be able to lead good lives and to act more kindly towards each other.

> I do not understand why the white men desire to put an end to our religious ceremonials. What harm can they do to our people? If they deprive us of our religion, we will have nothing left, for we know of no other that can take its place.

> We do not understand the white man's religion. The Black Robes (Catholic Priests) teach us one thing and the men-with-white-neckties (Protestant Missionaries) teach us another; so we are confused.

> We believe that the Sun god is all powerful, for every spring he makes the trees to bud and the grass to grow. We see these things with our own eyes, and, therefore, know that all life comes from him (Nabokov, 1991, p. 225).

Another aspect of Native religion that was prohibited during the first part of the 1900s was the use of plant sacraments. For centuries, Native people used plants to cure illness, enrich nutrition, and as sacramental objects during religious ceremonies. These sacramental plants, such as the peyote cactus that grows in parts of the Rio Grande River valley of Northern Mexico and Southern Texas, were banned by the government through the same regulations as Indian religious ceremonies. Indian agents were ordered to "seize and destroy" peyote and to classify it as an "intoxicating liquor."

Peyotism ranks among the oldest and largest continuously practiced tribal religions of the Western Hemisphere. It is a spiritual religion that is practiced by many tribes throughout the country. The peyote cactus is used in the ceremonies under the supervision of the religious leaders for the purpose of prayer. The plant is not ingested for entertainment purposes. In an effort to work within the system, the Indians of Oklahoma who used peyote in their religious ceremonies incorporated the Native American Church in Oklahoma in 1918. These efforts were to be unsuccessful, however, as many western states passed laws that prohibited the use, transportation, and possession of the cactus. Between 1916 and 1963, twelve different legislative bills were introduced in Washington to prohibit the use of peyote in the United States. None of them ever passed.

Individual states did, however, pass ordinances against the use, transportation, and possession of peyote. In more contemporary times, some of these states have repealed their laws against peyote and have given sanction to Native American Church groups and their members. The Native American Church originally incorporated in 1918 was renamed the Native American Church of the United States in 1944 in El Reno, Oklahoma. By that time there were organizations of Native American Church members in six other states.

EDUCATION

The "Friends of the Indians" encouraged the widespread implementation of a school system that would prepare Indians to be landowners and help them assimilate more quickly. Originally, the only schools in Indian Country were run either by the Indians themselves or were mission schools. The Indian-run schools, although very successful, were abruptly closed while the mission schools have persisted into the twentieth century.

To address the concerns and suggestions of the "Friends of the Indians," a provision for setting aside financial support for educating tribal members was included in treaties signed after early 1783. The first evidence of support from the Congress was in response to the efforts of Richard Henry Pratt, who founded Carlisle Indian School in 1879. A former U.S. Army officer, he was convinced that the Indian was educable and he used the Carlisle Boarding School to prove that his conviction was right.

Carlisle was an off-reservation boarding school where Indian children spent the greatest portion of the year. They were not allowed to speak their own language and forbidden to practice their traditional religion. If caught worshipping or speaking "Indian," they were punished. Most of the children came to school with long hair which was quickly cut in the European style. Rigid schedules were imposed on the students who studied, attended classes, and worked daily. The focus of the school curriculum and school day was to train Indian children in basic vocational skills.

During the next ten years, several boarding schools were opened around the country. Some of the most famous schools begun during this time period are Forest Grove, Oregon (1880) (which later became Chemawa), Albuquerque (1884), Chilocco (1884), Santa Fe (1890), Haskell (1884), Phoenix (1890), Pierre (1891), and Flandreau (1893). By the turn of the century there were over twenty off-reservation boarding schools operating in the United States. The first students of these schools to return home to the reservation were targets of ridicule. They had lost their knowledge of traditional ways of life and the training they received at school often had no application on the reservation.

The next type of school initiated by the Bureau of Indian Affairs was the on-reservation school or otherwise known as the day school. These schools were less costly and parents of the children complained less since their children could come home at night. Finally, because of the continuous encroachment of white people on Indian land, there was a need to build public schools on reservations for the children of white settlers who were leasing or purchasing land within the boundaries of the reservation.

Today, some students of the boarding school era say that they liked school and received a good education. These Indian people usually had happier, more

Illustration 11.1—Navajo Tom Toslino before (left) and after (right) attending Carlisle Boarding School. Photo by John N. Choate, Museum of New Mexico, Neg. #43501 and #43500.

successful experiences at the boarding school and now tend to be more assimilated into the dominant culture. Many other students had very different experiences, and they believe the boarding school impacted their lives in ways that were not healthy or good.

> As the weeks turned to months, I learned English more and more. It may appear that comprehension would be easier. It got easier to understand, all right. I understood that everything I had, and was a part of, was not nearly as good as the white man's. School was determined to undo me in everything from my sheepskin bedding to the dances and ceremonies which I had learned to have faith in and cherish (Suina, 1992, pp. 34–36).

The era of boarding schools began to decline by the mid-1930s. The Meriam Report and public interests caused the Bureau of Indian Affairs to change the way it educated the American Indian. The Meriam Report stated that the children attended school half a day and worked half a day. This is the only way the schools could stay open with their meager budgets. The children were fed a starvation diet, crowded into dormitories, not given sufficient medical care, and forced to work excessive hours. The government's response to the negative criticism of the boarding schools was to place blame on the minimal funding available to the schools. In an effort to cut costs and quiet the roar of dissatisfaction, more day schools were built on reservations and the number of Indian children in public schools increased. The boarding schools were not abandoned, though. The few that remained open were focused more for the older students and the standards of nutrition, housing, and work drastically improved. The final decline of boarding schools came as a result of the efforts of John Collier.

CITIZENSHIP

The United States' entrance into World War I in 1917 took attention and support away from domestic issues, such as Indian affairs, and turned the attention of the country to war. Approximately ten thousand American Indians enlisted in the armed forces and fought in the war. Congress acknowledged their service and passed the Indian Citizenship Act of 1924 to give American citizenship to all American Indians. The Act provided that:

> … all non-citizen Indians born within the territorial limits of the United States be, and they are hereby, declared to be citizens of the United States: Provided, that the granting of such citizenship shall not in any manner impair or otherwise affect the right of any Indian to tribal or other property (from *American Indian Tribal Government* by Sharon O'Brien, p. 80. Copyright © 1989 by the University of Oklahoma Press).

This unique citizenship meant that Indian people did not relinquish their right to their tribal membership when they became U.S. Citizens. The American Indian has rights and citizenship in three particular governmental entities—their tribe, the United States of America, and the state in which they reside. A few tribes had already been granted citizenship before 1924, and a few refused it. The latter believe that citizenship in their tribal nation is their first and only allegiance.

MERIAM REPORT

Toward the middle of the 1920s it became apparent that the methods employed to assimilate and "civilize" the Indians had not succeeded. In fact, reports of the time stated that those methods had contributed to the disastrous situation that existed. In 1926, two years after the granting of U.S. citizenship, the Secretary of the Interior, Hubert Work, commissioned the Brookings Institution to conduct a study of the conditions on reservations. The study, led by Dr. Lewis Meriam, produced a report at the end of the work entitled "The Problem of Indian Administration." The Report covered topics such as health, education, economics, family and community life, legal issues, and missionary activities among the Indian. The findings of the study revealed that Indian people throughout the country were living in poverty and sickness. The average annual per capita income was only one hundred dollars. Because of sickness, poor nutrition, and completely inadequate sanitation and medical care, the average life expectancy of American Indians was only forty-four years old. The Meriam Report called for radical revision in every area. According to the study, the Bureau of Indian Affairs was not meeting the needs of Indians, who were not being allowed an opportunity to participate in determining their own future. The report was not only critical; it also offered constructive suggestions for change. Some of these changes regarding Indian tribal organization and self-determination were not adopted until almost twenty years later.

LESSON PLAN: NATIVE AMERICAN RELIGION

Grade Level: Middle School

Basic Concepts: Tradition and change

Organizing Generalization: Throughout time, people have developed different religious practices. The right to practice religion in one's own ways is guaranteed by the U.S. Constitution.

Culture Area: Great Plains and Southwest

Time Period: Early 1900s and Present Day

Background: The Native American religion that uses peyote as a sacrament is believed to have to come to North America approximately one thousand years ago. It came from Central and South America and spread across the Great Plains and Southwest. The first Native American Church was incorporated in Oklahoma in 1918. Congress acknowledged the evidence brought before the Oklahoma legislature by the medicine men of the Native American Church and have never passed a law against the use of peyote. However, several western states did enact laws against the use of peyote, even for religious purposes. In 1917 Colorado, Nevada, and Utah enacted legislation outlawing the use of peyote. In following years Kansas, Arizona, Montana, North Dakota, Iowa, New Mexico, Wyoming, Idaho, Texas, California, New York, and South Dakota followed their lead. The laws were not actively enforced as there were not enough lawmen to enforce it and there was no strong influence from Washington to do so. In fact, by 1956, thirteen states had given twenty-eight charters to peyote churches (Vecsey, 1991).

Today, many contemporary Indian people still practice this religion and seek protection from the law for their right to freedom of religion. Most people who have opposed peyote's use through history have rarely taken part in Native American Church ceremonies. More knowledge about unfamiliar or mysterious religions will help people understand alternative ways of expressing religious beliefs and foster religious freedom.

Objectives:
Knowledge
Students will:
1. Demonstrate their understanding of the Native American Church and its use of peyote as a sacrament.
2. Identify the relationship between peyote and sacraments of other religions.
3. Recognize that the Native American Church is a living religion.

Skills
Students will:
1. Compare the use of peyote in the Native American Church and sacraments in other churches.
2. Debate (defend) whether or not Native American Church members should be allowed to use peyote as a religious sacrament.

Values
Students will:
1. Appreciate the value of freedom of religion for all and the right of the members of the Native American Church to use peyote.
3. Respect other religions.

Activities:

1. Gather students together and read aloud or have students read about the Native American Church ceremony. Encourage students to share how they feel about the reading and when they think it takes place. On a map of the Western Hemisphere, have students locate Central and South America, locating the Great Plains and Southwestern United States. Mark the general path that peyote usage took as it spread northward.

2. Have students list religious acts or rites (sacraments) of other religions with which they are familiar. Examples might include baptism, saying the rosary, communion, the bar mitzvah, "speaking in tongues," singing of hymns, chanting, making the sign of the cross, common prayer, pilgrimages, and weddings and funerals. Are any of them illegal or outlawed?

3. Read *Tinker and the Medicine Man* (Wolf, 1973) to the students. Discuss the fact that the use of peyote in North America began one thousand years ago and still continues today.

4. Divide the students into two groups and have them each prepare a defense for one side of the issue of the ban of peyote usage for religious purposes. Each student should prepare a written statement on his or her position and support it with research. Then have students debate the issue using examples from readings and other research.

5. Students should then write an individual statement supporting their personal stand on the issue.

Extensions:

It would be extremely helpful if a local Native American, especially a Native American Church member could come to the class and explain how they feel about their religion and their practicing of the ceremonies. Students would gain personal insight to the values, beliefs, and importance of this unique, contemporary religion.

Evaluation: Individual position papers and the class discussion and debate will demonstrate students' understanding of the relationship of peyote to the religion.

Materials/Resources:

Lame Deer, J. F. & Erdoes, R. *Lame Deer, Seeker of Visions.* New York: Pocket, 1976.

Underhill, R. M. *Red Man's Religion.* Chicago: University of Chicago, 1965.

Vecsey, C. (ed.) *Handbook of American Indian Religious Freedom.* New York: Crossroad, 1991.

Wolf, B. *Tinker and the Medicine Man.* New York: Random House, 1973.

NATIVE AMERICAN CHURCH CEREMONY

In the ritual the Native American Church uses the four elements: earth, air, fire, and water. The four herbs used are Peyote, Tobacco, Cedar, and Sage. A general description of the ritual follows:

The ritual developed by the Plains Indians has roughly the following form. A crescent shaped mound is raised in the back of a teepee, especially constructed for the purpose. In front of this a small fire, ignited with flint, is kept burning. A dozen or so participants sit in a circle around this, and behind the crescent sits the agreed ceremonial leader, the Road Chief. He is chosen by reason of his experience with Peyote, and while he has no authority, he initiates the singing of songs, the midnight and dawn breaks for water, and it is to him that members address requests to have a special prayer offered or to be allowed to leave the teepee.

On either side of the Road Chief are two assistants, the cedar chief and the drum chief, who begins the beating of a drum that is passed along the members and is kept up throughout the night. A meeting begins about 8 P.M., usually on a Saturday night, and continues until noon of the following day when the individual sponsoring the meeting provides a small feast. During the whole of this time the participants are supposed to center their gaze upon a Peyote plant placed atop the crescent and, in turn, to sing certain appropriate songs and to beat the drum as others sing.

Prayers are offered to the Great spirit, through his mediator, Father Peyote, and are made while smoking a pipe or cigarettes specially prepared with Indian tobacco. Visions and hallucinations are definitely discouraged, as they are thought to indicate a lack of the purity of spirit with which it is necessary to approach Peyote. Similarly, excessive nausea or vomiting upon eating the plant is taken as implying that the subject is not as acceptable to Father Peyote as he might be … .

Following the invocation offered by the Road Chief, four dried peyote buttons are passed to each participant, but after a suitable interval for these to be eaten, one may take as much as one wishes. Peyote is regarded as having powerful medicinal qualities by reason of its great spirit sanctity and Peyote tea. Tea is the usual form in which Peyote is offered to women and children and those sick or troubled persons for whom the meeting is held.

The rules regarding use by the Indians are brief and simple. In the legendary account of how Father Peyote made himself known to the Indian he is made to say: "There are several ways that you can use me, but unless you use me in only one way, the right way, I may harm you. Use me the right way and I will help you."

(Adapted from: Beck, P. V., Walters, A. L. and Francisco, N. *The Sacred.* Tsaile, AZ: Navajo Community College, 1992, p. 237.)

SUMMARY
COERCIVE ASSIMILATION CONTINUED: 1910–1934

The General Allotment Act was just one way in which the government attempted to force Indian people to assimilate into the Euro-American culture. Other ways to solve the "Indian problem" included Christianity and education. Toward the end of the 1800s, when the reservations were becoming standard throughout Indian Country, the U.S. government began to deny Native peoples the right to practice their traditional religions. By 1884 the government had banned the Sun Dance of the Plains Indians and other sacred ceremonies, as well as medicine men. Indians found guilty of participating in dances and religious ceremonies would be punished by withholding food and rations or by imprisonment for a period not exceeding thirty days.

Christianity was offered as an alternative to the traditional religions practiced by the various tribes. Reservations were flooded with missionaries, Indians agents, teachers, and priests representing the Christian faith. Indian people adjusted to this pressure by adapting the Christian holidays to their traditional ceremonies or by hiding their traditional ways and practicing Christianity openly.

Education was equally devastating to the people. Children were forced from their homes into off-reservation boarding schools which would prepare them to be farmers, laborers, and Christians. The environment at the boarding schools was often harsh and cruel. Indian youths lost their knowledge of traditional ways of life, their self-esteem, and their languages; the training they received at school often had no application on the reservation.

It was also during this period that American Indians supported World War I. Acknowledging their patriotism, Congress passed the Indian Citizenship Act of 1924 to give American citizenship to all American Indians. As U.S. citizens, Indian people maintain their right to membership in their own tribes.

TIME LINE: 1910–1930

1910
The United States government forbade the Sun Dance among Plains Indians, giving the use of self-torture as the reason.

1911
The Society of American Indians was formed as an activist pan-Indian group.

1914–1918
Many Native Americans enlisted in the armed forces during World War I.

1915
Congress passed appropriation act authorizing Bureau of Indian Affairs to buy land for landless Indians in California.

1917
For the first time in 50 years, Indian births exceeded Indian deaths.

1917
Papago Indian Reservation in Arizona was the last reservation to be established by executive order.

1917
Congress abolished practice of payment of subsidies to religious groups for Indian education.

1917–1920
The restrictions on allotments and the "Forced Patent" period began. Thousands of patents were issued, discontinuing federal guardianship of Indian lands. As a result, many Indians lost their lands to corrupt Anglos.

1918
Native American Church with ritual surrounding the use of peyote was incorporated in Oklahoma by members of Kiowa, Comanche, Apache, Cheyenne, Ponca, and Oto tribes. By 1930, it was estimated that half of the nation's Indians are Native American Church members.

1921
The Snyder Act made the Department of the Interior responsible for Indian education, medical, and social services.

1923
Department of the Interior formed the Committee of One Hundred to review Indian policy.

1924
Congress awarded American citizenship to all native-born Indians who have not yet obtained it. This ruling resulted in part from gratitude for the Indian contribution to the American effort in World War I.

1924
Division of Indian Health was created within the Bureau of Indian Affairs.

1926
National Council of American Indians was founded.

1928
Charles Curtis, a Kaw Indian and U.S. senator, was elected vice-president under Hoover.

1928
The Meriam Report deplored Indian living conditions and declared the allotment system a failure.

1930
The Senate Investigating Committee on Indian Affairs disclosed the use of kidnapping techniques by BIA school officials trying to educate Navajo children.

1930
Northern Cheyenne Reservation became last communally owned tract to be allotted.

Native Pottery from the Southwest

CHAPTER 12

Tribal Restoration, Phase One: 1934–1944

As John Collier, one of the leaders of the tribal restoration period, looked back upon his commissionership he spoke about seven basic principles that had guided his administration of Indian affairs. These principles were his philosophy of reform.

1. Indian societies must and can be discovered in their continuing existence, or regenerated, or become new and made use of.
2. The Indian societies, whether ancient, regenerated, or created anew, must be given status, responsibility, and power.
3. The land held, used, and cherished in the way the particular Indian group desires, is fundamental in any lifesaving program.
4. Each and all of the freedoms should be extended to Indians, and in the most convincing and dramatic manner possible. This would include protection of cultural liberty, religious liberty, and the freedom for children to learn from their elders.
5. Positive means must be used to ensure freedom: credit, education (of a broad and technical sort), and independence and responsibility.
6. The experience of responsible democracy is the most important of all experiences. In this one belief, we, the workers who knew so well the diversity of the Indian situation, were prepared to be strong and unwavering even at the risk of blunders and of turmoil.
7. The seventh principle I would call the first and the last. Research and then more research is essential to the program. Research can be made a tool of action essential to all the other tools, indeed, that it ought to be the master tool.

(adapted from Prucha, 1988, pp. 317–318)

I do believe ... that no one exceeds him in knowledge of Indian matters or his sympathy with the point of view of the Indians themselves, I want someone in that office who is the advocate of the Indians. The whites can take care of themselves, but the Indians need someone to protect them from exploitation. I want a man who will respect their customs and have a sympathetic point of view with reference to their culture. I want the Indians to be helped to help themselves. John Collier, with whatever faults of temperament he may have, has to a higher degree than any one available for that office, the point of view towards the Indians that I want in the Commissioner of Indian Affairs (Harold L. Ickes in a letter to Franklin D. Roosevelt. Prucha, 1988, 316–317).

It is often said that John Collier was the most important man in the history of American Indian policy. Although he was unable to fulfill his dream of Indian self-determination, self-government, and self-preservation, and he faced formidable public opposition including serious charges from Native people, his legacy of reform changed Indian life and U.S. Indian policy in ways that remain today.

President Franklin D. Roosevelt, heeding the advice of Harold Ickes, appointed John Collier as his Commissioner of Indian Affairs in 1933. As an admirer of Indian culture and an advocate of Indian rights, Collier was indeed uniquely qualified to bring reform to Indian policy. He founded the American Indian Defense Association in 1923 and was already well known for his fierce and dedicated interest in Native Americans. He was also a trained ethnologist and social scientist, and for eleven years he had been involved in the fight for the Pueblos. It was with his vision and commitment and under his direction that the policies of assimilation and allotment were reversed with the 1934 Indian Reorganization Act (Wheeler-Howard Act).

The Meriam Report, with language that was uncharacteristically straightforward, had soundly condemned the allotment policy with the following statement:

When the government adopted the policy of individual ownership of the land on the reservations, the expectation was that the Indians would become farmers. Part of this plan was to instruct and aid them in agriculture, but this vital part was not pressed with vigor and intelligence. It almost seems as if the government assumed that some magic in individual ownership of property would in itself prove an educational civilizing factor, but unfortunately this policy has for the most part operated in the opposite direction (Deloria and Lytle, 1988, pp. 12–13).

Seeking to diminish Indian criticism of some parts of the proposed Wheeler-Howard Act, Collier organized a series of meetings attended by tribal councils and business committees, superintendents, and officials from Washington. Some of the criticisms and fears included: individuals who held land allotments and wanted to keep them; proposals for self-government; tribal segregation (which meant regression to some); and the persistent rumors that the policies were "communistic." Many of the people in Washington believed that segregation was indeed a step backward and probably was "un-American."

Collier made some revisions and the amended law was passed on April 28, 1934. Although he had to compromise his proposal the Wheeler-Howard Act was, nonetheless, a significant change in policy and an important piece of legislation.

This act of fundamental reform can be summarized in the following way. The Indian Reorganization Act:

- Gave legal sanction to tribal landholding.
- Returned unsold allotted lands to tribes.
- Authorized the appropriation of 2 million dollars a year for the purchase of new lands for Indian tribes.
- Encouraged the organization of tribal governments with control over tribal funds, judicial systems, and tribal corporations for the management of communal property.
- Expanded educational opportunities through new facilities and loans, emphasizing day schools on reservations instead of off-reservation boarding schools.
- Advocated the hiring of Indians by the Bureau of Indian Affairs and Indian involvement in management and policy-making at national and tribal levels.
- Authorized a ten-million-dollar loan fund for the use of tribes and individual Indians.
- Extended the Indian trust status.
- Granted religious freedom to Indian people (Waldman, 1985, pp. 193–194).

The issue of religious freedom (which is still far from settled) was addressed by Collier when he insisted that boarding school children were no longer required to attend Christian services, and Native religious ceremonies and observances were no longer forbidden, but encouraged. He stated that, "No interference with Indian religious life or ceremonial expression will hereafter be tolerated. The cultural liberty of Indians is in all respects to be considered equal to that of any non-Indian group." Collier persuaded Congress to discontinue its efforts to suppress traffic in peyote. This afforded constitutional protection for the religious practices of the Native American church.

He also weakened the hold of the Bureau of Indian Affairs by enlisting the services of the Public Health Service, negotiating contracts with state departments of education for Indian children to attend public schools, and sponsoring the Johnson-O'Malley Act, which authorized the Office of Indian Affairs to enter into contracts with state and local agencies to provide various services.

Additionally, Collier supported joint Indian efforts including the founding of the National Congress of American Indians (NCAI) and the Indian Claims Commission. The Indian Claims Commission was designed to provide a reasonable process for handling tribal land claims and providing financial compensation for treaty violations. This commission lasted until 1978 and granted awards of 800 million dollars on sixty percent of the cases brought before it.

Understanding that communal life was fundamental to traditional Indian culture and lifeways, Collier wisely directed much of his effort to reversing the Euro-American emphasis on individualism which was embodied most directly in the Allotment Act. He believed that the strength of Indian nations was the continued survival of the tribal group despite the pressures they had endured through time. As an example, he assumed that Indians would cede their allotted lands to new tribal governments, thus helping to restore Indian societies. He wanted a return to cooperative rather than competitive endeavors.

These reforms proposed and initiated by John Collier met with substantial opposition. Fearing a return to paganism, some missionary organizations opposed his tolerance of Native religions. Those who made a business of exploiting Indian people opposed the efforts that ruined their businesses, and sought the support of politicians and the public in opposition to the new policies. Fervent patriots questioned the emphasis on restoring communal life and tribalism, and began to speak of "communism" and suspected alliances with the communistic Russia. Ultimately, Collier was charged with being an atheist, a communist, and a traitor and had to defend himself before the House Indian Affairs Committee. In addition, one of the most significant barriers to the implementation of Collier's policies was the ineffective bureaucracy of the dictatorial Bureau of Indian Affairs which maintained a "stone-wall" approach, stifling or delaying action with its inertia.

There was also significant opposition from Indian people. One of the provisions in the IRA was the referendums on the reservations by which tribes voted to accept the act or to exclude themselves from its provision. Eventually 181 tribes with a population of 129,750 accepted the law and 77 tribes with a population of 86,365 voted to reject it. Fourteen more groups did not hold elections and therefore were included in the act.

A model constitution that could be used by tribes as a starting point for their written documents was developed by the Office of Indian Affairs. Collier set up an Indian Reorganization Division within the Office of Indian Affairs and field representatives, field agents, and men on special detail were organized to work with the superintendents and leaders of the tribes that had voted to be included in developing their constitutions.

Deloria and Lytle (1988, p. 15) point out that the damage done to tribal governments through the years could not be undone quickly. Traditional governmental structures had been significantly weakened and much of the religious undergirding of the informal structures and systems had been eroded. The tribal constitutions that emerged as a result of this assistance from the Office of Indian Affairs were a form of a structured, legalistic European government; they did not restore traditional governments.

In addition, Congress had mandated that all constitutions be approved by the Secretary of the Interior. The approval of the Secretary of the Interior provided a sort of control over tribal affairs and issues, and problems that had been handled in the Indian way of consensus were now formalized into tribal resolutions and governmental approval. The Office of Indian Affairs still controlled Indian lives.

Approximately ninety-five tribes adopted constitutions, and about seventy-four formed corporations for conducting tribal businesses. There were also tribes, such as the Pueblos, that continued to manage their affairs in the old ways. The Oklahoma tribes were too fragmented at this time to renew tribal governments. According to Prucha (1986, p. 327) the Five Civilized Tribes in the eastern part of Oklahoma were too deeply integrated into the white society to be interested in tribal reorganization.

Although the Indian Reorganization Act did not extend—except in minor instances—to Alaska or Oklahoma, Congress passed the Oklahoma Indian Welfare Act in 1936. This act extended the basic principles to the Indians of Oklahoma, permitting them to organize as corporations and authorizing a revolving loan fund of 2 million dollars for them.

The largest Indian tribe, the Navajos, rejected the provisions of the Indian Reorganization Act. A Navajo leader, Jacob Morgan, led the resistance. It should be noted that the Navajos constituted over half of those who voted against the act. This rejection of the Navajos disturbed Collier.

It is important to remember that this was the time of depression throughout the country. President Roosevelt had implemented his New Deal to alleviate the severe economic depression and Collier's reform in Indian Country is often called the Indian New Deal. His efforts in this area made an immediate impact on the dismal poverty gripping the Indian reservations. He instituted an Indian Civilian Conservation Corps which operated with its own rules. Most of the projects dealt with soil erosion control, forestation, and range development; thus Indian people were provided income, were trained in better methods of using the land, and the land was preserved and protected.

Despite the tremendous impact of these conservation programs on the poverty of Native peoples, not all conservation efforts were well received. In fact, one such effort, the stock reduction program on the Navajo Reservation was the major issue that engendered the opposition of the Navajos to the Reorganization Act. Collier firmly believed that the reduction of Navajo stock was crucial to the preservation of the range. Navajo lands were overgrazed and seriously eroded. The Navajo people, however, have a special relationship with their livestock and they perceived that the stock reduction interfered with their traditional ways of providing for themselves and their well-being.

Indian education was dramatically impacted by John Collier. Boarding schools that sought to separate Indian children from their homes and their families and to educate them in the ways of the white world were systematically reduced in number. The boarding schools were replaced by day schools that allowed children to live at home. Efforts were also made to encourage the attendance of Indian children in public schools. The Johnson-O'Malley Act provided the legal structure for contracts between the federal government and the states for the education of Native children.

Of concern to Collier and those who led the efforts in the reform of Indian education was the acceptance of Indian children in public schools. They were rightly concerned not only by the issue of acceptance but also of appropriate curriculum and instruction. In fact, for these reasons, Office of Indian Affairs schools were often considered superior by officials. In many cases, impoverished Indian parents also appreciated the extra services provided by the Office of Indian Affairs such as lunches and clothing. Boarding schools were still needed in remote areas of reservations and were sometimes favored by Indian parents who found it difficult to provide for their children.

The health of Indian people was another target for Collier. Indian mortality rate was fifty percent higher than that of whites. Serious diseases such as tuberculosis and trachoma were rampant. Sanitation was often primitive and deficient. Basic services such as dental and prenatal care were inadequate. Progress was made during this period, but World War II drained medical personnel and funds and Indian health conditions and care remained scandalously inferior.

As part of the Indian New Deal, Collier initiated the passage of the Indian Arts and Crafts Act of 1935. This act had two purposes. Obviously one purpose was the restoration of Indians arts and crafts as part of the restoration of Indian cultures. The other purpose was linked directly to self-determination and economic well-being. Collier had long supported the promotion of Indian products but the depression had a serious negative impact on the sale of Indian work with the accompanying effect of reduced production.

The Indian Arts and Crafts Act provided for market research, technical assistance, coordination of concerned private and governmental agencies, supply management personnel, government marks of genuineness, and standards of quality. A board of five members was appointed by the Secretary of the Interior to direct these efforts. Although World War II seriously impacted the production of Indian arts and crafts, the board survived and its efforts to promote the sale of, and appreciation for, beautiful art of Native people remains today.

World War II had further dramatic effects on Indian people. The warrior tradition is strong and many young Indian people left the reservations to serve with distinction in the military. As citizens they were subject to Selective Service; a large number, however, volunteered for military service. In 1943 there were 18,000 Indians serving in the military and in 1944 there were 21,756 serving in all battle areas. Of particular pride were the Navajo Code Talkers who, using their Native language, were able to send messages that the enemy forces were unable to decode, and the many soldier/warriors who received citations for their meritorious service. In addition, many Indian people worked in war industries.

The massive war had significant influence on Indian education; it not only consumed funds that might have been appropriated for Indian education, but war efforts attracted many teachers and administrators who left for military service or higher paying wartime jobs. But most importantly, as part of their involvement in the war, Indians came into close direct contact with whites—they became comfortable with the freedom to interact with others and with the greater freedom from the governmental bureaucracies and restrictions on the reservations. They also became aware of the importance of education and upon their return not only demanded further educational opportunities, but a different type of education. They demanded more than a vocational education suitable for a rural, reservation lifestyle. They wanted to be educated to take their place in the larger, more urban society.

While the impact of John Collier produced improved health and education, restored tribal governments, respect and markets for Indian arts and crafts, cooperation between the bureau and other federal agencies, and restored reservation lands, he, nonetheless, encountered enduring opposition throughout his administration. When his goals were thwarted by Congress, he persisted through administrative means. His opposition rallied around the charges that he was restoring tribalism, separating Indians from the dominant white society, and preventing Indian assimilation. According to Prucha (1986, p. 333), "From 1937 to 1945 Collier was a man besieged."

Jacob Morgan, with considerable support from the Indian Rights Association, continued his opposition to Collier, the Navajo stock reduction program, and the reorganization of tribal councils. He was joined by a small Indian group, the American Indian Federation. This group opposed Collier, whom they charged with being an atheist, a communist, and unrepresentative of Indian people, and urged repeal of the Indian Reorganization Act.

And, of course, there were those whose goals were simply not the goals of the act or of John Collier. A special house investigative committee made the following statement. The goal of Indian education should be to make the Indian child a better American rather than to equip him simply to be a better Indian. The goal of our whole Indian program should be, in the opinion of your committee, to develop better Indian Americans rather than to perpetuate and develop better American Indians. The present Indian education program tends to operate too much in the direction of perpetuating the Indians as a special status individual rather than preparing him for independent citizenship (Prucha, 1986, p. 336).

John Collier resigned from his post on January 19, 1945. His influence on Indian policy was profound, though he was embroiled in controversy throughout his tenure. The forces that opposed him also nurtured the press for assimilation and the words of the house committee portended the future. It would be decades before Collier's words would have appeal to most Americans. It would be decades before most Americans could understand and agree with Collier that modernity was not necessarily the equivalent of white Americanism and that the two cultures—Indian and white—could exist side by side. As he said, "America is coming to understand this, and to know ..."

LESSON PLAN:
JOHN COLLIER AND THE NAVAJO STOCK REDUCTION PLAN

Grade Level: Middle School

Basic Concepts: Natural resources, conservation, conflict

Organizing Generalization: Conflict is an inevitable result when the economic base and lifeways of one group of people are threatened by another. Livestock, which was used for food, clothing, and weaving, was integral to the Navajo people. Although the stock reduction policy was not intended to harm the Navajo people, but to help them preserve their land, it threatened their ways of supporting themselves and created grave conditions among the Navajo people. Conflict raged between the people and their Tribal Council and the Office of Indian Affairs under the leadership of John Collier.

Culture Area: Southwest

Time Period: 1934

Background: Although John Collier had the best interests of the Navajo in mind when he enforced stock reduction to preserve the land from overgrazing and severe soil erosion, the policy was poorly enforced. Navajo people were devastated by the loss of their stock. It is necessary to understand that bureaucracy and insensitivity can enable any well-conceived policy to be not only ineffective, but to actually counteract the problem it was designed to solve. The understandable rage of the Navajo people against John Collier and the Tribal Council that supported him resulted in their voting against the Indian Reorganization Act. Teachers can easily integrate this lesson with the science and environmental curriculum. Navajo people still remember the forced stock reduction.

Objectives:
Knowledge
Students will:
1. Demonstrate their understanding of the need for stock reduction on the Navajo Reservation.
2. List the ways the policy of stock reduction was helpful and ways in which it was harmful.
3. Diagram the concept of "savory grazing" (see excerpt, p. 181).

Skills
Students will:
1. Compare the perspective of John Collier and the perspective of George Blueeyes.
2. Hypothesize how the objective of protecting the land could have been achieved without such harm to the people.

Values
Students will:
1. Appreciate the wisdom of the Navajo elders and their traditional ways.
2. Understand that short term solutions are often harmful in the long term.

Activities:
1. Younger students should first locate the Navajo Reservation on a map and discuss the physical environment, including climate, vegetation, average annual rainfall, and natural resources. They should

also be knowledgeable about the traditional Navajo way of life, including the raising of sheep and goats for food and wool for weaving and the importance of the horse to this way of life.

2. In discussing the Indian New Deal, emphasize Collier's conservation efforts and introduce the Navajo Stock Reduction. Ask students to form small groups and decide how (1) the Navajo herders and weavers and (2) the government scientists and officials might view this plan. Each group should write brief statements of its position for each of these two groups. Students should be able to support each position with sound reasoning.

3. Ask each group to read the following selection on the Navajo Stock Reduction. Do their hypotheses still seem reasonable? Now introduce the reading Hear the People. Again, make any revisions in the hypotheses.

4. Discuss the following questions:
   a. What did go wrong?
   b. What were the effects of the Stock Reduction? Lead students to consider the feelings of the people toward the Tribal Council and John Collier and the Indian New Deal.
   c. What other ways might be useful in solving the problem of overgrazing?

5. Introduce the concept of "savory grazing."

6. Discuss the value of the "old ways" versus the value of the "new ways." How can we avoid such harm again?

Extensions:
It is recommended that students integrate this lesson with science and environmental lessons.

Evaluation: Ask each student to write an "I learned" statement.

Materials/Resources:
Arthur, C., Bingham, S. and Bingham J. *Between Sacred Mountains*. Tucson: Sun Tracks and the University of Arizona Press, 1982.

Navajo Stock Reduction

John Collier did not mean evil for the Navajo People. There were at that time nearly 1,500,000 head of livestock in Navajo Country. Many of them were horses that nobody seemed to use. Several times, thousands of horses and other animals did die because they could find nothing to eat, as Charlie Yellow said.

Collier believed that dry years killed so much livestock because there were too many animals to begin with. Scientists from Washington told him that the limit for reservation land was only 500,000 sheep. They told Navajo livestock owners that 500,000 well-fed animals would probably grow more meat and wool than a million starving ones. The Tribal Council even agreed that this might be true.

Most livestock owners, however, did not believe Collier or his experts from Washington. When they refused to cut down the size of their herds, Collier decided to use force. Livestock owners first had to sell off horses, then goats, and finally ewe sheep. Thousands of animals were shot and left to rot.

Some people, like Charlie Yellow, managed to hide their sheep, but others who disobeyed the orders were caught and sent to jail.

Grazing laws were made for Navajo Country:
- Navajo land was divided into "grazing districts."
- Livestock could not be taken across district lines.
- No one could own livestock without a permit, and no one could hold permits for more than 350 sheep or goats (1 horse = 5 sheep; 1 cow = 4 sheep).
- No one could move livestock onto land traditionally used by someone else.

Washington hoped that the plant life of Navajo Country would become richer than before. To help people along until that happened they hired Navajos to build dams, schools and bridges, dig irrigation ditches and drill wells, so people who lost livestock could earn a living some other way.

Unfortunately nothing turned out right.

Because of grazing laws, people stopped moving around to look for grass. Each family settled in one place and tried to hold on to as much land as possible. As George Blueeyes said, "Everybody began to say, 'This is my land! Not yours! Go away where you came from!' "

The jobs that Washington paid for in Navajo Country did not make up for the lost livestock. After Stock Reduction many people had to leave home to find work or go on welfare.

Worst of all, Stock Reduction did not help the land itself. Grasses and plants that used to grow died away completely. Tumbleweed and snakeweed covered places where they never grew before. The sunflowers that turned the land yellow for miles in the old stories bloomed only by the roadsides and irrigation ditches. Medicine men, herders, scientists, and government officials all agree that something went wrong.

(Arthur, et al.,1982, p. 174)

NAVAJO STOCK REDUCTION

The sheep, the horses, and the cattle grew to great numbers, and the ground became bare like the floor. Now people speak of that time as "The Time the Horses Died of Starvation." What was left grew again and grew again to great numbers. Then John Collier came running with his Stock Reduction.

Our animals! He ate them up!

We were herding some distance from here when Collier's men caught up with us. Right there all the goats were killed, about a hundred of them. The sheep that survived grew and grew for several years. Then along came Collier again.

I took my sheep all the way down to a place called Cats Tails Come Out and hid them. All the horses and goats and many sheep around here were killed. Their bones still lie around. We live among their bones.

When they reduced the stock, many men, women, boys and girls died. They died of what we call … sadness for something that will never come back. Because of Stock Reduction, many people passed away.

(Arthur, et al., 1982, p. 245)

Savory Grazing

Allan Savory agrees with Navajo medicine men who say people, not animals, cause most problems. Most of all, land needs careful planning, cooperation among neighbors, and daily attention.

Animals eating the best plants day after day until they die is "overgrazing." Reducing stock doesn't help, because even a little stock will roam far to eat only the best plants—and kill them.

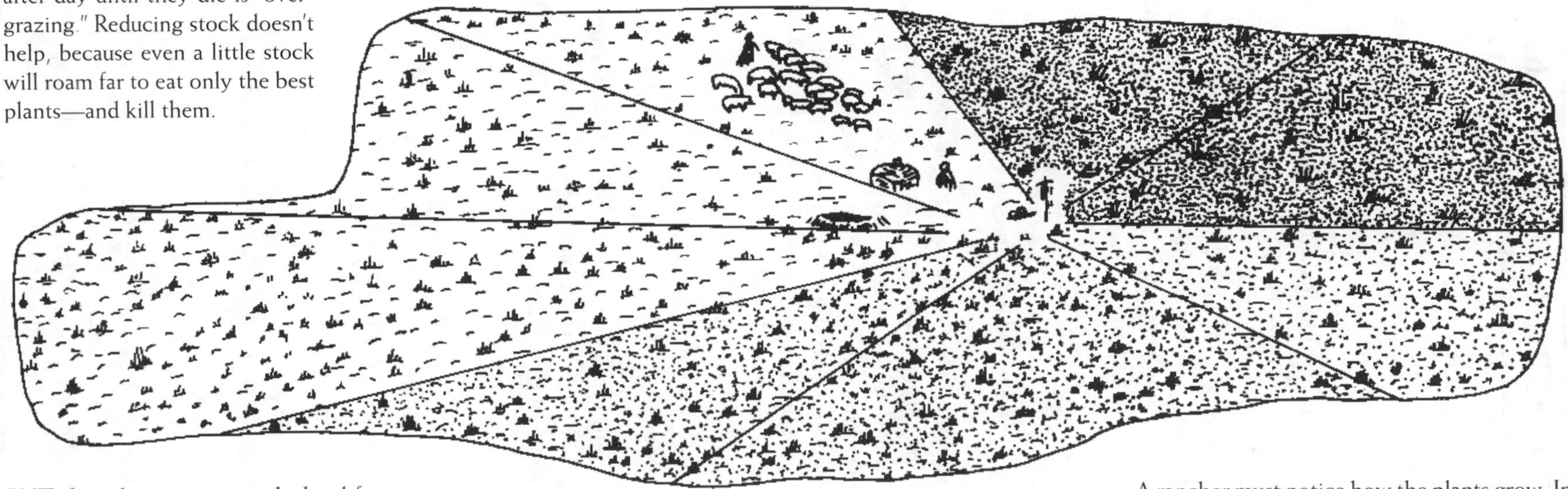

On well-managed land, grass will return without help from tractors. Good plants will increase and poor plants decrease until the land looks as it did when only wild animals lived on it. That is natural succession.

How long do most people graze stock in the same place? How often does stock cross the same land going to water and back to the corral? How often do neighbors use the same land without planning? These things hurt land more than herds that are too big.

BUT if stock moves in a tight herd from one area to another and doesn't spread over the land, plants have time to grow before they are bitten again. All the land is used equally. Careful herding or cheap, smooth-wire fences can make a herd graze in this way, as wild herds do.

Urine, manure, and trampling feet of a tightly packed herd fertilize soil, help seeds start, and open the ground for rain.

A rancher must notice how the plants grow. In spring, fall, and wet times, he can move a herd faster because plants grow quickly and need less rest. In dry times plants must rest more between grazing, so stock must move slower. In winter stock moves through all areas to use all the grass left standing.

Figure 12.1—Diagram of "Savory Grazing." Arthur, C., Bingham, S. and Bingham, J. Between sacred mountains. Tucson: Sun Tracks and the University of Arizona Press, 1982.

LESSON PLAN: THE POTTERY OF MARIA MONTOYA MARTINEZ, SAN ILDEFONSO PUEBLO

Grade Level: Grades 4–8

Basic Concepts: Beauty, harmony, and tradition

Organizing Generalizations: People strive to make their lives more beautiful by creating things that are aesthetically pleasing. When enough leisure time became available, the things of everyday life were adorned and decorated. Early Indian works of art are often expressed in the decoration and development of these things—pottery, baskets, and decorated clothing, household goods, and ceremonial objects. Beauty and harmony are expressed in Indian art and art is a way that brings cohesiveness to their cultures. The revival and recognition of the contribution of Indian arts and crafts has made a significant impact on the economic self-determination of Indian people.

Culture Area: Southwest

Time Period: 1887–1980 (The lifespan of Maria Montoya Martinez of San Ildefonso Pueblo)

Background: Recognizing the importance of beauty to Indian cultures, John Collier became deeply interested in preserving and promoting Indian art. He initiated the passage of the Indian Arts and Crafts Act of 1935 to stimulate national interest in traditional Indian art as a way of enabling Indian people to be economically independent. The Arts and Crafts Act achieved a success that remains today.

It is important for students to learn about Indian art and Indian artists as an integral part of traditional and contemporary American culture, but it is undoubtedly just as important for them to understand how art is integral to the Indian way.

Objectives:

Knowledge

Students will:

1. Recognize the unique contribution of the pottery of Maria Martinez.
2. Explain how art assisted in the economic recovery of San Ildefonso Pueblo.
3. Discuss the spiritual nature of Indian art.

Skills

Students will:

1. Use research skills to investigate a form of Indian visual art.
2. Use a creative way to present the results of their research.

Values

Students will:

1. Sense the power of Indian spiritualism, connection to Mother Earth and to the greater community.
2. Appreciate the art of Indian people.

Activities:

1. Have available pictures and samples of pueblo pottery.
2. Show the videotape, *Maria: Indian Pottery Maker of San Ildefonso.* This video was made before Maria's death and shows Maria and her son, Popovi Da, actually making pottery. It is particularly appropriate to discuss the great creativity and ingenuity of these Native potters.

3. Discuss the following statement: "Pottery holds the pueblo together economically. The ceremonials unite the community with tradition" (Peterson, 1977, p. 118). How does the impact of tourism and the continuing interest in Indian art impact San Ildefonso pueblo?

4. Introduce the idea of pottery as an embodiment of Indian values and an integral part of Indian culture. Ask students to read the following readings, *Maria* and *Indian Pottery and Indian Values*. This can be done independently or as partners, and as homework or in class.

5. Based on information gathered from the reading and the video, each student will write a brief cinquain about Maria or about Indian pottery. It will be helpful to some students if the class could brainstorm some words that could be used (clay, designs, harmony, beauty, patience). If students are not familiar with this structured form of verse, the teacher will need to review the basic structure.

6. Ask students to select a topic to research that is related to Indian art and that interests them. Form small interest groups to research a form of Indian visual art. Groups should present their research to the class using a visual form—for example, show samples, create a slide show, use the overhead, or make a scrapbook/notebook. All group work should demand individual as well as group accountability.

Extensions:

1. Visit local museums to view authentic pieces of art.
2. Invite local Indian artists to the classroom—consider all art forms including painting, sculpture, pottery, weaving and textiles, jewelry, basket-making, beadwork, leatherwork, and others.
3. Ask students to prepare reports on traditional and contemporary Indian artists in all of the culture areas.
4. Investigate the Santa Fe Institute of American Indian Art.
5. Make a piece of pottery.
6. Ask students to write a brief essay as a reflection on the following statement by Popovi Da.

> Fine art within our lives has been balanced and directed in a positive sense by the forces about us. If life is unbalanced, as it is now, by the pressure of mechanical things all about us, life seems to lose man in a cold world of steel where we are frustrated and afraid. This frustration will be reflected in our art. Should our civilization terminate today, future anthropologists would be puzzled by finding in our pueblos Japanese artifacts, complex distorted patterns of abstract paintings, and other evidence of the confusion of the world about us (Spivey, 1979, p. xix).

Evaluation: Student's cinquains and research reports should reflect an understanding of the spirituality of pueblo pottery.

Materials/Resources:

Batkin, J. "Three Great Potters of San Ildefonso and Their Legacy." *American Indian Art*, (Autumn 1991): 56–59.

Dockstader, F. J. *Indian Art in America: The Arts and Crafts of the North American Indian*. New York: Promontory Press, n.d.

Jacka, L. E. "Moments with Maria." *Native Peoples*. (Winter 1988): 24–29.

Spivey, R. L. *Maria*. Flagstaff, AZ: Northland, 1979.

U.S. National Park Service. Maria: Indian pottery maker of San Ildefonso (video). U.S. National Park Service, 1980.

American Indian Art. A quarterly publication that focuses on traditional, museum quality Indian art. The articles are scholarly in nature and would be valuable to teachers who are interested in more in-depth information on historical art of the Indian people. 7314 East Osborn Drive, Scottsdale, AZ 85251, (602) 994-5445.

Southwest Art. A monthly publication that is rich in information about contemporary Indian artists and in illustrations of their work. P.O. Box 460535, Houston TX 77256-0535, (713) 850-0990.

MARIA

But maybe God and the Great Spirit gave me (she claps her hands) that work (the hands to make pottery) … The spirit of the ones that passed away told me to love one another while we are on this earth. That's what God had told me, to keep it in my heart to love one another.

It's part of my work so that someday I could take it along with me. (The pottery she has made will stay here on this earth, but what goes into making them she will take along with her after death.)

I was never selfish with my work, for what God gave me. And so I help everybody. I used to teach at the government school in Santa Fe, the younger people from different pueblos. And now those ladies have … children, grandchildren, married. But some still come and visit me and thank me for what they learned from me. So I said, God gave me that hand, but not for myself, for all my people.

I just thank God because it's not only for me; it's for all the people. I said to my god, the Great Spirit, my Mother Earth gave me this luck. So I'm not going to keep it. I take care of our people. And I'm glad that those ladies learn and everything, and I'm happy.

Maria (Spivey, 1979, p. 149)

INDIAN POTTERY AND INDIAN VALUES
by Popovi Da (Maria Martinez's son)

We believe we are the first conservationists. We do not destroy or disturb the harmony of nature. To us this is beauty; it is our sense of aesthetics. We care for and husband our environment, trying to be all-forbearing like Mother Earth. We feel ourselves trustees of our environment and of our creative values. And this gives us a union with all existence, all the creatures which live in the world: wild animals, little crawling things, and even men.

We have multitudes of symbols—corn blossom, squash blossom, eagle and deer, rainbow and fire, and storm clouds; the design of plants, of all living things; the underworld which gave forth man and all the creatures—symbols whose secret meanings are only secret because they are within and cannot be easily expressed. This symbolism is perpetuated through memory alone, because we have no written language. But to be able to use our symbols and keep in harmony with our world we must work by fasting, continence, solitary vigil, and symbolic discipline. Out of the silences of meditation come purity and power which eventually become apparent in our art: the many spirits which enter about us, in us, are transformed within us, moving from an endless past not gone, not dead, but with a threshold that is the present. From this time sense, from this experience deep within, our forms are created. Even our small children sense this, and consequently create beautiful designs. Our simple lines have meaning.

We do what comes from thinking, and sometimes hours and even days are spent to create an aesthetic scroll in a design.

Our symbols and/or ceremonial representations are all expressed as an endless cadence, and beautifully organized in our art as well as in our dance.

A pueblo dance is a sacred drama and a tremendous religious experience to us. You behold a masterpiece of color, form and movement, sound, rhythm, a slow sequence of chants, beat of feet. This ceremony combines our spiritual and our physical needs. The dance expresses the union we feel between man and the whole of humanity or the union of all living things. At the same time, the dance gives to man, in his trusteeship of the corn, the health of the plant. The dance encourages the corn to grow.

(Spivey, 1979, pp. xvii–xix)

Summary
Tribal Restoration, Phase One: 1934–1944

One of the people who recognized the tragedy of the governmental policies of assimilation and allotment was John Collier. Appointed by President Franklin D. Roosevelt as Commissioner of Indian Affairs, Collier had been involved with Indian people for eleven years. It was with his vision and commitment and under his direction that the policies of assimilation and allotment were reversed with the Indian Reorganization Act of 1934.

Collier insisted that boarding school children were no longer required to attend Christian services and Native religious ceremonies and observances were no longer forbidden, but encouraged. He also weakened the hold of the Bureau of Indian Affairs by working with the Public Health Service and individual state departments of education. Collier supported the founding of the important National Congress of American Indians and the Indian Claims Commission.

Understanding that communal life was fundamental to traditional Indian culture and lifeways, Collier directed much of his effort to reversing the emphasis on individualism which was the focus of the General Allotment Act. The IRA also encouraged the organization of tribal governments with control over tribal funds and the organization of tribal corporations for the management of communal property. However, Congress mandated that all new tribal constitutions be approved by the Secretary of the Interior. In practice, this meant that the Office of Indian Affairs still controlled Indian lives.

There were many who opposed Collier's efforts; some tribes even voted to exclude themselves from the provisions of the law. In addition, the damage that had been done to tribal governments and the traditional ways that supported them had been significantly weakened; change would take time. Collier's influence was profound, but when he resigned in 1945 there were signs of problems ahead.

TIME LINE: 1933–1943

1933

John Collier was appointed commissioner of Indian Affairs by President Roosevelt, to administer the "New Deal" for Indians.

1934

The Wheeler-Howard Act (Indian Reorganization Act or Indian New Deal) reversed the policy of destroying tribal governments and landholdings through allotment and provides for tribal ownership of land and tribal self-government.

c. 1935–1940

A Navajo alphabet system was developed.

1936

Congress extended provisions of the Indian Reorganization Act to Alaskan Natives.

1936

Congress passed the Oklahoma Indian Welfare Act for the organization of the Indians who were excluded from the Wheeler-Howard Act.

1936

The Indian Arts and Crafts Board was established to help Indian artists.

1939

The Senecas issued a "Declaration of Independence" from the state of New York.

1941–1945

During World War II approximately twenty-five thousand Indians served in active duty and thousands more contributed to war efforts in war-related industries.

The famous Navajo Code Talkers used their language as a code the enemy was unable to decipher.

1943

Kateri Takakwitha, a seventeenth-century Mohawk, was declared venerable by the Roman Catholic Church. This is the first step toward sainthood.

Working the High Steel—A Contemporary Mohawk Helps Build a Skyscraper

CHAPTER 13

Tribal Restoration, Phase One Continued: 1944–1953

A friend of a returning Indian soldier explains simply, but eloquently, the veteran's conflict and struggle to survive in an urban environment.

It was kind of hard for him, you know, getting used to everything. We had to get down [to the factory] pretty early and put in a day's work. And then at night we would go down to Henry's place and fool around. We would get drunk and have a good time. There were always some girls down there, and on paydays we acted pretty big.

But he was unlucky. Everything went along all right for about two months, I guess. And it would have gone all right after that, too, if they had just let him alone. Maybe … you never know about a guy like that; but they wouldn't let him alone. The parole officer, and welfare, and the Relocation people kept coming around, you know, and they were always after him about something. They wanted to know how he was doing, had he been staying out of trouble and all. I guess that got on his nerves after a while, especially the business about drinking and running around. They were always warning him, you know? Telling him how he had to stay out of trouble, or else he was going to wind up in prison again. I guess he had to think about that all the time, because they wouldn't let him forget it.

Sometimes they talked to me about him, too, and I said he was getting along all right. But he wasn't. And I could see why, but I didn't know how to tell them about it. They wouldn't have understood anyway. You have to get used to everything, you know; it's like starting out someplace where you've never been before, and you don't know where you're going or why or when you have to get there, and everybody's looking at you, waiting for you, wondering why you don't hurry up.

And they can't help you because you don't know how to talk to them. They have a lot of words, and you know they mean something, but you don't know what, and your own words are no good because they're not the same; they're different, and they're the only words you've got. Everything is different, and you don't know how to get used to it. You see the way it is, how everything is going on without you, and you start to worry about it. You wonder how you can get yourself into the swing of it, you know? And you don't know how, but you've got to do it because there's nothing else. And you want to do it, because you can see how good it is. It's better than anything you've ever had; it's money and clothes and having plans and going someplace fast. You can see what it's like, but you don't know how to get into it; there's too much of it and it's all around you and you can't get hold of it because it's going on too fast.

You have to get used to it first, and it's hard. You've got to be left alone. You've got to put a lot of things out of your mind, or you're going to get all mixed up. You've got to take it easy and get drunk once in a while and just forget about who you are. It's hard, and you want to give up. You think about getting out and going home. You want to think that you belong someplace, I guess. You go up there on the hill and you hear the singing and the talk and you think about going home. But the next day you know it's no use; you know that if you went home there would be nothing there, just the empty land and a lot of old people going no place and dying off. And you've got to forget about that, too. Well, they were always coming around and warning him. They wouldn't let him alone, and pretty soon I could see that he was getting all mixed up.

(Excerpt from p. 143 from *House Made of Dawn* by N. Scott Momaday.© 1966, 1967, 1968 by N. Scott Momaday. Reprinted by permission of HarperCollins Pub. Inc.)

Although this was still considered a period of reorganization, and the Indian Reorganization Act had given new strengths to tribes, a new threat of extinction for Indian people was beginning to take shape. John Collier was an able defender of Indian people and tribal cultures. But Collier had to fight many formidable opponents. These opponents, although temporarily defeated, were not eliminated. This chapter will discuss the harbingers of change that led to a brief, but exceptionally destructive period of termination for Indian people.

With the resignation of John Collier in 1945, the mood of Congress began to change from the support of tribal culture and sovereignty to a movement to assimilate the American Indian into the "mainstream" of the American way of life. Earl Old Person, Blackfoot tribal chairman, asked, "Why is it so important that Indians be brought into the 'mainstream of American life'? What is the 'mainstream of American life'? I would not know how to interpret the phrase to my people in our language. The closest I would be able to come to 'mainstream' would be to say, in Indian, 'a big, wide river.' Am I then to tell my people that they will be 'thrown into the Big Wide River of the United States?'" (Nabokov, 1991, p. 336).

How did this mainstreaming or termination come into being? Let's look first at relocation, then the disaster of the Indian Claims Commission—both omens of what was to come.

Several contributing factors including intermarriage, grinding poverty and hardship, and the war, were initiating a change in ways of life for American Indians that would have an influence for years to come in the "mainstreaming" process and ultimately would make official termination policies seem attractive and possible to the government. These factors were often slow to evidence their disastrous effects. Relocation was one major result of the interplay of these factors.

Initially boarding schools of the previous generation had started a trend of intertribal marriage that would escalate into the late 1900s and would bring about conditions for even further changes in the lifeways of Native people. When young people of different tribes were at school together in their late teens and early twenties, they often met and married someone from another tribe. Then the decision came as to where they would live, in one or the other's home reservation or in an urban area, perhaps near both homes. They often selected cities, entering them shy and afraid of the unknown and unequipped to deal successfully with an urban environment.

City life began to appear to be a good option for many Indian people because of the unemployment, poverty, and hunger that were rampant on the reservations in many areas. The winter of 1947 was especially hard for the Navajos and Hopis. They were hit with such severe blizzards that many of their people died from starvation. Food had to be airlifted to save their lives. In the hope of finding better lives, many young people chose to move to the city. At first they went to the closest town or city, gradually moving farther from home into the major cities. There they could find new support systems initiated by the Indians themselves. In the process, they became "mainstreamed" (Steiner, 1968, p. 24).

World War II also contributed to the pattern of Indians moving to urban areas and to intertribal marriages. Soldiers were given a taste of life beyond the boundaries of the reservation. Over twenty-five thousand American Indians enlisted in the armed forces. (We have noted the heroic efforts of the Navajo Code Talkers, whose contribution is acknowledged around the world.) Based on their actions in the war, some soldiers were awarded honor in the old traditional ways by their tribes. Perhaps the greatest challenge experienced by Indian soldiers, though, was the one they faced when they returned home.

Most Indian soldiers had not been away from home before except when they attended boarding schools. As soldiers, they learned about the world, improved their communication skills, and learned about themselves. When they returned home from the war in 1945, many of these young men did not feel as comfortable at home as they once had, nor could they find employment or housing. Conflict between the ways of life they had experienced as soldiers and the traditional ways of reservation life caused internal conflict, and many returning soldiers became confused and disillusioned. They began moving to the cities to live and work and raise their families.

A tragic example of the contradiction that many Indian soldiers faced after the war was Ira Hayes, a Pima

Illustration 13.1—Ira Hayes, Pima Tribesman raising flag over Mount Suibachi, Iwo Jima Island, January 1945 (Library of Congress).

Indian from Arizona, who was one of the six soldiers who were photographed raising an American flag at Iwo Jima. Hayes, a Marine Private First Class, became a symbol of the "red man/noble warrior" for the army. He was pulled from the ranks and sent out around the country to inspire patriotism in other Americans. Always uncomfortable with the attention and notoriety, he returned home after the war. Like many other Indian veterans, he found himself between two worlds, not really belonging in either (Fixico, 1991). His early and unfortunate death was a result of this internal conflict.

During the period of time while John Collier was Commissioner of Indian Affairs, the programs established by his administration led to many changes in Indian Country. One of these programs had an unanticipated effect that resulted in relocation. The Indian Civilian Conservation Corp. (ICCC) implemented projects on reservations that were intended to enhance the life of the land or resources. For example, when the

ICCC initiated the Stock Reduction Program in Navajo country, many Navajos found themselves without a means of support on the reservation. Consequently many of them began seeking employment in the local urban areas of Gallup and Albuquerque. The Bureau of Indian Affairs then began a program to relocate them to Los Angeles, Denver, and Salt Lake City, helping them find housing and jobs.

Relocation from rural reservations to cities happened originally not as a result of a specific U.S. policy, but as an evolving result of changing conditions in life as it was experienced by individuals. Now the BIA was involved.

Well aware of the escalating movement of Indians to cities, the BIA believed that relocation was an important mainstreaming effort. In the next year, in 1949, under Dillon Meyer as commissioner, the BIA requested and received funding from Congress to increase placement services for other tribal members besides Navajos and in a larger number of cities. Each year the BIA asked for larger sums of money to support the relocation program and by 1952, relocation centers existed in Aberdeen, South Dakota; Billings, Montana; Portland, Oregon; Chicago, Phoenix, and New York (Fixico, 1991).

Indian people from all tribes were enticed to relocate with photographs of successful Indian families, employment, and housing. The posters portrayed a life that few Indians achieved. It was very easy to apply for relocation, and by 1952 over 12,500 Indians had moved to urban areas through the BIA relocation program.

Life in the cities was often not what the Indian people expected for they found fewer jobs, poorer housing, and little support once the first month was over. Most Indians came to the city without education or training and found only menial jobs. In many cases, the women found and kept jobs longer than their spouses. This in turn led to idle time for the unemployed men. Drinking with other unemployed male friends became a common way to spend time, and alcoholism increased. People became very dissatisfied with their lives, and the fabric that held many families together began to tear apart.

In 1956 it became apparent to Congress that the relocatees needed training to improve their opportunities for employment; it allocated money for relocation

Illustration 13.2—Relocation poster (courtesy of National Archives, Washington, D.C.)

and training. The amounts allocated by Congress increased each year. By 1957 another seventeen thousand Indian people had moved to the cities, bringing the total to over thirty thousand Indians relocating between 1949 and 1957. Through the years the name of the program was changed to the Employment and Training Assistance Program.

Perhaps the best expression of the personal experience of relocation was told by a young Indian woman who was relocated to Chicago. Her hopes, fears, and needs are expressed poignantly and eloquently.

Here I am in a big city, right in the middle of Chicago. I don't know anybody. I am so lonesome and I have that urge to go home. I don't know which direction to go—south, north, east, or west. I can't just take any direction because I don't know my way around yet.

I see strange faces around me and I keep wondering how I will survive in this strange environment. I keep pondering how I can get over this loneliness, and start adjusting to this environment. I know I have to start somewhere along the line and get involved in social activities and overcome the fear I am holding inside me and replace it with courage, dignity, self confidence, and the ambition to reach my goal.

Before I can adjust myself to this strange environment and get involved in things, I need friends who will help me overcome this urge to go home so I can accomplish my goal here in this unknown world which I entered (Fixico, 1991, p. 65).

"Come to Denver—The Chance of Your Lifetime!" read one of the many relocation posters that decorated the walls of Indian agencies all over the nation. The poster and other literature painted a picture of relocation to urban areas that few Indians experienced. By the late 1950s and early 1960s, almost half of all those who had relocated to cities returned to the reservation. They found the city frightening, with no support from extended family or guidance from elders. For those who stayed, they would be the beginning of an exodus of Indian people off of reservations to seek better lives than were possible at home. Those who adapted made new homes for their children and grandchildren. They became strangers to their families on the reservations and often never returned.

Indian centers were established in many urban areas through the efforts of Indians and others who saw that the support of the BIA generally ended after the first month of relocation and many could not survive alone. The centers were operated on federal grant money, foundation grants, and donations. They provided services such as health care, housing referral assistance, social services, employment referrals, and provided a hub for intertribal social activities. Once depression and substance abuse grew among relocatees, Indian centers also operated programs to assist in the treatment of alcoholism and depression. Many of these centers have survived the years and are still in operation today.

A unique culture that also began to become visible during these years, primarily as a result of relocation, was "Pan Indianism." Indians in urban centers found themselves wanting and needing to socialize and associate with each other. While Indians are known to have congregated often in bars during the relocation era, they also congregated at Indian churches, powwows, and urban Indian centers. Christianity had been a strong influence for decades on reservations, and many of the adults of the 1950s and 1960s were raised as Christians of various denominations. They sought out church congregations that also included other Indians. They also extended an old custom of gathering together for social dancing. The Indians of the Plains would provide the songs and everyone would dress in their traditional clothing to dance together. Families and friends shared an intertribal culture, loosely fashioned on the ways of the Plains tribes, that nurtured individual culture while supporting a new, shared culture.

The Indian Claims Commission was created by Congress in 1946 to settle tribal claims against the United States. In many respects, the payment for land that had been taken from the tribes could appear as though it was an action of belated fairness—that payment for Indian land would help to rectify a previous wrong. It could be perceived even as a major component to restoring tribal dignity and providing some economic security. This was not the case.

It was believed by Congress and others that if tribes were paid for the lands that were lost to the United States, the government could terminate the federal responsibility and relationship that existed between it and the tribes. This action was based on the theory that Indians would be better off if they could extinguish their ties to their land and become "regular" U.S. citizens.

There was no provision in the Act for tribes to regain the lost land or acquire new lands. Claims were accepted between 1946 and 1952. During that time, tribes filed 850 claims. Further, as the large sums of money were discharged to tribes, an issue developed over whether the payments should be made to individuals or the tribe as a whole. There were so many claims that the deadline was extended. The Commission was still in operation in 1962 with only 122 claims settled (Nabokov, 1991, p. 334). Criticisms of the Act have been summarized in the following way.

Tribes could not regain their old lands or acquire new ones. They could be granted only financial awards, which were based on the market value of the land at the time it was taken, not on its current value. In general, no interest was paid. Any gratuitous expenditures made by the federal government for the tribes were subtracted from the overall award, thereby penalizing the tribes for unrequested services. The average interval between filing of claims and receiving an award was fifteen years (from *American Indian Tribal Governments* by Sharon O'Brien, p. 84. Copyright © 1989 by the University of Oklahoma Press).

By the time the Commission was dissolved, it had awarded more than 800 million dollars to various tribes.

One very important and positive event occurred during this period of time. In 1944, during the administration of Commissioner John Collier, delegates representing many tribes gathered in Denver, Colorado, to join forces in facing the issues of past injustices and current and future conditions for American Indian people in the United States. They were optimistic that they could take an active and meaningful role in the determination of the future for American Indian people. The organization formed at that meeting, the National Congress of American Indians (NCAI), established regular meetings and began to develop a strategy for tribes to work together in taking back the control of their destinies. Formally incorporated in 1954, the preamble to the NCAI constitution states:

We, the members of Indian tribes of the United States of America invoking the Divine guidance of Almighty God in order to secure to ourselves—the Indians of the United States and the Natives of Alaska—and our descendants the rights and benefits to which we are entitled under the laws of the United States, the several states thereof, and the Territory of Alaska; to enlighten the public toward a better understanding of the Indian people; to preserve Indian cultural values; to seek an equitable adjustment of tribal affairs and tribal claims; to secure and to preserve rights under Indian treaties or agreements with, the United States; to promote the common welfare of the American Indian and to foster the continued loyalty and allegiance of American Indians to the flag of the United States do establish this organization and adopt the following Constitution and by-laws (from *American Indian Tribal Governments* by Sharon O'Brien, p. 236. Copyright © 1989 by the University of Oklahoma Press).

The organization was exclusively Indian, comprised originally of Indians primarily from Oklahoma and the Plains. As time passed other tribes joined and NCAI took a national role in lobbying for tribal rights and educating the public through its publications. NCAI assumed a central role in the relationship between Indians and the U.S. government, and it continues in modern times to be an example of a loosely knit confederation working for the benefit of all Indian people. In 1992 this organization represented 160 tribes and approximately 400,000 people.

The report of the Hoover Commission on the Reorganization of Government in 1949 recommended termination for tribes. In the late 1940s and early 1950s this policy was implemented through continuing relocation, a process of termination, and the Indian Claims Commission. The House Concurrent Resolution 108 was passed by Congress in 1953 and, in the same year, Public Law 280 gave Wisconsin, Minnesota, Nebraska, California, and Oregon civil and criminal jurisdiction over Indian reservations without the consent of tribes. Also in 1953, Congress repealed the special alcohol prohibition laws regarding Indians. Times were changing rapidly and the threat of total termination spread through Indian communities around the country.

The next chapter will explore further efforts of the BIA and the U.S. government to terminate tribes. The threat of termination, whether by relocation, buyout through the Indian Claims Commission proceedings, or directly through congressional act, haunted all nations of Indian people in the 1950s. For some, the threat became a reality.

What can I say to my Omaha people? That is my main question. For two nights I have stayed awake, looking for honest thoughts and true words to say. I knew my Omaha people would be afraid when they heard that the Bureau of Indian Affairs was thinking of making a great change in their lives. It is a poor life, but it is the only one they have to live. The only changes that will not frighten my Omaha people are the changes they make themselves. These respected officials of the Bureau of Indian Affairs told me my people do not have to be afraid. I stayed awake, trying to know if I could tell them there was nothing to fear. I cannot tell my people that. These honored officials met in Omaha April 15 and 16 to talk about whether it would be good administration to transfer many services to the county and state and perhaps to move our Indian Agency from the Reservation. When I heard that the officials were meeting about such a serious thing, I asked to be allowed to sit with them when they talked. They graciously said I could. I did, for two whole days. The officials said they would consult the people before any changes were made. They are being true to their word.

They are consulting, but I have to say this: After the people have been consulted, I am afraid the changes will be made, even if the people do consent to them or not. I think, probably, in Washington, D.C., someone has already decided that the changes will make for a cheaper administration. I think these officials are telling my people about how their life is to be changed, not asking whether they want it changed. ... If my Omaha people are allowed to make their own change, they will feel brave, proud, they will face the future standing up straight (Alfred W. Gilpin, Omaha Tribal Council Chairman, April 1954, as cited in Armstrong, 1971, p. 148).

LESSON PLAN:
RELOCATION AND URBANIZATION

Grade Level: Grades 5–8

Basic Concepts: Adaptation, change, independence, and survival

Organizing Generalization: When people migrate from one location to another and from one cultural setting to another, it is necessary to adapt to the new culture in order to survive. Some people adapt, while others never really do. Those who make successful adaptations often remain in the new home; those who are unable to adapt and therefore to survive in the new culture often develop maladaptive behaviors to cope or return to the original home.

Culture Area: All culture areas

Time Period: 1952–1958

Background: After World War II American Indians began moving to urban areas throughout America. Some of the first relocatees were voluntary—those who had served in the war and could not find adequate jobs and housing after the war on the reservation. Later, government programs relocated thousands of American Indians to cities in a massive effort to assimilate them into the dominant culture and terminate tribes. Each individual who relocated experienced a different world and adjusted in his or her own way to survive. Many returned home shortly after moving, while others carved out a new life in a new place and are now grandparents with extended families in the cities.

Objectives:

Knowledge
Students will:

1. Describe in their own words the major reasons that Indian people relocated to urban environments.
2. List qualities necessary for survival in the city.
3. List characteristics of reservations life that were missing in the city.

Skills
Students will:

1. Summarize the readings from various American Indians who relocated during the 1950s.
2. Compare the different responses to relocation in a class discussion.
3. Analyze why they are different.

Values
Students will:

1. Recognize the hardship on Indian people who were relocated through early government effort.
2. Recognize that many Indian people retain their culture when they relocate.
3. Appreciate the different ways people responded to the challenge of urban survival.

Activities:

1. Introduce this lesson, if appropriate to the age of the students, by reading the selection on page 189.
2. Organize students in small groups of four to six students. Pass out multiple copies of the comments of Indian people who were relocated and the accompanying worksheet. Ask each group to read these comments and complete the worksheet in preparation for a class discussion. Depending on the age of the students, other reference materials should be available for their use, including census data.

3. Each group should report its conclusions. Guide a class discussion that explores how the people felt, what worked and what didn't work for people, and how each did different things. Ask students how they would cope if they suddenly moved to a large city, or city in a foreign country, without family or friends. Have they had similar experiences in unfamiliar settings? Do people's culture end when they move away from the center of that culture? Classrooms in which there are students who are recent immigrants should discuss their experiences.

4. Summarize by discussing the positive and negative impacts of relocation on individuals and Native cultures.

Extensions:

1. Read *Urban Indians* (Fixico, 1991). This book explains the relocation period and urban Indians today in greater detail.

2. Students in urban areas may locate Native speakers through the Indian Center and ask them to share their story of how they or their family relocated to the urban area and how they stay in touch with their tribe and American Indian culture.

3. Write to an urban Indian center to see what services are available and learn about the urban Indian community.

4. Older students will enjoy the book *A Yellow Raft in Blue Water* (Dorris, 1988). This book was a Booklist Editor's Choice for adults and young adults and is fairly sophisticated reading. It provides insight to the stresses of reservation and urban life.

Evaluation:

Students should demonstrate through class discussions their understanding of the impact of relocation on Indian people in terms of assimilation, adaptation, and the survival of the culture.

Materials/Resources:

Dorris, M. *A Yellow Raft in Blue Water*. New York: Warner, 1988.

Fixico, D. L. *Urban Indians*. New York: Chelsea House, 1991.

Levine, S. and Lurie, N. O. (eds). *American Indians Today*. Baltimore: Penguin, 1968.

Moccasins on Pavement, the Indian Experience: A Denver Portrait. Denver: Denver Museum of Natural History, 1978.

Sorkin, A. *The Urban American Indian*. Lexington, KY: Lexington, 1978.

Steiner, S. *The New Indians*. New York: Delta, 1968.

Voices of Indian People
Who Relocated to Urban Areas After 1950

… many of those in the relocation program have had poor educational backgrounds and no training. Even worse, they have often been misled by over zealous placement personnel and have had no clear idea about what to expect once they reached places like Denver. Many whom I've talked to were given minimal assistance and counseling once they arrived. What can be expected from such situations?

George H. J. Abrams (Seneca) as cited in *Moccasins on Pavement*, 1978.

When I first came to Colorado I was so backward I didn't even know how to get off the bus. At home everyone knew everyone else and I thought it was wonderful that the bus driver in such a big city could remember where each person got on. I must have ridden ten blocks beyond my stop! I was so embarrassed. It seems funny now—at the time it wasn't. When you come from a place which has few paved roads, let alone buses, a pull cord may not be very obvious—it may be frightening.

Hazel Taylor (Oglala Sioux) as cited in *Moccasins on Pavement*, 1978.

It's really a vicious circle with no beginning and no end. A person comes to Denver because someone has told him about better jobs or schooling. When he gets here he realizes that he doesn't have the background and education to take advantage of these things. Not only that, but he doesn't even know where to go for help. He gets desperate and to calm his fears he starts hanging out in one of the Indian bars in town. At least here he sees other people like himself and he can be more comfortable. Maybe he panhandles to get a bottle or maybe he just gets picked up for fighting—that's what most Indian 'crimes' consist of. If he's lucky, he finds help before it's too late.

Pat Caverly (Rosebud Sioux) as cited in *Moccasins on Pavement*, 1978.

When I came to Denver I didn't think I'd have much trouble after a while. I had a lot of money, but that was before I bought that car. It was a '59 Ford. After we bought that car it seems like the money just go by. … So I think the most important thing that a man has is to have money. I have found in Denver that things are too high. Everything. Groceries, clothing, gas, and everything else is too high.

A Navajo relocatee as cited in Fixico, 1991.

I don't like living in Chicago. I'm here on the relocation training program, and I'm glad to learn a trade, but I sure don't like the city. The BIA doesn't give us enough money to live in Chicago. It's awfully expensive here. But it's not just that. People are different here—even the Indians. They don't talk to you … I got lost on the "el" [elevated train] and no one would help me. City people are in such a hurry. As soon as I finish school, I'm going away—maybe back to the reservation, but to a small town anyhow. I'd rather be in a small town and not have such a good job [than] stay in the city.

A twenty-five-year-old Indian man relocatee as cited in Fixico, 1991.

I came under the relocation program. I applied through the agency back on the reservation, and I came to Chicago to go to school. I went to a business school in a suburb, and I liked it out there. It was really beautiful, lived at the "Y." We don't any more.

I took secretarial training, and some of the teachers were good and some weren't. I used to think … I still think that sometimes they just passed us with good grades because they knew the BIA would go on paying. So maybe we didn't get a very good education always. But I must have learned all right because I applied for a job as a secretary, and I got it OK, and I am still doing it. I think the relocation program is a good thing, but the BIA just never seems to do anything right. They really don't seem to take an interest in the students, and they ran us through like cattle, but the idea is still good. And some of the advisors are real nice and helpful. Well, anyhow, I have a job now that pays enough and I can save some money. It is my hope to go to college someday.

A twenty-four-year-old Indian woman relocatee, as cited in Fixico, 1991.

The Center strives to assist all Indian people. Naturally some individuals need more help than others. I think that perhaps the most important function of the Center is to allow all of us to get together … the old and the young, the conservative and the activist, people from many different tribes. I know that if it hadn't been for the kind of mutual support we all derive from one another through the Center, I myself would have been lost long ago. Our job is to make sure not one single person is lost in the shuffle.

Ken Scott (Choctaw) as cited in *Moccasins on Pavement*, 1978.

Perhaps non-Indians would be surprised to know how much of our cultures we retain, even after years and years in the city. We are people with our feet in two worlds. Sometimes this can be very difficult, but for many Indian people it can be very rich and exciting. Our elders speak of life moving in great cycles, from infancy to death and beyond. They also speak of ages, from the beginning of creation to the present. This modern period, when half of all Indian people live in cities, is just another of these ages. We're going to make it, all right!

Ken Yellowmoon (Choctaw) as cited in *Moccasins on Pavement*, 1978.

It's not going to be easy. We may not succeed one hundred percent of the time, but we're going to keep trying. Our people are a whole lot stronger than most people realize. We've survived some pretty hideous situations before; we'll survive this too. And you know what? Everybody, not just Indians, will be better off for it. We still have a lot to offer, good things to contribute to the rest of America. We've contributed a lot already—why stop now? And just because we live in cities doesn't mean we stop being Indian. I'm proud of my tribal heritage—my kids will be too.

Jacque Gray (Osage) as cited in *Moccasins on Pavement*, 1978.

WORKSHEET
VOICES OF INDIAN PEOPLE
WHO RELOCATED TO URBAN AREAS AFTER 1950

Using the quotations of Indian people who relocated to urban areas as a reference, discuss the following topics with the people in your group. Also think of how you might react in a similar situation. How would you think, feel, and act? Try to come to some general agreement and answer the following questions.

1. What were some of the reasons that reservation people were not successful in the city?

2. How did the people who were not successful cope with their situations?

3. What assistance would have been helpful to them?

4. Do you think that most of those who were successful adapted or assimilated? What is the difference? What evidence did you use to decide? Do you need further information?

SUMMARY
TRIBAL RESTORATION, PHASE ONE CONTINUED: 1944–1953

Collier had to fight many opponents. These opponents, although temporarily defeated, were not eliminated. The mood of Congress began to change from the support of tribal cultures and sovereignty to a new movement to assimilate the American Indian into the "mainstream" of the American way of life.

Several factors including intermarriage, grinding poverty, hardship, and World War II accelerated more change in ways of life for American Indians and made official termination policies again seem attractive and feasible to the government. Relocation was one major result of the interaction of these factors.

Relocation began naturally, but it soon became a policy of the government. Young people from different tribes who had met at the off-reservation boarding schools married and frequently relocated in cities near their home reservations. They came to the cities shy, afraid, and unequipped to deal with an urban environment. Others came to cities because of the unemployment, poverty, and hunger that were so common on the reservations. Those who had served in the war were also attracted to city life.

Aware of the movement of Indian people to the cities, the BIA received funding from Congress to increase placement services for tribal members in several large cities.

Life in these cities was wretched for most Indian people. They found few jobs, poor housing, and little support. Alcoholism accompanied unemployment. Indian Centers were established in many urban areas through the efforts of Indians and others and provided health care, social services, employment referrals, and programs to deal with alcoholism and depression.

Relocation became another serious threat to the strength and sovereignty of tribal people and soon the word termination came to haunt them.

TIME LINE: 1944–1953

1944
The National Congress of American Indians (NCAI) was organized in Denver, Colorado.

1944
A House Indian Affairs Committee conducted an investigation of federal Indian policy.

1944
Native American Church was incorporated.

1945
John Collier resigned as Commissioner of Indian Affairs.

1946
An Indian Claims Commission was created by Congress to settle tribal land claims against the United States.

1948
Arizona was forced by the courts to give Indians the right to vote as in other states.

1948
Assimilative Crimes Act held that offenses committed on reservations, not covered under a specific federal statute but punishable under state law, were to be tried in federal courts.

1949
The Hoover Commission on the Reorganization of Government recommended termination of the federal-Indian trust relationship.

1950
Dillon Myer, Commissioner of Indian Affairs, supported termination as well as a relocation and urbanization program for reservation Indians, encouraging migration to cities and cultural assimilation.

1950
Navajo Rehabilitation Act called for appropriations to benefit tribes.

1952
A BIA program was established to work with individual tribes to achieve standards of living comparable to the rest of society, and to transfer certain BIA functions to the Indian people or to other local, state, or federal agencies.

1952
The BIA established a Voluntary Relocation Program to relocate Indian people to urban areas.

1953
Congress repealed Indian prohibition laws.

CHAPTER 14

Termination: 1952–1968

With the passage of the Menominee Termination Act in 1954, a tragic chapter in the tribe's history began. Although designed to free us from federal supervision, termination was a cultural, political, and economic disaster. Our land, our people, and our tribal identity were assailed in a calculated effort to force us into the mainstream of society. Like me, other Menominees were wounded to the heart when, unannounced, bulldozers began slashing and clearing trees from our beautiful lake shores and slicing the land into lots to be sold. This was the spark that lit a fire of determined resistance in us all, resulting in the formation of DRUMS (Determination of Rights and Unity for Menominee Shareholders). DRUMS led a successful effort to reverse termination and, with the signing of the Menominee Restoration Act on December 22, 1973, the future of the tribe, its land, and its people was assured. Working through the legal and political systems, we achieved a historic reversal of an ill-considered and damaging policy, thereby establishing precedents for other tribes in their struggles for self-determination.

Our experience has taught us that despite almost 300 years of disruption, tribal values run deep within each of us. We have two conclusions: first, INDIANS, remain true to your tribal values and traditions; second, the first Americans have a richness and depth of cultures which the world needs, and which our tribes will gladly share.

—Ada Deer, Menominee

Viola, H. J. *After Columbus: The Smithsonian Chronicle of the North American Indian.* Washington, D.C.: Smithsonian/Orion Books, 1990, p. 236.

The tragedy that Ada Deer laments began officially with House Concurrent Resolution (HCR) 108 which was adopted August 1, 1953. This resolution stated that "the policy of Congress is ... to make the Indians ... subject to the same laws and entitled to the same privileges and responsibilities as ... other citizens ... and to end their status as wards of the United States, and to grant them all the rights and privileges pertaining to American citizenship." Although this congressional resolution was not a law, it represented the beliefs and general opinions of Congress.

First, let's step back into the years preceding the House Resolution 108; the indicators of the mood of Congress were readily discernible.

Even before John Collier's term as Commissioner ended in 1946, his philosophy and policies were challenged and their effectiveness was questioned. In 1944, the Senate Committee on Indian Affairs approved a bill that recommended that the Wheeler-Howard Act (IRA) be repealed. The committee report specified eight conclusions:

1. Stopping the allotment program perpetuated governmental supervision over Indians and was incompatible with the American system of land tenure.
2. The indefinite extension of the trust period has caused many inheritance problems.
3. The return of surplus lands to tribes has been futile and expensive. It simply placed tribal land under BIA control.
4. The communal land set up under the IRA simply did not work. Indians possessed no land individually, and this was contrary to their wishes.
5. The land purchase program was grossly mismanaged. What land that had been purchased went into tribal ownership and had not been given to landless Indians.
6. The reservation system remained obnoxious and should be terminated
7. The revolving credit fund had placed too much power into the hands of the Indian Service. The bulk of the loans had gone to few tribes and only to those tribes that had sufficient security to handle their own affairs.
8. Loans to Indian students were no longer needed, since these students could obtain funds from general sources (Submitted by Mr. Bushfield, committe on Indian Affairs, "Repealing the So-Called Wheeler-Howard Act." Hearings on S.1218, 78th Congress, 2d Session, Senate Report #1031, June 22, 1944).

The reform efforts that Collier initiated certainly did not represent the beliefs of the committee members who wrote this report. The word termination was present in the report, and the mood and intent of Congress to terminate Indian cultures and their relationship with the federal government was evident.

In 1947, following World War II, in an understandable effort to reduce federal expenditures and in a Republican crusade to reduce the Democratic New Deal Programs, the Senate Civil Service Committee asked Acting Commissioner William Zimmerman to determine if Indian tribes were able to succeed independently. Zimmerman then classified tribes into three categories: (1) those tribes that could succeed immediately without federal assistance, (2) those tribes that would be able to live on their own in a reasonable amount of time, and (3) those tribes that would need continuing federal assistance, at least for the foreseeable future. Zimmerman used the following criteria to classify the tribes:

1. Degree of acculturation—including such factors as degree of white blood, literacy, business ability, acceptance of white institutions, and community acceptance by whites.
2. Economic condition of the tribe—ability of individuals to make a decent living.
3. Willingness of the tribe and its members to dispense with federal aid.
4. Willingness and ability of the state in which the tribe is located to assume the responsibilities.

He then prepared sample withdrawal plans—plans for the Klamath, Menominee, and Osage tribes the Bureau could consider that would end federal aid and that would also give the tribe a reasonable chance to be successful. According to Deloria, the suggestions of Zimmerman were basically sound and, if they had been carried out, they would have created a maximum of self-government and a minimum of risk until the tribes gained confidence and experience (1988, p. 59).

Interestingly, Zimmerman's suggestions were ignored when it was discovered that the budget of the Department of the Interior would be insignificantly affected by the termination of "even fifty thousand Indians." But the idea of termination of Indian tribes did not die; it would remain in the consciousness of those who would determine Indian policy in the future.

Next followed two major reports that were to influence the move toward termination. First, in 1949, the Hoover Commission released recommendations based upon a study of government programs, including Indian programs. In order to cut federal expenditures, and supposedly to be more efficient, the report recommended that the responsibility for Indians be transferred to the states as soon as it was practical. Second, the National Council of Churches released a report which recommended that Indians be given full citizenship by eliminating much of the discriminating legislation that bound them to the federal government.

It is also important to recognize that the language of termination was reasonable in tone. It was difficult for the average citizen to argue against reduction of federal spending or against the "civil rights" of Indians. During the presidential election of 1952 the two political parties made platform statements regarding Indian policy. The Democrats promised "to remove restrictions on the rights of Indians individually and, through their tribal councils, to handle their own affairs;" the Republicans promised that "All Indians are citizens of the United States and no longer should be denied full enjoyment of their rights of citizenship" (Debo, 1989, p. 351). Who could argue? However, those who were more informed could clearly see what the intent was to be—termination of Indian treaty rights and the government's trust responsibilities and the termination of Indian cultures and of Indians as a people. New words—same purpose.

Then in 1952, more direct efforts to terminate were evident. Dillon Myer, the Commissioner of the Bureau of Indian Affairs, sent a memo to Bureau employees that quite succinctly signaled a new era of termination. Myer presented a new policy that included what he called "withdrawal programming." Withdrawal programming meant that previous programs encouraging Indian development were abandoned. Myer stated, "I realize that it will not be possible always to obtain Indian cooperation....We must proceed, even though (this) may be lacking" (cited in Debo, 1989, p. 351).

It is important to remember that Dillon Myer, the commissioner who created both relocation and termination policies, was already well known for his efforts during World War II. Myer had been in charge of the Japanese internment camps which were developed following Pearl Harbor, and had been zealous (some say coercive) in his efforts to resettle and disperse the Japanese throughout the general population. Myer had a short tenure (1950–1952), but his purpose was perpetuated in the years to come.

Congress terminated the federal relationship with sixty-one tribes, bands, and communities from 1954 to 1962 (Waldman, 1985, p. 194).

The larger tribes such as the Navajo, which were more sophisticated politically and had clear treaty commitments, were not touched by termination. However, there was constant fear throughout Indian Country. In fact, the threat of termination was a tool that was used handily to exert pressure on tribes to conform to the wishes of the government.

> Unbearable pressures, lies, promises, and threats of termination were made whenever a tribe won funds from the United States because of past swindles by the federal government. Whenever a tribe needed special legislation to develop its resources, termination was often the price asked for the attention of the committee. And if a tribe compromised with the Senate committee it was on the road to termination. Quarter was asked but none given (Deloria, 1988, p. 63).

Fear was pervasive and had an impact in many subtle and not-so-subtle ways. But fear became reality for many tribes who were actually terminated.

THE PAIUTE

Five small bands of approximately two hundred land-poor and economically impoverished Paiutes were terminated. These people didn't know of the impending termination, and certainly lack of funds limited how they could respond. They were too poor to go to Washington to testify on their own behalf. The official reason for their termination was that they had never received much help from the government anyway. In reality, their land held the promise of oil and uranium. Their land was transferred to a Salt Lake City trust company. These Paiutes were demoralized regarding what had happened to them.

Two major tribes, the Menominee of Wisconsin (Northeast) and the Klamath of Oregon (Plateau) were terminated. What these tribes had in common was vast, rich timber lands. Let's look first at the Menominee, for their case was indeed a tragedy and a good example of the folly and dishonesty of U.S. policy.

THE MENOMINEE

Termination was presented to the reasonably successful Menominees as freedom from federal intervention—language that we have already seen was attractive. However, a strong motive also lay in white interests in the acquisition of timber on Indian lands. The Menominees had an impressive stand of virgin timber on its 234,000-acre reservation. There were also beautiful lakes, with good boating and excellent fishing. The timber was appraised at 36 million dollars in 1936. Nonetheless, the standard of living for the 3,270 Menominees was far below average. At the signing of the Menominee Termination Act, members received a payment of fifteen hundred dollars (of their own money) and were then released to their own resources.

Interestingly, the federal cost per year for the Menominees was $144,000, or $50.85 per person; the government would not save much money by terminating the Menominee. Another important point is related to their relative prosperity and self-sufficiency at that time—they were paying for all their own services.

> The sum of $520,714 was budgeted by the tribe for the reservation the year before termination. The tribe invested $285,000 in construction projects, $56,745 for education, $47,021 for welfare, and $130,000 for health. It set aside $42,615 for law and order activities. The federal government, which was obligated to provide all of these services, actually spent only $95,000 for roads and $49,000 for education, on a matching basis with the state and tribe (Deloria, 1988, p. 65).

The reservation was established as a separate county in Wisconsin against the wishes of the state of Wisconsin—the state envisioned the disaster that was to come.

On April 30, 1961, the property of the tribe, which had been held in trust by the federal government, was transferred to Menominee Enterprises, Inc., a tribal corporation. The services that had been provided for Indians were no longer available to individual Menominees, who were now under the laws of the state of Wisconsin.

After termination, chaos reigned and the tribe began to lose its valuable assets and sink deeper into abject poverty—their previous advances into independence destroyed. Tribal members lost jobs in the lumber industry, members lost their lands because they were unable to pay the new property taxes, they were unable to pay for their basic utility bills, and the loss of federally sponsored social, educational, and health services and facilities was disastrous to the health and welfare of the people. Their school and hospital were closed and a major tuberculosis epidemic broke out soon after termination.

Before long half of the residents were on welfare and approximately one-fourth of the members were unemployed. The sawmill, their major source of revenue, installed automated equipment to improve production, thus adding more people to ranks of the unemployed. People began to sell their land. Predictably, the lakefront land was exceptionally attractive to outside buyers. Once without their land, the Indians were truly destitute. The Menominees were on a path to extinction.

With the disaster readily apparent, Indian people, under the leadership of Ada Deer and others, and non-Indian supporters began to press for the restoration of trust status for the tribe and reservation status for the remaining lands. The activists (DRUMS—Determination of Rights and Unity for Menominee Shareholders) picketed real estate offices, held meetings to restore a sense of tribal identity and pride, and marched in protest to draw attention to the plight of the tribe. Finally, in 1974, Congress passed the Menominee Restoration Act.

The damage caused by the termination was great, and the Menominees are not yet completely healed and restored.

THE KLAMATH

The move toward termination was somewhat easier for the Klamath who were sharply divided among themselves. One faction favored holding onto its tribal lands; the other faction supported liquidation of the tribal estate and distribution of the proceeds in per capita payments. The Klamath Termination Act of August 13, 1954, did not provide enough preparation time for termination for one group, and another group perceived the delay as far too long.

The conservation of the Klamath forests was another issue. Obviously, clear cutting of the forests would be damaging to the land and to the Oregon economy. Consequently, termination was delayed to find a reasonable solution to these concerns. Later, it was determined that the Klamath forests would be harvested on a sustained-yield basis and sold at fair market prices.

Individual tribal members could vote to withdraw from the tribe and receive individual shares of the tribal assets or to remain in the tribe under a tribal management plan. In the election, 1,659 members voted to withdraw and only 474 chose to remain in the tribe. Most of the reservation was sold to the federal government to provide the money for the payments to the individual tribal members. The tribe divided these funds on a per capita basis. The Klamath members who chose to withdraw received $43,700 each in 1961.

The remaining land was committed to the U.S. National Bank of Portland as trustee for the remaining tribal members. Those who kept their shares in a corporate trust until 1975 received approximately $150,000 each.

> But the price was high; the reservation was gone and the tribe was nearly destroyed. Many of the Indians who withdrew were uneducated in ways to manage their money and they subsequently made arrangements with local banks to act as trustees. Others lost their money. Poverty and the accompanying educational, health and social problems were quick to follow. The Klamaths lost all federal recognition and assistance and were considered to be outcasts in the national Indian community (Deloria and Lytle, 1983, p. 21).

OKLAHOMA

Oklahoma tribes that were already without tribal lands were not directly affected by the termination. Yet their response to the termination of tribes and the loss of tribal lands was significant and enduring. According to Debo (1989, p. 408), Oklahoma Indians were slow to respond to the reality that "the liquidation of tribes and of tribal land to which it owed its existence had not

brought all the separated individuals into happy assimilation with the dominant society." Eventually, in 1963 the University of Oklahoma made a contract with the BIA office in western Oklahoma to create centers where white leaders and the Indians living on the fringes of the dominant society could come together in a united community program.

Two Indian women, Iola Taylor and LaDonna Harris, provided the vigorous and dedicated leadership that would eventually result in the formation of the Oklahomans for Indian Opportunity (OIO). The focus of the organization was on self-help and individual effort by Indian people themselves and on promoting acceptance of Indians in the white community. The OIO organized disparate tribes and created a unified organization with enormous influence. This organization was responsible for developing programs of (1) community improvements, implemented by Indians and non-Indians, (2) enlisting employers to train Indian workers, and (3) leadership activities for Indian high school students.

This activity is worthy of mention in a chapter on termination for at least one crucial reason. The purpose of the governmental policy of termination was assimilation and/or "civilizing;" its effects were disastrous. Oklahomans for Indian Opportunity created a place where Indian people learned the skills needed in a rapidly changing society, they learned these skills along with the whites, and their cooperative efforts made a contribution for the greater good.

Charles F. Wilkinson and Eric R. Biggs (cited in Deloria and Lytle, 1983, p. 20) summarized some of the basic consequences of terminations:

1. There were fundamental changes in land ownership patterns.
2. The trust relationship was ended.
3. State legislative jurisdiction was imposed.
4. State judicial authority was imposed.
5. Exception from state taxing power was ended.
6. Special federal programs to tribes were discontinued.
7. Special federal programs to individual Indians were discontinued.
8. Tribal sovereignty was effectively ended.

In 1958 Secretary of the Interior Fred Seaton announced on a radio talk-show interview in Gallup, New Mexico, that hereafter, no tribe would be terminated without its consent. The Congress and Washington politicians were embarrassed by this rather cavalier announcement, but it was clear that termination was unsuccessful and unacceptable, at least unofficially. This was welcome news to the terrified tribes.

In the presidential campaign of 1960, a new tenor was heard. Richard Nixon stated, "I want to emphasize here my deep and abiding respect for the values of Indian culture and for the undeniable right of Indian people to preserve their traditional heritage. Our overriding aim, as I see it, should not be to separate the Indians from the richness of their past or force them into some preconceived mold of human behavior. ... Every conceivable effort will be made to shape our actions and our policies in full harmony with the deepest aspirations of the Indian citizenry" (Debo, 1989, p. 405).

John Kennedy wrote, "There would be no change in treaty or contractual relationships without the consent of the tribes concerned. No steps would be taken to impair the cultural heritage of any group...There would be protection of the Indian land base...Indians have heard fine words and promises long enough. They are right in asking for deeds" (Debo, 1989, p. 405).

President Kennedy and President Johnson did not act on termination. Therefore, it wasn't until July 8, 1970, in an address to Congress that President Richard Nixon announced, "Because termination is morally and legally unacceptable, because it produces bad practical results, and because the mere threat of termination tends to discourage greater self-sufficiency among Indian groups, I am asking the Congress to pass a new Concurrent Resolution which would expressly renounce, repudiate, and repeal the termination policy as expressed in House Concurrent Resolution 108 of the 83rd Congress" (Deloria and Lytle, 1983, p. 20).

It is suggested that the feelings of the Indian people were summarized in an opinion of the Supreme Court [*Federal Power Commission v. Tuscarora Indian Nation*, 362 U.S. 99 (1960)]

The record does not leave the impression that the lands are the most fertile, the landscape the most beautiful or their homes the most splendid specimens of architecture. But this is their home—their ancestral home. There they, their children and their forebears were born. They, too, have their memories and their loves. Some things are worth more than money and the costs of a new enterprise (Deloria and Lytle, 1983, p. 21).

LESSON PLAN:
ADA DEER AND THE MENOMINEE

Grade Level: Grade 4–middle school

Basic Concepts: Leadership, political action, and collaboration

Organizing Generalization: Organized interest groups attempt to influence public policy when they believe such policy will affect their goals. In this lesson, students will learn about a Menominee woman, Ada Deer, and how with her leadership the Menominee people formed a powerful interest group to overturn the destructive termination policy of the U.S. government.

Culture Area: Northern Plains

Time Period: 1954 to the present

Background: Ada Deer, one of the first organizers of DRUMS, worked to gain the support of other interest groups and state and federal government officials, and to repeal the Menominee Termination Act of 1954. The Menominees' federally recognized status as an Indian tribe was restored in 1973. Legal help for DRUMS was provided by the Native American Rights Fund (NARF), of which Ada Deer became the chairwoman in 1989 (Viola, 1990, p. 236). It is important that Indian leaders, men and women, are recognized for their commitment, initiative, and enduring influence.

Objectives:

Knowledge
Students will:
1. Describe the accomplishments of Ada Deer.
2. List some of her personal characteristics.
2. Summarize her philosophy regarding political action and Indian leadership.

Skills
Students will:
1. Use a mapping strategy to indicate the groups that Ada Deer contacted and worked with to form a lobbying group for the restoration of the Menominee tribe.
2. Hypothesize why Ada Deer was willing to sacrifice personally and professionally to be politically active in various arenas.

Values
Students will:
1. Recognize that personal commitment to a cause requires self-sacrifice and intensive, intelligent effort.
2. Appreciate the need to develop Native leadership.

Activities:
1. Introduce Ada Deer as an Indian woman who was able to bring about important political action to end the termination of the Menominees. After distributing the abbreviated biography of Ada Deer, ask students to describe her interests, values, and characteristics, and to hypothesize about her personal and professional strengths.
2. Ask each student to read the excerpts from "Mobilizing to Win." Discussion questions should include:
   a. What knowledge and skills did Ada Deer bring to her leadership role in the Menominee restoration?

    b. What do you think her role was? What was her strategy? Why was she successful?

    c. Why is collaboration and the power of interest groups important in influencing public policy?

    d. What do you think Ms. Deer might have had to give up to work toward the end of termination?

    e. Is leadership in the Indian community any different from leadership in other areas or for other concerns?

3. It would be useful to ask students to map her strategy in the restoration efforts. This may require additional information.

4. Ask students, to form small groups of three to four and discuss the two separate documents—the biography and Ada Deer's own words about leadership. Then ask them individually to summarize her philosophy regarding political action and Indian leadership.

Extensions:

1. Do more in-depth research on DRUMS and how the Menominee tribe is recovering from termination.

2. Write The Committee for Ada Deer for further information about her, or correspond with her directly (address on page 212).

3. Provide biographies of prominent Indian leaders for further study.

Evaluation: Student summaries will provide evidence of their understanding of the significant role played by Ada Deer, how interest groups impact public policy, and the importance of Indian leadership.

Materials/Resources:

Materials for this lesson were obtained from The Committee for Ada Deer, 2575 University Avenue, Madison, WI 53705, (608) 231-1232.

Deer, A. "Mobilizing to Win." In S. Verble (ed.). *Words of Today's American Indian Women: OHOYO MAKACHI* Washington, DC: U.S. Department of Education, 1981, pp. 87–88.

Excerpts from "Mobilizing to Win"
by Ada Deer

Let me say that this all starts with ourselves—within ourselves—our own attitude and our own determination. I started thinking of the time when I became aware of the tribe and my responsibility to it. It was a growing thing. I was an 8th grade student sitting there with all the men. They kind of tolerated me and let me sit there. I didn't know anything about parliamentary procedure or any of the other things, but they let me come, and over a period of time I became very interested. Somewhere in the back of my mind I got the idea that I wanted to help and I wanted to be involved. I didn't know exactly what this would mean, but it was strengthened when I was the only person to win the tribal scholarship to attend college.

... And so I felt a great obligation to repay the tribe for the opportunity to go to college. The Menominee Termination Act occurred in 1954—it was finalized in 1961. Some of you may not know what termination is....Termination was a cultural, economic and political disaster. Our people are still recovering from this.

When termination occurred our people were no longer eligible for federal services, we were no longer a federally recognized tribe, the rolls were closed, our land became subject to taxation, we had no health services, no educational scholarships, nothing. It was a terrible, terrible feeling. There was this feeling of helplessness and powerlessness among our people.

In 1969, I came back to Wisconsin after spending many years in Minnesota. By this time I had a master's degree and ten years' experience. I started going to some tribal meetings and then I started looking into this matter of termination and how it was affecting the Menominees. The more I found out, the angrier I got. So, I decided to do something about it. There were other people along the way also, who felt it was important to do something about it.

We started meeting with a few of the people. We decided the first thing we needed was a lawyer. In Indian affairs you often need a lawyer. You have to get a good lawyer. I wish I had time to go into this, but the main point I want to emphasize to you about lawyers and professional people is that you as Indian people need to make the decisions. Don't let those non-Indians make decisions for you. You have to have confidence in yourself, you have to care about what the particular issue is, and you have to forge ahead. Many times people will tell you what you can't do. I think that's a double burden on us as Indians and as women. Because they're not accustomed to clear, determined thinking.

The more I thought about the suffering of the people—I could see the loss of the land—other people did, too, but they didn't know what to do about it. Well, I went to social work school to bring about social change and the opportunity to work with my tribe was the best example of how to put my skills to use.

To make a long story short, we accomplished it. And I tell you that if we as Menominees, a very small tribe of people, could accomplish what we did—any tribe should be able to do anything they want. It seemed like an impossible task to get a piece of legislation through the U.S. Congress, the government, senators, Congressmen, etc. But, nevertheless, we mobilized our resources, we talked to the press people, we talked to other people, the League of Women Voters, Common Cause, church groups, etc. I am only briefly summarizing the kinds of efforts that were necessary to bring this about.

We didn't do this by ourselves. We got excellent help from a number of groups and individuals. But it had to start somewhere—within myself, with a number of other people we worked with—and over a period of time we got a real movement of people among our tribe—the Drums Movement.

… I feel that over the years many people have identified the Menominee restoration with me as an individual but I want to emphasize that you can't do this by yourself; you have to have the movement of people. On the other hand, there has to be a focus for an effort. If you're the focus for the effort, then you have to be willing to pay the price for this. And in a way I had been developing all my life to get involved and to take part in this restoration....Over the years, in terms of leadership, you have to speak up, you have to speak out, you have to be willing to pay the price. I decided it was worth the price I had to pay both personally and professionally.

… We're too accustomed to having the BIA, missionaries, and other people telling us what to do. It takes some strength, some assertiveness, and some determination on our part to overcome this.

Deer, A. "Mobilizing to Win." In S. Verble (ed.). *Words of Today's American Indian women: OHOYO MAKACHI,* 1981 (pp. 87–88). Washington, D.C.: U.S. Department of Education.

Abbreviated Biography of Ada Deer

Personal Information:

Born on the Menominee Reservation on August 7, 1935.

Received a bachelor's degree from the University of Wisconsin in Madison in 1957.

Was the first person from her tribe to graduate from the university.

Received a master's degree from the Columbia University School of Social Work in 1961.

Studied law from 1971–1972.

Studied as a fellow of the Harvard Institute of Politics, JFK School of Government from 1977–1978.

Professional Employment:

1993–Assistant Secretary of Indian Affairs, Washington, D.C.

1977–1993 Lecturer, University of Wisconsin

1979–1981 Native American Rights Fund

1974–1976 Menominee Restoration Committee

1972–1973 National Committee to Save the Menominee People and Forest, Inc.

1970–1971 Program for Recognizing Individual Determination Through Education (PRIDE)

National Board Member:

1990 to present National Indian Advisory Committee

Honor Our Neighbors Origins and Rights (HONOR)

1990 to present Native American Rights Fund, Chair

1989 to present Quincentenary Committee, Smithsonian Institute

1989 to present Indian Community School

1989 to 1991 National Indian Advisory Committee

Job Training Partnership Act (JTPA)

1989–1990 Native American Rights Fund (chair)

Native American Rights Fund

1988–present Improving the Health of Native Americans

Robert Wood Johnson Foundation

1985 to present Encampment for Citizenship
1980 to present OHOYO Advisory Board
1988–1990 National Association of Social Workers, Wisconsin Chapter President
1988–1990 National Committee on Women's Issues
National Association of Social Workers

Awards and Honors:

1992 candidate for the U.S. House of Representatives from Wisconsin
1991 National Distinguished Achievement Award; American Indian Resources Institute
1987 Honoree, National Women's History Month Poster; National Women's History Project
1984 Vice Chair, National Mondale/Ferraro Presidential Campaign
1982 Candidate for the Democratic nomination
Office of Wisconsin Secretary of State
1982 Girl Scouts U.S.A. Women of the Year Award
1978 Directory of Significant 20th Century American Minority Women Fisk University
1976 CBS Bicentennial Minute
1975 Politzer Award, presented by the Ethical Culture Society
1974 White Buffalo Council Achievement Award
1974 Doctor of Public Service, Northland College
1974 Doctor of Humane Letters, University of Wisconsin

LESSON PLAN: YEAR OF THE AMERICAN INDIAN

Grade Level: Grades 4–middle school

Basic Concepts: Pride, recognition, and equity

Organizing Generalization: Every culture makes contributions to society and is worthy of respect. Native cultures have contributed to American governmental traditions, most professions, sports, and the arts in the past and the present.

Culture Area: All areas

Time Period: The lesson will require research throughout all time periods.

Background: The Senate and House of Representatives of the United States designated 1992 as the "Year of the American Indian." In this lesson students will create a celebration of Native American contributions and cultures. Termination was a time when the government wanted to eliminate Indian nations as separate nations and Indian cultures. It is beneficial for students to identify those aspects of Indian cultures that were valuable to save, the Native people who have brought honor to their tribes and to our country, and the contributions Indian people have made throughout history that deserve recognition and respect. In a sense, it is also a celebration of the failure of the policy of termination.

Objectives:

Knowledge

Students will:

1. Identify important Indian values, people, and contributions.
2. Discuss the need to maintain, not terminate them.

Skills

Students will:

1. Identify criteria as to what is "important" to recognize, and use the criteria to make their decisions.
2. Be creative in planning an appropriate celebration.
3. Practice skills of collaboration in implementing their planning celebration.

Values

Students will:

1. Recognize the impact of the opinions of others on self-esteem and pride.
2. Develop an appreciation of Indian values and contributions.

Activities:

1. Make a large poster or overhead of the congressional resolution. Discuss how termination was not successful in eliminating Indian tribes or Indian cultures. How is that failure evident today? What values of Indian people have enduring importance? Which Native individuals should be "recognized for their individual contributions"? What contributions have Native people made to society?
2. The lesson should be divided into two parts: gathering information, and planning an appropriate program, ceremony, or activity that celebrates the Year of the American Indian.
3. Students should work individually or in small groups to research Native values, individuals who have made important contributions and other contributions such as corn. Their notes can be recorded on index cards or added to a bulletin board or chalkboard list.

4. When adequate information has been gathered, students should plan and implement a celebration. The kind of celebration will depend on the time available and the age of the students.

5. Ask students to discuss the following:

   "Congress believes that such recognition of their contributions will promote self-esteem, pride, and self-awareness in American Indians young and old." Why is this important? Necessary? Older students should consider how Indian people have been represented in the press, media, and in inaccurate stories and textbooks. They should also be aware of insensitive stereotypes and blatant prejudice and how governmental policies of coercive assimilation, separation, allotment, and termination have affected Indian self-esteem and pride.

Extensions:

1. Encourage students to study the accomplishments of Indian people in their community and learn how they keep their traditions alive. Indian people might well be part of the celebration.

2. Ask students to review their textbooks and other reading material as to how Indian people are presented. Older texts are useful to show change.

3. Students can write a letter to the editor of their local paper stating their opinions regarding the Year of the American Indian.

Evaluation: Through the celebration, the students will demonstrate their knowledge of the distinct and important Native contributions to the United States and the rest of the world.

Materials/Resources:

1. Accurate biographies, videotapes, and articles such as those published in *Native Peoples* the *Native Monthly Reader*, and *National Geographic*.

2. Appropriate excerpts can be prepared for student use from the following books.

Weatherford, J. *Indian Givers: How the Indians of the Americas Transformed the World.* New York: Fawcett Columbine, 1988.

Weatherford, J. *Native Roots.* New York: Crown, 1990.

Year of the American Indian

Congress passed the following joint resolution authorizing the President to proclaim 1992 as the "Year of the American Indian."

Whereas American Indians are the original inhabitants of the lands that now constitute the United States of America;

Whereas American Indian governments developed the fundamental principles of freedom of speech and the separation of powers in government, and these principles form the foundation of the United States Government today;

Whereas American Indian societies exhibited a respect for the finite quality of natural resources through deep respect for the earth, and such values continue to be widely held today;

Whereas American Indian people have served with valor in all wars that the United States has engaged in, from the Revolutionary War to the conflict in the Persian Gulf, often serving in greater numbers, proportionately, than the population of the Nation as a whole;

Whereas American Indians have made distinct and important contributions to the United States and the rest of the world in many fields, including agriculture, medicine, music, language, and art;

Whereas it is fitting that American Indians be recognized for their individual contributions as artists, sculptors, musicians, authors, poets, artisans, scientists, and scholars;

Whereas the five-hundredth anniversary of the arrival of Christopher Columbus to the Western Hemisphere is an especially appropriate occasion for the people of the United States to reflect on the long history of the original inhabitants of this continent and appreciate that the "discoverees" should have as much recognition as the "discoverer,"

Whereas the peoples of the world will be refocusing with special interest on the significant contributions that American Indians have made to society;

Whereas the Congress believes that such recognition of their contributions will promote self-esteem, pride, and self-awareness in American Indians young and old; and

Whereas 1992 represents the first time that American Indians will have been recognized through the commemoration of a year in their honor;

Now, therefore, be it resolved by the Senate and House of Representatives of the United States of America in Congress assembled, That 1992 is designated as the "Year of the American Indian." The President is authorized and requested to issue a proclamation calling upon federal, state, and local governments, interested groups and organizations, and the people of the United States to observe the year with appropriate programs, ceremonies, and activities.

Velsey, C. (ed.) *Handbook of American Indian Religious Freedom.* New York: Crossroads, 1991.

SUMMARY
TERMINATION: 1952–1968

In 1947, Acting Commissioner of Indian Affairs William Zimmerman was asked to determine if Indian tribes were able to succeed independently. Zimmerman developed criteria to determine which tribes could succeed immediately without federal assistance. The idea of termination of federal trust status, though basically sound, again was disastrous for Indian people when it was eventually implemented.

From 1954 to 1962, under the direction of Dillon Myer, Commissioner of the Bureau of Indian Affairs, the government terminated the federal relationship with sixty-one tribes, bands, and communities. Larger tribes such as the Navajo that were more politically sophisticated and had treaty commitments were not touched by termination.

The Menominee was one of the larger tribes that endured actual termination. The Menominee had an impressive stand of virgin timber on its reservation along with beautiful lakes, good boating, and excellent fishing. Although the standard of living for the 3,270 Menominees was far below average, they paid for all their own services. The reservation was established as a separate county in Wisconsin, against the wishes of the state of Wisconsin, and taxes had to be paid to the state.

Unable to pay the taxes, chaos reigned and the tribe began to lose its valuable assets and sink deeper into abject poverty. Before long half of the residents were on welfare and approximately a quarter of the members were unemployed. People began to sell their land; they were on a path to extinction.

Indian people, under the leadership of Ada Deer and others, as well as non-Indian supporters began to work for the restoration of trust status for the tribe and reservation status for the remaining lands. Finally in 1974, Congress passed the Menominee Restoration Act.

The damage caused by termination was great and the Menominees and others are not yet completely healed and restored.

TIME LINE: 1952–1967

1952
Division of Programs was established with the BIA to work with individual tribes to achieve standards of living comparable to the rest of society and to transfer certain BIA functions to Indians themselves or the appropriate local, state, or federal agencies.

1952
BIA established Voluntary Relocation Program.

1953
Congress repealed special Indian prohibition laws.

1953
Congress passed the Termination Resolution that provided for the end of the special federal relationship with certain tribes.

1953
Congress empowered certain states to take over civil and criminal jurisdiction of Indian reservations without the consent of the tribes.

1954–1956
Congress removed federal services and protection from sixty-one tribes, bands, and communities.

1955
The Public Health Service of the Department of Health, Education, and Welfare assumed responsibility for Indian health and medical care from the BIA.

1956
The Adult Vocational Training Program, with an emphasis on service, trade, and clerical jobs for Indians, was established within the BIA.

1957
The Senecas opposed the building of the Kinqua Dam; the Tuscaroras fought the New York State Power Authority; the Mohawks reoccupied lands taken by white squatters.

1958
The Department of the Interior agreed to some modifications of the termination policy.

1959
Congress authorized the surgeon general to provide and maintain essential sanitation facilities for Indian communities.

1961
Department of the Interior changed federal land sales policy to allow Indian tribes the first opportunity to purchase lands offered for sale by individual Indians, countering the termination policy.

1961
Keeler Commission on Rights, Liberties, and Responsibilities of the American Indian recommended tribal self-determination and the development of tribal resources.

1961
Public Housing Act assisted Indians in improving homes, and the Area Redevelopment Act gives grants to communities.

1961
U.S. Commission on Civil Rights reported on injustices in Indian living conditions.

1962
New Mexico was forced by the federal government to give Indians voting rights.

1962
Manpower Development and Training Act provided vocational facilities and programs for Indians.

1964
Capital Conference on Indian Poverty was held in Washington, D.C.

1964
The Office of Economic Opportunity was created and sponsors anti-poverty programs.

1964
Civil Rights Act prohibited discrimination for reason of color, race, religion, or national origin.

1965
Voting Rights Act ensured equal voting rights.

1966
The Coleman Report on Indian Education was presented; the White House Task Force on Indian Health was formed; the Elementary and Secondary Education Act provided special programs for Indian children.

1967
The Indian Resources Development Act, which would have vested final authority over Indian land transactions in the Department of the Interior, was countered by the "Resolution of the Thirty Tribes" and subsequently defeated in Congress.

CHAPTER 15

Tribal Restoration, Phase Two: 1968–1975

DECLARATION OF THE FIVE COUNTY CHEROKEES—1966

Now, we shall not rest until we have regained our rightful place. We shall tell our young people what we know. We shall send them to the corners of the earth to learn more. They shall lead us.

Now, we have much to do. When our task is done, we will be ready to rest.

In these days, intruders, named without our consent, speak for the Cherokees. When the Cherokee government is the Cherokee people, we shall rest.

In these days, we are informed of the decisions other people have made about our destiny. When we control our destiny, we shall rest.

In these days, the high courts of the United States listen to people who have been wronged. When our wrongs have been judged in these courts, and the illegalities of the past have been corrected, we shall rest.

In these days, there are countless ways by which people make their grievances known to all Americans. When we have learned these new ways that bring strength and power, and we have used them we shall rest.

In these days, we are losing our homes and our children's homes. When our homeland is protected, for ourselves and for the generations to follow, we shall rest.

In the vision of our creator, we declare ourselves ready to stand proudly among the nationalities of these United States of America.

(Steiner, 1968, p. 15)

Deloria and Lytle (1984, p. 183) speak of the years between 1945 and 1965 as the barren years. The Bureau of Indian Affairs was stripped of its most effective personnel during the war, and the effects of the financial cost of the war were evident in many ways on the reservations. The war had been costly, and funds for domestic programs, including Indian programs, were dramatically reduced.

Indian support of the war had been pervasive; throughout the country Indian nations sent warriors to every battlefront and workers to the aircraft plants, shipyards, and to other industries and jobs that bolstered the war efforts. This exodus of the strong, young, and talented people meant that vigorous and youthful Indian leadership was absent, leaving only the children and the respected elders at home on the reservations. Without the strong leadership of the young, tribal governments were weakened.

Traditional ways were also altered. After the war, Indian lives were never quite the same, on or off the reservations. Many people stayed in their new jobs in the cities. They had experienced success, independence, acceptance, and the vagaries of the white world. They were not willing to acquiesce to the petty rules and regulations of reservation life; they knew the importance of education and vocational training, and, more importantly, many had learned how to survive in another, non-Indian world. Many came home to visit briefly, returning to the cities where they were more likely to find work and have more independence.

The policy of termination was the conservative position of the government following the war. As an outcome of war and termination (or the threat of termination), Native people became acutely aware of how slender was the thread that supported self-determination. The demands of the outside world, legislative acts, and shady politics could so easily terminate tribal governments and destroy the economic bases of traditional lifeways. Thus, it was during the 1950s, when termination was so threatening, that the concept of nationhood and Indian activism began to take root.

President Johnson's War on Poverty, under the Office of Economic Opportunity, provided major sums of money to tribal governments from a wide variety of federal agencies and had significant impact on Indian people. The philosophy of the Office of Economic Opportunity was that the poor should develop and manage the programs that were designed for them. This philosophy seemed to encourage tribal self-determination and the funds that were made available were very popular with Native American people.

In recent years, it has been pointed out that these programs were not developed and managed by the tribal governments; they were merely acting on behalf of the federal agency with whom they had contracted. Thus, most of the important decisions were not those of the tribes but belonged to the federal government. Self-determination was not a reality; the tribes simply acted on behalf of the government.

In 1961, a national conference sponsored by the National Congress of American Indians and anthropologists from the University of Chicago was held in Chicago. Perhaps the importance of the conference and the statement issued by those who attended was that it directed attention to unfilled treaty rights. However, though the statement appeared to present a strong voice in Indian destiny, it really did not express the deep, long-standing concerns of most Native peoples. Young Indian leaders began to meet together to assert their thoughts and beliefs. These concerns were subsequently given voice by a newly formed National Indian Youth Council (NIYC) which set as its goal the restoration of Indian pride.

> Although the NIYC began slowly, its message to Indians was unmistakable: Indians were no longer to bow their heads in humble obedience to the Bureau of Indian Affairs or the institutions of white society. The NIYC called upon Indians to look back at their own great cultural traditions and make decisions based on the values they had always represented. The Indian counterpart to Collier's idea of self-government had finally found its voice and was beginning to develop its ideology (Deloria and Lytle, 1984, p. 198).

The voice of the leaders of the NIYC was an assertive voice prepared for action, and it became the call for Indian activism. Steiner (1968) spoke of this new generation of young university-educated Indians as the "New Indians" who "have given voice to a human morality and tribal philosophy of life that melded the ancient with the modern." This voice is heard in the "Declaration of the Five County Cherokees" and in the words of Vine Deloria, Jr.

Our ideas will overcome your ideas. We are going to cut the country's whole value system to shreds. It isn't important that there are only 500,000 of us Indians ... What is important is that we have a superior way of life. We Indians have a more human philosophy of life. We Indians will show this country how to act human. Someday this country will revise its constitution, its laws, in terms of human beings, instead of property. If Red Power is to be a power in this country it is because it is ideological ... What is the ultimate value of a man's life? That is the question (McLuhan, 1971, p. 159).

It is well to remember that strident voices were heard from many groups during the 1960s. The nation stirred with unrest; fringe groups, ethnic and racial minorities, and women, supported by traditionally conservative groups such as the clergy, demanded their human and civil rights. This strong Indian voice had company and support in these times—their voices were among many others voices of protest. One of the first major efforts of Indian activism was the American Indian Movement (AIM) which was formed in Minneapolis in 1968. Initially, its purpose was to patrol the streets to prevent by their presence police brutality against Indian people. Ultimately, they became one of the most influential organizations in the rise of Indian political activism.

In 1968, President Johnson called for the establishment of the National Council on Indian Opportunity, to be chaired by the vice president and to include Indian leaders. He suggested that termination be replaced by Indian self-determination. This office was established in 1969, and in 1970 a federal policy of Indian self-determination was formulated.

THE AMERICAN INDIAN CIVIL RIGHTS ACT

The American Indian Civil Rights Act (ICRA) of 1968 was, in part, a response to the confusion caused by Public Law 280. This was the law that allowed most western states to assume jurisdiction over civil and criminal matters on the reservations without the consent of the tribes. Because PL 280 was so vague, it caused nothing but confusion and resentment.

Native people rightly believed that the law interfered with their tribal governments. The states were unwilling to assume the responsibilities of jurisdiction

without the support of federal funds or funds generated from the tribes in the form of taxes. Congress and the courts would not allow taxation of Indian property and protected Indian tax immunities. As a result, the states often refused to provide the protection of law enforcement. Tribes and individuals were left without the appropriate protection of the law.

The Civil Rights Act seemed as though it was necessary to eliminate the confusion created by PL 280 and to restore a system of law and order to the reservations. It is fairly simple to reiterate the provisions of the Civil Rights Act. The ICRA accomplished the following:

1. It extended the provisions of the Bill of Rights to reservation Indians.
2. It ruled that the states could not assume law and order jurisdiction on reservations without the consent of tribes.
3. It restricted tribal governments in the same way federal and state governments are restricted.

The introduction to the American Indian Civil Rights Handbook (1980) is useful in clarifying the intricacies of the ICRA.

Indians, like others, are entitled to...constitutional protections in regard to actions by Federal, State, and local governments. Most of the constitutional protections of individual rights do not, however, apply to the operations of tribal governments. Neither Indians nor non-Indians have the same rights with respect to tribal governments that they both have with respect to Federal, State, and local governments. Most of the rights that exist with respect to tribal governments come from either tribal constitutions or the Indian Civil Rights Act of 1968.

Many have felt that Congress should not have regulated Indian tribes by the Indian Civil Rights Act or similar legislation. These people argue that such regulation infringes on tribal sovereignty and imposes the values of United States culture on Indian cultures. Congress, however, only accepted this point of view to a very limited extent and did impose regulations—The Indian Civil Rights Act—on the conduct of the tribes.... The rights guaranteed to individuals by the Indian Civil Rights Act are similar, but not identical, to the rights provided by the Bill of Rights and the 14th amendment of the United States Constitution.

It would appear that the dangerous effects of PL 280 had been resolved, and perhaps, in some ways, they had, but the price was high for Indian people. The long-term impact was damaging, and the infringement on tribal sovereignty had serious consequences. The traditional ways that governed such things as real or perceived wrongs between people were now replaced by rigid requirements that identified which actions of the tribal government had impinged upon the rights of tribal members. The traditional ways of governing, of controlling the behavior of tribal members, were replaced by the ways of the white society. Traditional Indian society operated as a complex of responsibilities and duties. The ICRA changed this into a society based on rights against government and thus eliminated the traditional sense of responsibility that tribal members had for each other.

Generally, the ICRA was seen as a major step toward self-determination, but its hidden effects need to be considered in this assessment. The loss of tribal governments to settle some issues in the traditional ways will have a significant impact in the days to come—it was a major issue in the occupation of Wounded Knee.

THE RISE OF INDIAN ACTIVISM

In the beginning it was difficult to organize tribal groups for political action in a concerted and cooperative way; tribes tended to consider only their own tribal conditions and concerns before they would take action. Unity was nearly impossible as long as the traditional people primarily thought in terms of individual tribes.

The rise in the population in urban areas began to change this. Those Indian people who clustered together in the urban areas, and for whom it was not only necessary to band together, but easier as well, began to form a sense of pan-Indianism, common concerns and purposes, and, ultimately, powerful political alliances that brought about unity of action. Red power began to be a political reality.

Occupation of Alcatraz Island

On November 20, 1969, Indian people occupied Alcatraz Island in the San Francisco Bay and created "Indian Country." They declared that they were claiming the island for Indians and facetiously offered to buy it for slightly more than the twenty-four dollars worth of beads that the Europeans paid for Manhattan Island. The leaders, using the designation of Indians of All Tribes, proposed to turn the abandoned prison into an Indian cultural and educational center.

There was much media and public support for this effort of Indian unity. The federal government made no overt effort to dislodge them, but it did cut off electricity and water. According to the Indians, this certainly made the island seem more like a reservation.

The government made an alternative proposal to the Indians that offered to make Alcatraz a national park with an Indian theme and an Indian name and to give Indians preference in hiring personnel for the park. The offer was refused. Poor living conditions, social problems, and bickering ultimately weakened the occupation effort and after nineteen months, with only fifteen Indians left on the island, U.S. marshalls ended the occupation.

The occupation of Alcatraz was primarily symbolic; the war in southeast Asia consumed much of the public interest, and the Indians did not have the means to carry out their plans for the island. However, it is important to be aware of the power of the symbolism of Alcatraz. In *Alcatraz! Alcatraz!*, one of the most interesting, authentic, and readable accounts of the occupation, Adam Fortunate Eagle summarizes this symbolism with the following statement.

> Yet the most lasting result of Alcatraz may have been the growth of Indian pride throughout the country. News of the occupation swept through Indian communities; our continued resistance inspired wonder and pride. After decades of indignity and soul-sickening powerlessness beyond the understanding of any non-Indian, a group of Indians had seized an island in full view of millions and held it for nineteen months despite government efforts to destroy them. Everywhere, American Indians rejoiced (Fortunate Eagle, 1992, p. 150).

Trail of Broken Treaties Caravan

The Trail of Broken Treaties—press statement issued October 31, 1972:

> We need not give another recitation of past complaints nor engage in redundant dialogue of discontent. Our conditions and their cause for being

should perhaps be best known by those who have written the record of America's action against Indian People. In 1832, Black Hawk correctly observed: "You know the cause of our making war. It is known to all white men. They ought to be ashamed of it."

The government of the United States knows the reasons for our going to its capital city. Unfortunately, they don't know how to greet us ... We go because America has been only too ready to express its shame, and suffer none from the expression—while remaining wholly unwilling to change to allow life for Indian people. ...

We seek a new American majority—a majority that is not content merely to confirm itself by superiority in numbers, but which by conscience is committed toward prevailing upon the public will in ceasing wrongs and in doing right. For our part, in words and deeds of coming days, we propose to produce a rational, reasoned manifesto for construction of an Indian future in America. If America has maintained faith with its original spirit, or may recognize it now, we should not be denied (*Trail of Broken Treaties*, 1974, p. 3).

In the late summer and early fall of 1972, Indian leaders gathered on the Rosebud Sioux Reservation to discuss a way by which they could inform both the Democratic and Republican parties of the problems faced by Indian people and elicit from them, in that election year, concrete commitments for change. Led primarily by leaders of the American Indian Movement, it was decided to plan a pilgrimage to the nation's capital. Eight prominent Indian organizations were involved in the planning, and four others endorsed the purposes and plans for the "Trail of Broken Treaties" march to Washington. The intent was not violence. Co-chairman, Robert Burnette made the following eloquent statement at the conclusion of the planning sessions:

We should be on our finest behavior. We must ban all alcohol and drugs, with expulsions guaranteed to violators. If we can't take all the poor and the elderly and the despairing with us, then they should be with us in our minds. Today, Indian identity is defined and refined by a quality and a special degree of suffering. The Caravan must be our finest hour (*Trail of Broken Treaties*, 1974, p. 3).

Plans were made for caravans to leave Seattle, Los Angeles, and San Francisco; another left from Oklahoma, tracing the infamous "Trail of Tears." The caravans were to converge in St. Paul, Minnesota, where the people of the caravans would attend a national convention of the American Indian Movement, plan the schedule, and draft a set of goals. It was anticipated that 150,000 Indian people would be in Washington.

In St. Paul a document of twenty points was developed outlining the changes that were needed in federal policy. According to Deloria and Lytle (1984, p. 238), the first eight points, which dealt with the restoration of a treaty relationship with the United States, described a coherent process that the Indians wished to initiate.

The process also included restoring a constitutional treaty-making authority, establishing a commission to make new treaties, creating a commission to review treaty commitments and violations and to ensure justice with regard to the violations of treaty rights, resubmitting unratified treaties to the Senate, recognizing the legal right of Indians to interpret treaties, and address their right to the American people and Congress. The treaty relationship then would be flexible and just. The address to the American people was to ensure that the treaty process would be open and not deadlocked in bureaucracy.

The remaining points dealt with such issues as land and religious freedom, and would begin to reverse the damage done by previous governmental policies. These powerful twenty points would not only be economically sound but would also encourage Indians on the reservations to become more self-determining.

From the first moment of arrival in Washington, things did not go well for the people of the caravans. They were refused a police escort, the building that had been promised to house them was overrun with rats, and their requests to hold religious services at three Arlington Cemetery sites were rejected as conflicting with regulations. Officials ordered their subordinates not to cooperate with the Indian personnel. The people had no place to stay and federal officials would not talk to them. Urgent discussions began—to find food and housing and to arrange to present to the federal government the twenty demands that had been developed in St. Paul.

What ultimately turned this situation into a violent takeover of the building that housed the BIA was an unanticipated event. At 4 P.M. the security guards in the Bureau of Indian Affairs building changed shifts, and one lieutenant began to try to clear all Indians from his area. The Indians who were awaiting news of the negotiations refused to leave and heavily armed guards were called. Confusion and hostility reigned and the Indians forcibly occupied the building and the focus changed from the twenty points to the occupation.

Ultimately, the Indian negotiators won from the White House an agreement to create a task force to review the twenty demands. The task force was to exist for six months and its charge was to review federal Indian policy. Membership of the task force was to include officers of all agencies dealing with Indians and was to include consultation with Indian representatives on a continuing basis regarding the twenty demands. Financial assistance was required for the Indians to return home.

The governmental estimate of damage created during the takeover of the BIA was over 2 million dollars; the Indians questioned this amount. Many other questions were also left to be answered. Was the Trail of Broken Treaties effective? Did it represent Indian people?

Many tribal leaders disassociated themselves from the destruction and violence of the occupation.

> Paul Tafoya, Santa Clara Pueblo—That group does not actually represent the Indian tribes. The true representatives of the Indian people are located right on the Indian reservations.

> Southern Ute Tribal Council—(We) wish to express grave concern regarding the actions of certain Indian groups who have taken over the BIA ... The Tribal Council feels that the actions of these Indian groups are irresponsible and that the take-over of the BIA demeans and otherwise degrades the dignity and respect of Indians in the United States (*Trail of Broken Treaties*, 1974, p. 23).

Others had a different perspective.

> Peter MacDonald, Chairman of the Navajo Tribal Council—Other tribal chiefs who complained about the demonstrators have failed to analyze what really caused our people to rise up in frustration....Similar situations are sure to occur if nothing is done in a positive way to correct the problems that Indians have been complaining about for 100 years (*Trail of Broken Treaties*, 1974, p. 38).

Perhaps the final word should be the message left by an unknown Indian on the movie screen in the BIA building.

> I do not apologize for the ruin nor for the so-called destruction of this mausoleum for in building anew, one must first destroy the old! When history recalls our efforts here, our descendants will stand with pride, knowing their people were the ones responsible for the stand taken against tyranny, injustice, and the gross inefficiency of this branch of a decadent government (*Trail of Broken Treaties*, 1974, p. 27).

Occupation of Wounded Knee—1973

In 1973 the conditions of the Oglala Sioux were deplorable. Not including the people who had left the reservation to find work, unemployment on the reservation had reached fifty-four percent. Half of those who worked were employed by the tribal government or the BIA. There was no industry and a third of the people were dependent on welfare or other pensions for their survival. Oglala life expectancy was forty-six years. Alcoholism and suicide were pervasive. The time was right for protest.

AIM announced a victory celebration to be held on the Pine Ridge Reservation in South Dakota when the people from that state returned home from the Trail of Broken Treaties. Tribal chairman, Richard Wilson, was in disfavor with many of the tribal people and had banned AIM leaders, including Russell Means, from the reservation. Wilson stated that he believed that AIM intended to overtake the BIA building at Pine Ridge. He asked for federal assistance and, in response, the federal government bolstered the tribal police force. Very quickly, tribal police began to harass those people who were believed to be members of AIM. As a protest against such treatment and other serious charges, the people started to demand the removal of the tribal chairman, Richard Wilson. (This is a good example of the loss of the ability to solve tribal disputes in traditional ways.) The governmental support of Wilson extended beyond reason allowing him to remain as chairman during his impeachment.

In frustration, the people retreated to Wounded Knee to make a stand in what was to become the Occupation of Wounded Knee.

The valley of Wounded Knee is round, and around the perimeter lie seven bunkers—Last Stand, Hawk Eye, Little Big Horn, Denby, Little California, Crow's Nest, and Star—built to defend the village from an assault by Federal forces (*Voices from Wounded Knee*, 1974, p. 70).

AIM and the Oglala Sioux of Wounded Knee demanded a change of tribal leaders, a review of all Indian treaties, and an investigation into the treatment of Indians. They were barricaded, well-armed, and determined to create the Oglala Nation as a sovereign nation.

The FBI, U.S. marshals, the BIA, and state police came together to form a sort of illegal federal army that ostensibly was there to assist the local police in protecting chairman Wilson and the BIA building. The United States, including the BIA, federal marshals, and the FBI, and the corrupt tribal government, created a siege with all of its attendant horrors—no food, inadequate sanitation, and poor medical supplies. Still the Indian people held out. Supplies did come to Wounded Knee through anti-war groups, humanitarian groups, and other Indian people. Two Indians were killed during the siege.

The occupation on the site of the Wounded Knee massacre of 1890 lasted for seventy-one days. In the end, the government still did not acknowledge Oglala sovereignty. However, the chiefs thought there had been some movement in that direction and that the occupation had been somewhat effective. "The Wounded Knee community was tired." It was time to move on—to work on other strategies.

The end of the occupation was to be a stand-down—both sides laying down their arms. On May 9, Wallace Black Elk spoke to the people in the small church kitchen that had been the hub of the occupation. Breakfast had been prepared from the emergency food supply and the people gathered around the drum to sing the AIM song.

We have come to understanding, all of us.
white, black, yellow, and us red people.
I thank the powers of the four winds,
and to the Grandfather, Great Spirit,
and I thank the sacred Mother Earth, Grand-
    mother.
Thank you.
I ask you and bless all people here,
from the powers of the four winds,
and Grandfather, Great Spirit, we thank
    you this day
that we are alive.
Grandmother we thank you for keeping us
    alive.
Grandmother we stand here on your lap
    and once again
you cradle us in your arms, and feed us, and
    comfort us,
and heal us and forgive us.
    Mitakaye Oyasin—all my relations.

(Wallace Black Elk as cited in *Voices from Wounded Knee*, 1973–1974, p. 240).

Again, the occupation of Wounded Knee was historic and symbolic for Indian people; they experienced the power of unity and the taste of freedom.

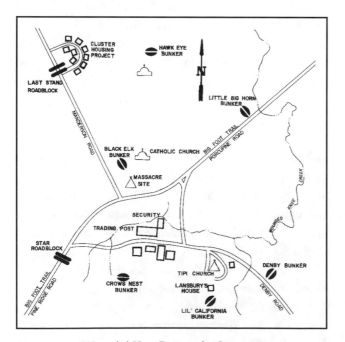

Map 15.1—Wounded Knee During the Occupation.

I think that everybody that was in there had a taste of freedom—what freedom is really about. And that put a deep impression on everybody that was in there.

Throughout their life they'll always remember this, that "I was free," at one time (*Voices from Wounded Knee*, 1973–1974, pp. 170–171).

INDIAN EDUCATION: A NATIONAL TRAGEDY—A NATIONAL CHALLENGE

In November 1969, a major report on Indian education was issued. This report "Indian Education: A National Tragedy—A National Challenge," has often been called the Kennedy Report because it was initiated in 1967 by Robert Kennedy. It is said that Kennedy was seeking to create a position for his presidential ambition by focusing national attention on civil rights issues. After the assassination of Robert Kennedy, the chairmanship of this subcommittee of the Senate Education Committee was eventually assumed by his brother, Edward Kennedy.

The subcommittee gathered an enormous amount of information not only on Indian education and the aspirations of Indian parents and communities for their children, but also on the social and economic environments in which Indian children lived and went to school. The title of the final report is a comprehensive summary of the social and economic conditions that impacted the lives of Indian children and on the education they were provided.

Sixty wide-ranging recommendations were made by the subcommittee and can be summarized as follows:

1. Indian people should control their educational institutions.
2. Indians need more education—at every level.
3. Funding should be increased for Indian education.

As could be expected, Indian people were pleased with the recommendations. So, what was the catch? The report was based primarily on the assumption that the education wanted and needed by Indian communities was the same kind of education that served all of America's schools—education for white, middle-class Americans. It did not propose a new and comprehensive reorganization of Indian educational programs to meet the specific needs of Indian children and communities. Rather, the basic premise promised more of what had not been working.

With strong Indian support, the Indian Education Act of 1972 was passed. The basic philosophy of education was not changed, but Indians were given more direct access to funds for operating their school programs.

Several Indian education groups were formed to work on the recommendations of the report and one of the provisions of the Indian Education Act was the creation of the National Advisory Council on Indian Education (NACIE). The intent of the legislation was to provide an informed and experienced body of Indian people who would provide oversight and direction for the future of Indian education. The council became a political issue—an Indian political issue and a national political issue—resulting in an ineffective council with divided loyalty. NACIE operates today with the same concerns and limitations.

LESSON PLAN:
THE OCCUPATION OF ALCATRAZ ISLAND

Grade Level: Middle school

Basic Concepts: Power and conflict

Organizing Generalization: Conflict can be used to influence public policy and lead to social and political change.

Culture Area: General

Time Period: The occupation of Alcatraz Island—1969

Background: Indian people seized control of Alcatraz Island in 1969 in an effort to draw attention to the problems of Indian people and in the hope that the occupation would influence the public and the government and bring change in a variety of forms. Their proclamation is a somewhat humorous statement on the historical treatment of Native people and their current condition and problems.

Objectives:

Knowledge

Students will:

1. Discuss the intention of the Indian occupation of Alcatraz Island.
2. Demonstrate knowledge of some of the important events and promises in Indian history that are expressed in the Alcatraz Proclamation.
3. Describe the conditions of most reservations in 1969.
4. Explain the impact of the occupation.

Skills

Students will:

1. Work in teams to research particular topics and report on their research.
2. Use evidence to support conclusions.

Values

Students will:

1. Understand the frustration and anger of Indian people.
2. Appreciate Indian humor.

Activities:

1. Present the Alcatraz Proclamation to the class on an overhead. Prepare an overhead with a map of the San Francisco Bay area and an additional overhead with a map of Alcatraz Island. Make certain students understand the facetious nature of the proclamation. Discuss the demands made by the Indians (Indian cultural and educational center).
2. Through discussion determine how much students understand the document, making a list of what words or phrases need to be clarified through research. For example, "in perpetuity—for as long as the sun shall rise and the rivers go down to the sea."
3. Divide the class into four research teams to gather information on the following areas: (a) the historical aspects alluded to in the proclamation, (b) the condition of the reservations during this period of time, (c)

life on the island during the occupation, and (d) the response of the public and the federal government.

4. Each of the four groups should prepare a brief ten- to fifteen-minute presentation to the class.
5. Discuss the final days of Alcatraz and the removal of the Indians.
6. Ask students to individually prepare a statement on the effectiveness of the occupation and support their statements with information from the presentations.

Extensions:
1. Research other incidents of civil disobedience during this period of time.
2. Interview leaders of the American Indian Movement regarding the purpose and effect of demonstrations and civil disobedience.

Evaluation: Students will demonstrate understanding of the importance of the occupation of Alcatraz in their individual statements.

Materials/Resources:
A collection of resource material should be made available for students. It will take some effort to gather appropriate materials that present an Indian perspective. *Alcatraz! Alcatraz!* by Adam Fortunate Eagle is an excellent book.

Fortunate Eagle, A. *Alcatraz! Alcatraz!* Berkeley, CA: Heydey Books, 1992.

PROCLAMATION:
TO THE GREAT WHITE FATHER AND ALL HIS PEOPLE

We the native Americans, reclaim the land known as Alcatraz Island in the name of all American Indians by right of discovery.

We wish to be fair and honorable in our dealings with the Caucasian inhabitants of this land, and hereby offer the following treaty:

We will purchase said Alcatraz Island for twenty-four dollars ($24) in glass beads and red cloth, a precedent set by the white man's purchase of a similar island about 300 years ago. We know that $24 in trade goods for these 16 acres is more than was paid when Manhattan Island was sold, but we know that land values have risen over the years. Our offer of $1.24 per acre is greater than the 47 cents per acre that the white men are now paying the California Indians for their land. We will give to the inhabitants of this island a portion of that land for their own, to be held in trust by the American Indian Affairs and by the Bureau of Caucasian Affairs to hold in perpetuity—for as long as the sun shall rise and the rivers go down to the sea. We will further guide the inhabitants in the proper way of living. We will offer them our religion, our education, our life-ways, in order to help them achieve our level of civilization and thus raise them and all their white brothers up from their savage and unhappy state. We offer this treaty in good faith and wish to be fair and honorable in our dealings with all white men....

We feel that this so-called Alcatraz Island is more than suitable for an Indian Reservation, as determined by the white man's own standards. By this we mean that this place resembles most Indian reservations in that:

1. It is isolated from modern facilities and without adequate means of transportation.
2. It has no fresh running water.
3. It has inadequate sanitation facilities.
4. There are no oil or mineral rights.
5. There is no industry and so unemployment is very great.
6. There are no health care facilities.

7. The soil is rocky and nonproductive; and the land does not support game.
8. There are no educational facilities.
9. The population has always exceeded the land base.
10. The population has always been held as prisoners and kept dependent upon others.

Further, it would be fitting and symbolic that ships from all over the world, entering the Golden Gate, would first see Indian land, and thus be reminded of the true history of this nation. This tiny island would be a symbol of the great lands once ruled by free and noble Indians.

(McLuhan, T. C. *Touch the Earth*. New York: Touchstone, 1971, pp. 164–165. Also in Fortunate Eagle pp. 44–46.)

LESSON PLAN:
THE OCCUPATION OF WOUNDED KNEE

Grade Level: Middle school

Basic Concepts: Civil disobedience, sovereignty, and redress

Organizing Generalization: Organized groups attempt to influence public policy when they believe that such policy will affect their goals. Civil disobedience, a form of overt and planned conflict, is one method that groups use in their effort to influence policy.

Culture Area: Plains

Time Period: The Occupation of Wounded Knee—1973

Background: The occupation of Wounded Knee on the Pine Ridge Reservation in South Dakota was an important event in recent Indian history. Although the demands of the Indian people centered around the Treaty of 1868 and the concept of sovereign Indian nations, other issues were also presented. These issues include poverty, unemployment, corruption in tribal government, social problems, health care, and education. It is important that students recognize that Indian people were making a stand for dignity and freedom and that this was and is symbolized by their right, by treaty, to sovereignty.

Objectives:

Knowledge
Students will:
1. State in their own words the meaning of the Treaty of 1868.
2. Summarize why Indian people in 1973 wanted the U.S. government to honor the treaty.
3. Summarize the position of the U.S. government regarding the treaty.
4. Define the term "sovereignty."

Skills
Students will:
1. Use research and analytical skills to review the formation of tribal governments under the Indian Reorganization Act.
2. Use reasoned supporting statements to support their personal stand on the statement of the Iroquois Confederacy.

Values
Students will:
1. Make a personal decision regarding whether or not they support the statement of the Iroquois Confederacy.
2. Examine how important freedom and respect is to all people, including themselves.

Activities:
1. Prepare students by locating Wounded Knee on a map and by reviewing with them the Trail of Broken Treaties and occupation of the Bureau of Indian Affairs building in Washington. It is also important students understand the concept of sovereign nation and how a dependent sovereign nation would interact with the U.S. government in a nation-to-nation relationship.

2. As a class, review the Indian Reorganization Act and Treaty of 1868 (see Appendix G).
3. Assign small teams to research what changes would occur if the people of Wounded Knee were to become a part of an Independent Oglala Nation.
4. Using an overhead transparency or chart compile a list of the changes that students suggest.
5. Review and discuss the statement of support offered by the Iroquois Confederacy. Why did the Oglala ask for support from the Iroquois? What was the statement designed to achieve? Why does the statement support the concept of sovereignty?
6. Ask students to make a list of the information they would need to make a reasoned decision as to whether or not they would, personally, support the statement of the Iroquois. What information would they need from the past? the present?
7. After gathering the information they need, including class discussions and independent or cooperative research, each student will write a personal statement, using reasoned and supported statements, as to whether or not they would support the statement of the Iroquois Confederacy.

Extensions:
1. Two very young Indian men lost their lives at Wounded Knee. Write a brief personal essay discussing the values you hold and those for which you would be willing to bear arms, challenge the law or the government, or lose your life.
2. Research the lives, contributions, and controversies surrounding such Indian activists as Russell Means and Dennis Banks.
3. Study the occupation of Wounded Knee in more depth—seek a variety of source materials.
4. Develop a personal journal as an Indian participant, media correspondent, or government agent during the occupation.
5. Inquire of *Akwesasne Notes* how it might support the effort to reprint the *Voices from Wounded Knee*, the book that presents the Indian perspective on the occupation.

Evaluation: Students' personal statements should demonstrate understanding of the concept of sovereignty and the concerns of Indian people for freedom and respect.

Materials/Resources:
The book, *Voices from Wounded Knee*, is the best resource available from the Indian perspective on the occupation of Wounded Knee. Unfortunately, it is out of print, and the publisher, *Akwesasne Notes*, is seeking funds to reprint the book. It is worth searching interlibrary loan services and other resources to locate this book.
Voices from Wounded Knee. Rooseveltown, NY: *Akwesasne Notes*, Mohawk Nation, 1974.

Let It Be Known This Day, March 11, 1973, That the Oglala Sioux People Will

Revive the Treaty of 1868 and that it will be the basis for all negotiations.

Let the declaration be made that we are a sovereign nation by the Treaty of 1868.

We intend to send a delegation to the United Nations as follows: Chief Frank Fools Crow; Chief Frank Kills Enemy; Eugene White Hawk, District Chairman (of the Wounded Knee District Council); Meredith Quinn, international advisor; Matthew King, interpreter ...

... [We want] to abolish the Tribal Government under the Indian Reorganization Act. Wounded Knee will be a corporate state under the Independent Oglala Nation.

In proclaiming the Independent Oglala Nation, the first nation to be called for support and recognition is the [Iroquois] Six Nation Confederacy. [We] request that the Confederacy send emissaries to this newly proclaimed nation immediately to receive first-hand all the facts pertaining to this act ...

(*Voices from Wounded Knee*, 1974, p. 55)

Statement Sent by the Grand Council of the Iroquois Six Nation Confederacy to the U.S. Government

The Six Nation Iroquois Confederacy stands in support of our brothers at Wounded Knee ...

We are a free people. The very dust of our ancestors is steeped in our tradition. This is the greatest gift we gave to you, the concept of freedom. You did not have this. Now that you have taken it and built a constitution and country around it, you deny freedom to us. There must be some one among you who is concerned for us, or if not for us, at least for the honor of your country.

... The solution is simple: be honest, be fair, honor the commitments made by the founding fathers of your country. We are an honorable people—can you say the same? You are concerned for the destruction of property at the BIA building and at Wounded Knee. Where is your concern for the destruction of our people, for human lives? Thousands of Pequots, Narragansetts, Mohicans, thousands of Cherokees on the Trail of Tears, Black Hawk's people, Chief Joseph's people, Captain Jack's people, the Navajos, the Apaches, Sand Creek Massacre (huddled under the American flag seeking the protection of a promise), Big Foot's people at Wounded Knee. When will you cease your violence against our people? Where is your concern for us?

... The balance of the ledger is up to you. Compare the damage of the BIA and Wounded Knee against the terrible record and tell us that we are wrong for wanting redress. We ask for justice, and not from the muzzle of an M-16 rifle. Now what is to occur?

... We have not asked you to give up your religions and beliefs for ours.
We have not asked you to give up your language for ours.
We have not asked you to give up your ways of life for ours.
We have not asked you to give up your government for ours.
We have not asked that you give up your territories to us.

Why can you not accord us with the same respect? For your children learn from watching their elders, and if you want your children to do what is right, then it is up to you to set the example. That is all we have to say at this moment. Oneh

(Voices from Wounded Knee, 1974, pp. 94–95)

SUMMARY
TRIBAL RESTORATION, PHASE TWO: 1968–1975

The years between 1945 and 1965 have often been called the barren years. The nation was recovering from the war. Funds for domestic programs including Indian programs had been reduced. The war also deeply affected tribal governments when they lost the strong leadership of their young to war efforts.

One of the outcomes of termination (or the threat of termination) was the recognition that self-determination for Indian people was tentative and always threatened. During this time the concept of nationhood and Indian activism began to form.

Young Indian leaders began to meet together to speak of their thoughts and beliefs. They formed the National Indian Youth Council which set as its goal the restoration of Indian pride. The voice of the leaders of this group was an assertive voice, prepared for action, and became the call for Indian activism. One of the first major efforts of Indian activism was the American Indian Movement (AIM) formed in Minneapolis in 1968. AIM became one of the most influential and visible organizations in the rise of Indian political activism.

The American Indian Civil Rights Act (ICRA) was passed in 1968, extending the provision of the Bill of Rights to reservation Indians. It ruled that the states could not assume law and order jurisdiction on reservations without the consent of tribes, and it restricted tribal governments in the same way federal and state governments are restricted.

This was the time of the occupation of Alcatraz Island, which claimed the island for Indians and offered to buy it for slightly more that twenty-four dollars' worth of beads, and the Train of Broken Treaties Caravan in 1972. These actions focused on developing Indian unity of purpose and pride and bringing the critical issues of Indian people to the public.

TIME LINE: 1968–1974

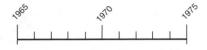

1968

Civil Rights Act extended provisions of the Bill of Rights to reservation Indians; decreed that the states cannot assume law and order jurisdiction on reservations without the consent of tribes; and restricted tribal governments in the same way federal and state governments are restricted.

1968

American Indian Movement (AIM) was founded in Minneapolis.

1968

President Johnson called for the establishment of the National Council on Indian Opportunity to be chaired by the vice president and to include Indian leaders. He suggested that termination should be replaced by Indian self-determination.

1968

Navajo Community College, the first four-year college on a reservation, was chartered in Arizona.

1968

The Mohawks of St. Regis, Ontario, attempted to block the St. Lawrence Seaway International Bridge to protest the Canadian government's failure to honor the treaty that guaranteed the Mohawks unrestricted travel between Canada and the United States. The right to travel across the border was honored after this demonstration.

1969

Indians occupied Alcatraz Island in San Francisco Bay. The occupation lasted until 1971.

1969

AMERIND was founded to protect Indian rights and improve Indian working conditions.

1969

Indian Task Force (thirty-six tribes) opposed federal termination policy in response to the Department of the Interior statements that Indians were overprotected by trust status of reservations.

1969

Josephy Report on federal Indian policy argued against termination.

1969

Kennedy Report on Indian Education recommended greater Indian self-determination.

1969

Environmental Policy Act was enacted to protect Indian resources.

1969

National Council on Indian Opportunity was created in the office of the vice president.

1969

Court upheld land "freeze" order of the Secretary of the Interior on behalf of Indians.

1970

A federal policy of Indian self-determination was formulated.

1970

Blue Lake Wilderness Area in New Mexico was returned to Taos Pueblo.

1971

Model Urban Indian Center program was created by federal government to provide essential services for urban Indians.

1972

Trail of Broken Treaties Caravan (organized by AIM) developed a position paper concerning the plight of Indians and marched on Washington. Demonstrators occupied and destroyed offices of the BIA.

1972

More than one thousand Sioux protested the death by suicide ruling in a racial incident in Gordon, Nebraska. Officials were forced to perform an autopsy, and the verdict was changed to manslaughter. Two of the white vigilante killers were convicted.

1972

Indian Education Act was passed to provide educational programs for Indians.

1972

State and Local Fiscal Assistance Act provided loans for Indians.

1973

On the Pine Ridge Reservation in South Dakota, AIM and armed Oglala Sioux occupied the site of the Wounded Knee massacre of 1890 for seventy-one days. They demanded a change of tribal leaders, a review of all Indian treaties, and an investigation into the treatment of Indians. Two Indians were killed in the siege.

1974

A group of Mohawks occupied Eagle Bay at Moss Lake in the Adirondacks, claiming original title to it, and founded Ganienkeh, the "Land of Flintstone."

1974

The first trial stemming from the occupation of Wounded Knee took place in Minnesota.

1974

Indian Financing Act provided loans to Indians for business projects.

1974

Navajo-Hopi Land Settlement Act tried to resolve dispute between the two tribes.

1974

Housing and Community Development Act provided Indian housing.

CHAPTER 16

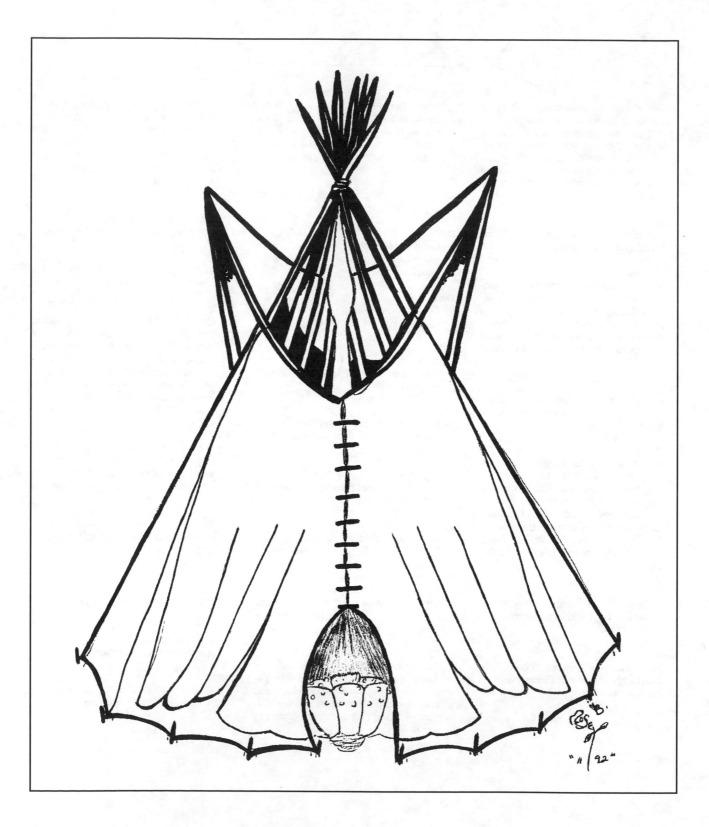

Tribal Restoration, Phase Two Continued: 1975–Present

A people's dream died at Wounded Knee.
The nation's hoop is broken and scattered.
There is no center any longer, and the
sacred tree is dead.

Black Elk, Oglala Medicine Man

This is the tale of Wanbli Numpa Afraid of Hawk, an eight year old Oglala Lakota who rode the final year of the Big Foot Memorial Ride.

But even after all these years our people were still in pain from Wounded Knee, my dad said, and he wanted to do something to help. So five years ago, he went with my uncles, Alex White Plume and Birgil Kills Straight, to see a medicine man named Curtis Kills Ree. They asked Curtis what could be done to end the Lakota's sadness.

The medicine man told them that the massacre had broken the sacred hoop of the world. The hoop is the unity of all life for the Lakota. When our people were killed at Wounded Knee, there was such sadness that the Lakota people lost their way for one hundred years. They forgot how to be strong together as a tribe. To mend the sacred hoop, he said, my dad and uncles had to take horses and wagons on the same path Big Foot and his people traveled. They had to leave at the same time Big Foot left, travel the same way his people did, sleep in the same places, and feel the same cold. They had to do this five times for five years. The last year would be the one hundredth anniversary of the massacre, and then the hoop would be mended. The journeys would wipe away the tears of sadness so that Lakota children , like me, could lead the Lakotas as one tribe into the future.

The first four winters, I watched my dad leave with our horses for the ride. I wanted to go so much, but I was too young. It was a hard and dangerous ride. But in the winter of 1990, I was eight years old and I was strong enough to go. For four years I had prepared for this and now it was time to become a man. Three months before the ride, I told my mother and dad I wanted to go because this was the last ride and the one hundredth anniversary, and I wanted to pray for our ancestors who died.

In the old days Lakota boys took tests to become men. They had to shoot arrows at targets, hunt bison, or steal horses from the enemy. Now, the Big Foot ride was my test and I made a sacred promise to finish the ride. My dad was very proud and so was my mother, but she was worried because I was her only boy.

I was scared too. But I though that if my great lala did it when he was a boy, so could I …The prayers helped me. We came over the top of the ridge and looked down at Wounded Knee Creek. I could see hundreds of people there waiting to honor us. I felt really proud. The wind was biting me, but now I knew I could make it. We rode down the road and lots of cars followed behind us. 'We rode to Big Foot's grave and made a big circle next to it. Uncle Birgil said a prayer thanking the spirits for our safety and a prayer to the ancestors who were killed...

On December 29, 1890, Big Foot and his people were killed at Wounded Knee. Exactly one hundred years later, the day after the ride, we went back to the grave site to honor the dead. We were all stiff and tired from the ride, but we got on our horses again for the ceremony. Hundreds of Lakota people were there to listen and watch. … Birgil prayed with sage in the center and I could feel the suffering around me. There were women covered with blankets crying near the ancestors' graves. I saw how much everyone was hurt for the last hundred years. But I also felt very proud. I rode a difficult ride, was bucked off, and got cold, but I hung in there. I was a Big Foot rider now, not a little kid. … When I get older I want to tell my children and grandchildren about Wounded Knee and how we mended the sacred hoop. I will never forget the Si Tanka Wokiksuye (The Big Foot Memorial Ride).

(Used by permission of T. Wood, with Afraid of Hawk, W. N. *A Boy Becomes a Man at Wounded Knee*. New York: Walker, 1992.)

While the years before 1975 seemed to hold incredible change, only few would realize how the 1970s would change the future for all American Indians. Young Indian people attended college for the first time in the late 1960s and early 1970s. They graduated into professional fields including law, medicine, engineering, and education. During the coming years these newly educated Indians would take the lead in the courts, battling for the "promises" that were made to Indian people and tribes for over three hundred years. Indian educators would operate schools that would address not only the English language and basic skills for survival and success in the modern world, but also the wisdom of the elders and the American Indian language and culture. Indian physicians would begin to help heal the physical wounds of being a conquered people, and prepare the way for a new future, combining the wisdom of the past healers and modern medicine. Indian engineers and lawyers would guide their tribes in the use of their natural resources and technology. They would protect the tribe and determine how best to develop the land.

This new leadership within Indian Country enabled Indian people to finally act on the determination of their destiny instead of reacting to actions made by the U.S. Congress and its administrative arm, the Bureau of Indian Affairs. The newly educated leadership would take their battles to the halls of Congress, introducing legislation supporting rights for Indian individuals and tribes. They would argue in court to establish positive precedents for upholding the legislation. The 1970s and 1980s are two decades characterized by Indian people taking a self-determining role in their futures. Indian people throughout the country began to talk about their oppression and to face the challenge head on to change the course of events of the last century. Times were changing.

THE INDIAN SELF-DETERMINATION ACT OF 1975

Perhaps the most important single piece of legislation that marked the shift from imposing policy to self-determining policy is the Indian Self-Determination Act of 1975. This act allows tribes to administer all federal programs on the reservation. The act also allowed tribes to structure themselves in whatever way they saw fit, rather than as set forth in the Reorganization Act of 1934.

Since the late 1800s, much of the process of caring for extended family members, providing food, clothing, and shelter, and other life necessities had fallen to the Bureau of Indian Affairs and other outside agencies. This was, of course, because the normal livelihood of the various Indian tribes had been taken away by the U.S. government. The Indian Self-Determination Act began to give these responsibilities back to the tribes. The Act enables the tribes to manage their own schools, tribal administrations, law enforcement, housing, health, social services, and community development programs. It changed the role of the tribes and American Indian individuals as it created more opportunity for Indian people to determine their own destiny and provide for their own people.

The act also encouraged more tribes to organize and to begin receiving federal support as it allowed tribes to choose between organizing in traditional or contemporary structures. While many tribes organized as part of the Reorganization Act of 1934, many resisted because the act of 1934 required all tribes to structure their government only as set forth in the law. There was no provision for the historical and traditional ways that the tribes governed themselves. The 1975 act opened the door for tribes to be self-determining and still receive the benefits promised in treaties.

AMERICAN INDIAN POLICY REVIEW COMMISSION

The American Indian Policy Review Commission (AIPRC) was also initiated in 1975 to study the status of Indian tribes and the federal policies that determined their lives. The results were no different than those in several other studies commissioned since the Merriam Report in 1924. Indian people were still suffering the ravages of poverty, with high unemployment rates and minimal family incomes. Tribes needed more authority to enable them to meet the needs of their members. The AIPRC echoed the recommendations of years before to increase tribal autonomy and define the relationship between the federal, state, and tribal governments. The final report of the commission, issued in 1977, opposed forced assimilation and supported Indian self-determination.

[The trust relationship] includes an obligation to provide these services, required to protect and enhance Indian lands, resources, and self-government, but also includes those economic and social programs which are necessary to raise the standard of living and social well-being of the Indian people to a level comparable to [that of] the non-Indian population (*Akwesasne Notes*, 1986).

INTERNATIONAL TREATY RIGHTS CONFERENCE

With renewed self-confidence and self-identity, traditional chiefs and religious leaders from various Indian tribes joined together as the International Treaty Council to bring their message of injustices committed by the U.S. government to the International Treaty Rights Conference in Geneva, Switzerland in 1977. The Indian International Treaty Council was recognized as a non-governmental organization of the United Nations, and the representatives were allowed to state their case. Representatives of the indigenous people of Central, South, and North America grouped together to present their message. Participation in the conference was very dangerous for some who were testifying. Some members of the group were being watched by their country's government and were sure to be punished for their participation. Photographers continually tried to document who was speaking to keep as evidence in trials as traitors when they returned home. Some countries, such as Brazil, refused to let representatives travel to Geneva to state their case (*Akwesasne Notes*, 1986).

While there has been no direct response to the testimony given in Geneva, educating the world about the hidden injustices is an important part of bringing change to Indian Country. Since that time the Native people of North America have continued to join Native people throughout the world to bring their message of human rights for all to the world forum. International Treaty Conferences are held annually on various reservations to bring the North American tribes together to discuss issues and develop strategies for determining a bright future for Indian people. Representatives continue to travel to Geneva to tell the story of the lives of Native people to the world.

INDIAN CHILD WELFARE ACT

By 1977, although tribes had worked for years to change the trend, twenty-five to thirty-five percent of all Indian children had been taken from their homes by bureaucratic authorization (O'Brien, 1989, p. 89). The tribes were subject to state custody laws and often unprepared non-Indian social workers would impose inappropriate standards on the Indian homes, judge them unsatisfactory, and take away the children. The guidelines used conflicted with tribal customs and culture and the families were not easily able to get their children back from the system. Congress began a study of the plight of the Indian child and found that the removal of children from their Indian homes was often because they were poor and Indian. Congress noted that state courts "have often failed to recognize the essential tribal relations of Indian people and the cultural and social standards prevailing in Indian communities and families" (Indian Child Welfare Act. 25 U.S.C. Sec. 1901[5]).

The forced separations were disastrous for both child and family, but the tribe and family could do little. Congress passed the Indian Child Welfare Act (ICWA) in 1978 "recognizing that there is no resource that is more vital to the continued existence and integrity of Indian tribes than their children." The act gives tribes authority over all Indian child custody proceedings unless parents expressly request state jurisdiction. The purpose of the Indian Child Welfare Act is "to protect the best interests of Indian children and to promote the stability and security of Indian tribes and families" (Indian Child Welfare Act. 25 U.S.C. Sec. 1902).

Basically, the ICWA states that if a child resides on a reservation or is a ward of the tribal court, the tribe has complete jurisdiction. When the child resides off the reservation the tribe and the state have concurrent jurisdiction. The case must be initiated in state court and the state must notify the tribe of the proceedings. If the tribe or either parent requests, the state court must transfer the case to the tribe unless there is good cause. The state court may not terminate parental rights without proof, beyond a reasonable doubt, that if the child continued with the biological parents, he or she would suffer serious emotional or physical harm. Before the state can place an Indian child, it must give placement priority to first, the child's extended family, then the other members of the child's tribe, and finally, other Indian families. The same preference must be applied to foster care placement.

The act appropriates money to tribes for programs that benefit children and families, but, like much legislation, in many ways it lacks the enforcement to make it effective. Since over two-thirds of the American Indians today live off the reservation, without adequate funding for urban as well as tribal programs, there will always be Indian children who do not receive the full benefits of the Indian Child Welfare Act. States are often unwilling or unable to give children the services and benefits to which they are entitled. Even when trying to abide by the guidelines of the act, local social service departments are often unable to find licensed American Indian foster homes or adoptive homes. Tribes are often overwhelmed also, with similar placement limitations and not enough counseling and other family support services. Finally, many cases are not clear regarding who should or can take responsibility for the child. These issues create a barrier for the proper application of the Indian Child Welfare Act. And once again, the child is the victim.

AMERICAN INDIAN FREEDOM OF RELIGION ACT

Another piece of legislation that began to restore to tribes and American Indians the rights that they had been denied for hundreds of years was the American Indian Freedom of Religion Act (AIFRA) of 1978. Since the First Amendment to the Constitution of the United States says that "Congress shall make no law respecting an establishment of religion or prohibiting the free exercise thereof...", one would think that the rights of American Indians to worship as they have since time immemorial were naturally protected. This is not so, however, and our brief look at history thus far has proven that to be true. At the time that the AIFRA passed into law, it was a significant turning point in self-determination for American Indians. There was a clear reversal of the policy that had been the driving force behind the Bureau of Indian Affairs and the fear and hatred of Indian religion that had existed since the beginning of contact in 1492.

The act states that "henceforth it shall be the policy of the United States to protect and preserve for American Indians their inherent right of freedom to believe, express, and exercise the traditional religions of the American Indian, Eskimo, Aleut, and Native Hawaiians, including but not limited to access to sites, use and possession of sacred objects, and the freedom to worship through ceremonials and traditional rites."

This sets the framework for the modern day struggles that Native people still face while practicing their traditional religion, in trying to regain possession of the remains of their ancestors, or religious items in museums and other non-Indian possession. While the law directs the "various Federal departments, agencies, and other instrumentalities responsible for administering relevant laws to evaluate their policies and procedures in consultation with Native traditional religious leaders in order to determine appropriate changes necessary to protect and preserve Native American religions cultural rights and practices," there has not been response in all levels of federal policies and procedures and Indian people are still suffering the illegal denial of their First Amendment and AIFRA religious freedoms.

A case in point is the Oregon case of Smith and Black regarding the firing of two American Indian Church members for ingesting peyote while off duty during a religious ceremony. They were also denied unemployment compensation for the same reason. When Smith and Black appealed the decision, the Oregon Supreme Court held that the decision denied Smith and Black's free exercise of religious rights and dismissed the lower court's ruling. The state of Oregon appealed to the U.S. Supreme Court, which told the Oregon Supreme Court to decide if possession and use of peyote violated the Oregon law without exception. Since Oregon law had not been amended to respect the 1978 AIFRA, peyote was prohibited under any circumstances. The court further stated, however, that the "outright prohibition of good-faith religious use of peyote by adult members of the Native American Church would violate the First Amendment directly as interpreted by Congress" (Michaelsen, 1991, p. 121).

The difference of implementation of the AIFRA between the actual policy, local and state law, and the various courts leaves American Indians with no clear cut message regarding the First Amendment Rights. A last word available in this case takes once more the opposing position. The U.S. Supreme Court, in 1990, upheld the Oregon State Supreme Court decision that use of drugs was cause for a denial of benefits. In the majority opinion, Justice Antonin Scalia wrote that peyote's sacramental character could carry no weight against neutral law passed by the state against "criminal" activities. If such a ruling were to curtail the practice of American Indian (and other minority) religion, then so be it (Vecsey, 1991, pp. 58–59).

When the AIFRA was being considered for passage in the House, Morris Udall, while on the side of the act, made the statement that the act was "the sense of Congress ... merely a statement of policy" with "no teeth in it" (Vecsey, 1991). Udall made this statement to help the measure pass but perhaps without realizing how true his words were. Case after case regarding the use of sacred sites, the return of religious items and the remains of Indian ancestors, and the practice of religious ceremonies continue to determine the actual meaning of the AIFRA for Indian people.

INDIAN ACTIVISM: THE LONGEST WALK

The winter of 1978 was the beginning of the Longest Walk from the west coast of the United States to Washington, D.C. Indian people from around the country joined in the walk to bring attention to the continued lack of honoring of treaties with Indian nations and the deplorable conditions on most reservations. Traditional leaders joined with the youth and other tribal members to voice their concerns to the American public. Once they reached Washington, D.C., they held gatherings to share their message and call upon others to join together in a united voice.

LEONARD PELTIER: A MODERN-DAY WARRIOR

The specific conditions in most Indian areas depend on the relationship between the Indians and the other population. Where fishing rights or other individual or commercial rights are involved there is often friction. Friction also occurs as result of the relationship between the full bloods and the half bloods on a reservation. Frequently small, seemingly isolated incidents escalated until they were of national importance and well out of proportion. The story of Leonard Peltier and the shooting of an Indian man and two FBI agents on the Pine Ridge Reservation in South Dakota is a grave example. Leonard Peltier is an Anishinabe-Lakota, born in North Dakota, who grew up on the Turtle Mountain Reservation.

On June 26, 1975, in the late morning, two FBI agents drove onto Indian land near Oglala, South Dakota, a small village on the Pine Ridge Reservation. Here a shoot-out occurred in which both agents and an Indian man were killed. Although large numbers of FBI agents, Bureau of Indian Affairs (BIA) police, state troopers, sheriff's deputies, and vigilantes surrounded the property within an hour of the first shots, the numerous Indians involved in the shoot-out escaped into the hills.

The death of the agents inspired the biggest manhunt in FBI history. Of the four men eventually indicted for the killings, one was later released because the evidence was "weak," and two others were acquitted in July 1976 when a jury concluded that although they had fired at the agents, they had done so in self-defense. The fourth man, Leonard Peltier, indicted on the same charges as his companions but not tried until the following year, after extradition from Canada, was convicted on two counts of murder in the first degree, and was sentenced to consecutive life terms in prison, although even his prosecutors would dismiss as worthless the testimony of the only person ever to claim to have witnessed his participation in the killings. This testimony was also repudiated by the witness, who claimed to have signed her damning affidavit under duress, as part of what one court of appeals judge would refer to as a "clear abuse of the investigative process by the FBI."

Whatever the nature and degree of his participation at Oglala, the ruthless persecution of Leonard Peltier had less to do with his own actions that with underlying issues of history, racism, and economics, in particular Indian sovereignty claims and growing opposition to massive energy development on treaty lands and the dwindling reservations (Matthiessen, 1991, p. xx).

Matthiessen detailed the events that led up to the shooting and the various court trials and episodes in a book, *The Spirit of Crazy Horse* which was originally published in 1983. The book explains how Leonard Peltier was denied due process and how various governmental agencies participated in the shooting and subsequent events. Two months later the author and publisher were sued for libel by former South Dakota Governor William Janklow for 24 million dollars. In January 1984, the author, publisher, and attorney were sued by special Agent David Price of the FBI for an additional 25 million dollars. The book was taken off the market. Finally, eight years later and eight court decisions later, the book has returned to the shelves of bookstores. The original opinion of the publisher that the book was free of libel was born out. The real victim is Leonard Peltier who still has been denied the benefit of due process.

The following message was written by Dino Butler while in jail during trials for the shooting of the two FBI agents on the Pine Ridge reservation in 1975. "Joseph" refers to Joe Killsright Stuntz who also died along with the two FBI agents, Jack Coler and Ron Williams, during the shootout.

> June 26, 1975, was the day I became a red man. It was the day that truth was born in my mind and heart, uniting me with my spirit and the spirits of all our ancestors. It was the day I learned about life without death. There was no fear in me for the first time in my life, and I knew I could never die, for the fear of death no longer limited my perception of life, which is everlasting. That is what my brother Joseph taught me that day, and I know he has not been lost in the past but awaits me in the future.

> I know that I can continue on no matter what burden I must carry. I will always stand with honor and dignity in the dust of my ancestors upon Mother Earth amongst my people—all people. I shall never be defeated by our enemy—that is my freedom. That is what Annie Mae taught me.

> We must always fight for what we believe in. We must never tire in our fight. It does not really matter how we fight, what matters is what we are fighting for. It is our right to live: that is our first right. That is why we fight for our unborn, for it is through them that our nations live on. If we have to shed blood for them—the unborn—it is only right. As it was right on June 26, 1975 (Mattheissen, 1991, p. 558).

Leonard Peltier's uncompromising spirit to fight the injustice of his imprisonment and the continued efforts of individuals on the outside have kept his case alive. A fifth appeal for a new trial, based on the atrocities of his past cases, was filed in March 1992, and is currently waiting a date before the U.S. Eighth Circuit Court of Appeals. Ramsey Clark, former U.S. Attorney General, will be arguing his appeal.

The attention of millions of people from around the world has focused on Leonard Peltier and his fight for due process and the protection of his human and civil rights. Their letters demanding a new trial have been joined by sixty Democratic and Republican members of Congress, fifty members of the U.S. House of Representatives, fifty-one members of the Canadian Parliament, the Archbishop of Canterbury, Bishop Desmond Tutu, and many other political and religious leaders. In 1986, Peltier was awarded the International Human Rights Prize by the Human Rights Commission of Spain. Most recently, Robert Redford produced the film *Incident at Oglala* which tells the story of Leonard's case.

> Today, the case of Leonard Peltier is a symbol—in both a positive and negative sense—to indigenous people everywhere who are struggling against illegal expropriation of their lands and destruction of their cultures. Peltier's uncompromising resistance fueled the growth of an international movement that had focused attention not only on his case, but on broader issues of indigenous land rights and political imprisonment in the United States (Jaimes, 1992, p. 306).

TRIBALLY CONTROLLED COLLEGES

As tribes and individuals became more educated and took an active role in the modern day governance of their people, they could see the need for culturally based, high quality kindergarten through twelfth-grade schools and college level classes in the rural, reservation areas. It was a dream of Raymond Nakai when he was elected tribal chairman in the late 1960s. He decided to make his dream a reality. With the help of Robert and Ruth Roessel, he established the Rough Rock Demonstration School for grades kindergarten through twelve, and in 1968 the first Board of Regents for the Navajo Community College announced its intent and philosophy regarding education and the role that the Navajo Community College would play.

Congress passed the Navajo Community College Act of 1971 providing federal funding for a tribally controlled college. The first tribally run college, the Navajo Community College, was born. Today there are over two thousand students attending the Navajo Community College in Tsaile, Arizona, or one of the five community campuses.

Seven years later, Congress passed the Tribally Controlled Community College Act of 1978. This act authorized funding for other tribally controlled colleges. Today there are twenty-seven tribally controlled colleges located in Montana, North Dakota, South Dakota, Washington, California, Arizona, New Mexico, Michigan, Wisconsin, Minnesota, Nebraska, Kansas, and Saskatchewan. Fourteen of the twenty-seven are fully accredited and several more are in the process of accreditation. One college, Sinte Gleska in South Dakota, offers an accredited bachelor's degree and is working toward offering graduate-level degrees.

These community colleges are all members of the American Indian Higher Education Consortium, a national organization that provides training and support for colleges, coordinates information for the network of colleges, and acts as an advocate on behalf of the members. The tribal colleges are community colleges that provide culturally based curriculum and instruction. They serve the rural Indian communities and offer new alternatives to help students stay in school and graduate. Tribal colleges provide a lifeline to students, offering comforts similar to those of non-Indian colleges but which are often culturally based. They are small and usually close to the homes of students. The average age of tribal college students is twenty-seven and most are females with children. Most Indian students are first-generation college students. According to Bob Moore, a Rosebud Sioux who attended Sinte Gleska College, "If a student starts to fail, there is a sense of family, of helping each other, instead of saying 'it would open a spot if he dropped out'" (Ambler, 1991b, p. 24).

Tribally controlled colleges have and will continue to play a major role in the future of Indian people by preparing them to manage for themselves every facet of tribal business and providing professional services to their people. The colleges have also contributed to the personal empowerment of Indian adults. Their role in the future is one of increasing importance as they help develop the human resources of American Indian people. One graduate praised the founders of the colleges: "Vision is the ability to see results before an action is taken. We, as graduates, are the products of our leaders' vision" (Ambler, 1991b, p. 24).

While the acts of Congress since 1975 seem to be supportive of individual and tribal rights, there is one important factor that either enhances or limits the implementation of any act: money. During the Carter administration, Indian programs received funding at a level that they began to grow and prosper. They were on the way to self-determination. However, during the Reagan years in the White House major funding cutbacks hurt everyone in Indian Country. Under Reagan, funding for Indian tribes fell drastically; not only were Indian programs cut, but also all programs such as Economic Development Administration, the Community Services Administration, Comprehensive Employment and Training Act, and others received harsh cutbacks. Since tribes participated in these economic development programs, they felt those cuts also.

EDUCATION

Education is an area that saw great changes during the 1970s and 1980s. Rebounding from an era of boarding schools and lack of Indian participation in the policy boards that governed schools, Indian people throughout the country established their own contract tribal schools with the assistance of the 1975 Indian Self-Determination Act. They began a process of educating more Indian teachers, developing curriculum that included Native language and culture, and involved parents directly in the education of their young.

Reauthorizations of the Indian Education Act of 1972 also included options that allowed not only tribes but also Indian organizations to operate schools and programs that benefited American Indians. Survival schools were established in urban areas that focused on the empowerment of Indian people through education. Examples of the success of these schools are the Heart of the Earth Survival School and Red Earth School, both located in the twin cities area of Minnesota.

On March 8, 1990, former Secretary of Education Lauro F. Cavazos issued the charter for the Indian Nations At Risk Task force. The fifteen members he appointed in April of that year were charged with studying the status of Native education in the United States and issuing a report including recommendations that would improve the quality of education of American Indian and Alaska Native children. After months of research including regional meetings where Indian people could give testimony, they issued a report that contained a list of basic recommendations. These are the recommendations that were used in the focusing and direction setting process of the White House conference on Indian Education.

The Indian Education Act of 1988 included language allowing the president to call a White House Conference on Indian Education. Once the president set the process in motion, and established a staff to implement the legislation, Indian people throughout the country began meeting in small groups and in large meetings to discuss the critical issues facing Indian people in the field of education. Indian people congregated on a state-by-state basis to develop reports that expressed the specific needs of their Indian communities.

Delegates were then selected by the president, the Speaker of the House of Representatives, and the president *pro tempore* of the Senate. These delegates attended a White House Conference on Indian Education in Washington, D.C., on January 20–21, 1992. The act charged the conference participants with exploring the feasibility of establishing a National Independent Board of Education and combining all education programs for Indians under this board and making recommendations for improving education programs to make them more relevant to Indians. Delegates to the conference voted not to have a National School Board. They developed a broad set of recommendations that ranged from more well-trained Indian teachers, Native language, culture, and history classes included in the curriculum, and money for more scholarships for higher education. At the time of this printing, the final report was not yet available.

POPULATION TRENDS

The 1980 U.S. Census listed 1,418,195 American Indians residing in the United States. The 1990 U.S. Census lists American Indians at 1,959,234. This is an increase of half a million Indian people in ten years. The average mortality rate for both males and females has increased, but both live longer than they have for a century or more. There is still a high infant mortality rate, often due to the lack of adequate medical facilities and staff in rural areas and the high cost of good health care.

Increasing numbers of people make political influence more of a reality. In particular, the larger reservations such as the Navajo Reservation exert considerable political power. There has been talk about the Navajo Nation forming the fifty-first state!

It also places critical stress on reservations whose land cannot sustain a subsistence economy for larger numbers of people. Overgrazing, a problem on the Navajo reservation in John Collier's time, becomes more of a threat when there are more people relying on the land for their livelihood.

THE CURRENT STATUS OF AMERICAN INDIAN PEOPLE

Now American Indians are on the verge of a time when they can assert themselves and take an active part in determining the future of their people. While that future is still too dependent on the United States, there is more opportunity to participate in the delineation of the future than any other time in the last century. The Native American Rights Fund, the American Indian Science and Engineering Society, the Council of Energy Resource Tribes, the American Indian Higher Education Association, the National Indian Education Association, and other organizations have taken a leadership role in Congress advocating favorable laws, arguing cases in the courts that support and define Indian tribal sovereignty, and educating Indian children as well as others about the real history of Indian people and the role that they have to play in modern times.

The 1992 Quincentennial

Some Indian people decided to speak out against the 1992 celebration of the Columbian Quincentennial. They believe that the last five hundred years have been disastrous for Indian people and that it is a mockery to celebrate the man and the time that enslaved and destroyed entire civilizations. Others have focused their efforts in other ways. For example, Oklahoma designated 1992 as the Year of the Indian to bring attention to the current status of Indians and promote a brighter future. In any case, the quincentennial brought renewed attention to the history of America's indigenous people and brought to public attention the triumphs and tragedies of their struggles to restore prosperity and pride.

American Indian people have not disappeared nor have they been assimilated. As a nation of diverse people, we are becoming increasingly aware that their traditional ways of humility, honor, respect for children, elders, and the earth, and cooperation have much to teach a hostile, harried, and wasteful world.

LESSON PLAN: BIG FOOT MEMORIAL RIDE

Grade Level: Grades 5–8

Basic Concepts: Conflict, loss, healing/reconciliation, culture, and change

Organizing Generalization: Conflict between societies can lead to feelings of loss—loss of land, culture, resources, or pride—on the part of one or both sides. Societies both in present day and in the past hold ceremonies and other activities to heal the wounds left by past conflicts and losses. These events help mend the emotional and spiritual aspects of the society as well as prepare for physical and material healing.

Culture Area: Plains

Time Period: 1890–1990

Background: By the end of the nineteenth century the Indian wars of the West were mostly over. The great buffalo herds had been wiped out, and the Indian people who once roamed the Plains were confined to reservations. They faced starvation and death. Several bands of the Lakota had refused to be confined to reservations, and they fled to Canada under the leadership of Chief Sitting Bull. Sitting Bull returned to the Plains and his people, believing promises from the U.S. government that he would receive a pardon. Not long after his return, the police surrounded his tipi and tried to bring him into custody. A brief scuffle broke out and Sitting Bull was killed. It was December 15, 1890. In fear for their own lives, the remaining Lakotas fled.

When word reached Chief Big Foot, who was camped on the Cheyenne River a little over fifty miles away, in fear he led his people south to Pine Ridge where he felt Oglala Chief Red could help protect them. It was bitter cold and his people didn't have enough food or clothing for the ride. But they left anyway and faced the 150-mile journey. About forty miles from Pine Ridge, the band ran into the U.S. Calvary sent to round them up and bring them back to the reservation. Big Foot was sick with pneumonia and he raised a white flag to the soldiers. Even though they were hungry and cold, they all rested for the night at Wounded Knee. The next day the soldiers had the Indians turn in all of their guns and weapons. During the process of collecting the weapons a shot rang out and the soldiers began firing on the Indians. The Indians were helpless without weapons. When the dust settled, over three hundred men, women, and children had been massacred, including Big Foot. Only about fifty Lakota escaped. The Seventh Calvary received twenty-seven medals of honor for killing Big Foot's band. "For the Lakota, it was a massacre that tore open the heart of the Indian people for the next hundred years" (Wood, 1992, p. 4).

Almost one hundred years later, a small group of Lakota men sought the advice of a medicine man to find out how to help heal the people. In order to begin the healing process, they began the Big Foot Memorial Ride that culminated on the one hundredth year anniversary of the death of Big Foot. This is one example of the renewal and healing that is going on all through Indian Country.

Objectives:

Knowledge

Students will:

1. Recall the events that led up to the 1890 Wounded Knee Massacre.
2. Identify the relationship between the original Battle of Wounded Knee and the Big Foot Memorial Ride.
3. Describe how children who were at Wounded Knee both in 1890 and 1990 might have felt.

Skills

Students will:

1. Draw a map of South Dakota labeling the sacred Black Hills, Pine Ridge, Wounded Knee, Big Foot's Cheyenne River encampment, and other points of interest.

2. Compare the living conditions of the Lakota people in 1890 and 1990.
3. Hypothesize about how living conditions of the Lakota might change over the next one hundred years in ways that would continue the healing process.

Values

Students will:

1. Understand why the Lakota people call the incident at Wounded Knee a massacre.
2. Recognize the meaning of the relationship between the 1890 Wounded Knee and the Big Foot Memorial Ride.
3. Express the significance of the phrase "Mending the Sacred Hoop" to the Lakota people.

Activities:

1. Students can read the book *A Boy Becomes a Man at Wounded Knee* by Ted Wood. If only one copy is available, read it to the students and have the book available for individual viewing.
2. Have students draw a map of South Dakota and locate the Black Hills, Pine Ridge, Wounded Knee, the Cheyenne River Encampment, and other sites of interest.
3. In small groups, have students research the life of the Lakota both in the late 1800s and in modern times. The small groups can report in class to share information.
4. Have a class discussion regarding the past and present conditions of the Lakota. Explore the events of the incident at Wounded Knee and the Memorial Ride. Talk about the experiences of Wanbli Numpa Afraid of Hawk. Focus on the healing nature of the ride.
5. Have students brainstorm other cultures that have ceremonies or other memorials of their past that contribute to the healing of those involved or impacted.
6. Make a class mural that depicts Wounded Knee in 1890 and the ride in 1990.

Extensions:

1. Read "Wounded Knee: Mending the Sacred Hoop" by Chaymaine White Face Wisecarver.
2. Research other tribes and look for examples of healing ceremonies or events of modern times (Choctaw re-creation of the Trail of Tears, memorials for the death of loved ones, and others).
3. Students can read *Bury My Heart at Wounded Knee* by Dee Brown.

Evaluation: Through discussion students should demonstrate a knowledge of the Wounded Knee incident and the Big Foot Memorial Ride. They should also demonstrate an understanding of the significance of the two events to the Lakota people.

Materials/Resources:

Brown, D. *Bury my Heart at Wounded Knee.* New York: Holt, Rinehart, and Winston, 1970.
Brown, D. "Wounded Knee: An Indian History of the American West." Adapted by Amy Erlich from *Bury My Heart at Wounded Knee.* New York: Holt, Rinehart, and Winston, 1974.
"A Lakota Times Special: Wounded Knee Remembered 1890–1990." January 8, 1991, *Lakota Times.*
Stein, R. C. *The Story of Wounded Knee.* Chicago: Childrens Press, 1983.
Wisecarver, C.W.F. "Wounded Knee: Mending the Sacred Hoop." *Native Peoples* (Spring 1990): 8–16.
Wood, T., with Afraid of Hawk, W. N. *A Boy Becomes a Man at Wounded Knee.* New York: Walker, 1992.

Videotapes

VCA—Wiping the Tears (Producer). *Wiping the Tears of Seven Generations.* Leonia, NJ: Producer. This is an award-winning video of the Big Foot Memorial Ride. Available for $29.95 (plus $4.00 shipping) from VCA—Wiping the Tears, 50 Leyland Dr., Leonia, NJ 07605. A portion of the proceeds goes to Lakota educational institutions.

SUMMARY
TRIBAL RESTORATION, PHASE TWO CONTINUED: 1975–PRESENT

Young Indian people attended college for the first time in the late 1960s and early 1970s. They graduated into professional fields such as law, medicine, engineering, and education. During the coming years these newly educated American Indians would battle in the courts for the "promises" that had been made to Indian people and tribes for over three hundred years.

Indian educators would operate schools that would address not only the English language and basic skills for survival and success in the modern world, but also the wisdom of the elders and American Indian languages and culture. Indian physicians would begin to help the physical and emotional wounds of being a conquered people, combining the wisdom of ancient healers and modern medicine. Indian engineers and lawyers would guide their tribes in the use of their natural resources and modern technology. Indian people throughout the country began to talk about their oppression and face the challenge to change the course of events of the last century. Times were changing.

The most important piece of legislation that marked the shift to self-determining policy was the Indian Self-Determination Act of 1975. This act allowed tribes to administer all federal programs on the reservation and to structure themselves in whatever way they saw fit, rather than as dictated in the Reorganization Act of 1934.

Other important legislation leading to increased self-determination has included (1) the American Indian Policy Review Commission (1975), (2) the Indian Child Welfare Act (1978), (3) the American Indian Freedom of Religion Act (1978), (4) the Tribally Controlled Community College Act (1978), and (5) the Indian Education Act (1972).

The 1990 U.S. Census listed the number of American Indians at 1,959,234.

TIME LINE: 1975–1992

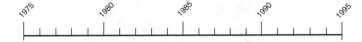

1975
Violent confrontation on the Pine Ridge reservation in South Dakota between AIM members and FBI agents resulted in the death of two agents. Leonard Peltier was later convicted.

1975
American Indian Policy Review Commission analyzed the unique relationship of Indians with the federal government.

1975
Indian Self-Determination Act permitted tribes to participate in all federal social programs and services related to Indians.

1975
Council of Energy Resource Tribes (CERT) formed to protect and manage energy resources on reservations.

1975
AIM leaders Dennis Banks and Russell Means were convicted on assault and riot charges. In 1978, Governor Jerry Brown gave Dennis Banks sanctuary in California.

1977
The Final Report of the American Indian Policy Review Commission opposed forced assimilation and supported Indian self-determination.

1977
Indian activists presented a resolution to the International Human Rights Conference in Geneva, Switzerland, calling on the United Nations to recognize Indian tribes as sovereign nations. The International Treaty Council was recognized as a nongovernmental organization of the United Nations.

1978
Indian Education Act gave greater decision-making powers to Indian school boards.

1978
Indian Child Welfare act established standards for federal foster care programs and provided assistance to tribes for child and family service programs. The Act also established the principle that Indian children belong to the tribes and should not be adopted by non-Indian families.

1978
Indian activists organized the "Longest Walk" to Washington, D.C.

1978
Women of All Red Nations (WARN) was organized.

1978
Congress passed the American Indian Freedom of Religion Act that stipulated that Indian religions are protected by the First Amendment.

1978
The Indian Claims Commission ended. Since formation of the Commission in 1946, 800 million dollars was granted to Indian tribes. Tribes won awards on sixty percent of the claims.

1980
According to the federal census, the Native American population in the United States was 1,418,195.

1981
President Reagan initiated a policy of cutbacks of funds for Indian social programs. Over forty percent of funds were cut.

1982
Congress passed the Indian Government Tax Status Act.

1983
Dennis Banks, the AIM leader, left California and took refuge on the Onondaga Reservation in New York.

1984
Dennis Banks surrendered to state and local officials in Rapid City, South Dakota. He was sentenced to three years in prison.

1984
President Reagan's Commission on Indian Reservation economics accused the BIA of excessive regulation and incompetent management with the agency consuming more than two-thirds of its budget on itself and recommended assigning the agency's program to other federal agencies. The Commission also recommended a shift away from tribal goals toward increased private ownership and individual profit motive, as well as waiving of tribal immunity from certain lawsuits.

1985
National Tribal Chairman's Association voted to reject the proposals of Reagan's Commission, fearing a new attempt by the federal government to terminate tribal sovereign status and gain control of tribal resources.

1988
The Indian Gaming Act was passed by Congress.

1990
The land claims of the Seneca were addressed by the Seneca Nation Settlement Act which was passed by Congress.

1990
The Native American Graves Protection and Repatriation Act was passed by Congress.

1990
According to the federal census, the Native American population in the United States was 1,959,234.

1992
A major White House Conference on Indian Education was held in Washington D.C., in response to deep concerns regarding the academic achievement of American Indian children.

1992
Indian people throughout the Americas protested the celebration of the Columbian Quincentennial.

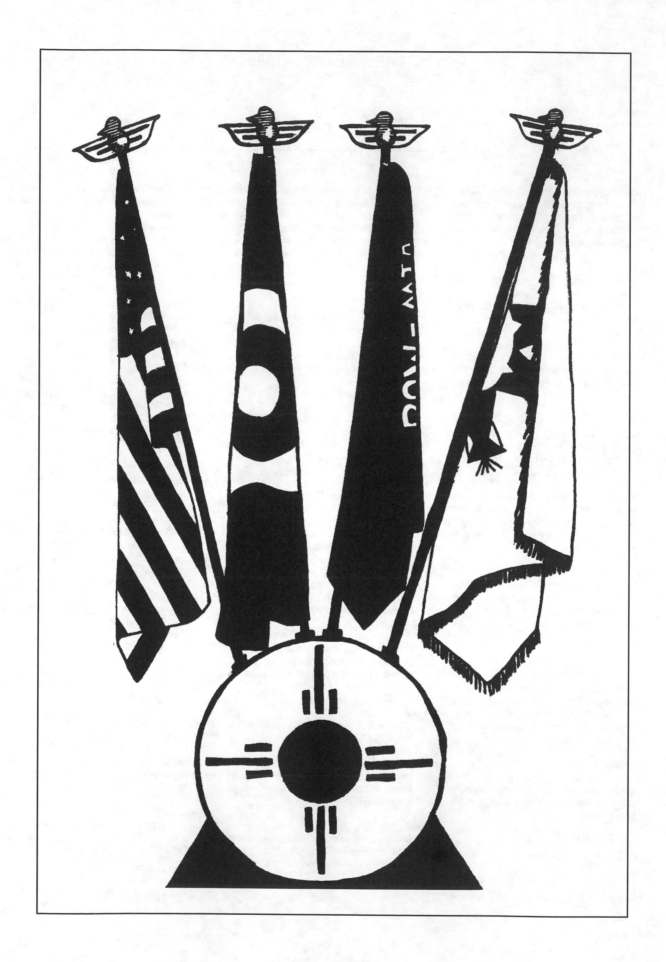

CHAPTER **17**

Contemporary Issues

These are the personal comments of Zuni people who went to Denver to receive one of their War Gods which was returned to them:

When I first went up to Denver, and I saw this war God on display in a square glass case—and they just told us it was on the third floor, I believe. So we went up there, and we started looking around for it, and it just so happened—I don't know, maybe because I am an Indian, or what, I don't know—but when I first saw it, it was standing there. And he looked, to me it appeared there was a sign of relief from the idol. And I guess in a way he said, "Finally, somebody, some Zuni, contacted me." But I could see the facial features on the War God itself, it was—it looked like it was sad to me. That was my personal experience.

—Councilman Barton Martza, Zuni Pueblo

Museums misunderstand it. And the white society must also learn that some of our traditional culture is for Zunis only. And in the case of these War Gods, like the one I visited in Denver, I was standing there and all it had was a little blurb on it, and if that is the museum's idea of educating the people, I think they are misrepresenting themselves. And what some of our beliefs are, like I said, they are for Zunis only. And I think that if an individual wants to know something about Zuni, that individual should buy all these books that are already out, or come down here to Zuni and learn—to ask what to do and what not to do. And not just going out there and picking up our sacred idols and going back and selling them, and then explaining that for education.

—Councilman Barton Martza, Zuni Pueblo

If education is contained in the thoughts of museums, they have never sent a delegate or anybody to find out the meaning of these figures and what is behind them. There are a lot of things that have to be done in preparing them to be placed in their specific shrine areas. They are just not taken over there by the individuals responsible for this task—they also have to go through the ritual whenever they are delivered to these shrine areas...Zuni people, not just the religious sector, but all who know that these have been taken out of their specific areas, they feel bad about it. And then when they see something like that on display in some museum without any type of an explanation of what they are, you know, that is not educating anybody—it's just a curiosity. And this is something that we don't like to see. They are our guardians, and I think that just that word covers a lot of territory.

—Governor Robert E. Lewis, Zuni Pueblo

(Used by permission of Ferguson, T. J. & Eriacho, W. "Ahayuda Zuni War Gods: Cooperation and Repatriation." *Native Peoples* [Fall 1990]: 6–12. The war god was returned to Zuni Pueblo by the American Museum of Natural History in New York in a well known repatriation effort.)

The next two chapters will address some of the contemporary issues and challenges for Native peoples in the United States as they meet the twenty-first century. Most of the issues that American Indian people have faced since 1492 are still problems being addressed today in new and more powerful ways. Old wrongs need to be made right and emerging concerns need to be addressed.

In traditional Navajo beliefs, when the twins born of Changing Woman slayed the monsters in order to make the world safe for the people, four monsters remained—age, poverty, disease, and death. These monsters were left to keep people from becoming complacent and to remind them that nature is more powerful than people. In many ways, Indian people must continue to face these monsters whose powers now have additional complexity and the problems they create have renewed urgency. There are also new monsters terrorizing the people, such as prejudice, discrimination, and cultural erosion which need to be slain.

In the Quincentennial year, the United States faced the reality that Native people have neither vanished nor assimilated. In fact, five hundred years after Europeans first set foot in the Caribbean, American Indians have renewed their efforts to regain their land and treaty rights, restore their cultures, practice their religions, educate their children, instill respect for their traditional ways, live in health, become economically self-sufficient, and take their rightful place in their homeland—Indian Country.

We will explore individual case studies of how Indian people are working to slay many of the monsters that have plagued them and to work toward a relationship with the land, the government, and other people to ensure a life of beauty and harmony for them and for their children.

DEVELOPMENT OF POLITICAL INFLUENCE

Political influence, the ability to form coalitions, exert pressure, demonstrate leadership, and have power to affect social, economic, and political systems, is crucial to Indian people as they confront their future. Indian leadership is manifested individually and collectively and is becoming an influence on these systems and thus making a difference to the physical, emotional, and political well-being of Native people.

Indian Leaders

There are many examples of personal leadership in Indian Country. Ben Nighthorse Campbell is a prominent Indian leader serving in the U.S. Senate. Campbell, a Democrat from Colorado, got into politics somewhat "accidentally"—he went to a political meeting when his plane was grounded by a snowstorm. After convincing voters that he wasn't a hippie because of his long hair—worn "Indian style"—he won the election to the Colorado legislature. Proving to be a hard-working, thoughtful, and independent state legislator, Campbell was elected to the U.S. House of Representatives in 1986.

The only Native American serving in Congress, Campbell has distinguished himself as an independent representative of Indian people. As a demonstration of his statesmanship, he led the 1992 Rose Bowl Parade in full traditional regalia, serving as co-grand marshal with Cristobal Colón, a descendant of Christopher Columbus. He is also a prominent rancher and successful designer and producer of contemporary Indian jewelry and has won many awards for his artistry.

Also in a prominent national leadership role is Wilma Mankiller who is Chief of the Cherokee Nation of Oklahoma, the second largest Indian tribe in the United States. Wilma Mankiller's ancestors came to Oklahoma along the Trail of Tears. Born in the Cherokee town of Tahlequah in 1945, she lived in a home without most modern conveniences such as indoor plumbing. She is keenly aware of her heritage as well as the needs of poor people in rural areas.

Early in her adult life, she actively worked for Indian political causes. After working for improved housing, health, and education programs, she became the tribe's first woman chief in 1985. She is a hard worker and a fighter for the things that are needed by the Cherokee people and under her leadership the Cherokee Nation has made a dramatic economic recovery. In 1970 the Oklahoma Cherokees were nearly financially destitute; today they have a 70-million-dollar budget.

Chief Mankiller believes that a strong sense of being Indian will help the Cherokee culture remain alive and the people will keep their tribal social and cultural ways. One of her major goals is to lead the Cherokee people to trust their own thinking, find their own solutions to their problems, and move forward with confidence.

Indian Organizations

Indian leadership is seen in many professional organizations that affect the quality of life for the people. Some of the more prominent examples of influential Indian organizations include those that focus their efforts on the preservation of natural resources on Indian land, Indian legal issues, and the education of Indian children.

The American Indian Movement (AIM) is the organization that symbolizes the most vocal, active, and militant coalition of Indian people defending and fighting for their rights. It is AIM that seeks publicity and attacks popular and unpopular Indian causes. AIM's presence is notable and assertive. Although public acts of defiance and civil disobedience like the occupations of Alcatraz, the Bureau of Indian Affairs, and Wounded Knee bring publicity to just causes and provide a unifying effect for Indian people, other acts of AIM are also powerful in raising public consciousness and effecting change. For example, recent acts of AIM leadership include protest regarding the celebration of the Columbus quincentennial and the establishment of an Indian Anti-Defamation organization. AIM continues to exert its leadership and lend its voice to the more militant efforts toward change.

The Council for Energy Resource Tribes (CERT) was founded in 1975 and is a sort of "Indian OPEC" that represents forty-four Indian tribes. Indian lands hold vast amounts of coal, oil, gas, uranium, and other natural resources such as lumber and water. The goals of CERT are (1) to ensure that the Indian people receive an equitable return for their resources, and are able to utilize those resources as a foundation upon which to develop stable tribal economies, (2) to assist the tribes in protecting their natural, social, and cultural environment from the adverse impacts of energy resource development, and (3) to aid each tribe in acquiring the capability to manage its resources.

These goals intend to bring tribes from their traditional passive roles in their business dealings to joint partnerships, by requiring Indian preference in employment and manpower training, and demanding fixed terms of duration and other factors that will not allow others to exploit their resources, thus enabling them to obtain a sound economic prosperity. Tribes must learn to manage their valuable resources with expertise and dignity.

The executive headquarters of CERT is located in Washington, D.C., and deals with administration, policy analysis, and communications. The Technical Assistance Center in Denver responds to tribal requests for technical assistance in virtually any area of resource management.

David Lester, Executive Director of CERT, stated, "We've done a better job [in managing Indian resources] than the feds or the states anywhere we've had a chance to manage" (*Denver Post*, August 18, 1992, p. A1). According to Lester, the tribes have learned three lessons in fifty years of Washington-based economic development: The survival of Indian nations depends on the development of a stable, diversified economic base, avoidance of non-Indian practices, and a stable political climate in tribal government.

Recognizing that education is the key to the future and that Indian children are not faring well in traditional American schools, the National Indian Education Association (NIEA) is active in promoting political advocacy, informed leadership, and professional coalitions on behalf of Indian students. In a way that is unique to Indian people, education is closely tied to Indian treaties and Indian law—and the issues of federal, state, and tribal financing of schooling is complex. NIEA brings together students, parents, teachers, administrators, and school board members in an active organization that focuses on the improvement of Indian education.

Native American Rights Fund (NARF) is one of the most powerful organizations in Indian Country today. In a publication that celebrates twenty successful years for the organization, David Getches, the founding director, stated, "NARF has brought most of the landmark cases in Indian law of this era—virtually all of them successful ... . It has established the foundations of Indian sovereignty ... NARF stands for the ability of the law to serve the most vital needs of people" (Sanders, 1990, p. 3).

> When we started the Native American Rights Fund twenty years ago, our objective was to bring competent and ethical legal representation to Native Americans who were unable to afford such representation. We believed that Indians—if given this opportunity—could receive justice from the American legal system.
>
> Our mission had always been to secure for Indians the sovereignty, natural resources and human dignity that the laws of the majority society promised. At the heart of these laws lies the goal of all Native people—to maintain their status and traditional ways of life (John Echohawk as cited in Sanders, 1990, p. 2).

NARF attorneys travel from reservation to reservation and from tribe to tribe. The following Five Priorities of the Native American Rights Fund are the guideposts for their work and recognize that although the tribes have different languages, different cultures, and different histories, Indian people have the same needs.

The Five Priorities of the Native American Rights Fund (NARF) (Sanders, 1990, p. 5).

1. The Preservation of Tribal Existence
2. The Protection of Tribal Natural Resources
3. The Promotion of Human Rights
4. The Accountability of Governments
5. The Development of Indian Law

Many strong examples of leadership in public positions exist in the American Indian community. However, it is important to recognize that the qualities of leadership are formed, nurtured, and demonstrated in small ways within families, tribes, and communities. Although visible, national leadership is emerging, many Indian people demonstrate leadership in private and powerful ways. A single Indian woman who adopts a child is a leader. A man who remains sober is a determined leader in his family and community. An Indian youth who studies to go to college is a leader in his school and among his fellow students. Medicine people and hard-working teachers are models and leaders. The fifty-five Indian delegates at the Democratic National Convention in 1992 are leaders. Leadership is not just manifested in a few public roles, but is revealed daily in the lives of ordinary Indian people who go to work, raise their families, and meet commonplace problems.

DEVELOPMENT OF ECONOMIC SELF-SUFFICIENCY

Poverty, one of the four monsters that plague Indian people, is being fought in many ways—CERT, NARF, NIEA are organizations that fight for economic self-sufficiency in differing ways. These organizations are focused on developing tribal leadership and gaining the keys to self-sufficiency.

Now let's turn to some of the major issues in the fight for economic self-sufficiency that are important in Indian country. Perhaps the foremost issue is gaming.

Gaming

Gaming or gambling has now become one of the major sources of revenue for many tribes. Bingo has become a part of reservation life.

American Indians have always enjoyed games and gambling. Their own unique types of games such as the moccasin game, dice games, hand games (much like the traditional Button, Button, Who Has the Button), and ball games were usually played at social gatherings, and the items or amounts wagered were affordable. These were social games and were an integral part of each tribe's culture. Gambling is different. Remember that most lands set aside for Indian people were perceived to be of no value to others and therefore were reserved for Indian people. As a consequence, it is easy to recognize how gambling, a lucrative industry that does not depend on natural resources, is attractive to tribes. The sovereignty of tribes and their freedom from taxes on reservations have made the profits from gambling irresistible to both Indians and non-Indians. Gambling is now big business on Indian reservations.

Bingo created the first lure, and the Seminole Tribe of Florida was the first to offer million-dollar prizes. High stakes gambling quickly got the attention of other tribes and the outside world. The unique ability of reservations to offer gambling, without taxes and, to a limited degree, without the concurrence of the state in which the tribes were located, was irresistible to Indians who were desperately seeking economic development on Indian lands. Today, there are Indian-owned casinos that offer poker, blackjack, wheel games, slot machines, pull-tab paper games, and others.

In 1988 Congress passed the Indian Gaming Regulatory Act (IGRA) and established an Indian Gaming Commission. The Bureau of Indian Affairs was given increased responsibility to oversee Indian gambling. The rules and requirements for non-Indian involvement were strict in an effort to ensure that gambling on Indian reservations was without corruption and would benefit Indian people. By 1992 the National Indian Gaming Commission was not fully operational, and the BIA was criticized for being passive in regulating the industry and too slow in approving casino plans.

By opening an office in the BIA to oversee gaming contractors, monitor background checks, and approve plans for distributing gaming income, Secretary of the Interior Manuel Lujan initiated steps in 1992 to prevent abuses in the Indian gambling industry. The Justice Department has stated that it has found no evidence that organized crime has infiltrated Indian-run casinos, but some individuals have been charged with operating illegal gambling. Lujan's intent was to ensure that tribes can maintain gaming as a viable economic enterprise while implementing controls.

Gambling has indeed brought some measure of economic self-sufficiency to reservations. Recent reports indicate that American Indian games are the fastest growing segment of the gambling industry, with an economic impact of more that 1 million dollars annually. The jobs created by the casinos, restaurants, cigarette and tobacco sales, gasoline sales, and the provision of appropriate security for the areas have decreased unemployment dramatically on many reservations. Consequently, welfare loads have been considerably reduced. For example, according to Brasher (1992, p. 3), Indian-run gaming has taken many Indians and non-Indians off welfare rolls in Minnesota and South Dakota. On the Mille Lacs Reservation in Minnesota, where a major casino opened in April 1992, participation in government food programs has decreased twenty-three percent.

The budget of the Oneida Tribe (Wisconsin) grew from 5 million dollars a decade ago to 85 million dollars in 1992. Supported by bingo, the tribe owns Radisson Hotel, an environmental lab, and five convenience stores, and the tribe is buying land. Tribes have been able to provide higher education opportunities, build schools, hospitals and health clinics, and community buildings, offer retirement benefits for tribal members, finance new business enterprises, and construct new housing thus impacting education, health, and well-being for Indian people.

So what are the problems? There are several. Savilla states:

> And who better to find those loop-holes than the fast buck lawyers who under the cover of tribal sovereignty, self-determination and self-sufficiency, derive their fees from efforts to establish casino-style gambling on reservations and on land taken into "trust" by the U.S. even though it is located miles from the tribal reservation. These lawyers for litigation fees, encourage tribes to push their sovereign rights to the limit in order to attract test cases in federal courts filed by state and local governments who rightly or wrongly, feel threatened by Indian gambling (1992, pp. 6–7).

However, shady lawyers are not the predominant problem. The over-arching problem resides in the tangle of legal relationships between state, federal, and tribal governments. Intergovernmental squabbles are intense and often result in significant conflict. Federal rules allow tribes to run casino-style gambling if their state allows such gaming in any form outside the reservation, but only if the tribes and the state negotiate a compact allowing the games. Forced by the federal government into making compacts with the tribes, many states have resisted, for a number of reasons. The reasons most often cited are those of alleged corruption and even Mafia infiltration in Indian gaming.

Another reason might well be that the business experience and revenue that come with tribal gaming also create a new power relationship between tribes and states. According to Tim Giago, editor of the *Lakota Times*, tribes see gaming as a means to true independence (1992, p. 1–1). With successful gaming operations they can now deal with state governments from a position of financial and political strength. This independence may well be seen as a threat to state governments who do not want to extend the same government-to-government relationship that tribes have with the federal government to state governments.

And there are other problems as well. Recently there has been concern that the laws regarding Indian gaming, along with a precedent-setting non-Indian casino already operating within the National Park Service system, increase the likelihood of gambling within some of the nation's best-known parks. Several parks are considered vulnerable because parts or all of them are on reservation land. For example, some of the most beautiful National Parks in the Southwest such as Canyon de Chelly National Monument, Chaco Canyon National Historic Park, Navajo National Monument, and the Grand Canyon are located partially or completely on reservation land. There is undoubtedly going to be a major conflict between the rights of tribes to establish gaming on their lands and the mandate of the National Park Service to protect these lands so as to leave them unimpaired for the enjoyment of future generations (Miniclier, 1992b).

And finally, tribes struggle to balance the hope of economic self-sufficiency with potential costs to the quality of life such as the possibility of the intrusion of crime, prostitution, corruption, and other of the more shady aspects of gambling on reservation life.

Natural Resources

The protection of tribal natural resources is closely related to the preservation of tribal existence. Natural resources are necessary to sustain tribal life. Such issues are the ownership, control, and preservation of Indian lands, water rights, and fishing and hunting rights. In each of the issues, tribes are in direct conflict, again, for the lands and resources that are theirs and the needs or desires of others to acquire, use, and profit from these resources.

Battles are waged on many fronts. Tribes in the eastern part of the country are challenging old treaties to regain their land; nearly all western tribes are involved in either litigation or negotiations to establish their reserved water rights which guarantee water for both present and future uses with priority over most non-Indian uses; and tribes fight to hunt and fish in traditional areas for both subsistence and commercial purposes (Sanders, 1990, pp. 15–20). None of these is a simple problem. For example, the salmon on the West Coast are now an endangered species; they cannot live and reproduce in river waters that are warm and that are running low. Droughts throughout the region have required the diversion of river water to protect irrigated crops and to supply cities. Do we save the salmon? At what cost?

Storing of High-Level Nuclear Waste

The conflict between economic sufficiency and protection of land and lifeways is demonstrated in the issue of the storage of high-level nuclear waste on reservation lands. Fourteen tribes have applied for grants to study the feasibility of storing nuclear waste in Monitored Retrievable Storage (MRS) sites. These facilities would store radioactive fuel rods from eleven nuclear reactors for forty to fifty years until a permanent site is constructed.

The tribes who applied for one-hundred-thousand-dollar grants under Phase I include the Mescalero Apache (New Mexico) which recently applied for an additional 3 million dollars in Phase II funding, Prairie Island Mdewakanton Sioux (Minnesota), Skull Valley Band of Goshutes (Utah), Lower Brule Tribe (South Dakota), Akhiok-Gaguyak Tribe and Tetlin Village (Alaska), Chickasaw Indian Nation, Sac and Fox Nation, Eastern Shawnee Tribe, Apache Development Authority, Absentee Shawnee Tribe, Alabama/Quassarte Tribe, and the Ponca Tribe (Oklahoma). The Chickasaw and the Sac

and Fox Nations, under opposition from their tribes, returned the money and declined to undertake the studies.

Tribal leaders from Washington, Oregon, South Dakota, Arizona, Nevada, Minnesota, Utah, and Oklahoma have denounced the interest of some tribal governments to study storing high-level nuclear waste on their reservations. Lance Hughes, director of Native Americans for a Clean Environment in Tahlequah, Oklahoma, expressed the concern of many tribal leaders who remember the tragic lessons learned in the past—including Los Alamos, New Mexico; Rocky Flats, Colorado; Hanford, Washington; and Idaho's National Engineering Laboratory.

> Many Indian people all over the country have died or suffered terribly from the production of nuclear fuel rods. And we all know the final destination for these fuel rods. So why would any tribe participate in a system that has killed Indian people, stolen land and then contaminated our communities? It's totally immoral .... This is a very serious issue facing Indian Nations. We cannot participate in a system that kills us (Taliman, 1992a, p. 10).

Even on the Mescalero Apache Reservation there is organized opposition to the MRS funds and the proposed nuclear waste storage site. Tribal members opposed to Mescalero President Wendell Chino's decision to study the feasibility of a MRS site on the reservation are speaking out about "Chernobyl Chino's MRS." One leader has summarized the viewpoint of those in opposition by stating that building a MRS would be "contrary to the Apache outlook and beliefs to protect the environment, the wildlife, the clean, pure air and water."

Tribal President Chino has stated that he is approaching the project as a business venture that would yield a billion dollars for the tribe over a ten- to twenty-year period. David Leroy, U.S. nuclear waste negotiator, has said that the benefits to the tribe could include construction of railroads, highways, waterways, airports, public schools, health care facilities, recreation facilities, environmental programs, and economic development programs (Taliman, 1992b, p. 11).

Although these tribes have only committed themselves to studying, not building, a MRS site, the question is wrenching. Tribes badly need economic development—but, again, at what cost?

In yet another case, the Navajo Nation is fighting construction of a 160-acre asbestos waste dump that will desecrate sacred land and pose serious health risks to residents of the reservation. Under the leadership of President Peterson Zah, Navajos plan to block the landfill through political and legal battles with the State of New Mexico Environmental Department. A permit to an individual contractor allows the burial of up to fifty thousand cubic yards of waste annually in two-hundred-foot-long trenches fifty feet deep and twenty feet wide. The asbestos will be buried in plastic bags or barrels and the trenches will be covered by a minimum of three feet of dirt.

The site is located on private land near Dzilth-Na-O-Dith-Hle, a sacred mountain where Navajo people believe their ancestors first emerged. Residents of the area also fear the health and safety of the people are at risk because of the known cancer risks associated with asbestos. The conflict originates in the "checkerboard" status of the land surrounding the sacred land. The checkerboard land status of the area includes a mixture of tribal, federal, and state lands situated next to allotment lands owned by individual Navajo families. This mixture of land holding makes jurisdictional issues exceptionally difficult (Taliman, 1992c, p. 13).

RESTORATION OF
TRIBAL LANDS AND ARTIFACTS
Tribal Lands

The return of tribal lands has special significance when we recognize the importance of sacred lands and rights of Native people to religious freedom.

> Since time immemorial, Indian tribal Holy Men have gone into the high places, lakes, and isolated sanctuaries to pray, receive guidance from the Spirits, and train younger people in the ceremonies that constitute the spiritual life of the tribal community. In these ceremonies, medicine men represented the whole web of cosmic life in the continuing search for balance and harmony and through various rituals in which birds, animals, and plants were participants, harmony of life was achieved and maintained (Deloria, 1991, p. 1).

The spread of the population into sparsely settled areas has threatened sacred Indian lands as has the introduction of corporate farming and the continuing extension of the mining and timber industries. Some battles for sacred land have been won as in the case of Blue Lake of the Taos people. Others, however, continue. According to Deloria (1991, p. 2), the great gulf that exists between traditional western thinking about religion and the Indian perspective makes it difficult for many to understand why it is so important that Indian ceremonies be held, and they be conducted only at certain locations, and that they be held under conditions of extreme secrecy and privacy.

To assist Westerners in understanding the sacredness of lands (acknowledging that this does not represent the nature of reality) Deloria finds four major categories of description:

- Lands are sacred because the site is where, within a particular history, something of great importance took place. Wounded Knee, South Dakota, is such a place. In this classification, the site is all-important, but it is sanctified each time ceremonies are held and prayers offered.

- Lands are sacred because the site is where something specifically religious has happened. Examples would include the mountains in the Southwest where the Pueblo, Hopi, and Navajo peoples completed their migrations, were told to settle, or were where they first established their spiritual relationships with other forms of life who participate in the ceremonials.

- Lands are sacred because they are places where Higher Powers, on their own initiative, have revealed themselves to human beings. These sites are holy in and of themselves. Blue Lake and Bear Butte are sacred lands in and of themselves.

- The fourth classification is based upon the premise that there are higher spiritual powers that are in communication with human beings and that humans must always be ready to receive new revelations at new locations. This is important because some federal courts have insisted that traditional religious practitioners restrict their identification of sacred locations to those places that have been historically visited by Indians, implying that there could be no revelation of new, sacred places and new ceremonies. Deloria says this has a "God is dead" connotation that has no meaning to Native peoples.

There are several prominent battles for sacred lands including the Badger Two Medicine in Montana where oil drilling has been proposed in an area sacred to the Blackfeet and other tribes; Mt. Graham in Arizona where telescopes are proposed which would destroy an Apache sacred site; and the Medicine Wheel in Wyoming where the Forest Service has proposed to build a parking lot and observation platform on the site of the Wheel which is sacred to many tribes.

Although there are several prominent court cases involving the return of tribal lands, one of the most prominent is the Sioux and their struggle to regain their sacred Black Hills. According to Pevar (1992, p. 41), the Sioux experience typifies how the United States broke treaties to obtain Indian land. In 1851 the Sioux signed a treaty that guaranteed a large reservation as a permanent home; the government violated this treaty. The claims of the Sioux are based upon a subsequent treaty claim dating back to 1868 which took most of their land, left the sacred Black Hills, and promised that no additional land would be taken from them. When gold was discovered in 1874, the Black Hills was removed from the reservation. The taking of land continued.

The return of Sioux land is an issue that is still not settled. The issue has drawn international attention and some efforts have been made to negotiate with the Sioux. However, the Sioux people continue to refuse acceptance of a monetary land settlement of 17 million dollars made by the U.S. Indian Court of Claims in 1980 which has grown to over 330 million dollars since then.

> History itself has shown the Indians something more. Without a land base, there is no cohesive people, there is no tribe, there are no longer Indians, only lost, wandering individuals being sucked into the non-Indian world. For a tribe to continue to exist, for Indians and Indianness to continue, there must be a recognized, protected, and revered tribal home (Josephy, 1986, p. 130).

Another enduring battle that has not yet reached resolution involves the Seneca, one of the tribes of the Iroquois Confederacy. The battles of the Iroquois Six Nations Confederacy for their land are among the longest and most complicated Indian land claim struggles. Currently, of most interest are the claims of the Seneca Nation. It should be noted that in 1965 the Kinzua Dam was completed, flooding approximately ten thousand acres of the Seneca Reservation, including ancestral homes, farms, hunting grounds, fishing sites, community buildings, and burial plots; this is land that cannot be restored or returned.

In October 1784, the government made a treaty with the Six Nations at Fort Stanwix in which the Indians relinquished claim to all lands west of a north-south line running from Niagara River in New York to the border of Pennsylvania and the land on which Fort Oswego had been built. In return, the United States guaranteed three of the four hostile nations (Mohawks, Senecas, and Cayugas) most of their traditional homelands. The Oneida and Tuscarora were also guaranteed possession of the lands on which they were currently settled. This is approximately half of the state of New York. Subsequent efforts to erode, occupy, allot, or secure these lands were numerous, complicated, and frequently successful.

However, in 1919 the State of New York formed a commission headed by attorney Edward A. Everett to conduct a comprehensive study of land title questions in New York and to make recommendations as to how they might be made clear. Everett submitted a totally unexpected (and unwelcome to the state) conclusion: the Six Nations still possessed legal title to all 6 million acres of the Fort Stanwix treaty area.

In 1941 the Justice Department filed a suit in behalf of the Senecas. The suit sought to enforce a resolution of the Seneca Nation whereby cancelling hundreds of low-cost ninety-nine year leases taken in the city of Salamanca which is located on the reservation and at the northern part of the Kinzua Dam. The case was unsuccessful. Now this action has taken a most interesting turn of events. The leases in the town of Salamanca expired at the end of 1991. The Seneca have stipulated their intent not to renew the leases and to begin eviction proceedings against non-Indian lease and mortgage holders in the area, unless the new arrangements included terms in their favor. They have asked for clarification of the Seneca title, a shorter leasing period, fair rates for property rental, and jurisdiction over the land and the cash income derived from it. In addition, they have asked that compensation be made for all non-payment and underpayment of fair rental values of Seneca property accruing from the last lease. One can only imagine the furor of the non-Indians.

> As of now, their basic terms have been met and Congress has passed the Seneca Nation Settlement Act of 1990 including a settlement of $60 million for rental fees that the Seneca should have received over the past ninety-nine years (Churchill, 1992, p. 162).

Repatriation

Repatriation is a very old concern to Indian people and a recent concern to others. In direct terms, repatriation means returning an object to the place from which it came, to its point of origin. In the case of American Indian art, the definition has to do with removing certain types of pieces of tribal importance or value from nontribal hands and returning them to the representatives of the groups from which they were originally taken and to which they still rightfully belong.

In instances of direct theft, there are few people who would not support the repatriation of Native American material. For example, recently a shield that had been stolen in the mid-1970s was returned to the Hopi village of Oraibi by the officials of the Heard Museum in Phoenix. The piece had been obtained in 1976 as a donation from a Phoenix realtor. For the Hopis the shield was an important religious object that had been taken from the tribe unlawfully. The Coyote Clan leader sent by Oraibi to retrieve the shield stated that the shield "will be closely guarded by us, and in return it will guard us" (McCoy, 1992, p. 23).

According to McCoy (1992, p. 23), in the case of cultural patrimony, repatriation is more controversial. Again, in terms of American Indian art, cultural patrimony refers to an object that is not the property of an individual but of the group as a whole. Usually, these pieces are central to tribal religious beliefs and while they may be "works of art" to curators, collectors, and dealers, they are the artifacts that help to define a culture and keep it intact.

An example of the return of an object of cultural patrimony was the return of six thirty-inch-tall cottonwood carvings of the Zuni war god to the tribe by the Denver Museum of Natural History. These objects had been donated to the museum in 1968 and had been kept in storage since. It was only in 1991 that the governor

of Zuni issued a warning about three stolen war god effigies: "These war gods are communally owned sacred artifacts, and were removed without permission of Zuni authorities. No one other than the Zuni tribe has the right of possession" (McCoy, 1992, p. 23). The importance of war gods to the Zuni is made clear in the words that introduced this chapter; people in the art world are responding appropriately.

> In the first place, it was because of monetary desires that whoever took them away from here turned them over to somebody through sale, and that somebody perhaps even sold or maybe even donated them to these museums—that's the reason why they are scattered out. We are thankful for the museums that have been courteous and kind enough to return them. Because they have been replaced in the specific areas they were whenever they were taken away from here (Governor Robert E. Lewis, Zuni Pueblo, cited in Ferguson and Eriacho, 1990, p. 12).

It is clear that either private or public possession of items of cultural patrimony is not acceptable and that some "pieces of art" are, in reality, communal sacramental objects, not the property of individuals. American Indian people do not regard these objects as artifacts of a vanished past, "but as lively reflections of a people's spirit, as manifestations of whatever it is that binds them together and makes them something most of us are not: members of tribes" (McCoy, 1992, p. 23).

The disturbance of human remains is another issue. In 1989 Nebraska set a national precedent by enacting legislation that required state-sponsored institutions to return to requesting tribes all reasonably identifiable Indian skeletal remains and burial offerings for reburial. NARF, representing the Pawnee Tribe of Oklahoma and the Winnebago Tribe of Nebraska, led this successful legislative effort. In 1990 the Nebraska State Historical Society returned the skeletal remains and burial offerings of 398 individual Pawnees who were reburied in Pawnee ancestral homelands near Genoa, Nebraska.

The ancestors of the Pawnee, Wichita, and Arikara tribes who have been on public display in the "Salina Burial Pit" in Kansas were reburied in a tribal religious ceremony in 1990. This was made possible by legislation passed by the Kansas Legislature, again spearheaded by NARF.

Provisions that require The Smithsonian Institution to return Native human remains to a tribe upon request are included in the National American Indian Museum Act enacted in 1989. The Smithsonian must return Native human remains when the preponderance of the evidence indicates that the remains are culturally affiliated with the requesting tribe. Objects that have been buried with the remains are to be returned as well. The Smithsonian holds approximately nineteen thousand Native bodies.

On November 23, 1990, a most important piece of legislation was passed by Congress. The Native American Graves Protection and Repatriation Act has four components:

- Federal agencies and private museums which receive federal funding must inventory their collections of Native American human remains and funerary objects. The tribe must be notified and, upon request of the tribe, the ancestral remains and funerary objects must be returned for reburial or other disposition by the tribe.

- Indian tribes have ownership of cultural items which are excavated or discovered on federal or tribal land and they have the right of disposition of Indian human remains discovered in these areas.

- Trafficking in Native American human remains discovered in these areas is prohibited.

- Federal agencies and private museums which receive federal funds must create a summary of sacred objects or objects of cultural patrimony in their possession. If a tribe can prove a right of possession to these objects then the object must be returned upon request of the tribe (Native American Rights Fund Annual Report, 1990, pp. 16 and 17).

RECOGNITION AND RECLAMATION OF U.S. TREATY RIGHTS AND TRUST RESPONSIBILITIES

Part of recognizing and reclaiming U.S. treaty rights and trust responsibilities is demanding accountability in the federal offices that have responsibilities for Indian affairs. Indian people are determined to have a stronger voice in their own destiny and to streamline the BIA and make the agency more accountable. Peterson Zah, President of the Navajo Nation has stated that the BIA frequently has allocated money based on favoritism and politics rather than need.

Verna Williamson, tribal council president of the Isleta Pueblo alleged, "The BIA is slow, unaccountable, cumbersome, unresponsive, and afraid of making decisions." According to Williamson, before the BIA instituted Indian preference in hiring practices, it was staffed "with a lot of condescending white people. Now there are a lot of condescending Indians who think that they are above the rest of us because they don't live on a reservation," and the bureau is just as ineffective (Miniclier, 1992a, p. 1A and 4A).

Other problems are evident. The BIA can't account for 71 million dollars congress appropriated for an alcohol and substance abuse program. Two agencies of the BIA office in Albuquerque spent approximately 3.9 million dollars in a federal housing program and had such poor control that the project "was highly vulnerable to fraud and waste."

U.S. Senator Daniel Inouye (Hawaii) has suggested abolishing the bureau and giving Indians control of their own lives and destiny. This recommendation has its critics in government bureaucrats, traditional older Indians, and the Bush Republican administration. While the government and Indian people struggle with this question, one thing remains quite clear. Indians are beginning to reverse the centuries of oppression and are working to gain control of their lives.

The struggles for the rights of Indian people has been made more public by the Quincentenary, by a more informed general public, by the alarming statistics which point to a people deprived of their rights, their culture, and their pride over the years, and by strong Indian leadership. Educators have a responsibility to teach all young people not about the defeated Indians or the vanishing race, but about how Indian people are striving to reclaim their heritage and their rights ... and how, in a democracy, those are goals that can be achieved.

LESSON PLAN: ENVIRONMENTAL ISSUES
AND TRADITIONAL NATIVE DECISION-MAKING

Grade Level: Grades 5–8

Basic Concepts: Environment, natural resources, conservation, and interdependence

Organizing Generalization: When the physical environment and natural resources of any area in the world are used, misused, damaged, or changed, it affects all living things.

Culture Area: All areas

Time Period: Present

Background: In traditional Indian belief systems, Mother Earth is sacred—as are the things around us that sustain our lives—the sun, moon, wind, rain, rivers, mountains, trees, rocks, birds, fish, and animals. When these things of nature are destroyed or damaged, the earth, the environment, and the people are hurt. For Indian people, issues of the earth, tradition, and culture are all related. Traditional people of the Iroquois Nation considered the seventh generation when they made decisions. How would a particular decision impact the earth and those things on it seven generations from now? Students will examine the problems and issues that Native American people face today and hypothesize the long-term impacts of alternative solutions.

Objectives:
Knowledge
Students will:
1. Gain understanding of one major environmental issue that faces Native American people today.
2. Recognize that every environmental decision has both short-term and long-term consequences.

Skills
Students will:
1. Generate alternative solutions to an environmental issue.
2. Hypothesize the long-term effects of alternative decisions.
3. Practice information-gathering and decision-making skills.

Values
Students will:
1. Respect the need to make thoughtful decisions.
2. Appreciate the wisdom of traditional Indian people.

Activities:
1. Discuss the Iroquois Principle of the Seventh Generation. Using the chart on page 271, help students understand the Principle of the Seventh Generation.
2. There are many complex contemporary environmental issues that face Indian people today including, soil erosion, air, water, and land pollution, preservation of fish and game, storage of nuclear waste, foresting, recreational use of land, water management (dams). Identify issues that have interest for the students; local issues are usually most intriguing and have information more readily available. A news article that both indicates the interest and action of Native people in the environmental field as well as provides possible resources is included to stimulate students' involvement.

3. Depending on the age of the students, as a class or in small groups, identify one or more environmental issues to research in depth. Assist students in identifying a question such as, "Should the Mescalero Apache store nuclear waste in Monitored Retrievable Storage (MRS) sites on tribal lands?" Using brainstorming techniques generate alternative answers to the question(s).

4. Now, using the Principle of the Seventh Generation, evaluate each alternative answer as to its possible and probable impact on the seventh generation.

Extensions:
1. Write a brief essay on the wisdom of the Principle of the Seventh Generation.
2. Take any historical issue seven generations in the past and apply this principle "backwards." For example, what issue was important in 1842? What decision was made? What was the effect on the seventh generation in 1992? What factors would have been predictable? Not predictable?

Evaluation: Individual students should write letters to the tribe or major agency, such as the Department of the Interior, Forest Service, or Bureau of Land Management, which is involved in the decision stating its position on the question. Each letter should present a reasoned argument and be based on the Principle of the Seventh Generation.

Materials/Resources:
Newspapers (Indian and non-Indian), magazine articles, and environmental groups, NARF, and CERT.

1991 PROTECTING MOTHER EARTH

Indigenous Environmental Network—Over 500 participants from 57 different tribes and reservations gathered June 6–9, 1991, in the Paha/Sapa Black Hills for the 1991 Protecting Mother Earth: The Toxic Threat to Indian Lands Conference. This historic event was twice as large as last years' founding conference held in the Navajo Nation at Dilkon, AZ. The gathering successfully made giant steps forward in uniting Indigenous people and their allies in the struggle to protect Mother Earth.

This years' conference took place near Bear Butte, the Lakota and Cheyenne sacred mountain. The conference was hosted by the Native Resource Coalition (Pine Ridge Reservation), the Good Road Coalition (Rosebud Reservation), and was co-sponsored by many Indigenous organizations. Conference participants joined in many cultural activities, as well as in workshops to learn how to better protect our land, traditions, culture, and people. Many elders and spiritual leaders shared their traditional perspectives, providing guidance and assistance for our efforts.

Illustration 17.1—Jane Yazzie, a Navajo from Dilkon, AZ, was presented a "Protecting Mother Earth" statue in recognition of her environmental stewardship and the successes of C.A.R.E. (Citizens Against Ruining our Environment). This Navajo community rejected a hazardous waste incinerator and a toxic waste dump which was to be located on their land and which had been misrepresented to them as a "recycling facility." (permission from Native Monthly Reader)

At the conference the Indigenous delegates created and formalized the "Indigenous Environmental Network" as a tool and clearinghouse for activities of Indigenous people who want to work together in this common goal. The delegates also wrote and approved an "Environmental Code of Ethics and Conference Statement" which will be presented to the large environmental groups and the public, demanding respect for Indigenous people, their land, sovereignty, and self-determination

If you would like more information contact: Indigenous Environmental Network, Box 399, Southwold, Ontario, Canada NOL 2G0 or call Jackie Warledo (918) 742-2125 or Chris Peters (916) 625-4247.

(Used by permission of *Native Monthly Reader* (1991–1992): 2)

SEVEN GENERATIONS

		PRESENT
1. Great grandparent	87 years	(Your great grandparents)
2. Grandparent	62 years	(Your grandparents)
3. Parent	37 years	(Your parents)
4. Child	**12 years**	**(You as you are now)**
		FUTURE
5. Parent	37 years	(You as a parent)
6. Grandparent	62 years	(You as a grandparent)
7. Great Grandparent	87 years	(You as a great grandparent)

In 1992, if your great grandparents were eighty-seven years old, your grandparents sixty-two years old, your parents were thirty-seven years old, and you were twelve years old, you would be:

- Approximately thirty-seven years old in 2017 when you are a parent

- Approximately sixty-two years old in 2042 when you are a grandparent

- Approximately eighty-seven years old in 2067 when you are a great-grandparent

Your great grandparents would have been born in 1905. Throughout their lives, they made decisions for children and families who would be living many years in the future!

Using twenty-five years as a generation, in what year were the decisions made that are affecting your life right now?

In what year will you be eligible to vote?

If you honor the Principle of the Seventh Generation, approximately what years do you need to consider in casting your first vote?

THE SEVENTH GENERATION

In our way of life, in our government, with every decision we make, we always keep in mind the Seventh Generation to come. It's our job to see that the people coming ahead, the generations still unborn, have a world no worse than ours—and hopefully better. When we walk upon Mother Earth we always plant our feet carefully because we know the faces of our future generations are looking up at us from beneath the ground. We never forget them.

(Oren Lyons, Haudenosaunee. Wall and Arden, 1990, p. 68)

Over and over we were told: Turn around and look, there they are, the Seventh Generation—they're coming up right behind you. "Look over your shoulder," Tadodaho Leon Shenandoah told us. "Look behind you. See your sons and your daughters. They are your future. Look father, and see your sons' and your daughters' children even unto the Seventh Generation. That's the way were were taught. Think about it: you yourself are a Seventh Generation!"

(Wall and Arden, 1990, p. 120)

LESSON PLAN:
BLACK HILLS OF SOUTH DAKOTA AND THE SIOUX

Grade Level: Grades 7–9

Basic Concepts: Religious freedom and sacred land

Organizing Generalization: All religions have lands, sites, ceremonies, and artifacts that are sacred to them. The rights to these sites, ceremonies, and artifacts are guaranteed to the citizens of the United States.

Culture Area: Plains

Time Period: 1980 to present

Background: The Black Hills of South Dakota is one of the most sacred places on earth. It remains so, despite the abomination of Mount Rushmore, the tourists, and the gold mines. The Black Hills are called "O'onakezin" which means they are a place of shelter. They are sometimes called "Wamakaognaka E'cante" which means that they are "the heart of everything that is."

> Today the largest gold mine in this part of the world, making 85% of all the gold in the United States, is located in the Black Hills. The 'heart of everything that is' lies open and bleeding, scarred by men and their machines, seeking profits for their own generation while forgetting the generations to come (Charging Eagle and Zeilinger, 1987).

Since 1980, the Sioux have sought return of the Black Hills. The U.S. government has offered them money for the land, which they have repeatedly refused—they demand the return of their sacred land. For tribes in which destructive and degrading poverty is the norm, this refusal of large sums of money is difficult, but nonetheless endured by the Sioux who place their sacred land and their right to worship as they deem proper above their material comforts and economic security.

Objectives:
Knowledge
Students will:
1. Recall the major points of the Treaty of 1868 to the present as they relate to the ownership of the Black Hills.
2. Demonstrate their understanding of the sequence of events in the controversy of the ownership of the Black Hills.
3. Construct a reasoned position on whether or not the Black Hills should be returned to the Sioux.

Skills
Students will:
1. Develop a time line.
2. Use research skills.
3. Practice skills of debate and reasoned argumentation.

Values
Students will:
1. Appreciate the reverence that the Sioux hold for the Black Hills.
2. Respect the decisions of the Sioux to refuse over 300 million dollars for this land.

Activities:

1. Use the brief newspaper clipping to introduce this lesson. Ask students to make a list of the information that they would need to be able to decide fairly who should own the Black Hills. Explain to them that they are going to thoroughly research and debate the issue, and present their arguments and recommendations to their congressional representatives.

2. Divide the class into two to six research teams. Teams can research specific topics, such as the resources of the Black Hills, the religious beliefs of the Sioux regarding this land, the treaties, the arguments presented to the Indian Claims Commission and so on. This division into teams will depend on the age and abilities of the students.

3. Students should view the videotapes *The Black Hills Claim* and *The Treaty of 1868*. Present the videotapes twice, first to gain an overall understanding of the history and the issues, and second to take specific notes.

4. Make a large class time line that traces the sequence of the important events in this controversy.

5. Write NARF for additional information or for resources to use in gaining further understanding. One possibility would be to arrange for a telephone interview with a NARF attorney. Students should write their questions in advance of an interview.

6. Seek other resources for additional information.

7. Students should find a reasonable way to synthesize their arguments—a debate which begins with a position statement might be one way, a mock court trial might be another.

8. Seek a way to prepare written final statements for or against the return, or perhaps a proposed compromise.

9. Students will write letters to their congressional representatives, presenting their arguments.

Extensions:

1. Research the history of Mount Rushmore. How do Indian people feel about Mount Rushmore? What about the monument that is being made of Chief Crazy Horse?

2. Research such issues as tourism and gaming on or near the Black Hills.

3. Read about George Custer. Connell, E. S. *Son of the Morning Star*. San Francisco: North Star, 1984. (Custer "discovered" gold in the Black Hills.)

Evaluation: Students will be evaluated on the quality of their letters and the arguments presented either for or against the return of the Black Hills to the Sioux Nation.

Materials/Resources:

Charging Eagle, T. and Zeilinger, R. *Black Hills: Sacred Hills*. Chamberlain, SD: Tipi Press, 1987.

Churchill, W. "The Earth Is Our Mother: Struggles for American Indian Land and Liberation in the Contemporary United States." In M. Annette Jaimes (ed.) *The State of Native America: Genocide, Colonization, and Resistance*. Boston: South End, 1992, 162–69. This brief explanation provides a broad overview of the sequence of events in the Black Hills land claim and is exceptionally valuable for the teacher. A time line could easily be made from this information.

Lazarus, E. *Black Hills/White Justice*. New York: HarperCollins, 1991.

Videotapes

The Black Hills Claim. (1987). NETCHE (Producer). Available from the Native American Public Broadcasting Consortium.

The Treaty of 1868. (1987). NETCHE (Producer). Available from the Native American Public Broadcasting Consortium.

SIOUX NATION TRIBES LOOKING AT ACQUIRING BLACK HILLS LANDS

Pine Ridge, South Dakota (ICC)—A delegation of Great Sioux Nation members recently went to Washington D.C. to see if they might be able to acquire land designated as disposable within the Black Hills that has been the subject of a treaty claim dating back to 1868.

The eight member tribes hope to obtain title to those lands by special legislation while preserving their claims to the entire treaty land area. The Sioux continue to refuse acceptance of a monetary land settlement of $17 million made by the U.S. Indian Court of Claims in 1980 which has grown to over $330 million since then.

(Used by permission of *News from Indian Country* (Mid-August 1992): 1.

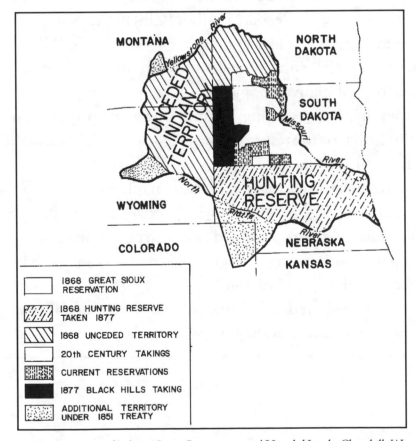

Map 17.2—Map of Lakota Nation Reservations and Unceded Lands. Churchill, W.
(1992), p. 165.

SUMMARY
CONTEMPORARY ISSUES

In 1992, the United States faced the reality that Native people have not vanished nor have they assimilated. In the five hundred years since Columbus first set foot in the Caribbean, American Indians have renewed their efforts to regain their land and treaty rights, restore their cultures, practice their religions, educate their children, instill respect for their traditional ways, live in health, become economically self-sufficient, and take their rightful place in their homeland—Indian Country.

There are many examples of strong Indian leadership today. In 1992 Ben Nighthorse Campbell, Colorado Democrat, was elected to the Senate. Wilma Mankiller is the principal Chief of the Cherokee Nation and provides leadership at the national level. Indian organizations such as the American Indian Movement (AIM), the Council for Energy Resource Tribes (CERT) the Native American Rights Fund (NARF), and the National Indian Education Association (NIEA) are providing leadership in political, legal, educational, and economic areas that are important to the self-determination of Native people.

New industries, including gaming, are bringing new prosperity to some reservations. Tribes are fighting for the return of invaluable water rights and the right to hunt and fish on their traditional lands.

The return of tribal lands and artifacts has great religious importance. The sacred Blue Lake of the Taos people has been returned and legal battles are raising issues of certain rights and lands that were accorded to Indian people in forgotten treaties. The Sioux are still engaged in securing the return of their sacred Black Hills which was guaranteed to them in the Treaty of 1868.

Recent laws have required the return of Native American material of tribal importance to the tribes to which they belong.

CHAPTER 18

Contemporary Issues

The stories of the People
tell how the world began.
The stories of the People
tell how the stars filled the skies,
    that the earth is alive,
    where not to fish,
    when to give thanks.

No one asked "Why?"

The stories of the People
guide their way of life.
The stories of the People
guide them in times of success and loss,
    in times of happiness and sorrow,
    in times of famine and abundance.

No one asked "Why?"

The stories of the People
link past to present to future.
The stories of the People
are passed from father to child,
    from elder to youth,
    from teacher to student.

No one asked "Why?"

Time came when the stories were broken,
when the People forgot.
Time came when the stories were broken,
when the language was forbidden,
      the ceremonies were outlawed,
      the thread became thin.

No one asked "Why?"

The stories of the People
cannot be silenced.
The stories of the People
cannot be silenced.
      They are being passed
      from generation to generation.

No one asked "Why?"

The stories of the People
will foretell the future.
The stories of the People
will guide them through unknown danger.
The stories of the People
protect them from the evil of the world.
The stories of the People
keep the spirit alive.
The thread now grows stronger.

Listen, can you hear the stories?

                —Lisa Harjo

As American Indian people step into the twenty-first century, they are well aware of their position in the world and the role they play. Their strength comes from strong convictions about the knowledge and wisdom that has been handed down generation to generation. This wisdom and knowledge is imbedded in the stories of the people. Tribes enter the next century with strong ties to this heritage and they not only talk about it, but they live it in their everyday lives.

This chapter will explore several aspects of American Indian life and how the future will be woven with the threads of the present and the past. Education, health, and the maintenance of traditional languages and cultures are naturally related. There are many examples of these principles that we will discuss in every tribe, but, as in the rest of the book, we will focus on the Haudenosaunee (Iroquois), the Muskogee (Five Civilized Tribes), the Navajo and Pueblo people of the Southwest, and the Lakota (Sioux).

CULTURE

The Haudenosaunee, People of the Longhouse and the Iroquois Confederacy, practice their traditional beliefs daily. Today, they live in several communities and reservations that are spread across New York, Wisconsin, Oklahoma, and Canada. While some of the communities have elected tribal councils that conform to the requirements of Canada and the United States, they also have maintained the traditional Grand Council. Those members of the Six Nations who live in the traditional way are often also followers of the Longhouse religion. These Confederacy members have not acknowledged United States citizenship, but rather honor their tribal membership and the Confederacy membership as their only allegiance.

They believe that the Iroquois Confederacy is made up of nations. This is the way that it has always been. One way this traditional teaching is demonstrated in the present is in the issuance and use of Iroquois Confederacy passports. According to Onondaga Chief Oren Lyons, members of the six Confederacy tribes have traveled to over twenty countries using the passports. These passports signify the nation to nation status that is inherent in the concept of Indian nation sovereignty (Arden, 1987, pp. 67, 70).

The tradition that accompanies the wampum is also ancient wisdom that is very important in modern times. John Mohawk, a member of the Seneca Nation, expressed the meaning of the wampum as he spoke during a conference held at Cornell University on the topic of the Great Law. Wampum represents the peoples' best thinking put into belts. The interpretation of the value of wampum is particularly interesting. When Europeans first observed the Iroquois, they thought the wampum was money. It took many laborious hours to make using a stone drill on the shells. However, the wampum were made not to trade for goods, but to be made into belts that commemorated an agreement between or solution produced by the people. It represented the fact that the people had sat down together and found a way to solve their problems. The wampum belt was brought out at meetings of the Council and at other meetings to bring the people to a shared mind that would encourage problem solving. The belts are sacred, and they represent sacred bonds between people.

> I also remember the tradition of the people of the Five Nations that our power to create peace and a peaceful resolution depends on our ability to see the other side, the other people's humanity. That unless we believe that they are sane, competent, and coherent people, unless we can put away our fear and our hatred of them, we cannot use our minds to solve problems with them (Mohawk, 1987).

This philosophy is necessary in the twenty-first century to help people of the world join together to create a future for all of us. This is an example of how the traditions of the past will guide the way into the future. The wisdom of the Great Tree of Peace has guided the Iroquois for thousands of years. Nations around the world recognize its power and respect it.

In 1985, using Haudenosaunee passports, a group of representatives of the Six Nations, including Chief Oren Lyons, traveled to Bogota, Colombia, to meet with Nicaragua's Sandinista president and representatives of the Miskito Tribe, an Indian tribe which refused to succumb to the rule of the Sandinista. At the meeting, Chief Lyons said: "We are the Haudenosaunee. We are made up of Six nations ... each of us equal ... each of us sovereign ... and we come together in a confederacy. Our business is peace, not war ... . We must be of one mind" (Arden, 1987, pp. 69–70). He spoke about how no problem was too big to cause disunity. He spoke in a measured tone in the manner of the old ones. Those in the room were stunned. The teachings of the Great Tree of Peace once again touched the hearts and minds of the people.

Since the members of the Iroquois Confederacy have been moved from their original homeplace, they hold fast to their beliefs and look for a return of the land. In 1974, a group of Mohawks seized an unused summer camp on New York State park land. They occupied the land and lived there for three years. At that time, they agreed to exchange that piece of land for another piece of state land in the northern Adirondacks. The community lives there to this day. The community is Ganienkeh, or land of flint. The people in this community live according to the law of the Great Tree of Peace. Today they operate a school and other community facilities with no assistance from the U.S. government. They encourage the use of traditional language and culture to fashion their lives in this modern day.

LANGUAGE

Native languages hold the key to culture. They are the link to the past and the future. There are many in Indian Country who feel that without Native languages, there will be no true Indians. The language is necessary to practice the traditional religion. Soon youths will know the songs but not the meanings. Then they will forget the songs. And all will be forgotten.

The first blows to Native religion were struck by the government-run boarding school system. The use of Native languages was prohibited throughout the country, and children were punished both physically, and emotionally for talking to each other in Indian languages. On many occasions, one student didn't understand the English of the teacher and asked another student for clarification in his or her language. Both students were punished, regardless of the situation. Even after the number of boarding schools was reduced and day schools were built in reservation communities, Native languages were still prohibited. Fluency in English for success in the modern world was valued above the maintenance of tribal language.

In Busby, Montana, members of the Cheyenne Nation are taking active steps on many reservations and in many tribes to change the trend of losing their Native language. With leadership from Ted Risingsun, Sylvester Knows-His-Gun, Sr., and others, the language has been written down by linguists and language curriculum for children in grades kindergarten through three has been implemented in the schools. However, the road to this accomplishment was long and difficult, and there is still much to be done to keep the language alive among the people (West, 1992, pp. 1, 17).

For Ted Risingsun, a future without the Cheyenne language would mean an end to the great oral tradition which is so much a part of his life. At sixty-five, he still shares stories of his youth and of his ancestors with his friend since childhood, Mr. Know-His-Gun, Sr. They talk of events in the 1800s as though they happened yesterday. The path taken by the Cheyenne, first taking control of their own schools, then developing their own language materials and curriculum, and then implementing them in the schools has taken almost twenty years. Their ultimate goal is to have the Cheyenne language taught and used in all grades.

A report of the Indian Nations at Risk Task Force issued in early 1992 stated that among the other barriers that Indian children have to overcome is "the loss of Native-language ability and the wisdom of the older generations." It is said that Indian languages could, and have, disappeared in a heartbeat. Along with the languages will go the wisdom of the ancients when there is no longer anyone to carry on.

Another factor that contributes to loss of Native language is that many Indian people cannot find work on their own reservations or pueblos. So they leave for the cities and often, in a few short years, forget their language from lack of use and need. This is the plight that faced the people of Isleta Pueblo in the Southwest. The adobe buildings of the Isleta Pueblo, strung along the banks of the Rio Grande in present-day New Mexico, are home to almost twenty-four hundred residents. In this small community, modern technology has come to the aid of the tribe and is helping to keep Isletan, a dialect of the Tiwa language, alive and well (Donahue, 1990. p. 21).

The active learners in this setting are not kindergarten through third-graders, or even older students, but preschoolers in the Headstart Program. They flick on their computers with confidence and engage in a revolutionary computer program developed by Isletan, Ted Jojola. Professor Jojola, a Native who chairs University of New Mexico's Native American Studies Department, first dreamed of using computers while watching his own son grow up and learn to talk. He was entrenched in the television and learned English from what he saw and heard. The program that Jojola developed combines graphics of the words with sound displays that name the words for the child to model. The program was begun in 1985 and is now utilizing one computer in each of their five classrooms and three computers, including one with a large screen, in their office.

The Zuni Tribe is also pioneering this technology for teaching Native languages. So far they have compiled five storybooks and English definitions for seven hundred Indian words. Their electronic dictionary is in use in Zuni language classrooms in middle school. The goal of the Zuni Literacy Project is to create audible videotapes of Zuni folktales and to install computers in its elementary school and two high schools. Joining the Isleta and the Zuni are the Acoma and the San Juan tribes of New Mexico and many others throughout the country. The challenge is there for all Native people in the modern world.

This is an excellent use of the ability of modern technology to maintain and promote tribal language and culture; it is the ultimate in combining the wisdom of the old and the technology of the new. However, there are drawbacks on both sides. Many Isleta traditionalists object to the recording of the historically oral Isleta language and fear that the culture and history will be taken away through the greater use of technology and access to their language by outsiders. For over four hundred years, the tribe's culture has been under attack. When an Isletan folktale, *Giant from the Black Mesa*, was being used for a computer videotape recently, the elders objected. They said the "tale alluded to cornbread, a food Isletans often eat during religious ceremonies" (Donahue, 1990, p. 25). As a result, all plans for the development and use of a video about the folktale have been abandoned. This means the responsibility of teaching Native languages and stories to children rests in the hands of the parents and grandparents. The problem with this option, however, is that many Indian parents of today do not speak their language fluently.

One of the problems of the use of technology is cost and, as a consequence, availability. Much of the computer hardware that is available to tribes and schools is inadequate to run the software programs that will meet the needs of the students. Therefore, the students are handicapped by the equipment that is available. This also inhibits the development of programs and expansion of creativity regarding instruction in Native languages.

If Native languages are not taught in the schools, many believe the languages will be lost. Others fear that too much of the tribal culture will be diluted or diminished as others outside of the tribe learn the language and are exposed to the stories and history. However, the natural mechanisms for teaching language within communities such as extended families, parents fluent in the language, and the real need to speak the language in order to communicate are missing because of recent history. Without concentrated effort, the languages will be lost. As Sylvester Know-His-Gun says, "My kids don't know how to talk Cheyenne, and every once in a while they get on me and say, 'Why didn't you teach us?' and I don't know what to tell them."

HEALTH

The winds of change have blown in Indian Country for thousands of years, but until the last five hundred years, change was an ordinary response to the seasons and the natural world. During the last five hundred years, change has been imposed on Native people by outside forces. And this change came too fast and without warning or support for appropriate responses. One of the significant areas of life that has been affected by the changes of the last five centuries is health. Forced removal from historical homesites and ways of life has caused Native people to accept new foods and customs that have had ill effects on their health.

Native people throughout North America survived for thousands of years eating a natural diet of whole grains, fruits, vegetables, and meat or fish when available. These foods were largely replaced with processed foods such as refined white flour, white sugar, lard, canned vegetables, and little or no fresh meat. As a result, Indian people have begun to suffer a variety of diseases and conditions that are linked to nutrition and way of life. Additionally, the use of alcohol and drugs has greatly impacted Native communities.

The major killers of American Indians are heart disease, diabetes, cancer, alcoholism, and accidents. Statistics indicate that while the lifespan for American Indians has increased significantly, it is still much shorter than that of other Americans. Another alarming statistic is that suicide is very prevalent in Native American communities, with the greatest incidence in teenagers. A closer look at a few of these conditions and the lives of American Indians will give some insight to the conditions present in most American Indian communities.

Diabetes

Almost one of every thousand of the Tohono O'odham (formerly known as the Papago of the Southwest culture area) will die of diabetes. This is the highest mortality rate for this disease recorded in the nation. According to the Indian Health Service, it is ten times higher than the national rate and it is increasing. Almost unknown to the O'odham fifty years ago, diabetes has reached epidemic stage. Diabetes is a condition in which the body doesn't create enough insulin or doesn't use it properly in the digestion of sugar. Excess sugar in the blood can damage organs, nerves, and blood vessels. Insulin, a hormone of the pancreas, aids in the digestion of sugar by allowing blood sugar to be deposited in cells where it is used for energy. When cells become resistant to insulin, or when there is not enough insulin, high blood sugar can result in diabetes.

There are considered two types of diabetes: Type I in which the body cannot make insulin and injections are needed, and Type II in which the body manufactures too much insulin. Cells become resistant to it and do not allow the sugar to be digested. Type II diabetes is the most common type of diabetes for American Indians.

When the Native people such as the O'odham were put on reservations and introduced to a diet that was high in fat and sugar and readily available year-round, they often changed their lifestyles also. They became more sedentary as their basic needs could be met with less effort, and there were no periods of famine as in the past. These two factors contributed to rise in obesity and a disastrous Type II diabetes epidemic.

Robert Hackenberg, a professor at the University of Colorado in Boulder and director of a grant aimed at developing new strategies for the O'odham people to cope with and conquer the diabetes epidemic, says that researchers widely agree on a hypothesis that many aboriginal people developed a "thrifty gene" as an evolutionary survival mechanism. The gene allowed the Native people, such as the O'odham to store excess caloric energy in fatty tissues when food was abundant. This store could then be used by the body in lean times. Without this gene many tribes would have become extinct when famine existed in the extreme climates (Johnson, 1992, p. 1A).

The grant that Dr. Hackenberg currently directs focuses its efforts on three hundred junior and senior high school students and their parents. The team working with the grant is convinced that weight control, low fat diet, and exercise can greatly reduce the chance that the young will have diabetes when they get older. Cindy Chico, now twenty-eight years old, has kept her diabetes under control since first diagnosis at thirteen years of age. She has never used medication, relying on diet and exercise to keep her healthy. She has replicated the state of health that the members of her tribe enjoyed until recent times.

Substance Abuse

Alcoholism is a disease that has infected many American Indians. While the obvious reason for drinking may be depression, poverty, and hopelessness, there may also be a genetic reason that predisposes certain intolerance of or reaction to alcohol. Before interaction with the Europeans, alcoholic beverages were known to Indians of both North and South America. The fermented wine of older times was made from cactus, persimmons, and other fruit. The Europeans distilled liquor differently and made a liquor with a much stronger alcohol content. They used corn and potatoes instead of fruit. Indian people seemed to have a different reaction to the stronger alcohol and over the years have developed a much higher percent of alcoholism. Current studies are investigating the correlation of heredity and environment with the incidence of alcoholism.

A result of the high incidence of alcoholism is fetal alcohol syndrome (FAS), a great sorrow among Indian people. When mothers drink during pregnancy, their babies are greatly harmed. The children, if they live, can develop seizures, poor eyesight and hearing, mental retardation, physical deformities, and a host of other problems. It appears that the FAS child's ability to make reasoned decisions and to solve problems is greatly impaired. For a people who believe that the children are the future, this is an alarming reality.

Alcoholism manifests itself in other destructive ways. The most common method of suicide is from drug overdose. The high incidence of suicide among American Indians is a symptom of the hopelessness and lack of control that many Indians feel, especially the youth. They cannot see that they can determine their futures. Their experiences with the world have often been unfriendly, with extreme social stress and disruption. They feel that they have few, if any, alternatives. Most of those Indians who succeed at suicide are male while more females only attempt suicide.

According to the Indian Health Service, accidental death is the leading cause of death for Indian people living on reservations and in rural areas. Often these deaths are from motor vehicle accidents. Among the Dineh' (Navajo), for instance, accidents have been the leading cause of death since the 1950s, causing four to five times as much death as among the general U.S. population. Males are more likely to be killed in accidents than females. In 1975–1977, seven times more Navajo Indians died from accidental motor vehicle death than the U.S. average. Some researchers believe that there is a relationship between the high number of single passenger/single vehicle accidents and suicide. When they investigated this type of crash, they found the drivers were more likely to be male and have records of drunk driving, driving without a license, personal problems, or recent major life changes.

Communities across the land are rising to the challenge of combatting alcoholism, both on reservations and in urban areas. Programs that provide intervention, prevention, and treatment for alcoholics are funded by tribes, the Indian Health Service, and private sources. As an example, many national conferences and associations that in the past offered wine and cheese receptions and alcoholic beverages at their functions now host only nonalcoholic activities and model and promote sobriety among the Native people. While many Native people use the twelve-step program of Alcoholics Anonymous with great success, others are turning to the traditional American Indian religion. Participating in ceremonies, following the instructions of the elders, and learning to live in accordance with the traditional philosophy of living help Indian people heal themselves.

EDUCATION

It is clear that American Indian people are at a crossroad. The children of today must learn the ways of their people, including language and culture, and they must know how to apply this knowledge in the modern world. Native American children must also learn the skills and knowledge of the larger world to enable them to survive and succeed. In an interview with John Echo Hawk, executive director of the Native American Rights Fund, he stated that the future for Indian people would be determined through education and the court system (Harvey, Harjo, and Jackson, 1991, p. 59). Education is important for Indians as well as non-Indians, as non-Indians often play an integral part in determining the future for Indian people.

Indian self-determination in the modern context is a direct result of the education and leadership of Indian professionals, in science and engineering, law and medicine, education and other fields. These leaders have learned the tools of their profession and are still practicing members of their traditional religious practices. They recognize that they are Indians who have acquired powerful tools through education.

> You are an Indian first, last, and always. You may have a degree in anthropology, law, or nuclear engineering, but that is your profession, and how you make your living; it is not you! ... Your first responsibility is to be a human being, an Indian. Once you accept that fact and use it as a positive factor, you can do whatever professional tasks are required of you but you will know when to draw the line between professional responsibilities and the much greater responsibility to be a person. You can earn money but you cannot be happy or satisfied unless you become yourself first (Deloria, 1991, p. 15).

The Indian world view is a unified one. Everything is connected; communities, people, and all living things are related. Therefore, there is a direct relationship between Indian people and their communities. This may be essential to the success of tribally controlled and operated kindergarten through twelfth-grade schools and colleges. Schools like Rough Rock Community School on the Navajo Reservation and the Little Wound School in Kyle, South Dakota (Sioux), allow Indian students to learn within the context of the Indian community. The curriculum is culturally based and focused to enhance that student's personal knowledge and perspectives. Native languages are being taught in many Indian-controlled schools, promoting the old ways alongside the new. Elders have become mentors and teachers in the schools and communities. Children are learning and succeeding.

Even in the urban context, schools geared for the unique needs of Indian students have been established and thrive. The Heart of the Earth Survival School in Minneapolis and the American Indian Magnet School in St. Paul, Minnesota, are two examples of intertribal urban schools that offer a more holistic education in an American Indian cultural environment. They emphasize the community even though it is in an urban context.

> The American Indian Magnet School is conveying to students a network of values, norms, rituals, roles, heroes, heroines, ceremonies, personal anecdotes, stories, and myths. The school attracts students, staff, and volunteers who do more than emphasize a Native American philosophy, we espouse it and live it. We do so for the betterment of our children, ourselves, and our world—one world (Pewewardy, 1992, pp. 56–57).

The great success of tribal colleges to retain and graduate Indian students is linked to the fact Indian students thrive when their learning is purposeful and related to their lives. Education in many non-Indian educational institutions is fractured and compartmentalized. The learning is not related to life needs and experiences.

This greater success of Indian students in tribally controlled kindergarten through twelfth-grade schools and colleges will have an increasing impact on Native communities, tribes, and lands. As time passes, the impact of formal education on the American Indian and the impact of the American Indian on education will become apparent. A few signs of the significance of the impact are already evident. Oglala Lakota College currently offers a master's degree that is equivalent to a degree in business administration. The Managers as Warriors program is based on Lakota values, spirituality, and language. According to Debra White Plume, in the winter of 1992 there were twenty-seven students enrolled. The program, currently funded through a grant from the Kellogg Foundation, became part of the regular Oglala Lakota College offerings in 1993. As more tribally based colleges offer programs like the Managers as Warriors program, they will nurture the leadership that will guide the Indian nations into the twenty-first century.

Native cultures are living cultures, and where they have been weakened through disease, massacre, forced assimilation, relocation, termination, education, religious conversion, and nurtured dependency, they are experiencing new power and vitalization. Determined American Indian people are recovering lost languages, cultures, and lifeways as they adapt to advancing technology and a global world. This determination and the challenge of renewal is beautifully expressed in the following words.

> A renaissance is taking place among Native American people. This renaissance is not of a material nature. It is a spiritual renaissance, a retrieving and reviving of our original covenant with the Creator. We are reaffirming our relationship and stewardship with our Mother Earth. While we are inspired and directed to do this for our children and ourselves, we also realize that many, not all, of our Elders have fallen asleep, forgotten, or have never known our rightful spiritual heritage. Therefore, it is up to those of us who have, in whatever measure, the teachings, philosophy, and traditions, including the rituals, to work for their revival and continuance (Eddie Benton-Banaise as cited in Wall and Arden, 1990, pp. 50–51).

LESSON PLAN:
THE NAVAJO NATION: A NAME CHANGE

Grade Level: Grades 4–6

Basic Concepts: Change and adaptation

Organizing Generalization: When people assert their independence as a group or even as individuals, they demonstrate the importance of their language, culture, and values, and their impact on their image of themselves and how others perceive them.

Culture Area: Southwest

Time Period: 1992

Background: The Navajo people have been called "Navajo" since they were first encountered by the Spaniards more than three hundred years ago. The Spanish called these newly found people, who farmed and raised animals, Navajo, a Tewa word that means "cultivators of the fields." Initially, the name was spelled "Navaho." In 1954, tribal members voted to change the spelling to "Navajo." The word Navajo or Navaho has been used by countless businesses as a trademark or product name as it stimulates an image of the rugged outdoors. Now the Navajo have decided to put their name to a vote of the tribe, this time to change it to "Dineh," a Navajo word which means "the people."

Objectives:
Knowledge
Students will:

1. Demonstrate their understanding of who the Navajo people are today and where they live.
2. Explain the origin of the word Navajo.
3. List reasons why the name change is wanted by many Navajo people.
4. Recognize the importance of names to a group of people or individual in their perception of themselves and how others perceive them.

Skills
Students will:

1. Research information on the present-day Navajo.
2. Locate their home on a map of the Southwest.

Values
Students will:

1. Appreciate the importance of group participation in the name selection process.
2. Empathize with the need for the people of the Navajo Nation to have a name that is Navajo.

Activities:

1. Students can conduct individual or group research projects to answer some basic questions: Who are the Navajo? Where do they live? What is the current population? What is their form of tribal government? What is their current economic, educational, and governmental status? Pass out a map of the Southwest for the students to locate the Navajo Reservation. Discuss the results of the investigations in class.

2. Discuss name changes that students might be familiar with such as:
   a. Changing names in marriage (this custom is changing).
   b. Changing the names of places as a way of honoring a person (Cape Canaveral to Cape Kennedy).
   c. Changing the names of sports teams to eliminate names that do not show respect to a group of people (a current issue for Indian people, e.g., Washington Redskins, Atlanta Braves).
   d. Changing names of immigrants to more Anglicized versions.
   e. Changing names as a matter of choice (e.g., Tohono O'odham).
   f. Changing names as a matter of coercion (e.g., in boarding schools for Indian children).

3. Discuss that the name United States came from people who were asserting their independence and who chose the term to describe who they were. The term "United States" is based in the concept of democracy imbedded in Great Law of Peace of the Iroquois Confederacy. Why is our name the United States of America?

4. Have students get into small groups. Distribute copies of the newspaper article about the possible name change, asking students to read it to themselves.

5. Ask each group to predict the outcome of the Navajo election, stating reasons for their prediction.

6. After hearing the opinions expressed by the group, ask students to imagine that they are Navajo and cast their vote. Is this vote different than they would vote if they were not Navajo? Why or why not?

Extensions:
1. Research other Native tribes that have changed their names back to their traditional name or who use the more ancient name when referring to themselves. (Todono O'odham—Papago, Lakota—Sioux). Or, find the original names of other tribes that still retain the names given to them by their conquerors.
2. Ask students to write an essay on the meaning of their own names.

Evaluation: Students should demonstrate through class discussions their knowledge and understanding of the impact of the name change process on individuals and groups.

Materials/Resources:
Newspaper article on Navajo name change (included in the text).
Arthur, C., Bingham, S., and Bingham, J. Between Sacred Mountains. Tucson: Sun Tracks and the University Press, 1982.
Gilpin, L. The Enduring Navaho. Austin: University of Texas, 1988.
Locke, R. F. The Book of the Navajo. Los Angeles: Mankind, 1992.

Videotapes
Peace River Films and KAET-TV (Producers). (1985). Seasons of a Navajo. Available from the Native American Broadcasting Consortium

Navajos May Become 'Dineh' to Rest of Globe
Tribal Leaders Urge Change to Traditional Name

For centuries, the Navajos have referred to themselves as Dineh, or "The People."

Now, their president and other tribal leaders think it's time for the rest of the world to catch up.

Tribal President Peterson Zah, who has sponsored a resolution for the tribe to change its name, said the proposed switch to Dineh—pronounced Dee-NEH—is a matter of tribal sovereignty. All people, he said, have a right "to determine by what name they are called."

"The name 'Navajo' was given to us by outsiders, and it is only right that we decide for ourselves what we should be called," Zah said.

The word "Navajo" comes from a word used by another Indian tribe, the Tewas in central New Mexico, and means "cultivators of the fields." The Spaniards who explored the Southwest more than three hundred years ago picked it up, and the people have been called Navajo ever since.

Duane Beyal, Zah's spokesman, said, "I don't see why there is so much concern by the media about this. We haven't received any calls from Navajos."

Many of the questions posed to Beyal stem not from the right of the tribe to change its name, but the possibility for confusion.

"The rest of you can be confused," he said, "as long as the Navajo people aren't confused."

If the Navajos go through with the name switch, they will join the Tohono O'odham, which changed from the name Papago when adopting a new constitution in 1985. Leaders of the tribe in southern Arizona said the decision was made to fit the tribe's traditional view of themselves as "Desert People."

The Navajo proposal already has received unanimous approval from council and chapter officials in the Shiprock District, the biggest in the tribal government.

"I would think the (full) council would be in agreement to use our traditional name," said Ray Baldwin Louis, press spokesman for the tribe's legislative branch.

Beyal said the tribe is planning to let members first decide whether they favor the name before taking the measure before the Navajo Nation Council in the winter session, which begins in January.

It would be up to individual entities carrying the Navajo name but outside the tribe's control, such as schools, to follow the name change, he said.

The change would "absolutely not" have any effect on Navajo County's name, said Marlin Gillespie, a county supervisor.

Some radio and television announcers already have had problems with the word "Dineh," pronouncing it with a long "i" as "DIE-neh."

Beyal said to alleviate some of the confusion, the council may decide to spell it "Deneh."

Tribal attorneys said Thursday that records indicate that the council only discussed the name once previously. After a three-hour debate in 1954, members voted to spell it "Navajo" instead of "Navaho."

The name also was an issue when Peter MacDonald was chairman. He once told tribal attorneys to check into the possibility of registering the name as a trademark so that the tribe could determine who used it.

His idea went nowhere, as tribal attorneys reported back that the word had become so generic that it would be impossible to register.

That was good news for the Mazda Corp., which three years ago picked the name for one of its vehicles. But what's in store for the car now that the word "Navajo" could be history?

Fred Aikins, a spokesman for Mazda, said the company thinks it's an "interesting prospect" that the Navajos want to change their name. But, he said, it won't have any effect on the company's use of the name.

"It's a name that has a lot of positive connotations," he said. "It brings up feelings of being powerful and rugged—a feeling of the outdoors."

Beyal said, "It's totally up to them what they do," adding that it's possible the tribe might go ahead and register the new name to have some say in who could use it.

LESSON PLAN: INDIAN POWWOWS

Grade Level: Grades 5–8

Basic Concepts: Culture and adaptation

Organizing Generalization: People join together in groups to practice social or religious rituals and ceremonies to perpetuate values and customs and to instill a sense of pride and self-esteem in the participants. People also learn about the culture through participating in the ceremonies.

Culture Area: All areas, especially the Plains

Time Period: Contemporary

Background: Over the last fifty years, many tribes have established powwows in an effort to maintain and perpetuate in a modern world traditional values such as sharing, happiness, and respect. While powwows have had an even longer past for some tribes of the Great Plains, for the most part, they are fairly contemporary, and represent the coming together and sharing among different tribes as well as within a particular tribe or community. Many Indian people follow the powwows each summer as they are held throughout Indian Country. They are like a giant family reunion with friends, food, and fun. Different tribes come together to dance and sing and share their traditions with their young and others.

Objectives:
Knowledge
Students will:

1. Identify important Indian values that are demonstrated in powwows.
2. Describe the role that the powwow plays in perpetuating these values.

Skills
Students will:

1. Identify different powwow customs and the associated tribal group.
2. Compare different powwows and their customs.
3. Identify various customs that are common to different powwows.

Values
Students will:

1. Value the importance of powwow in maintaining culture for American Indians.
2. Appreciate the role that the powwow plays in bringing people together to nurture positive self-concepts and happiness.

Activities:

1. Show the video *Powwow*. After the video, generate a list of adjectives that describe the powwow. Next, watch *Dancing to Give Thanks*, a videotape by the Nebraska Educational Television. Ask students to list customs or traditional practices that they see in both videos regarding the powwow. What happens at a powwow?
2. Organize students in small groups and ask them to brainstorm familiar customs in a modern context and what values they convey (e.g., treatment of the national flag—respect, honor). Now lead the discussion to consideration of the values that the powwow customs represent.

3. Invite an American Indian to the classroom to talk about powwow and possibly show a powwow outfit and demonstrate dance steps or songs. Have students develop a set of questions related to customs and values before the guest comes. Why are certain things done? What do certain behaviors mean?

4. Ask students to discuss the following: "There is no line drawn. We are all in this world and must live together. There is more to the powwow than the contemporary version that is seen in the media. We do not look upon the powwow as a side show. We are not providing entertainment. We are interpreting an Indian awareness by incorporating religious and cultural aspects into this event."

Extensions:

1. The most exciting extension would be to attend a real powwow. They are held frequently on reservations, at Indian Centers, universities, and museums. Visitors are always welcome.

2. Play tapes of Indian powwow music for students to listen to, both as part of the activity and during other times of the day including during fun activities. A music teacher can help students recognize and understand the unique aspects of Indian music.

3. Students can find sources for dance steps and can learn to do several of them to the beat of the music.

4. Learn to distinguish between the different categories of competitive dances.

5. Investigate the different kinds of powwow regalia including contemporary and traditional from many tribal groups.

6. Plan a class powwow with the foods, music, and fun of a real powwow.

7. Make a mural or diorama of a powwow.

8. Learn appropriate powwow etiquette.

9. Distinguish between a powwow and other ethnic, cultural, or religious festival, fair, or social dance.

Evaluation: In discussion, students should demonstrate their understanding of the importance of the powwow as a social and cultural event in contemporary Indian life. Ideally, they should be able to demonstrate their understanding of the importance of the powwow by their respectful behavior at a powwow.

Materials/Resources:

Coombs, L. *Powwow*. Cleveland, OH: Modern Curriculum, 1992.

Horse Capture, G. *Powwow*. Cody, WY: Buffalo Bill Historical Center, 1989.

Red Hawk, R. *A Trip to a Powwow*. Newcastle, CA: Sierra Oaks, 1988.

Roberts, C. "Rocky Boy." *Native Peoples* (Summer 1988): 2–7.

Videotapes:

Nebraska Educational Television (Producer). (nd.) *Dancing to Give Thanks*. Available from the Native American Public Broadcasting Consortium.

Powwow. Available from Social Studies School Service catalog, 1992.

Powwow Terminology

Fancy dance: a modern style of dancing with much body movement and fancy footwork. The beat of the drum is moderate to fast.

Gourd dance: a ceremonial dance primarily for men, but women also participate. The dance is one originated by the Cheyenne, Kiowa, and Comanche, but has been taken up by many other tribes. Dancers wear red and blue robes, beaded and fringed sashes, mescal bead bandoliers, and carry gourd rattles and feather fans. The dancers remain stationary, but occasionally move in a clockwise direction.

Head dancer: a dancer appointed to lead all other dancers during a powwow. This position is one of honor. For any given set of songs, no other dancer will dance until the head dancer begins.

Honor song: a song that fulfills an individual or family's request to highlight and focus attention on individual accomplishments. The song itself, sung by a particular group of singers, may be one of tribal, family, or individual significance.

Host drum: a group of singers designated to start the powwow.

Inter-tribal: general term referring to open powwow dancing by all participating dancers; all tribes.

Jingle dress: a dance originated with the Ojibway in the Great Lakes area. Each dress is decorated with metal cones that make the jingle sound. These cones originally came from snuff can lids.

Northern drum: refers to Northern Plains tribes' style of singing. Songs are characteristically sung at a higher pitch.

Northern fancy: refers to the Northern style of men's fancy war dance in which overall body movement is paramount and includes spins, jumps, high leg kicks, and often times somersaults and splits. Songs are sung at a moderate-fast tempo.

Northern traditional: refers to the style of dancing and dress of the traditional warrior societies of the Northern Plains tribes. Dancers do not wear the colorful bustles of the fancy dancer. Many dancers, depending on their tribe, wear only one bustle at the lower back, cloth or buckskin leggings, a breechcloth, and a roach headdress with two eagle feathers.

Round dance: a social dance in which all dancers and spectators participate. Movement is clockwise in a circular fashion with dancers stepping continually to the left in time with the beat of the drum.

Southern drum: refers to the Oklahoma style of singing. Songs are characteristically sung at a lower pitch.

Southern fancy: Oklahoma style of men's fancy war dance with lots of body movement and rapid dancing. Songs are moderate to very fast in tempo.

Summary
Contemporary Issues

American Indian people are conscious of how their future must be created from the present and the past. In their world view, health, education, language, and culture are naturally related. And the strength of the people comes from the strong convictions about the knowledge and wisdom that has been handed from generation to generation.

Ancient traditions are being revived and strengthened as are Native languages. There are many in Indian Country who believe that without Native languages, there will be no true Indians. The language is necessary to practice the traditional religion. Soon the youth will know the songs, but not the meanings. Then they will forget the songs.

Language is being retained through the efforts of elders and linguists and dictionaries, storybooks, and school curriculum are being developed to teach tribal languages. Frequently computers are used in teaching language and culture, although not with the total support of traditional tribal members.

Forced removal from historical homesites and ways of life caused Native people to accept food and customs that have had ill effects on their health. The major killer of American Indians are heart disease, diabetes, cancer, alcoholism, and accidents. Suicide is all too prevalent. Fetal alcohol syndrome is also a major problem.

Indian children of today must learn the ways of their people, including language and culture, and know how to apply this knowledge in the modern world. They must also learn the skills and knowledge of the larger world to enable them to survive and succeed. Education is the key to a strong future for Indian people.

Their cultures are living cultures that are experiencing new power and vitalization. Determined Indian people have survived and will continue to do so.

George Horse Capture

As he does everywhere, the Great Spirit in his infinite wisdom bestows a balance here, too. So, if there is a bad part, there is also a good part. It's good being Indian. As we drive across the country and see the trees and coulees and the sage brush and grass covering the prairie, we know this is Indian Country, and long ago buffalo covered it from horizon to horizon. We know this has always been our land. We will never emigrate to the British Isles or to Australia or to anywhere. This is our home, good or bad. It is our earth and these hills are our hills. It doesn't matter who owns the deed to the land, because these paper holders change and they will always change. But these hills and mountains and valleys and coulees and bluffs are ours, the Indian people's. They have always been ours and they always will be. We know this. It makes us feel good. No one can change this, and it does not matter if we are poor or not. ... We know where we came from and we know where we are going to be buried. We have a center to our lives. Out of all this chaos, there is a certain order.

Horse Capture, G. P. Powwow. Cody, WY: Buffalo Bill Historical Center, 1989.

Definitions of "Indian Country"

To most American Indian people, the term "Indian Country" simply means where Indian people, their people, live. It is a term of respect that means home, family, friends—being at home in their own place, wherever that may be. And most Indian people believe that this country is Indian Country.

The following definitions of the term "Indian Country" represent legal definitions.

> (a) all land within the limits of any Indian reservation under the jurisdiction of the United States government, notwithstanding the issuance of any patent, and, including rights-of-way running through the reservation, (b) all dependent Indian communities within the borders of the United States whether within the original or subsequently acquired territory thereof, and whether within or without the limits of a state and (c) all Indian allotments, the Indian titles to which have not been extinguished, including rights-of-way running through the same.

Deloria, V., Jr., and C.M. Lytle. *American Indians, American Justice*. Austin: University of Texas, 1983.

Indian Country is a romantic phrase that evokes nostalgia for the Old West as depicted in the movies. Indian Country once meant exactly that, the country of Indians, a place where Indians lived and where the trade and intercourse acts controlled. It was a geographical definition with clear-cut jurisdictional overtones. It could be marked on a map with some accuracy. ...

Today, except when used for questions of federal criminal jurisdiction, Indian Country is about as provisional as "Marlboro country," that is, it is an image, or a state of mind, or a sociological phenomenon to many. Indian Country is an incredibly complex jurisdictional issue disguised in a colorful phrase.

Ragsdale, F. L., Jr. "The Deception of Geography." In Vine Deloria, Jr. (ed.) *American Indian Policy in the Twentieth Century*, Norman: University of Oklahoma, 1985.

The concept of Indian Country has been elevated by federal law above other ideas because it transcends mere geographical connotations and represents that sphere of influence in which Indian traditions and federal laws passed specifically to deal with the political relationship of the United States to American Indians have primacy. The term originated in the popular designations of the lands beyond the frontier, as the unknown populated by tribes and bands of Indians who rejected contact with "civilized" populations. That the idea moved from a popular conception to a highly technical legal term is testimony to the ability of the law to incorporate customs with its intellectual framework.

Deloria, V. Jr. & Lytle, C. M. (1983). *American Indians, American Justice*. Austin, TX: University of Texas, p. 58.

All references cited in Sutton, I. (1991). Preface to Indian Country: Geography and law. *American Indian Culture and Research Journal*, 15 (2), pp. 8 & 10.

The Challenge to the Speech of Chief Seattle

The Denver Post—Wednesday, April 22, 1992

CHIEF SEATTLE GIVEN FORKED TONGUE?
Famed environmental speech of 1854 was altered by professor

Montpelier, Vt.

An environmental warning cry that Earth Day celebrants may read today is attributed to an 1854 speech by Chief Seattle. But the real author of the speech is still living.

"I never tried to pretend that Chief Seattle said the things I wrote," said Ted Perry, 54, a film writer and professor at Middlebury College. "I'm partly to blame in the fact that I was presumptuous enough to try to write what Chief Seattle might have said."

Chief Seattle, a head of the Suquamish tribe near Puget Sound in Washington state, had a reputation as a strong leader, eloquent speaker and diplomat with the whites. The city of Seattle was named after him.

Perry said he took a speech by the chief, as written down by a white man, and strengthened its environmental theme while writing for an environmental film called "Home," produced by the Southern Baptist Radio and Television Commission in 1971.

"I was inspired by Chief Seattle and I told the producers to identify me as the author of the words he said. "But they said it would be more authentic if people thought Chief Seattle had said it."

Chief Seattle called the Earth his mother and the rivers his brothers, lamented the slain buffalo shot by white men and warned that the "dogs of appetite will devour the rich Earth and leave only a desert," in Perry's version.

Historians pointed to historical inconsistencies in Perry's version, noting that things he referred to such as the completion of the railroads and the mass slaughter of buffalo occurred after Seattle's death.

The embellished version is revered by many as a piece of great significance to the environmental movement.

The Denver Post—Friday, April 24, 1992

CHIEF SEATTLE'S WORDS
Editorial

The celebration of Earth Day has been clouded this week by the revelation that one of the oracles of the environmental movement, Chief Seattle, may have been far less prophetic than commonly believed.

A widely cited version of a speech the Indian leader made in 1854, it now turns out, was actually written by a screenwriter in Texas for a TV movie produced in 1971. The fiction was uncovered by historians who questioned Chief Seattle's supposed allusions to railroads, "talking wires" and the slaughter of the buffalo—developments that occurred years later in the 19th century.

As distortions of history go, this one is probably no more serious that TV's shift of the Grand Tetons to northern Minnesota for a mini-series on John Charles Fremont a few years ago. What seems more troubling about the embellished translation—which also has been circulated in the best-selling book, "Brother Eagle, Sister Sky"—is its apparent romanticization of the Native American concept of nature.

While there's little doubt that the 19th century Indians found spiritual meaning in "every shining pine needle, every sandy shore," as the scriptwriter put it, it's quite another matter to ascribe to them or to their leaders the kind of sophisticated intellectual understanding so hyped by Earth Day organizers.

Probably what guided the indigenous tribes was less a '60s-style ecological consciousness than a strong survival instinct—a point raised last year by critics of "Dances with Wolves," Hollywood's latest paean to the myth of the noble savage.

Perhaps this week's disclosure, by spotlighting the same concern, may lead to a fuller understanding of the Indians' true vision—and to a greater appreciation for the habits of stewardship they practiced.

Alphabet of Things That
the Americas Gave to the World

A   avocado, amaranth, asphalt

B   buffalo, beaver pelts, brazilian dye

C   canoe, corn, caucus, chocolate, cocoa, cassava, chicle, cotton, cashews, chayotes, catfish, chilis, cayenne

D   democracy, dyes, dog sleds

E   ecology

F   fertilizer, food preservation

G   gum, guano deposits, grits

H   hammock, hominy, hickory nut

I   impeachment, ipecac

J   jerky, Jerusalem artichoke

K   kidney beans, kayaks

L   libraries, long pants, llamas

M   milpa, moccasins, manioc, medicines

N   nuts, names (half the state names of USA)

O   Oklahoma

P   potatoes, parrots, pumpkins, peanuts, popcorn, pineapple, passenger pigeon, pear cactus, parkas, peppers, pomegranate, passion fruit, papaya, pecan, paprika

Q   quinine, quinoa

R   rubber

S   squash, silver, sisal, sunflowers, sweet potatoes, succotash

T   turkey, tapioca pudding, tomatoes, tortillas, tobacco, tar

U   USA Constitution (influenced by the Iroquois)

V   vanilla

W   wild rice, witch hazel, words (many words in English and Spanish), white potatoes

X   xylophone (the marimba of both African and American origin)

Y   yams

Z   zero, zucchini

From: B. Bigelow, B. Miner, and B. Peterson. Rethinking Columbus *Milwaukee, WI: Rethinking Schools, 1992.*

The Choctaw and Chickasaw Respond

In response to the Dawes Commission, delegates of the Choctaw and Chickasaw Nations in Indian territory addressed the following to the President of the United States and the Senate and the House of Representatives.

We desire to recall a little history of our people. The Choctaw and Chickasaw (Southeast area) people have never cost the United States a cent for support. They have always and are now self-sustaining. It will be admitted that but little over a half a century ago the Choctaws and Chickasaws were happily located east of the Mississippi River. Their possessions were large and rich and valuable. The whites began to crowd around and among us in the east, as they now are in the west. The Government of the United States urged us to relinquish our valuable possessions there to make home for their own people and to accept new reservations west of the great river Mississippi, assuring us that there we would be secure from the invasion of the white man. Upon condition that the Government would protect us from such renewed invasion and would give us the lands in fee and convey them to us by patent, and would, by solemn treaty guarantee that no Territorial or State Government should even be extended over us without consent, and as it was to yield up and surrender our old homes, we consented, and with heavy hearts we turned our backs upon the graves of our fathers and took up the dismal march for our new western home, in a wilderness west of the Mississippi River. After long and tedious marches, after suffering great exposure and much loss of life, we reached the new reservation, with but one consolation to revive our drooping spirits, which was that we were never again to be molested. There, in the jungle and wilds, with nothing but wild animals and beasts for neighbors, we went to work in our crude way to build homes and Governments suited to our people.

In 1855, at the request of the United States we leased and sold the entire west part of our reservation amounting to over 12 million acres, for the purpose of homes for the white man and of locating thereon other friendly Indians. Again in 1866, at the urgent request of the Government we gave up all that part leased for the occupancy of friendly Indians, and ceded it absolutely for the same purpose. And again, in 1890 and 1891, we relinquished...3 million acres... to be occupied by the whites. Now in less than five years we are asked to surrender completely our tribal governments and to accept a Territorial Government in lieu thereof; to all our lands in severalty, and to become citizens of the United States and what is worse, an effort is being made to force us to do so against our consent. Such a radical change would, in our judgement, in a few years annihilate the Indian. ...

We ask every lover of justice, is it right that a great and powerful government should, year by year, continue to demand cessions of land from weaker and dependent people, under the plea of securing homes for the homeless. While the great government of the United States, our guardian, is year by year admitting foreign paupers into the Union, at the rate of 250,000 per annum, must we sacrifice our homes and children for this pauper element?

We have lived with our people all our lives and believe that we know more about them than any Commission, however good and intelligent, could know from a few visits... on the railroads and towns, where but a few Indians are to be seen and where but few live.... They [the white man] care nothing for the fate of the Indian, so that their own greed can be gratified.

Words of John Collier

As the Indian societies move from their four-centuries-long advance, expression along many lines of literature, of the arts, of religion and of philosophy will come into being. The ancient-modern Indian affirmation of the deathless man-nature relationship will flow into poetry and symbolic art of cosmic intensity, tranquility and scope.

The movement will be inward and outward at one and the same time-inward to the world-old springs, buried or never buried, which still flow because the societies have not died; outward to the world of events and affairs.

There will come to dawn in the nations, the Indians playing their part, two realizations. The first, that their soils, waters, wild life, the whole web of life which sustains them are being wasted—often irreparably and fatally. The other, that their local community life, their local democracy, their values which are required for beauty, wisdom and strength—their very societies—are wasting away even as their natural resources are wasting. As these realizations increase, the nations will turn to their Indian societies increasingly, seeking the open secrets they have to reveal.

All these good things will come to pass if the nations will maintain and increase their enterprise and research into Indian need and Indian power. More slowly, less decisively they will come about even if the nations regress in their Indian programs. For the delaying action of the Indian societies and of that spirit they represent is ended. They have proved that they cannot be destroyed, and they are now advancing into the world.

Collier, J. *The Indians of Americas*. New York: W.W. Norton, 1947.

Termination Acts

Indian Group	State	Tribal Memberships	Tribal Land	Date of Act	Effective
Menominee	Wisconsin	3,270	233,881	6/17/54	1961
Klamath	Oregon	2,133	862,662	8/13/54	1961
Western Oregon (61 tribes and bands)	Oregon	2,081	3,158	8/13/54	1956
Alabama-Coushatta	Texas	450	3,200	8/23/54	1955
Mixed-blood Ute	Utah	490	211,430	8/27/54	1961
Southern Paiute	Utah	232	42,839	9/1/54	1957
Wyandotte	Oklahoma	1,157	94	8/1/56	1959
Peoria	Oklahoma	640	0	8/2/56	1959
Ottawa	Oklahoma	630	0	8/3/56	1959
California Rancherias	California	1,107	4,315	8/18/58	1969
Catawaba	South Carolina	631	3,388	9/21/59	1962
Ponca	Nebraska	442	834	9/5/62	1966
		13,263	1,365,801		

SOURCE: Data from Theodore W. Taylor, The States and Their Indian Citizens (Washington; Bureau of Indian Affairs, 1972), p. 180; Charles F. Wilkinson and Eric R. Biggs, "Evolution of the Termination Policy," American Indian Law Review 5, No. 1 (1977): 151.

Excerpts from the Fort Laramie Treaty of 1868

ARTICLE I. From this day forward all war between the parties to this agreement shall forever cease. ...

ARTICLE II. The United States agrees that the wit, viz: commencing on the east bank of the Missouri River where the forty-sixth parallel of north latitude crosses the same, thence along the low-water mark down said east bank to a point opposite where the northern line of the State of Nebraska strikes the river, thence west across said river, and along the northern line of Nebraska to the one hundred and fourth degree of longitude west from Greenwich, thence north on said meridian to a point where the forty-sixth parallel of north latitude intercepts the same, thence due east along said parallel to the place of the beginning...shall be, and the same is set apart for the absolute and undisturbed use and occupation of the Indians herein named...and the United States now solemnly agrees that no persons except those herein designated and authorized so to do...shall ever be permitted to pass over, settle upon, or reside in the territory described in this article...

ARTICLE XII. No treaty for the cession of any portion or part of the reservation herein described which may be held in common shall be of any validity or force as against the said Indians, unless executed and signed by at least three fourths of all adult male Indians, occupying or interested in the same...

ARTICLE XVI. The United States hereby agrees and stipulates that the country north of the North Platte river and east of the summits of the Big Horn mountains shall be held and considered to be unceded Indian territory, and also stipulates and agrees that no white person or persons shall be permitted to settle upon or occupy any portion of the same, or without the consent of the Indians, first had and obtained, to pass through the same. And it is further agreed by the United States that within ninety days after the conclusion of peace with all bands of the Sioux nation, the military posts now established in the territory of Montana shall be closed.

Voices From Wounded Knee, 1973. Rooseveltown, NY: *Akwesasne Notes,* Mohawk Nation, 1974, p. 134.

Indian Activism

MAJOR ACTIVIST ORGANIZATIONS AND ACTIVITIES

1944	National Congress of American Indians founded
1961	National Indian Youth Council founded
1961	American Indian Chicago Conference
1964	Fish-ins in the state of Washington
1968	American Indian Movement founded
1968	International Bridge blocked at St. Regis
1969–1971	Occupation of Alcatraz
1972	Trail of Broken Treaties Caravan to Washington, D.C.
1972	Occupation of BIA Offices in Washington, D.C.
1973–1975	Occupation of Wounded Knee
1974	International Indian Treaty Council founded
1974	Ganienkeh—(Moss Lake)—Mohawk Occupation of state lands in the Adirondacks
1975	Council of Energy Resource tribes founded
1977	Leonard Peltier convicted (Wounded Knee)
1978	Women of All Red Nations founded
1978	The Longest Walk
1978–1983	Dennis Banks' sanctuary
1984	Dennis Banks' refuge
1984	Dennis Banks' surrender
1992	Pan-Indian protest against the celebration of the Columbian Quincentennial

Religious Freedom

The religious practices of Indians are threatened in the following situations:

- the degradation of geographical areas deemed sacred sites (Blue Lake);

- the maltreatment of Indian burials, particularly bodily remains;

- the prohibition against capture, kill, and use of endangered or protected species (eagles);

- the regulations regarding the collection, transport, and use of peyote (Native American Church);

- the alienation and display of religious artifacts (Zuni war gods);

- the prevention of Indian rituals and behavior, particularly in authoritarian institutions (schools, military service and prisons).

Vecsey, C. (ed.) *Handbook of American Indian Religious Freedom*. New York: Crossroads, 1991.

Blue Lake

What the white man does to us follows a pattern. First they come to us offering presents which we do not need. Then they offer to buy our land which is not ours to sell. The land does not belong to anyone. It was put here to be thanked and used gently. The land belongs to itself, just like the moon and the stars.

But to the white man such an idea is crazy. To him everything has to be used up. Then it is worth something. That is why they will do anything to take our homes and destroy us. All of our brothers to the east had this happen and many of our brothers to the west also. What can we do? If we fight, they will not educate our children to their way which is all we are left with now. If we do not fight, they will help themselves to our life.

This time the white man wants our water which flows out of our sacred Blue Lake. It flows through our land and down into the pueblo where we use it for drinking and cooking and washing. It nourishes our crops as well. It is all we have. The white man does not need it. It is so small anyway, just enough for us and for our children. We have been careful with the water which flows from Blue Lake and it will last forever.

When the white man gave Blue Lake back to us, some of us said, it will not end here. The white man is angry because he had to give up this land which was ours to begin with, ever since we were put here as a people by the Great Father. We said, the white man will think of some new way to get what he wants. And now that has happened.

Wood, N. *Many Winters*. New York, NY: Doubleday, 1974, p. 65.

Coil Pottery Making

Additional Resources

MAGAZINES/JOURNALS

American Indian Art
7314 East Osborn Drive
Scottsdale, AZ 85251
(602) 994-5445

Daybreak Star Reader
United Indians of all Tribes
Daybreak Star Arts Center—Discovery Park
Seattle, WA 98199
(206) 285-4425

Native Monthly Reader
P.O. Box 217
Crestone, CO 81131
(719) 256-4848
Fax (719-256-4849)

Native Peoples
P.O. Box 3620
Phoenix, AZ 85067-6820
(602) 277-7852

These three journals are scholarly in content and are excellent resources for those who teach Native American students or teach Native Studies courses.

American Indian Culture and Research Journal
American Indian Studies Center
3220 Campbell Hall
University of California, Los Angeles
405 Hilgard Avenue
Los Angeles, CA 90024-1548

American Indian Quarterly
3415 Dwinelle Hall
University of California
Berkeley, CA 94720

Journal of Indian Education
Center for Indian Education
College of Education
Arizona State University
Tempe, AZ 85287-1311

NEWSPAPERS

Akwesasne Notes
Rooseveltown, NY 13683-0196
(518) 358-9531

Lakota Times
1920 Lombardi Drive
Rapid City, SD 57701
(605) 341-0011

Navajo Times
P.O. Box 310
Window Rock, AZ 86515

News From Indian Country
RT. Box 2900-A
Hayward, WI 54843

United Tribes News
3315 University Drive
Bismarck, ND 58504
(701) 255-3285

FILMS AND VIDEOS

Native American Public Broadcasting Consortium
P. O. Box 83111
Lincoln, NE 68501-3111
(402) 472-3522

COMPUTER PROGRAM

American Indian Resource Services
P.O. Box 1624
Dallas, TX 75354-1624

IBM (DOS) & MAC
$89.95 plus $1.50 Shipping

Includes such information as: Complete listing of all BIA area offices, agencies, and BIA supervised schools; complete address, telephone, & FAX listings of all federally recognized tribes; address listings of American Indian newspapers, magazines, and organizations that serve the Indian community; and address listings of museums and arts & crafts organizations with Indian ownership of collections.

American Indian Statistics 1990

- **U.S. POPULATION:** 2 million (1.96 million in 1990 census), up 37.9 percent since 1980.
- **U.S. DISTRIBUTION:** 62.3 percent off reservation, 37.7 percent on Indian lands.
- **U.S. TRIBES:** 510 including 200 village groups in Alaska.
- **U.S. LANDS:** 56.2 million acres of reservations and trust lands.
- **LANGUAGES:** About 250 tribal languages spoken within the United States.
- **MEDIAN AGE:** 23.5 years for Indians, compared with 30 years for the entire nation.
- **BIRTHS:** 27.5 per 1,000 compared with 15.7 nationally.
- **DEATHS:** 571.7 per 100,000 compared with 435.5 nationally.
- **MEDIAN HOUSEHOLD INCOME:** $20,025, compared with $30,056 nationally.
- **POVERTY RATE:** 23.7 percent of Indian families, compared with 10.3 percent nationally.
- **UNEMPLOYMENT:** 14.4 percent, but 45 percent (estimated) among Indians on or adjacent to reservations.
- **SUICIDES:** 15 per 100,000 (down from peak of 29 in 1975), compared with 11.7 nationally.
- **DROPOUT RATE:** 35.5 percent, compared with 28.8 percent nationally.
- **HIGHER EDUCATION:** 89,000 now enrolled.
- **CITIZENSHIP:** Granted in 1924.
- **OTHER RIGHTS:** New Mexico Indians didn't win right to vote until 1962; federal permission granted Indians to drink alcohol in 1950's.
- **TOP 10 STATES BY INDIAN POPULATION:** Oklahoma, California, Arizona, New Mexico, Alaska, Washington, North Carolina, Texas, New York, Michigan.
- **TOP 10 RESERVATIONS BY INDIAN POPULATION:** Navajo (Arizona/New Mexico/Utah), Pine Ridge (South Dakota), Fort Apache, Gila River, Papago (Arizona), Rosebud (South Dakota), San Carlos (Arizona), Zuni Pueblo (Arizona/New Mexico), Hopi (Arizona), and Blackfeet (Montana).

Sources: United States Bureau of Indian Affairs, United States Bureau of Census (1990).

Resources and References

INTRODUCTION

Ortiz, S. *The People Shall Continue.* Revised edition. San Francisco: Children's Book Press, 1988.

Standing Bear, L. *Land of the Spotted Eagle.* Lincoln: University of Nebraska, 1978.

CHAPTER 1

Deloria, V. Jr. (ed.). *American Indian Policy in the Twentieth Century.* Norman: University of Oklahoma, 1985.

Guidelines for Geographic Education: Elementary and Secondary Schools. Washington, D.C.: Joint Committee on Geographic Education of the National Council for Geographic Education and the Association of American Geographers, 1984.

Harvey, K. D., Harjo, L. D., and Jackson, J. K. *Teaching About Native Americans.* Washington, D.C.: National Council for the Social Studies, 1990.

Jones, B. F., Pierce, J. and Hunter, B. "Teaching Students to Construct Geographic Representations." *Educational Leadership* (December 1988/January 1989): 20–25.

Lame Deer, J. (Fire) and Erdoes, R. *Lame Deer Seeker of Visions.* New York: Pocket, 1976.

Morris, G. and Means, R. "Why AIM Opposes Columbus Day and Columbus Day Parades." *Denver Post,* October 12, 1991:7B.

Ortiz, Simon J. *The People Shall Continue.* San Francisco: Children's Book Press, 1988.

Spicer, E. H. *The American Indians.* Cambridge, MA: Belknap Press of Harvard University Press, 1982.

Viola, H. J. (ed.) *After Columbus: The Smithsonian Chronicle of the North American Indian.* Washington, D.C.: Smithsonian/Orion Books, 1990.

Waldman, C. *Encyclopedia of Native American Tribes.* New York: Facts on File, 1988.

CHAPTER 2

Commager, H. S. and Muessig, R. H. *The Study and Teaching of History.* Columbus, OH: Charles E. Merrill, 1980.

Glatthorn, A. A. *Curriculum Renewal.* Alexandria, VA: Association for Supervision and Curriculum Development, 1987.

Spencer, P. *Three Strands in the Braid: A Guide for Enablers of Learning.* San Anselmo, CA: Tribe of Two Press, 1984.

Spencer, P. *Who Speaks for Wolf?* San Anselmo, CA: Tribe of Two Press, 1983. (Paula Spencer is from the Iroquois tradition.)

Storm, H. *Seven Arrows.* New York: Ballantine Books, 1972. (Although Storm professes to be Northern Cheyenne, there has been controversy regarding his Native heritage.)

Waldman, C. *Atlas of the North American Indian.* New York: Facts on File, 1985.

CHAPTER 3
References and Resources for Adults

Akwesasne Notes. "Basic Call to Consciousness." Rooseveltown, NY: *Akwesasne Notes,* Mohawk Nation, 1986.

Begley, S. "The First Americans." *Newsweek* (Fall/Winter 1991): 15–16.

Brescia, W. "Choctaw Oral Tradition Relating to Tribal Origin." In C. K. Reeves, (ed.), *The Choctaw Before Removal.* Jackson: University Press of Mississippi, 1985.

Brown, V. P. and Owens, L. *The World of the Southern Indians.* Birmingham, AL: Beechwood, 1983.

Canby, T. Y. "The Anasazi: Riddles in the Ruins." *National Geographic* (November 1982): 554–592.

Graves, W. (ed.). "1491: America Before Columbus." *National Geographic* (October 1991): 4–9.

Jennings, J. D. "Across an Arctic Bridge." In J. B. Billard (ed.), *The World of the American Indian.* Washington, DC: National Geographic Society, 1989, pp. 29–69.

Jennings, J. D. *Prehistory of North America,* 2nd edition. New York: McGraw-Hill, 1984.

Kopper, P. (ed.) *The Smithsonian Book of North American Indians: Before the Coming of the Europeans.* Washington, DC: Smithsonian Books, 1986.

Taylor, C. F. *The Native Americans.* New York: Smithmark, 1991.

Waldman, C. *Atlas of the North American Indian.* New York: Facts on File, 1985.

Resources for the Classroom

Archaeology. Milwaukee, WI: Raintree, 1986.

Baylor, B. *When Clay Sings.* New York: Macmillan, 1972.

Bleeker, S. *The Pueblo Indians: Farmers of the Rio Grande.* New York: William Morrow, 1955.

Branigan, K. *Prehistory.* New York: Franklin Watts, 1986.

Bruchac, J. *Native American Stories.* Golden, CO: Fulcrum, 1991.

Caduto, M. J. and Bruchac, J. *Keepers of the Animals.* Golden, CO: Fulcrum, 1991.

Caduto, M. J. and Bruchac, J. *Keepers of the Earth.* Golden, CO: Fulcrum, 1988.

Carey, V. S. and Barnett, I. *Quail Song.* New York: G.P. Putnam's Sons, 1990.

Cornplanter, J. J. *Legends of the Longhouse.* Ontario, Canada: Iroqrafts Ltd., 1986.

Etling, M. and Folsom, M. *The Secret Story of Pueblo Bonito.* New York: Scholastic, 1963.

Erdoes, R. *The Rain Dance People: The Pueblo Indians, Their Past and Present.* New York: Alfred A. Knopf, 1976.

Fradin, D. B. *Archaeology.* Chicago: Childrens Press, 1983.

Marriott, A. *The First Comers: Indians of America's Dawn.* New York: Longmans, Green, 1960.

Marton, E. *Mysteries in American Archaeology.* New York: Walker, 1986.

Ortiz, A. "Origins." *National Geographic* (October 1991): 6–7.

Pickering, R. B. *I Can Be An Archaeologist.* Chicago: Childrens Press, 1987.

Red Hawk, R. *Grandfather's Origin Story: The Navajo Indian Beginning.* Newcastle, CA: Sierra Oaks, 1988.

Secrets from The Past. Washington, DC: National Geographic Society, 1979.

Silverberg, R. *The Mound Builders.* Columbus: Ohio University Press, 1986.

Smith, G. "Utah's Rock Art: Wilderness Louvre." *National Geographic* (January 1980): 97–117.

Smith, H. E. Jr. *All About Arrowheads and Spear Points.* New York: Henry Holt & Company, 1989.

Stuart, G. E. "Mounds: Riddles from the Indian Past." *National Geographic* (December 1972): 783–801.

Tamarin, A. and Glubok, S. *Ancient Indians of the Southwest.* Garden City, NY: Doubleday, 1975.

Trimble, S. *The Village of Blue Stone.* New York: Macmillan, 1990.

Wood, N. and Wood, M. *Hollering Sun.* New York: Simon and Schuster, 1972.

Yue, D. and Yue, C. *The Pueblo.* Boston: Houghton Mifflin, 1986.

Simulations/Videotapes

Site Anasazi: CA. A.D. 900–1300. (1989) Available from Social Studies School Service 1992 catalog. Suitable for middle grades.

Dig 2: A Simulation in Archaeology. Interact. Available from Social Studies School Service 1992 catalog. Suitable for middle grades.

Sioux Legends. Available from Social Studies School Service 1992 catalog. Legends reflecting the philosophy and religion of the Sioux people are presented in this videotape which features Native Americans reenacting three tales of creation.

CHAPTER 4
References and Resources for Adults

Appleton, L. A. *American Indian Design and Decoration.* New York: Dover, 1971.

Billard, J. (ed.) *The World of the American Indian.* Washington, DC: National Geographic Society, 1989.

Campbell, J. *The Power of Myth.* New York: Doubleday, 1988.

Davidson, S. *How Can One Sell the Air?: The Manifesto for the Earth.* Summertown, TN: Book Publishing Company, 1980.

Dockstader, F. J. *Indian Art in North America.* Greenwich, CT: New York Graphic Society, 1961.

Friend, D. and The Editors of Life. *The Meaning of Life: Reflections in Words and Pictures on Why We Are Here.* Boston: Little, Brown, 1991.

Harvey, K. D., Harjo, L. D., and Jackson, J. K. *Teaching About Native Americans.* Washington, DC: National Council for the Social Studies, 1990.

Kopper, P. (ed.). *The Smithsonian Book of North American Indians.* Washington, DC: Smithsonian, 1986.

McLuhan, T. C. *Touch the Earth.* New York: Promontory, 1987.

Waldman, C. *Atlas of the North American Indian.* New York: Facts on File, 1985.

Resources for the Classroom

Garaway, M. K. *The Old Hogan.* Cortez, CO: Mesa Verde, 1986.

Jeffers, S. *Brother Eagle, Sister Sky.* New York: Dial, 1991. (Although these words are attributed to Chief Seattle, this has recently been disputed. Nonetheless, it is a beautiful book.)

Sneve, V. *Dancing Teepees.* New York: Holiday House, 1989.

Yue, C. and Yue, D. *The Igloo.* Boston: Houghton Mifflin, 1988.

Yue, D. and Yue, C. *The Pueblo.* Boston: Houghton Mifflin, 1986.

Yue, D. and Yue, C. *The Tipi.* New York: Alfred A. Knopf, 1984.

CHAPTER 5
References and Resources for Adults

Cowley, G. "The Great Disease Migration." *Newsweek* (Fall/Winter 1991): 54–56.

Crosby, A. W. Jr. *The Columbian Exchange: Biological and Cultural Consequences of 1492.* Westport, CT: Greenwood Press, 1972.

Deak, G. "Everything You Need to Know About Columbus." *American Heritage* (October 1991): 40–54.

Foote, T. "Where Columbus Was Coming From." *Smithsonian* (December 1991): 28–41.

Giago, T. *The Christian Science Monitor* (March 17, 1992): 12.

Graves, W. (ed.) "America before Columbus." *National Geographic* (October 1991): 4–99.

Hawke, S. D. and Davis, J. E. *Seeds of Change.* Palo Alto, CA: Addison-Wesley, 1991.

Kopper, P. (ed.). *The Smithsonian Book of North American Indians Before the Coming of the Europeans.* Washington, D.C.: Smithsonian Books, 1986.

MacLeish, W. H. "1492 America: The Land Columbus Never Saw." *Smithsonian,* (November 1991): 34–52.

Nabhan, G. P. "Native American Cornucopia." *Native Peoples* (Spring 1992): 10–16.

Sale, K. *The Conquest of Paradise: Christopher Columbus and the Columbian Legacy.* New York: Alfred A. Knopf, 1990.

Schwartz, J. "The Great Food Migration." *Newsweek* (Fall/Winter 1991): 62.

Scofield, J. "Christopher Columbus and the New World He Found." *National Geographic* (November 1975): 584–

626.

Sharp, S. *Columbus and the Americas 1492–1991: Discovery and Encounter.* Petaluma, CA: Pomegranate Calendars & Books, 1991.

Thornton, R. *American Indian Holocaust and Survival.* Norman: University of Oklahoma, 1987.

Viola, H. J. and Margolis, C. (eds.). *Seeds of Change: A Quincentennial Commemoration.* Washington, D.C.: Smithsonian Institution Press, 1991.

Viola, H. J. and Smith, R. M. (eds.) "When Worlds Collide: How Columbus' Voyages Transformed Both East and West." *Newsweek,* special Columbus issue, a joint project with the Smithsonian Institute's Natural History Exhibit "Seeds of Change." (Fall/Winter 1991).

Waldman, C. *Atlas of the North American Indian.* New York: Facts on File, 1985.

Weatherford, J. *Indian Givers: How the Indians of the Americas Transformed the World.* New York: Fawcett Columbine, 1988.

Weatherford, J. *Native Roots.* New York: Crown, 1991.

Zinn, H. *A People's History of the United States.* New York: Harper & Row, 1981.

Resources for the Classroom

Fradin, D. B. *Columbus Day.* Hillside, NJ: Enslow Publishers, 1990.

Hawke, S. D. and Davis, J. E. *Seeds of Change.* Palo Alto, CA: Addison-Wesley, 1991.

Las Casas, B. *The Log of Christopher Columbus' First Voyage to America in the Year 1492 as Copied out in Brief by Bartholomew Las Casas.* Hamden, CT: Linnet, 1991.

Levinson, N. S. *Christopher Columbus: Voyager to the Unknown.* New York: Lodestar/Dutton, 1990.

Meltzer, M. *Columbus and the World Around Him.* New York: Franklin Watts, 1990.

Roop, P. & Roop, C. I, *Columbus: My Journal 1492–3.* New York: Walker, 1990.

Yolen, J. *Encounter.* San Diego: Harcourt Brace Jovanovich, 1992.

This list can be expanded to include books about such topics as horses, corn, and slavery, the "seeds of change." Books such as the following make important contributions to young children's understanding of the legacy of Columbus.

Aliki, *Corn Is Maize.* New York: Thomas Crowell, 1976. (Corn)

Goble, P. *The Gift of the Sacred Dog.* New York: Bradbury Press, 1980. (Horse)

Miles, M. *Annie and the Old One.* Boston: Atlantic Monthly Press, 1971. (Sheep)

CHAPTER 6
References and Resources for Adults

Bolton, H. E. *Coronado: Knight of Pueblos and Plains*. New York: Whittlesey House/McGraw-Hill; and Albuquerque: University of New Mexico, 1949.

Debo, A. *A History of the Indians of the United States*. Norman: University of Oklahoma, 1989.

Deloria, V. Jr. and Lytle, C. M. *American Indians, American Justice*. Austin: University of Texas, 1983.

Diaz, B. *The Conquest of New Spain*. (H. M. Cohen, trans.). New York: Viking/Penguin, 1963.

Durham, J. "Columbus Day." In B. Slapin and D. Seale (eds.), *Books Without Bias: Through Indian Eyes*. Berkeley, CA: Oyate, 1989, pp. 46–47.

Josephy, A. M. Jr. *The Indian Heritage of America*. New York: Alfred A. Knopf, 1985.

Judge, J. "Between Columbus and Jamestown: Exploring Our Forgotten Century." *National Geographic* (March 1988): 330–363.

Leon-Portilla, M. (ed.). *The Broken Spears: The Aztec Account of the Conquest of Mexico*. Boston: Beacon, 1966.

Santos, J. S. *The Pueblo Indians*. San Francisco: The Indian Historian Press, 1976.

Shears, B. L. and Wyaco, R. "Hawikku: A Fabled City of Cibola." *Native Peoples* (Summer 1990): 20-24.

Spicer, E. H. *A Short History of the Indians of the United States*. Malabar, FL: Robert E. Kreiger, 1983.

Suina, J. H. "Pueblo Secrecy Result of Intrusion." *New Mexico Magazine* (January 1992): 60–63.

Udall, S. L. "The Battle of Hawikuh." *Native Peoples* (Summer 1990): 25–29.

Viola, H. J. *After Columbus: The Smithsonian Chronicle of the North American Indians*. Washington, DC: Smithsonian/Oricle, 1990.

Waldman, C. *Atlas of the North American Indian*. New York: Facts on File, 1985.

Weigle, M. and White, P. *The Lore of New Mexico*. Albuquerque: University of New Mexico, 1988. This is an excellent book for teachers who want to explore the intricate multicultural environment of New Mexico. Three cultures, Spanish, Anglo, and Indian are presented in the rich folklore tradition.

Wissler, C. *Indians of the United States*. New York: Doubleday, 1989.

Wood, N. *Many Winters*. New York: Doubleday, 1974.

Resources for the Classroom

Anderson, J. *The First Thanksgiving Feast*. New York: Clarion/Houghton Mifflin, 1984.

Blackburn, J. *The Bloody Summer of Seventeen Forty-two: A Colonial Boy's Journal*. St. Simons Island, GA: Fort Frederica, 1985.

Brown, M.W. (ed.) *Homes in the Wilderness: A Pilgrim's Journal of Plymouth Plantation in 1620 by William Bradford & others of the Mayflower Company*. Hamden, CT: Shoe String, 1988.

Celsi, T. N. *Squanto & the First Thanksgiving*. Milwaukee: Raintree, 1989.

Fradin, D. B. *Thanksgiving*. Hillside, NJ: Enslow, 1990.

Fritz, J. *The Double Life of Pocahontas*. New York: Putnam, 1983.

Kessel, J. K. *Squanto and the First Thanksgiving*. Minneapolis: Carolrhoda, 1983.

O'Dell, S. *The Serpent Never Sleeps*. Boston: Houghton Mifflin, 1987.

Scott, J. A. *Settlers on the Eastern Shore: 1607–1750*. New York: Facts on File, 1990.

Seawall, M. *The Pilgrims of Plimoth*. New York: Atheneum, 1986.

Tomchek, A. H. *The Hopi*. Chicago: Childrens Press, 1987.

CHAPTER 7
References and Resources for Adults

Armstrong, Virginia I., ed. *I Have Spoken: American History Through the Voices of the Indians*. Swallow Press/Ohio University Press: Athens, OH, 1971, repr. 1992.

Graymont, B. *The Iroquois*. New York: Chelsea House, 1988.

Josephy, A. Jr. *The Patriot Chiefs*. New York: Penguin, 1989.

Landau, E. *The Sioux*. New York: Franklin Watts, 1989.

O'Brien, S. *American Indian Tribal Governments*. Norman: University of Oklahoma, 1989.

Spencer, Paula. *Kui Tatk*. Washington, DC: Native American Science Education, 1987.

Spicer, E. *A Short History of the Indians of the United States*. Malabar, FL: Robert E. Krieger, 1983.

Waldman, C. *Atlas of the North American Indian*. New York: Facts on File, 1985.

Resources for the Classroom

Armstrong, Virginia I., ed. *I Have Spoken: American History Through the Voices of the Indians*. Swallow Press/Ohio University Press: Athens, OH, 1971, repr. 1992.

Carey, V. *Quail Song*. New York: G. P. Putnam's Sons, 1990.

Cwiklik, R. *King Philip and the War with the Colonists*. Englewood Cliffs, NJ: Silver Burdett, 1989.

Feest, C. F. *The Powhatan Tribes*. Englewood Cliffs, NJ:

Chelsea House, 1990.

Lyons, G. *The Creek Indians*. New York: Simon & Shuster, 1978.

Morris, R. B. *The Indian Wars*. Minneapolis: Lerner, 1985.

Ochoa, G. *The Fall of Quebec and the French and Indian War*. Englewood Cliffs, NJ: Silver Burdett, 1990.

Paul, P. *Dance with Me Gods*. New York: Lodestar, 1982.

Roman, J. *King Philip: Wampanoag Rebel*. New York: Chelsea House, 1992.

Sando, J. *The Pueblo Indians*. San Francisco: The Indian Historian Press, 1976.

Siegel, B. *Fur Trappers and Traders*. New York: Walker, 1981.

Yue, C. and Yue, D. *The Pueblo*. Boston, Houghton Mifflin, 1986.

Videotapes

Connecticut Public Television (producer). (n.d.). *The New Pequot: A Tribal Portrait*.

Lewis, A. J. (producer). (1986) *Gannagaro*. Rochester, NY: WXXI-TV.

Videotapes available through Native American Public Broadcasting Consortium.

CHAPTER 8
References and Resources for Adults

Brown, J. P. *Old Frontiers*. Kingsport, TN: Southern Publishers,

Carter, F. *The Education of Little Tree*. Albuquerque: University of New Mexico, 1989. Recent research has questioned whether or not this book is actually autobiographical.

Cushman, H. B. *History of the Choctaw, Chickasaw, and Natchez Indians*. Stillwater, OK: Redlands, 1962.

Debo, A. *A History of the Indians of the United States*. Norman: University of Oklahoma, 1989.

Ehle, J. *Trail of Tears: The Rise and Fall of the Cherokee Nation*. New York: Anchor Books/Doubleday, 1988.

Ellis, J. *Walking the Trail*. New York: Delacourte, 1991. More a story of one man's journey than the Trail of Tears, this, nonetheless, is good reading.

Ford, P. L. (ed.) *The Writings of Thomas Jefferson*, volume III. New York: 1892.

Foreman, G. *Sequoyah* , Norman: University of Oklahoma, 1980.

Humphrey, W. *No Resting Place*. New York: Dell, 1989.

Spicer, E. H. *A Short History of the Indians of the United States*. Malabar, FL: Robert E. Krieger, 1983.

Spicer, E. H. *The American Indians*. Cambridge, MA:

Belknap, 1982.

Viola, H. J. *After Columbus: The Smithsonian Chronicle of the North American Indians*. Washington, DC: Smithsonian/ Orion, 1990.

Waldman, C. *Atlas of the North American Indian*. New York: Facts on File, 1985.

Williams, J. *Trails of Tears*. Dallas: Hendrick-Long, 1992.

Resources for the Classroom

Bealer, A. W. *Only the Names Remain: The Cherokee and the Trail of Tears*. Boston: Little, Brown, 1972.

Bedford, D. R. *Tsali*. San Francisco, CA: Indian Historian Press, 1972.

Carter, F. *The Education of Little Tree*. Albuquerque: University of New Mexico, 1989.

Claro, N. *The Cherokees*. New York: Chelsea House, 1991.

Cwiklik, R. *Sequoyah and the Cherokee Alphabet*. Englewood Cliffs, NJ: Silver Burdett, 1989.

Kelly, L. C. *Federal Indian Policy*. New York: Chelsea, 1990.

Lee, M. *The Seminoles*. New York: Franklin Watts, 1989.

Pate, G. S., Hollowell, J., Ging, B. *The Trail of Tears: An Inquiry Simulation*. Tucson: GSP, 1982. (Available from Social Studies School Service catalog, 1992)

Sharpe, J. D. *The Cherokees Past and Present*. Cherokee, NC: Cherokee Publications, 1988.

Stein, R.C. *The Story of the Trail of Tears*. Chicago. Childrens Press, 1985.

Underwood, T. B. *Cherokee Legends and the Trail of Tears*. Cherokee, NC: Cherokee Publishing, 1989.

Underwood T. B. *The Story of the Cherokee People*. Cherokee, NC: Cherokee Publications, 1961.

Waldman, C. *Who Was Who in Native American History*. New York: Facts on File, 1990.

CHAPTER 9
References and Resources for Adults

Andrist, R. K. *The Long Death: The Last Days of the Plains Indians*. New York: Collier/Macmillan, 1964.

Arthur, C., Bingham, S., and Bingham J. *Between Sacred Mountains*. Tucson: Sun Tracks and the University of Arizona, 1982.

Brown, D. *Bury My Heart at Wounded Knee*. New York: Pocket Books, 1981.

Brown, D. *Wounded Knee: An Indian History of the American West*. New York: Holt, Rinehart, and Winston, 1974.

Connell, E. S. *Son of the Morning Star: Custer and the Little Bighorn*. San Francisco: North Point, 1984.

Eckert, A. W. *A Sorrow in our Heart: The Life of Tecumseh*.

New York: Bantam, 1992.

Fuchs, E. and Havinghurst, R. J. *To Live on This Earth: American Indian Education.* Albuquerque: University of New Mexico, 1972.

Josephy, A. M. Jr. *The Indian Heritage of America.* New York: Alfred A. Knopf, 1985.

McLuhan, T. C. *Touch the Earth.* New York: Promontory, 1987.

O'Brien, S. *American Indian Tribal Governments.* Norman: University of Oklahoma, 1989.

Svaldi, D. *Sand Creek and the Rhetoric of Extermination: A Case Study in Indian-White Relations.* Lanham, MD: University Press, 1989.

Thompson, T. (ed.) *The Schooling of Native America.* Washington, DC: U.S. Department of Education, 1978.

Vanderwerth, W. C. *Indian Oratory.* New York: Ballantine Books, 1971.

Resources for the Classroom

Brown, D. *Wounded Knee: An Indian History of the American West.* New York: Holt, Rinehart, and Winston, 1974.

Capps, B. *The Great Chiefs.* Alexandria, VA: Time-Life Books, 1975.

Dippie, B. *Custer's Last Stand.* Missoula: University of Montana Publications in History, 1976.

Freedman, R. *Buffalo Hunt.* New York: Holiday House, 1988.

Gilpin, L. *The Enduring Navaho.* Austin: University of Texas, 1988.

Halliburton, W. J. *The Tragedy of Little Bighorn.* New York: Franklin Watts, 1989.

Iverson, P. *The Navajos.* New York: Chelsea, 1990.

Locke, R. F. *The Book of the Navajo.* Los Angeles: Mankind, 1992.

Luther, T. *Custer High Spots.* Ft. Collins, CO: The Old Army Press, 1972.

Marrin, A. *War Clouds in the West: Indians & Cavalrymen, 1860–1890.* New York: Atheneum, 1984.

McGaw, J. B. *Chief Red Horse Tells About Custer.* New York: Lodestar/E.P. Dutton, 1981.

O'Dell, S. *Sing Down the Moon.* New York: Dell, 1970.

Schultz, D. *Month of the Freezing Moon.* New York: St. Martin's, 1990.

Shorto, R. *Tecumseh and the Dream of an American Indian Nation.* Englewood Cliffs, NJ: Silver Burdett, 1989.

Wills, C. *The Battle of the Little Bighorn.* Englewood Cliffs, NJ: Silver Burdett, 1990.

Wood, L. H. *The Navajo Indians.* New York: Chelsea, 1991.

Videotapes

National Endowment for the Humanities (producer). (1982) *An Ancient Gift.* Flagstaff, AZ: Northern Arizona Museum.

Nez Perce: Portrait of a People. National Park Service. This documentary traces the history of the Nez Perce people from their first interactions with white men through the series of treaties which left them with less and less land, and on to the present system of tribal self-government. Available from Social Studies School Service 1992 catalog.

Peace River Films and KAET-TV (producers). (1985) *Seasons of a Navajo.* Available from the Native American Public Broadcasting Consortium.

Tahtonka. (1982) This videotape presents the connection between the Sioux people and the buffalo (*tahtonka*), tracing Native American culture from the pre-horse era through the Battle of Wounded Knee in 1890. Appropriate for middle grades and up. Available from Social Studies School Service 1992 catalog.

Tellens (producer). (1982). *Navajo.* Flagstaff, AZ: Museum of Northern Arizona.

Wiping the Tears of Seven Generations. Leonia, NJ: VCA—Wiping the Tears. This is an awarding-winning video of the Big Foot Memorial Ride. It depicts hundreds of Lakota riding horseback in temperatures of 70 degrees below zero commemorating the victims of the Wounded Knee Massacre. Available from VCA—Wiping the Tears, 50 Leyland Drive, Leonia, NJ 07605. A portion of the proceeds go to Lakota educational institutions.

CHAPTER 10
References and Resources for Adults

Andrist, R. K. *The Long Death: The Last Days of the Plains Indian.* New York: Macmillan, 1964.

Armstrong, Virginia I., ed. *I Have Spoken: American History Through the Voices of the Indians.* (Swallow Press/Ohio University Press: Athens, OH, 1971, repr. 1992).

Brown, D. *Bury My Heart at Wounded Knee.* New York: Holt, Rinehart, and Winston, 1981.

Burke, C. H. To All Indians (letter). Washington, D.C.: U.S. National Archives (File: 10429-22-063 Part I), 1923.

Cloud Bringing Rain and Culp, M. "Our Blue Lake Lands." *Native Peoples* (Spring 1992): 38–43.

Debo, A. *A History of Indians of the United States.* Norman: University of Oklahoma, 1989a.

Debo, A. *And Still the Waters Run: The Betrayal of the Five Civilized Tribes.* Norman: University of Oklahoma, 1989b.

Gordon-McCutchan, R. C. *The Taos Indians and the Battle*

for Blue Lake. Santa Fe, NM: Red Crane Books, 1991.

Jensen, R. E., Paul, R. E. & Carter, J. E. Eyewitness at Wounded Knee. Lincoln: University of Nebraska, 1991.

Josephy, A. M. Jr., Thomas, T. and Eder, J. Wounded Knee: Lest We Forget. Cody, WY: Buffalo Bill Historical Center, 1990.

Keegan, M. Taos Pueblo and its Sacred Blue Lake. Santa Fe, NM: Clear Light, 1991.

Mails, T. E. The Mystic Warriors of the Plains. Garden City, NY: Doubleday, 1972.

Mooney, J. The Ghost-Dance Religion and the Sioux Outbreak of 1890. Lincoln: University of Nebraska, 1991.

McLuhan, T. C. Touch the Earth. New York: Simon & Schuster, 1971.

Prucha, F. P. Americanizing the American Indians. Lincoln: University of Nebraska, 1978.

Prucha, F. P. The Great Father (abridged). Lincoln: University of Nebraska, 1986.

Spicer, E. H. The American Indians. Cambridge, MA: Belknap Press of Harvard University Press, 1982.

Wilson, M. "Naming Beverly's Baby." Native Peoples (Fall 1987): 2–5.

Wisecarver, C. W. F. "Wounded Knee: Mending the Sacred Hoop." Native Peoples (Spring 1990): 8–16.

Resources for the Classroom

Black, S. Sitting Bull. Englewood Cliffs, NJ: Silver Burdett, 1989.

Brown, D. Wounded Knee: An Indian History of the American West (adapted by Amy Ehrlich from Bury My Heart at Wounded Knee). New York. Holt, Rinehart & Winston, 1974.

Fleischer, J. Sitting Bull: Warrior of the Sioux. Mahwah. NJ: Troll, 1979.

Keegan, M. The Taos Indians and Their Sacred Blue Lake. New York: Julian Messner, 1972.

Kissinger, R. K. Quanah Parker: Comanche Chief. Gretna, LA: Pelican, 1991.

Marrin, A. War Clouds in the West: Indians & Cavalrymen 1860–1890. New York: Atheneum, 1984.

Stein, R. C. The Story of Wounded Knee. Chicago: Childrens Press, 1983.

Waldman, C. Who Was Who in Native American History. New York: Facts on File, 1990.

Wood, T. With Afraid of Hawk, W. N. A Boy Becomes a Man at Wounded Knee. New York: Walker, 1992.

Videotapes

Sitting Bull: Tatankaiyotake (Video). (1988). Life Video. Artwork and documentary photos provide the visual images for this survey of the life and influence of the Great Sioux chief. The video includes the Battle of the Little Bighorn, the death of Sitting Bull, and the Wounded Knee Massacre. Suitable for middle grades and up. Available for $69.95 from Social Studies School Service 1992 catalog.

CHAPTER 11
References and Resources for Adults

Beck, P. V., Walters, A. L. and Francisco, N. The Sacred. Tsaile, AZ: Navajo Community College, 1992.

Carter, F. The Education of Little Tree. Albuquerque: University of New Mexico, 1989.

Echo-Hawk, W. "Loopholes in Religious Liberty: The Need for a Federal Law to Protect Freedom of Worship for Native People." In NARF Legal Review, Boulder, CO: Native American Rights Fund, Summer, 1991.

Fuchs, E. and Havinghurst, R. J. To Live on This Earth: American Indian Education. Albuquerque: University of New Mexico, 1972.

Henry, J. (ed.) The American Indian Reader: Education. San Francisco: The Indian Historian, 1972.

Lame Deer, J. (Fire) and Erdoes, R. Lame Deer Seeker of Visions. New York: Pocket, 1976.

McLuhan, T. C. Touch the Earth. New York: Promontory 1, 1987.

Nabokov, P. (ed.) Native American Testimony. New York: Viking, 1991.

Neihardt, J. G. Black Elk Speaks. New York: Simon & Schuster, 1932.

O'Brien, S. American Indian Tribal Governments. Norman: University of Oklahoma Press, 1989.

Standing Bear, L. My People the Sioux. Lincoln: University of Nebraska, 1975.

Steward, O. Peyote Religion: A History. Norman: University of Oklahoma, 1987.

Szasz, M. C. Education and the American Indian. Albuquerque: University of New Mexico, 1974.

Thompson, T. The Schooling of Native America. Washington, DC: U.S. Department of Education, 1978.

Underhill, R. M. Red Man's Religion. Chicago: University of Chicago, 1965.

Vecsey, C. (ed.) Handbook of American Indian Religious Freedom. New York: Crossroad, 1991.

Viola, H. J. After Columbus: the Smithsonian Chronicle of the North American Indians. Washington, DC: Smithsonian/Orion Books, 1990.

Resources for the Classroom

Hood, F. M. Something for the Medicine Man. Chicago:

Melmont, 1962.

Liptak, K. *North American Indian Medicine People.* New York: Franklin Watts, 1990.

Selam, L. Suwaptsa. In J. Henry (ed.) *The American Indian Reader: Education.* San Francisco: The Indian Historian Press, 1972.

Suina, J. "And Then I Went to School: Memories of a Pueblo Childhood." In B. Bigelow, B. Miner, and B. Peterson (eds.) *Rethinking Columbus.* Portland, OR: Rethinking Schools, 1992.

Wolf, B. *Tinker and the Medicine Man.* New York: Random House, 1973.

CHAPTER 12
References and Resources for Adults

Arthur, C., Bingham, S., and Bingham J. *Between Sacred Mountains.* Tucson: Sun Tracks and the University of Arizona, 1982.

Collier, J. *Indians of the Americas.* New York: New American Library, 1947.

Deloria, V., Jr. and Lytle, C. M. *American Indians, American Justice.* Austin: University of Texas, 1983.

Highwater, J. *Song from the Earth: American Indian Painting.* Boston: New York Graphic Society, 1976.

Locke, R. F. *The Book of the Navajo.* Los Angeles: Mankind, 1979.

Marriott, A. *Maria: The Potter of San Ildefonso.* Norman: University of Oklahoma, 1948.

Prucha, F. P. *The Great Father.* Lincoln: University of Nebraska, 1986.

Spicer, E. *A Short History of the Indians of the United States.* Malabar, FL: Robert E. Kreiger, 1983.

Spivey, R. L. *Maria.* Flagstaff, AZ: Northland, 1979.

Waldman, C. *Atlas of the North American Indian.* New York: Facts on File, 1985.

Resources for the Classroom

Arthur, C., Bingham, S., and Bingham J. *Between Sacred Mountains.* Tucson: Sun Tracks and the University of Arizona, 1982.

Batkin, J. "Three Great Potters of San Ildefonso and Their Legacy." *American Indian Art* (Autumn 1991): 56–69.

Dockstader, F. J. *Indian Art in America: The Arts and Crafts of the North American Indian.* New York: Promontory Press, n.d.

Highwater, J. *Many Smokes, Many Moons: A Chronology of American Indian History Through Indian Art.* Philadelphia: J. B. Lippincott, 1978.

Hofsinde, R. *Indian Arts.* New York: William Morrow,

1971.

Jacka, L. E. "Moments with Maria." *Native Peoples* (Winter 1988): 24–29.

Kawano, K. "Faces of the Code." *Native Peoples* (Summer 1989): 24–28.

Kawano, K. *Warriors: Navajo Code Talkers.* Flagstaff, AZ: Northland, 1992.

Peterson, S. *The Living Tradition of Maria Martinez.* Tokyo: Kodansha International, 1977.

Videotapes

McCarthy, T. (Producer). (1986). *Navajo Code Talkers.* KENW-TV. (Available from Native American Public Broadcasting Consortium).

U.S. National Park Service. (1980). *Maria: Indian Pottery Maker of San Ildefonso.* U.S. National Park Service.

CHAPTER 13
References and Resources for Adults

Armstrong, Virginia I., ed. *I Have Spoken: American History Through the Voices of the Indians.* Swallow Press/Ohio University Press: Athens, OH, 1971, repr. 1992.

Deloria, V. Jr., and Lytle, C. *The Nations Within: The Past and Future of American Indian Sovereignty.* New York: Pantheon, 1984.

Fixico, D. L. *Urban Indians.* New York: Chelsea House, 1991.

Levine, S., and Lurie, N .O. (eds) *American Indians Today.* Baltimore: Penguin, 1968.

Moccasins on Pavement, The Indian Experience: A Denver Portrait. Denver: Denver Museum of Natural History, 1978.

Momaday, N. S. *House Made of Dawn.* New York: Harper & Row, 1968.

Nabokov, P. (ed.) *Native American Testimony.* New York: Penguin, 1991.

O'Brien, S. *American Indian Tribal Governments.* Norman: University of Oklahoma, 1989.

Spicer, E. H. *A Short History of the Indians of the United States.* Malabar, FL: Robert E. Krieger, 1983.

Sorkin, A. *The Urban American Indian.* Lexington, KY: Lexington, 1978.

Steiner, S. *The New Indians.* New York: Delta, 1968.

Viola, H. J. *After Columbus: The Smithsonian Chronicle of the North American Indians.* New York: Crown, 1990.

Resources for the Classroom

Dorris, M. *A Yellow Raft in Blue Water.* New York: Warner, 1988.

Fixico, D. L. *Urban Indians.* New York: Chelsea House, 1991.

CHAPTER 14
References and Resources for Adults

Debo, A. *A History of the Indians of the United States.* Norman: University of Oklahoma, 1989.

Deer, A. (1981). "Mobilizing to Win." In S. Verble (ed.). *Words of Today's American Indian Women: OHOYO MAKACHI,* 1981, (pp. 87–88). Washington, DC: U.S. Department of Education.

Deloria, V. Jr. *Custer Died for Your sins: An Indian Manifesto.* Norman: University of Oklahoma, 1988.

Deloria, V. Jr. and Lytle, C. M. *American Indians, American Justice.* Austin: University of Texas, 1983.

Deloria, V., Jr. and Lytle, C. *The Nations Within: The Past and Future of American Indian Sovereignty.* New York: Pantheon, 1984.

Viola, H. J. *After Columbus: The Smithsonian Chronicle of the North American Indian.* Washington, DC: Smithsonian/ Orion Books, 1990.

Waldman, C. *Atlas of the North American Indian.* New York: Facts on File, 1985.

Weatherford, J. *Indian Givers: How the Indians of the Americas Transformed the World.* New York: Fawcett Columbine, 1988.

Weatherford, J. *Native Roots.* New York: Crown, 1990.

"Year of the American Indian." *Native Monthly Reader* (1991–1992): 3.

Resources for the Classroom

Franklin. R. J. and Bunte, P. A. *The Paiute.* New York: Chelsea, 1990.

Merrell, J. H. *The Catawbas.* New York: Chelsea, 1989.

Ourada, P. *The Menominee.* New York: Chelsea, 1990.

CHAPTER 15
References and Resources for Adults

Basic Call to Consciousness. Rooseveltown, NY: *Akwesasne Notes,* Mohawk Nation, 1986.

Burnette, R. and Koster, J. *The Road to Wounded Knee.* New York: Bantam, 1974.

Coyote, F., et al. *I Will Die an Indian.* Sun Valley, ID: Institute of the American West, 1980.

Deloria, V. Jr. and Lytle, C. *The Nations Within: The Past and Future of American Indian Sovereignty.* New York: Pantheon, 1984.

Fortunate Eagle, A. *Alcatraz! Alcatraz!* Berkeley: Heyday, 1992.

Josephy, A. M., Jr. *Red Power.* Lincoln: University of Nebraska, 1971.

McLuhan, T.C. *Touch the Earth.* New York: Touchstone, 1971.

Pevar, S. L. *The Rights of Indians and Tribes.* Carbondale: University of Illinois Press, 1992.

Steiner, S. *The New Indians.* New York: Harper Colophon, 1968.

Trail of Broken Treaties: B.I.A. I'm Not Your Indian Anymore. Rooseveltown, NY: *Akwesasne Notes,* Mohawk Nation, 1974.

U.S. Commission on Civil Rights. *American Indian Civil Rights Handbook.* Washington, DC: U.S. Government Printing Office, 1980.

Voices from Wounded Knee, Rooseveltown, NY: *Akwesasne Notes,* Mohawk Nation, 1973–1974.

Resources for the Classroom

Voices from Wounded Knee, Rooseveltown, NY: *Akwesasne Notes,* Mohawk Nation, 1973–1974. Because transcriptions of actual conversations are a significant part of the book, some of the strong language of frustration and hostility could be considered inappropriate for young people. However, the teacher will find much teaching material in the book.

CHAPTER 16
References and Resources for Adults

Ambler, M. "The Nation's First Tribal College." *Native Peoples* (Winter 1991a): 22–23.

Ambler, M. "Tribal Colleges Change Lives." *Native Peoples* (Winter 1991b): 18–21, 24.

Basic Call to Consciousness. Rooseveltown, NY: *Akwesasne Notes,* 1986.

Brown, D. *Bury My Heart at Wounded Knee.* New York: Holt, Rinehart, and Winston, 1970.

Brown, D. "Wounded Knee: An Indian History of the American West." Adapted by Amy Erlich from *Bury My Heart at Wounded Knee.* New York: Holt, Rinehart, and Winston, 1974.

Cahape, P., and Howley, C. B. (eds.) *Indian Nations at Risk: Listening to the People.* Charleston, WV: ERIC Clearninghouse on Rural and Small Schools, 1992.

Deloria, V. Jr. "The Place of Indians in Contemporary Education." *American Indian Journal* (February 1976).

Jaimes, M. A. (ed.) *The State of Native America.* Boston: South End, 1992.

Josephy, A. M., Jr. *Now that the Buffalo's Gone.* Norman: University of Oklahoma, 1986.

Matthiessen, P. *In the Spirit of Crazy Horse.* New York: Viking Penguin, 1991.

Michaelsen, R. S. "Law and the Limits of Liberty." In C.

Vecsey (ed.), *Handbook of American Indian Religious Freedom*. New York: Crossroad, 1991.

O'Brien, S. *American Indian Tribal Governments*. Norman: University of Oklahoma, 1989.

Pevar, S. *The Rights of Indians and Tribes: The Basic ACLU Guide to Indian and Tribal Rights*, 2nd edition. Carbondale and Edwardsville: University of Illinois, 1992.

Stein, R. C. *The Story of Wounded Knee*. Chicago: Childrens Press, 1983.

Vecsey, C. (ed.). *Handbook of American Indian Religious Freedom*. New York: Crossroad, 1991.

Wisecarver, C.W.F. "Wounded Knee: Mending the Sacred Hoop." *Native Peoples* (Spring 1990): 8-16.

Resources for the Classroom

Benton-Banaise, E. *Generation to Generation*. Hayward, WI: Indian Country Communications, 1991.

Brown, D. *Bury My Heart at Wounded Knee*. New York: Holt, Rinehart, and Winston, 1970.

Brown, D. "Wounded Knee: An Indian History of the American West." Adapted by Amy Erlich from *Bury My Heart at Wounded Knee*. New York: Holt, Rinehart, and Winston, 1974.

Wood, T. with Afraid of Hawk, W. N. *A Boy Becomes a Man at Wounded Knee*. New York: Walker, 1992.

Videotapes

VCA—Wiping the Tears (Producer). *Wiping the Tears of Seven Generations*. Leonia, NJ: Producer.

CHAPTER 17
References and Resources for Adults

Brasher, P. "Thousand Drop Commodity Food for Jobs and/or Food Stamps." *News from Indian Country* (Late March 1992): 3.

Campbell, B. N. "A Native American in Congress." *Native Monthly Reader* (1991–1992): 1.

Churchill, W. "The Earth Is Our Mother: Struggles for American Indian Land and Liberation in the Contemporary United States." In M. Annette Jaimes (ed.) *The State of Native America: Genocide, Colonization, and Resistance*. Boston: South End, 1992.

Cloud Bringing Rain and Culp, M. "Our Blue Lake Lands." *Native Peoples* (Spring 1992): 39–43.

Deloria, V., Jr. "The Place of Indians in Contemporary Education." *American Indian Journal* (February 1976).

Deloria, V., Jr. "Sacred Lands and Religious Freedom." *NARF Legal Review*, (Summer 1991): 1–6.

Ferguson, T. J., and Eriacho, W. Ahayu:da "Zuni War Gods: Cooperation and Repatriation." *Native Peoples* (Fall 1990): 6–12.

Giago, T. "Raids on Indian Casinos Reopen Old Tribal Wounds." *Denver Post* (May 17, 1992): 1-1, 5-1.

Josephy, A. M., Jr. *Now That the Buffalo's Gone*. Norman: University of Oklahoma, 1986.

Lazarus, E. *Black Hills/White Justice*. New York: HarperCollins, 1991.

McCoy, R. "Repatriation." *American Indian Art Magazine* (Autumn 1992): 23.

Miniclier, K. "Drumbeat of Criticism Pounds at BIA." *Denver Post* (August 2, 1992a): 1A, 4A.

Miniclier, K. "Effects of Gaming Invasion Spread." *Denver Post* (September 13, 1992b): 1C, 4C.

"Name Offers Graphic Link to Cherokee Past." *The Fresno Bee* (March 21, 1991).

"Native American Rights Fund." Native American Rights Fund Annual Report. Boulder, CO: Native American Rights Fund, 1990.

"Peace on Earth." *Native Peoples* (Fall 1991): 7. This advertisement is a part of a national campaign by the Smithsonian Institution in support of the National Museum of the American Indian (see Appendix 000).

Pevar, S. L. *The Rights of Indians and Tribes*. Carbondale & Edwardsville: Southern Illinois University, 1992.

Sanders, S. "Our First Twenty Years." Boulder, CO: Native American Rights Fund, 1990.

Savilla, E. M. "High Stakes on Gambling in Indian Country." *News from Indian Country* (Late April 1992): 6–7.

Taliman, V. "Mescalero People Fear 'Chino Dump.'" *News from Indian Country* (Late March 1992b): 11.

Taliman, V. "Sacred Ground Slated for Asbestos Dump." *News from Indian Country* (Late March 1992c): 13.

Talliman, V. "The Toxic Waste of Indian Lives." *News from Indian Country* (Mid-May 1992d): 6–7.

Taliman, V. "Tribes Take MRS Funding." *News from Indian Country* (Late April 1992a): 10.

Vecsey, C. (ed.) *Handbook of American Indian Religious Freedom*. New York: Crossroad, 1991.

Wall, S. and Arden, H. *Wisdomkeepers*. Hillsboro, OR: Beyond Words, 1990.

Watts, J. G. "Sacred Circle." *Native Peoples* (Summer 1991): 34–39.

Work, J. C. *Prose and Poetry of the American West*. Lincoln: University of Nebraska, 1990.

Resources for the Classroom

Charging Eagle, T. and Zeilinger, R. *Black Hills: Sacred Hills*. Chamberlain, SD: Tipi Press, 1987.

Harlan, J. *American Indians Today*. New York: Franklin Watts, 1987.

Hirschfelder, A. *Happily May I Walk: American Indians and Alaska Natives Today*. New York: Scribners, 1986.

Videotapes

The Black Hills Claim. (1987). NETCHE (Producer). Available from the Native American Public Broadcasting Consortium.

The Treaty of 1868. (1987). NETCHE (Producer). Available from the Native American Public Broadcasting Consortium.

Those who want continuing resources for the classroom regarding contemporary issues must rely on newspapers, magazines, journals, and other up-to-date sources. Teachers are obliged to present the Indian perspective on such vital issues as gaming, environmental concerns, political action, and repatriation.

CHAPTER 18
References and Resources for Adults

Arden, H. "From One Sovereign People to Another." *National Geographic* (September 1987): 370–73.

Arden, H. "The Fire That Never Dies." *National Geographic* (September 1987): 375–403.

Arthur, C., Bingham, S., and Bingham, J. *Between Sacred Mountains*. Tucson, AZ: Sun Tracks and the University Press, 1982.

Deloria, V., Jr. "Higher Education and Self-Determination." *Winds of Change* (Winter 1991): 18–25.

Deloria, V., Jr. "Property and Self Government as Educational Initiatives." *Winds of Change* (Autumn 1990): 26–31.

Deloria, V., Jr. "Traditional Technology." *Winds of Change* (Spring 1990): 12–17.

Donahue, B. "Computer Program Helps Revive Ancient Language." *Winds of Change* (Spring 1990): 20–23.

Dorris, M. *The Broken Chord*. New York: Harper and Row, 1989.

Dorris, M. "Pregnancy and Alcohol." *Winds of Change* (Autumn 1990): 36–40.

Gill, K. "Is There a Genetic Basis to the Development of Alcoholism Among Native Americans?" *Winds of Change* (Winter 1992): 68–70.

Gilpin, L. *The Enduring Navaho*. Austin: University of Texas, 1988.

Harvey, K. D., Harjo, L. D., and Jackson, J. K. *Teaching About Native Americans*. Washington, DC: National Council for the Social Studies, 1991.

Johnson, R. "Diabetes Ravages Arizona Indians." *Denver Post* (June 21, 1992): 1A, 8A–9A.

Josephy, A. *Now That the Buffalo's Gone*. Norman: University of Oklahoma Press, 1984.

Locke, R. F. *The Book of the Navajo*. Los Angeles: Mankind, 1992.

Matthews, A. *Where the Buffalo Roam*. New York: Grove Press, 1992.

May, P. "Suicide and Self-Destruction Among American Indian Youths." *American Indian and Alaska Native Mental Health Research Journal* (June 1987): 51–69.

Mohawk, J. "A Symbol More Powerful than Paper." *Northeast Indian Quarterly* (Winter–Spring 1987–1988).

Pewewardy, C. and Bushey, M. "A Family of Learners and Storytellers." *Native Peoples* (Summer 1992): 56–60.

Silko, L. M. *Ceremony*. New York: Penguin, 1986.

Simonelli, R. "Indian Education in America." *Winds of Change* (Summer 1991): 12–17.

Vecsey, C. (ed) *Handbook of American Indian Religious Freedom*. New York: Crossroad, 1991.

Waldman, C. *Atlas of the North American Indian*. New York: Facts on File, 1985.

Wall, S. and Arden, H. *Wisdomkeepers*. Hillsboro, OR: Beyond Worlds Publishing, 1990.

Weatherford, J. *Indian Givers*. New York: Fawcett Columbine, 1988.

West, P. "Indians Work to Save a Language—and Their Heritage." *Education Week* (September 30, 1992): 1, 16–17.

Resources for the Classroom

Benton-Banaise, E. *Generation to Generation*. Hayward, WI: Indian Country Communications, 1991.

Coombs, L. *Powwow*. Cleveland, OH: Modern Curriculum, 1992.

Horse Capture, G. *Powwow*. Cody, WY: Buffalo Bill Historical Center, 1989.

Red Hawk, R. *A Trip to a Powwow*. Newcastle, CA: Sierra Oaks, 1988.

Roberts, C. "Rocky Boy." *Native Peoples* (Summer 1988): 2–7.

Wall, S. and Arden, H. *Wisdomkeepers*. Hillsboro, OR: Beyond Worlds Publishing, 1990.

Videotapes

Nebraska Educational Television (Producer). (nd.) *Dancing to Give Thanks*. Available from the Native American Public Broadcasting Consortium.

Peace River Films and KAET-TV (Producers). (1985). *Seasons of a Navajo*. Available from the Native American Broadcasting Consortium.

Powwow. Available from Social Studies School Service catalog, 1992.

Bibliography

Akwesasne Notes. (1986). *Basic Call to Consciousness* (3rd printing). Rooseveltown, NY: Akwesasne Notes. Mohawk Nation.

Ambler, M. (1991, Winter). The nation's first tribal college. *Native Peoples*. 4 (2), pp. 22–23.

Ambler, M. (1991, Winter). Tribal colleges change lives. *Native Peoples*, 4 (2), pp. 18–21 & 24.

Anderson, J. (1984). *The First Thanksgiving Feast*. New York, NY: Clarion/Houghton Mifflin.

Andrist, R. K. (1964). *The Long Death: The Last Days of the Plains Indians*. New York, NY: Collier/Macmillan.

Appleton, L. A. (1971). *American Indian Design and Decoration*. New York: Dover.

Archaeology. (1986). Milwaukee, WI: Raintree.

Arden, H. (1987, September). From one sovereign people to another. *National Geographic*, 172 (3), pp. 370–73.

Arden, H. (1987, September). The fire that never dies. *National Geographic*, 172 (3), pp. 375–403.

Armstrong, V. I. (1971). *I Have Spoken*. Athens, OH: Swallow Press/Ohio Univ. Press.

Arthur, C., Bingham, S. & Bingham J. (1982). *Between Sacred Mountains*. Tucson, AZ: Sun Tracks and the University of Arizona.

Batkin, J. (1991, Autumn). Three great potters of San Ildefonso and their legacy. *American Indian Art*. 16 (4), pp. 56–69.

Baylor, B. (1972). *When Clay Sings*. New York, NY: Macmillan.

Bealer, A. W. (1972). *Only the Names Remain: The Cherokee and the Trail of Tears*. Boston, MA: Little, Brown.

Beck, P. V., Wallers, A. L. & Francisco, N. (1992). *The Sacred* (2nd printing). Tsaile, AZ: Navajo Community College.

Bedford, D. R. (1972) *Tsali*. San Francisco, CA: Indian Historian Press.

Begley, S. (1991, Fall/Winter). The first Americans. *Newsweek* (Columbus Special Issue), pp. 15–16.

Ben Nighthorse Campbell, A Native American in Congress. (1991–1992). *Native Monthly Reader*, 3 (6). p. 1.

Benton-Banaise, E. (1991). *Generation to Generation*. Hayward, WI: Indian Country Communications.

Black, S. (1989). *Sitting Bull*. Englewood Cliffs, NJ: Silver Burdett.

Blackburn, J. (1985). *The Bloody Summer of Seventeen Forty-Two: A Colonial Boy's Journal*. St. Simons Island, GA: Fort Frederica.

Bleeker, S. (1955). *The Pueblo Indians: Farmers of the Rio Grande*. New York, NY: William Morrow.

Bolton, H. E. (1949). *Coronado: Knight of Pueblos and Plains*. New York, NY: Whittlesey House/McGraw-Hill and Albuquerque, NM: University of New Mexico.

Branigan, K. (1986). *Prehistory*. New York, NY: Franklin Watts.

Brasher, P. (1992, Late March). Thousands drop commodity food for jobs and/or food stamps. *News From Indian Country, VI*, (6), p. 3.

Brescia, W. (1985). Choctaw oral tradition relating to tribal origin. In C. K. Reeves, C. K. (Ed.), *The Choctaw Before Removal*. Jackson, MS: University Press of Mississippi.

Brown, D. (1971). *Wounded Knee: An Indian History of the American West* (adapted by Amy Ehrlich from *Bury My Heart at Wounded Knee*). New York, Holt, Rinehart & Winston.

Brown, D. (1981). *Bury My Heart at Wounded Knee* (reprint). New York, NY: Pocket Books.

Brown, J. P. (1938). *Old Frontiers*. Kingsport, TN: Southern Publishers.

Brown, M. W. (Ed.) (1988). *Homes in the Wilderness: A Pilgrim's Journal of Plymouth Plantation in 1620 by William Bradford & Others of the Mayflower Company.* Hamden, CT: Shoe String.

Brown, V. P. & Owens, L. (1983). *The World of the Southern Indians.* Birmingham, AL: Beechwood.

Burnette, R. & Koster, J. (1974). *The Road to Wounded Knee.* New York, NY: Bantam.

Caduto, M. J. & Bruchac, J. (1988). *Keepers of the Earth.* Golden, CO: Fulcrum.

Caduto, M. J. & Bruchac, J. (1991). *Keepers of the Animals.* Golden, CO: Fulcrum.

Cahape, P. & Howley, C. B. (Eds.). (1992). *Indian Nations at Risk: Listening to the People.* Charleston, WV: ERIC Clearinghouse on Rural and Small Schools.

Campbell, J. (1988). *The Power of Myth.* New York, NY: Doubleday, pp. 42–43.

Canby, T. Y. (1982, November). The Anasazi: Riddles in the ruins. *National Geographic, 162* (5), pp. 554–592.

Capps, B. (1975). *The Great Chiefs.* Alexandria, VA: Time-Life Books.

Carey, V. S. & Barnett, I. (1990). *Quail Song.* New York, NY: G.P. Putnam's Sons.

Carter, F. (1989). *The Education of Little Tree* (7th printing). Albuquerque, NM: University of New Mexico.

Celsi, T. N. (1989). *Squanto & the First Thanksgiving.* Milwaukee, WI: Raintree.

Charging Eagle, T. & Zeilinger, R. (1987). *Black Hills: Sacred Hills.* Chamberlain, SD: Tipi Press.

Churchill, W. (1992). The earth is our mother: Struggles for American Indian land and liberation in the contemporary United States. In M. Annette Jaimes (Ed.). *The State of Native America: Genocide, Colonization, and Resistance.* Boston, MA: South End, pp. 162–169.

Claro, N. (1991). *The Cherokees.* New York, NY: Chelsea.

Cloud Bringing Rain & Culp, M. (1992, Spring). Our Blue Lake lands. *Native Peoples, 5* (3), pp. 38–43.

Collier, J. (1947). *Indians of the Americas.* New York, NY: New American Library.

Commager, H. S. & Muessig, R. H. (1980). *The Study and Teaching of History.* Columbus, OH: Charles E. Merrill.

Connell, E. S. (1984). *Son of the Morning Star: Custer and the Little Bighorn.* San Francisco, CA: North Point.

Coombs, L. (1992). *Powwow.* Cleveland, OH: Modern Curriculum.

Cornplanter, J. J. (1986). *Legends of the Longhouse* (reprint). Ontario, Canada: Iroqrafts Ltd.

Cowley, G. (1991, Fall/Winter). The great disease migration. *Newsweek* (Special Edition), pp. 54–56.

Coyote, F., and others. (1980). *I will Die an Indian.* Institute of the American West.

Crosby, A. W. Jr. (1972). *The Columbian Exchange: Biological and Cultural Consequences of 1492.* Westport, CT: Greenwood Press.

Cushman, H. B. (1962). *History of the Choctaw. Chickasaw, and Natchez Indians.* Stillwater, OK: Redlands.

Cwiklik, R. (1989). *King Phillip and the War with the Colonists.* Englewood Cliffs, NJ: Silver Burdett.

Cwiklik, R. (1989). *Sequoyah and the Cherokee Alphabet.* Englewood Cliffs, NJ: Silver Burdett.

Deak, G. (1991, October). Everything you need to know about Columbus. *American Heritage,* pp. 40–54.

Debo, A. (1989). *A History of the Indians of the United States* (11th printing). Norman, OK: University of Oklahoma.

Debo, A. (1989). *And Still the Waters Run: The Betrayal of the Five Civilized Tribes* (5th printing). Norman, OK: University of Oklahoma.

Deer, A. (1981). Mobilizing to win. In S. Verble (Ed.). *Words of Today's American Indian Women: OHOYO MAKACHI* (pp. 87–88). Washington, D.C.: U.S. Department of Education.

DeJong, D.H. (1993). *Promises of the Past: A History of Indian Education.* Golden, CO: North American Press.

Deloria, V. Jr. (1976, February). The place of Indians in contemporary education. *American Indian Journal, 2,* (21).

Deloria, V. Jr. (1988). *Custer Died for Your Sins: An Indian Manifesto* (2nd printing). Norman, OK: University of Oklahoma.

Deloria, V. Jr. (1990, Spring). Traditional technology. *Winds of Change, 5* (2), pp. 12–17.

Deloria, V., Jr. (1990, Autumn). Property and self government as educational initiatives. *Winds of Change, 5* (4), pp. 26–31.

Deloria, V. Jr. (1991, Summer). Sacred lands and religious freedom. *NARF Legal Review, 16* (2), pp. 1–6.

Deloria, V., Jr. (1991, Winter). Higher education and self-determination. *Winds of Change. 6* (1), pp. 18–25.

Deloria, V. Jr. (Ed.). (1985). *American Indian Policy in the Twentieth Century.* Norman, OK: University of Oklahoma.

Deloria, V. Jr. & Lytle, C. (1981). *The Nations Within: The Past and Future of American Indian Sovereignty.* New York, NY: Pantheon.

Deloria, V. Jr. & Lytle, C. M. (1988). *American Indians, American Justice* (4th printing). Austin, TX: University of Texas.

Diaz, B. (1963). *The Conquest of New Spain* (H. M. Cohen, Trans.). New York, NY: Viking/Penguin.

Dippie, B. (1976). *Custer's Last Stand.* Missoula, MT: University of Montana Publications in History.

Dockstader, F. J. (1961). *Indian Art in North America.* (4th printing.). Greenwich, CT: New York Graphic Society.

Dockstader, F. J. (n.d.). *Indian Art in America: The Arts and Crafts of the North American Indian*. New York, NY: Promontory Press.

Donahue, B. (1990). Computer program helps revive ancient language. *Winds of Change, 5,* pp. 20–23.

Dorris, M. (1988). *A Yellow Raft in Blue Water*. New York, NY: Warner.

Dorris, M. (1989). *The Broken Chord*. New York, NY: Harper and Row.

Dorris, M. (1990, Autumn). Pregnancy and alcohol. *Winds of Change, 5* (4), pp. 36–40.

Echo-Hawk, W. (1991, Summer). Loopholes in religious liberty: The need for a federal law to protect freedom of worship for Native people. In *NARF Legal Review*, Boulder, CO: Native American Rights Fund.

Eckert, A. W. (1992). *A Sorrow in Our Heart: The Life of Tecumseh*. New York, NY: Bantam.

Ehle, J. (1988). *Trail of Tears: The Rise and Fall of the Cherokee Nation*. New York, NY: Anchor Books/Doubleday.

Ellis, J. (1991). *Walking the Trail*. New York, NY: Delacourte.

Erdoes, R. (1976). *The Rain Dance People: The Pueblo Indians, Their Past and Present*. New York, NY: Alfred A. Knopf.

Etling, M. & Folsom, M. (1963). *The Secret Story of Pueblo Bonito*. New York, NY: Scholastic.

Feest, C. F. (1990). *The Powhatan Tribes*. Englewood Cliffs, NJ: Chelsea.

Ferguson, T. J. & Eriacho, W. (1990, Fall). Ahayu:da Zuni war gods: Cooperation and repatriation. *Native Peoples, 4* (1), pp. 6–12.

Fixico, D. L. (1991). *Urban Indians*. New York, NY: Chelsea.

Fleischer. J. (1979). *Sitting Bull: Warrior of the Sioux*. Mahwah, NJ: Troll.

Foote, T. (1991, December). Where Columbus was coming from. *Smithsonian 22* (9), 28–41.

Foreman, G. (1980). *Sequoyah* (6th printing.) Norman, OK: University of Oklahoma.

Fortunate Eagle, A. (1992). *Alcatraz! Alcatraz!* Berkeley, CA: Heyday.

Fradin, D. B. (1983). *Archeology*. Chicago, IL: Childrens Press.

Fradin, D. B. (1990). *Columbus Day*. Hillside, NJ: Enslow Publishers.

Fradin, D. B. (1990). *Thanksgiving*. Hillside, NJ: Enslow Publishers.

Franklin. R. J. & Bunte, P. A. (1990). *The Paiute*. New York, NY: Chelsea.

Freedman, R. (1988). *Buffalo Hunt*. New York, NY: Holiday House.

Friend, D. & The Editors of Life. (1991). *The Meaning of Life: Reflections in Words and Picture on Why We Are Here*. Boston, MA: Little, Brown.

Fritz, J. (1983). *The Double Life of Pocahontas*. New York, NY: Putnam.

Fuchs, E. & Havinghurst, R. J. (1972). *To Live on This Earth: American Indian Education*. Albuquerque, NM: University of New Mexico.

Garaway, M. K. (1986). *The Old Hogan*. Cortez, CO: Mesa Verde.

Gattuso, J. (Ed.). (1993). *A Circle of Nations: Voices and Visions of American Indians*. Hillsboro, OR: Beyond Words.

Giago, T. (1992, March 17). *The Christian Science Monitor*. p. 12.

Giago, T. (1992, May 17). Raids on Indian casinos reopen old tribal wounds. *Denver Post*, pp. 1–1 & 5–1.

Gill, K. (1992, Winter). Is there a genetic basis to the development of alcoholism among Native Americans? *Winds of Change, 7* (1), pp. 68–70.

Gilpin, L. (1988). *The Enduring Navaho* (7th printing). Austin, TX: University of Texas.

Glatthorn, A. A. (1987). *Curriculum Renewal*. Alexandria, VA: Association for Supervision and Curriculum Development.

Gordon-McCutchan, R. C. (1991). *The Taos Indians and the Battle for Blue Lake*. Santa Fe, NM: Red Crane Books.

Graves, W. (Ed.) (1991, October). 1491: America before Columbus. *National Geographic, 180* (4).

Graymount, B. (1988). *The Iroquois*. New York, NY: Chelsea.

Guidelines for Geographic Education: Elementary and Secondary Schools. (1984). Washington, D.C.: Joint Committee on Geographic Education of the National Council for Geographic Education and the Association of American Geographers.

Halliburton, W. J. (1989). *The Tragedy of Little Bighorn*. New York, NY: Franklin Watts.

Harlan, J. (1987). *American Indians Today*. New York, NY: Franklin Watts.

Harvey, K. D., Harjo, L. D., & Jackson, J. K. (1990). *Teaching About Native Americans*. Washington, D.C.: National Council for the Social Studies.

Hawke, S. D. & Davis, J. E. (1991). *Seeds of Change*. Palo Alto, CA: Addison-Wesley.

Henry, J. (Ed.). (1972). *The American Indian Reader: Education*. San Francisco, CA: The Indian Historian Press.

Heth, C. (Ed.). (1992). *Native American Dance: Ceremonies and Social Traditions*. Washington, D.C. National Museum of the American Indian Smithsonian Institution/Starwood.

Highwater, J. (1976). *Song from the Earth: American Indian Painting.* Boston, MA: New York Graphic Society.

Highwater, J. (1978). *Many Smokes. Many Moons: A Chronology of American Indian History Through Indian Art.* Philadelphia, PA: J. B. Lippincott.

Hirschfelder, A.B. (1982). *American Indian Stereotypes in the World of Children: A Reader and Bibliography.* Metuchen, NJ: Scarecrow.

Hirschfelder, A. (1986). *Happily May I Walk: American Indians and Alaska Natives Today.* New York, NY: Scribners.

Hirschfelder, A.B. & Singer, B.R. (1992). *Rising voices: Writings of Young Native Americans.* New York, NY: Charles Scribner's Sons.

Hofsinde, R. (1971). *Indian Arts.* New York, NY: William Morrow.

Hood, F. M. (1962). *Something for the Medicine Man.* Chicago, IL: Melmont.

Horse Capture, G. (1989). *Pow-wow.* Cody, WY: Buffalo Bill Historical Center.

How Can One Sell the Air?: The Manifesto for the Earth. Summertown, TN: Book Publishing Company.

Humphrey, W. (1989). *No Resting Place.* New York, NY: Dell.

Iverson, P. (1990). *The Navajos.* New York, NY: Chelsea.

Jacka, L. E. (1988, Winter). Moments with Maria. *Native Peoples,* pp. 24–29.

Jaimes, M. A. (Ed.). 1992. *The State of Native America.* Boston, MA: South End.

Jeffers, S. (1991). *Brother Eagle, Sister Sky.* New York, NY: Dial.

Jennings, J. D. (1984). *Prehistory of North America* (2nd edition). New York, NY: McGraw-Hill.

Jennings, J. D. (1989). Across an Arctic bridge. In J. B. Billard (Ed.), *The World of the American Indian* (pp. 29–69). Washington, DC: National Geographic Society.

Jensen, R. E., Paul, R. E. & Carter, J. E. (1991). *Eyewitness at Wounded Knee.* Lincoln, NE: University of Nebraska.

Johansen, B. (1982). *Forgotten Founders.* Ipswich, MA: Gambit Publishers.

Johnson, R. (1992, June 21). Diabetes ravages Arizona Indians. *Denver Post,* pp. 1A, 8A–9A.

Jones, B. F., Pierce, J. & Hunter, B. (December 1988/January 1989). Teaching students to construct graphic representations. *Educational Leadership,* pp. 20–25.

Josephy, A. M. Jr. (1971). *Red Power.* Lincoln, NE: University of Nebraska.

Josephy, A. M. Jr. (1985). *The Indian Heritage of America* (14th printing). New York, NY: Alfred A. Knopf.

Josephy, A. M. Jr. (1986). *Now That the Buffalo's Gone.* Norman, OK: University of Oklahoma.

Josephy, A. M. Jr. (1989). *The Patriot Chiefs.* New York, NY: Penguin.

Josephy, A. M. Jr., Thomas, T. & Eder, J. (1990). *Wounded Knee: Lest We Forget.* Cody, WY: Buffalo Bill Historical Center.

Judge, J. (1988, March). Between Columbus and Jamestown: Exploring our forgotten century. *National Geographic, 173* (3), pp. 330–363.

Kawano, K. (1992). *Warriors: Navajo Code Talkers.* Flagstaff, AZ: Northland.

Kawano, K. (Photographer). (1989, Summer). Faces of the code. *Native Peoples, 2* (4), pp. 24–28.

Keegan, M. (1972). *The Taos Indians and Their Sacred Blue Lake.* New York, NY: Julian Messner.

Keegan, M. (1991). *Taos Pueblo and Its Sacred Blue Lake.* Santa Fe, NM: Clear Light.

Kelly, L. C. (1990). *Federal Indian Policy.* New York, NY: Chelsea.

Kessel, J. K. (1983). *Squanto and the First Thanksgiving.* Minneapolis, MN: Carolrhoda.

Kickingbird, K. (1987). *Indians and the U.S. Constitution: A Forgotten Legacy.* Washington, D.C.: Institute for Development of Indian Law

Kissinger, R. K. (1991). *Quanah Parker: Comanche Chief.* Gretna, LA: Pelican.

Kopper, P. (Ed.). (1986). *The Smithsonian Book of North American Indians: Before the Coming of the Europeans.* Washington, D.C.: Smithsonian Books.

A Lakota Times Special: Wounded Knee Remembered 1890–1990. (1991, January 8). *Lakota Times.*

Lame Deer, J. (Fire) & Erdoes, R. (1976). *Lame Deer Seeker of Visions* (9th printing). New York, NY: Pocket.

Landau, E. (1989). *The Sioux.* New York, NY: Franklin Watts.

Las Casas, B. (1991). *The Log of Christopher Columbus' First Voyage to America in the Year 1492 as Copied Out in Brief by Bartholomew Las Casas.* Hamden, CT: Linnet.

Lazarus, E. (1991). *Black Hills/White Justice.* New York: HarperCollins.

Lee, M. (1989). *The Seminoles.* New York, NY: Franklin Watts.

Leon-Portilla, M. (Ed.). (1966). *The Broken Spears: The Aztec Account of the Conquest of Mexico.* Boston, MA: Beacon.

Levine, S. & Lurie, N. O. (Eds.). (1968). *American Indians Today.* Baltimore, MD: Penguin.

Liptak, K. (1990). *North American Indian Medicine People.* New York, NY: Franklin Watts.

Locke, R. F. (1992). *The Book of the Navajo* (5th edition). Los Angeles, CA: Mankind.

Luther, T. (1972). *Custer High Spots*. Ft. Collins, CO: The Old Army Press.

Lyons, G. (1978). *The Creek Indians*. New York, NY: Simon & Shuster.

Lyons, O., Mohawk, J., Deloria, V. Jr., Berman, H., Berkey, C., Grinde, D. Jr., Hauptman, L. & Venables, R. (1992). *Exiled in the Land of the Free: Democracy, Indian Nations and the U.S. Constitution*. Available from the Four Winds Trading Co. (800-456-5444).

MacLeish, W. H. (1991, November). 1492 America: The land Columbus never saw. *Smithsonian*, 22 (8), 31-52.

Mails, T. E. (1972). *The Mystic Warriors of the Plains*. Garden City, NY: Doubleday.

Mankiller, W. (1993). *Mankiller: A Chief and Her People*. New York, NY: St. Martins.

Marrin, A. (1984). *War Clouds in the West: Indians & Cavalrymen • 1860–1890*. New York, NY: Atheneum.

Marriott, A. (1948). *Maria: The Potter of San Ildefonso*. Norman, OK: University of Oklahoma.

Marriott, A. (1960). *The First Comers: Indians of America's Dawn*. New York, NY: Longmans, Green.

Marton, E. (1986). *Mysteries in American Archeology*. New York, NY: Walker.

Matthews, A. (1992). *Where the Buffalo Roam*. New York, NY: Grove Press.

Matthiessen, P. (1991). *In the Spirit of Crazy Horse*. New York, NY: Viking Penguin.

May, P. (1987, June). Suicide and self-destruction among American Indian youths. *American Indian and Alaska Native Mental Health Research Journal*. 1 (1), pp. 51–69.

McCarthy, G. & Marso, M. *Discovering Archaeology: Learning Through Arte-facts*. D.O.K. Publishers.

McCoy, R. (1992, Autumn). Repatriation. *American Indian Art Magazine*, p. 23.

McGaw, J. B. (1981). *Chief Red Horse Tells About Custer*. New York, NY: Lodestar/E.P. Dutton.

McLuhan, T.C. (1987). *Touch the Earth*. New York, NY: Promontory.

Merrell, J. H. (1989). *The Catawbas*. New York, NY: Chelsea.

Miniclier, K. (1992, August 2). Drumbeat of criticism pounds at BIA. *Denver Post*, pp. 1A, 4A.

Miniclier, K. (1992, September 13). Effects of gaming invasion spread. *Denver Post*, pp. 1C, 4C.

Moccasins on Pavement, the Indian Experience: A Denver Portrait. (1978). Denver, CO: Denver Museum of Natural History.

Mohawk, J. (1987, Winter). A symbol more powerful than paper. *Northeast Indian Quarterly*, 4 (4), foreword.

Momaday, N. S. (1968). *House Made of Dawn*. New York, NY: Harper & Row.

Mooney, J. (1991). *The Ghost-Dance Religion and the Sioux Outbreak of 1890*. Lincoln, NE: University of Nebraska.

Morris, G. & Means, R. (1991, October 12). Why AIM opposes Columbus Day and Columbus Day parades. *Denver Post*, p. 7B.

Morris, R. B. (1985). *The Indian Wars*. Minneapolis, MN: Lerner.

Nabhan, G. P. (1992, Spring). Native American cornucopia. *Native Peoples*, 5 (3), pp. 10–16.

Nabokov, P. (Ed.). (1991). *Native American Testimony*. New York, NY: Viking.

Name offers graphic link to Cherokee past. (1991, March 21). *The Fresno Bee*.

Native American Rights Fund. (1990). *Native American Rights Fund Annual Report*. Boulder, CO: Author.

Neihardt, J. G. (1932). *Black Elk Speaks*. New York, NY: Simon & Schuster.

O'Brien, S. (1989). *American Indian Tribal Governments*. Norman, OK: University of Oklahoma.

O'Dell, S. (1970). *Sing Down the Moon*. New York, NY: Dell.

O'Dell, S. (1987). *The Serpent Never Sleeps*. Boston, MA: Houghton Mifflin.

Ochoa, G. (1990). *The Fall of Quebec and the French and Indian War*. Englewood Cliffs, NJ: Silver Burdett.

Ortiz, A. (1991, October). Origins. *National Geographic*, 180 (4), pp. 6–7.

Ortiz, A., Brandenburg, H., Pascua, M. P., Stuart, G. E., Bruchac, J., Creamer, W. & Haas, J. (October, 1991). 1491: America Before Columbus. *National Geographic*, 180 (4), 4–99.

Ortiz, S. (1988). *The People Shall Continue* (revised edition). San Francisco, CA: Children's Book Press.

Ourada, P. (1990). *The Menominee*. New York, NY: Chelsea.

Paul, P. (1982). *Dance with Me Gods*. New York, NY: Lodestar.

Peace on Earth. (1991, Fall). *Native Peoples*, 5 (1), p. 7.

Peterson, S. (1977). *The Living Tradition of Maria Martinez*. Tokyo: Kodansha International.

Pevar, S. (1992). *The Rights of Indians and Tribes: The Basic ACLU Guide to Indian and Tribal Rights* (2nd edition). Carbondale, IL: University of Illinois Press.

Pewewardy, C. & Bushey, M. (1992, Summer). A family of learners and storytellers. *Native Peoples*, 5 (4), pp. 56–60.

Pickering, R. B. (1987). *I Can Be an Archaeologist*. Chicago, IL: Childrens Press.

Prucha, F. P. (1978). *Americanizing the American Indians* (reprint). Lincoln, NE: University of Nebraska.

Prucha, F. P. (1988). *The Great Father* (2nd printing). Lincoln, NE: University of Nebraska.

Prucha, F. P. (1990). *Documents of United States Indian Policy* (2nd edition). Lincoln, NE: University of Nebraska.

Red Hawk, R. (1988). *A Trip to a Powwow.* Newcastle, CA: Sierra Oaks.

Red Hawk, R. (1988). *Grandfather's Origin Story: The Navajo Indian Beginning.* Newcastle, CA: Sierra Oaks.

Roberts, C. (1988, Summer). Rocky Boy. *Native Peoples,* pp. 2–7.

Roman, J. (1992). *King Philip: Wampanoag Rebel.* New York, NY: Chelsea.

Roop, P. & Roop, C. (1990). *I. Columbus: My Journal 1492–3.* New York, NY: Walker.

Sale, K. (1990). *The Conquest of Paradise: Christopher Columbus and the Columbian Legacy.* New York, NY: Alfred A. Knopf.

Sanders, S. (1990). *Our First Twenty Years.* Boulder, CO: Native American Rights Fund.

Sando, J. (1976). *The Pueblo Indians.* San Francisco, CA: The Indian Historian Press.

Santos, J. S. (1976). *The Pueblo Indians.* San Francisco, CA: The Indian Historian Press.

Savilla, E. M. (1992, Late April). High stakes on gambling in Indian Country. *News From Indian Country, VI,* (8), pp. 6–7.

Scharf, G. *The Great Law of Peace and the Constitution of the United States of America.* North Bend, WA: Gregory Schaff, n.d. Order from Dr. Gregory Schaff, 44626 S.E. 151 Place, North Bend, WA 98045.

Schultz, D. (1990). *Month of the Freezing Moon.* New York, NY: St. Martin's.

Schwartz, J. (1991, Fall/Winter) The great food migration. *Newsweek* (Special Issue), p. 62.

Scofield, J. (1975, November). Christopher Columbus and the new world he found. *National Geographic, 148* (5), pp. 584–626.

Scott, J. A. (1990). *Settlers on the Eastern Shore: 1607–1750.* New York, NY: Facts on File.

Seawall, M. (1986). *The Pilgrims of Plimoth.* New York, NY: Atheneum.

Secrets from the Past. (1979). Washington, D.C.: National Geographic Society.

Selam, L. (1972). Suwaptsa. In J. Henry (Ed.), *The American Indian Reader: Education.* San Francisco, CA: The Indian Historian Press.

Sharp, S. (1991). *Columbus and the Americas 1492–1991: Discovery and Encounter.* Petaluma, CA: Pomegranate Calendars & Books.

Sharpe, J. D. (1988). *The Cherokees Past and Present* (8th printing). Cherokee, NC: Cherokee Publications.

Shears, B. L. & Wyaco, R. (1990, Summer). Hawikku: A fabled city of Cibola. *Native peoples, 3* (4), pp. 20–24.

Shemie, B. (1989). *Houses of Snow, Skin and Bones: Native Dwellings of the Far North.* Montreal: Tundra.

Shemie, B. (1991). *Houses of Hide and Earth: Native Dwellings of the Plains Indians.* Montreal: Tundra.

Shemie, B. (1992) *Houses of Bark: Native Dwellings of the Woodland Indians.* Montreal: Tundra.

Shemie, B. (1992). *Houses of Wood: Native Dwellings of the Northwest Coast.* Montreal: Tundra.

Shorto, R. (1989). *Tecumseh and the Dream of an American Indian Nation.* Englewood Cliffs, NJ: Silver Burdett.

Siegel, B. (1981). *Fur Trappers and Traders.* New York, NY: Walker.

Silko, L. M. (1986). *Ceremony.* New York, NY: Penguin.

Silverberg, R. (1986). *The Mound Builders.* Columbus, OH: Ohio University.

Simonelli, R. (1991, Summer). Indian Education in America. *Winds of Change, 6* (3), pp. 12–17.

Simpson, L. B. (1966). *The Encomienda in New Spain.* Berkeley, CA: University of California, pp. 127–128.

Slapin, B. & Seale, D. (1989). *Books Without Bias: Through Indian Eyes.* Berkeley, CA: Oyate.

Smith, C. (Ed.). (1992). *Native Americans of the West.* Brookfield, CT: Millbrook.

Smith, G. (1980, January). Utah's rock art: Wilderness Louvre. *National Geographic, 157* (1), pp. 97–117.

Smith, H. E. Jr. (1989). *All About Arrowheads and Spear Points.* New York, NY: Henry Holt & Company.

Sneve, V. (1989). *Dancing Teepees.* New York, NY: Holiday House.

Sorkin, A. (1978). *The Urban American Indian.* Lexington, KY: Lexington.

Spencer, P. (1983). *Who Speaks for Wolf?* Austin, TX: Tribe of Two Press.

Spencer, P. (1984). *Who Speaks for Wolf: Teacher's Guide.* Austin, TX: Tribe of Two Press.

Spencer, P. (1987). The Great Tree of Peace—Symbol of the Iroquois Confederacy—Part of our national heritage. *Kui Tatk,* 1987, Fall. Order from Native American Science and Education Association, 1333 H. Street N.W. Washington, D.C. 20005.

Spicer, E. H. (1982). *The American Indians.* Cambridge, MA: Belknap Press of Harvard University Press.

Spicer, E. H. (1983). *A Short History of the Indians of the United States* (reprint). Malabar, FL: Robert E. Kreiger.

Spivey, R. L. (1979). *Maria.* Flagstaff, AZ: Northland.

Standing Bear, L. (1975). *My People the Sioux* (7th printing). Lincoln, NE: University of Nebraska.

Standing Bear. L. (1978). *Land of the Spotted Eagle* (reprint). Lincoln,

Stein, R. C. (1983). *The Story of Wounded Knee*. Chicago, IL: Childrens Press.

Stein, R. C. (1985). *The Story of the Trail of Tears*. Chicago, IL. Childrens Press.

Steiner, S. (1968). *The New Indians*. New York, NY: Delta.

Steward, O. (1987). *Peyote Religion: A History*. Norman, OK: University of Oklahoma.

Storm, H. (1972). *Seven Arrows*. New York, NY: Ballantine Books.

Stuart, G. E. (1972, December). Mounds: Riddles from the Indian past. *National Geographic, 142* (6), pp. 783–801.

Suina, J. (1992). And then I went to school: Memories of a Pueblo childhood. In B. Bigelow, B. Miner, & B. Peterson (Eds.), *Rethinking Columbus* (4th edition) (pp. 34–36). Portland, OR: Rethinking Schools.

Suina, J. H. (1992, January). Pueblo secrecy result of intrusion. *New Mexico Magazine, 70* (1), pp 60–63.

Suzuki, D. & Knudtson, P. (1992). *Wisdom of the Elders: Sacred Native Stories of Nature*. New York, NY: Bantam.

Svaldi, D. (1989). *Sand Creek and the Rhetoric of Extermination: A Case Study in Indian-White Relations*. Lanham, MD: University Press.

Szasz, M. C. (1974). *Education and the American Indian*. Albuquerque, NM: University of New Mexico.

Taliman, V. (1992, Late April). Tribes take MRS funding. *News From Indian Country, VI,* (8), p. 10.

Taliman, V. (1992, Late March). Mescalero people fear "Chino Dump". *News From Indian Country, VI,* (6), p. 11.

Taliman, V. (1992, Late March). Sacred ground slated for asbestos dump. *News From Indian Country, VI,* (6), p. 13.

Talliman, V. (1992, Mid-May). The toxic waste of Indian lives. *News From Indian Country, VI,* (10), pp. 6–7.

Tamarin, A. & Glubok, S. (1975). *Ancient Indians of the Southwest*. Garden City, NY: Doubleday.

Taylor, C. F. (1991). *The Native Americans*. New York, NY: Smithmark.

Thompson, T. (Ed.). (1978). *The Schooling of Native America*. Washington, D.C.: U.S. Department of Education.

Thornton, R. (1987). *American Indian Holocaust and Survival*. Norman, OK: University of Oklahoma.

Tomchek, A. H. (1987). *The Hopi*. Chicago, IL: Childrens Press.

Trail of Broken Treaties: B.I.A. I'm Not Your Indian Anymore (2nd edition). (1974). Rooseveltown, NY: Akwesasne Notes, Mohawk Nation.

Trimble, S. (1990). *The Village of Blue Stone*. New York, NY: Macmillan.

Udall, S. L. (1990, Summer). The battle of Hawikuh. *Native Peoples, 3* (4). pp. 25–29.

Underhill, R. M. (1965). *Red Man's Religion*. Chicago, IL: University of Chicago.

Underwood T.B. (1961). *The Story of the Cherokee People*. Cherokee, NC: Cherokee Publications.

Underwood, T.B. (1989). *Cherokee Legends and the Trail of Tears* (18th printing). Cherokee, NC: Cherokee Publishing.

United States Commission on Civil Rights. (1980, September). *American Indian Civil Rights Handbook*. Washington, D.C: Author.

Vanderwerth, W. C. (1971). *Indian Oratory*. New York, NY: Ballantine.

Vecsey, C. (Ed.). (1991). *Handbook of American Indian Religious Freedom*. New York, NY: Crossroad.

Viola, H. J. (Ed.) (1990). *After Columbus: The Smithsonian Chronicle of the North America Indian*. Washington, D.C.: Smithsonian/Orion Books.

Viola, H. J. & Margolis, C. (Eds.). (1991). *Seeds of Change: A Quincentennial Commemoration*. Washington, D.C: Smithsonian Institution Press.

Viola, H. J. & Smith, R. M. (Eds.) (1991, Fall/Winter). When worlds collide: How Columbus voyages transformed both east and west. *Newsweek* (Columbus Special Issue, a joint project with the Smithsonian Institute's Natural History Exhibit "Seeds of Change").

Voices from Wounded Knee, 1973. (1974). Rooseveltown, NY: Akwesasne Notes, Mohawk Nation.

Waldman, C. (1985). *Atlas of the North American Indian*. New York, NY: Facts on File.

Waldman, C. (1988). *Encyclopedia of Native American Tribes*. New York, NY: Facts on File.

Waldman, C. (1990). *Who Was Who in Native American History*. New York, NY: Facts on File.

Wall, S. & Arden, H. (1990). *Wisdomkeepers*. Hillsboro, OR: Beyond Words.

Watts, J. G. (1991, Summer). Sacred circle. *Native Peoples, 4* (4), pp. 34–39.

Weatherford, J. (1988). *Indian Givers: How the Indians of the Americas Transformed the World*. New York, NY: Fawcett Columbine.

Weatherford, J. (1991). *Native Roots*. New York, NY: Crown.

Weigle, M. & White, P. (1988). *The Lore of New Mexico*. Albuquerque, NM: University of New Mexico.

West, P. (1992, September 30). Indians work to save a language—and their heritage. *Education Week*, pp. 1, 16–17.

Williams, J. (1992). *Trail of Tears*. Dallas, TX: Hendrick-Long.

Wills, C. (1990). *The Battle of the Little Bighorn*. Englewood Cliffs, NJ: Silver Burdett.

Wilson, M. (1987, Fall). Naming Beverly's baby. *Native Peoples*, pp. 2–5.

Wisecarver, C. W. F. (1990, Spring). Wounded Knee: Mending the sacred hoop. *Native Peoples*, 3 (3), pp 8–16.

Wissler, C. (1989). *Indians of the United States* (reprint). New York, NY: Doubleday.

Wolf, B. (1973). *Tinker and the Medicine Man*. New York, NY: Random House.

Wolfson, E. (1992). *The Iroquois: People of the Northeast*. Brookfield, CT: Millbrook.

Wolfson, E. (1992). *The Teton Sioux: People of the Plains*. Brookfield, CT: Millbrook.

Wood, L. H. (1991). *The Navajo Indians*. New York, NY: Chelsea.

Wood, N. & Wood, M. (1972). *Hollering Sun*. New York, NY: Simon and Schuster.

Wood, T. with Afraid of Hawk, W. N. (1992). *A Boy Becomes a Man at Wounded Knee*. New York, NY: Walker.

Work, J. C. (1990). *Prose and Poetry of the American West*. Lincoln, NE: University of Nebraska.

Year of the American Indian. (1991–1992). *Native Monthly Reader*, 3 (5), p. 3.

Yolen, J. (1992). *Encounter*. San Diego, CA: Harcourt Brace Jovanovich.

Yue, C. & Yue, D. (1988). *The Igloo*. Boston, MA: Houghton Mifflin.

Yue, D. & Yue, C. (1984). *The Tipi*. New York, NY: Alfred A. Knopf.

Yue, D. & Yue, C. (1986). *The Pueblo*. Boston, MA: Houghton Mifflin.

Zinn, H. (1981). *A People's History of the United States*. New York, NY: Harper & Row.

SIMULATIONS/VIDEOS

Connecticut Public Television (Producer). (n.d.). *The New Pequot: A Tribal Portrait*. Available from Native American Public Broadcasting Consortium.

Dig 2: A Simulation in Archaeology. Interact. Available from Social Studies School Service Catalog, 1992.

Educational Communications (Producer). (1974). *Menominee* (Video). Available from Native American Public Broadcasting Consortium.

Lewis, A. J. (Producer). (1986). *Gannagaro*. Rochester, NY: WXXI-TV. Available from Native American Public Broadcasting Consortium.

Madison, C. (Producer). (1983). *Huteetl: Koyukon Memorial Potlatch* (Video). Available from the Native American Public Broadcasting Consortium.

McCarthy, T. (Producer). (1986). *Navajo Code Talkers* (Video). KENW-TV. Available from Native American Public Broadcasting Consortium.

National Endowment for the Humanities (Producer). (1982). *An Ancient Gift* (Video). Flagstaff, AZ: Northern Arizona Museum.

Nebraska Educational Television (Producer). (nd.) *Dancing to Give Thanks* (Video). Available from the Native American Public Broadcasting Consortium.

NETCHE (Producer). (1987). *The Treaty of 1868* (Video). Available from the Native American Public Broadcasting Consortium.

NETCHE (Producer). (1987). *The Black Hills Claim* (Video). Available from the Native American Public Broadcasting Consortium.

Nez Perce: Portrait of a People. National Park Service. Available from Social Studies School Service 1992 catalog.

Pate, G. S., Hollowell, J., Ging, B. (1982). *The Trail of Tears: An Inquiry Simulation*. Tucson, AZ: GSP. Available from Social Studies School Service catalog, 1992.

Peace River Films and KAET-TV (Producers). (1985). *Seasons of a Navajo* (Video). Available from the Native American Public Broadcasting Consortium.

Powwow (Video). Available from Social Studies School Service 1992 catalog.

Sioux Legends (Video). Available from Social Studies School Service 1992 catalog.

Site Anasazi: CA. A.D. 900–1300. (1989). Available from Social Studies School Service 1992 catalog.

Sitting Bull: Tatankaiyotake (Video). (1988). Available from Social Studies School Service 1992 catalog.

Tahtonka (Video). Available from Social Studies School Service 1992 catalog.

Tellens (Producer). (1982). *Navajo* (Video). Flagstaff, AZ: Museum of Northern Arizona.

United States National Park Service. (1980). *Maria: Indian Pottery Maker of San Ildefonso* (Video). United States National Park Service.

VCA—Wiping the Tears. *Wiping the Tears of Seven Generations* (Video). Leonia, NJ: Producer. This is an award-winning video of the Big Foot Memorial Ride. Available for $29.95 (plus $4.00 shipping) from VCA—Wiping the Tears, 50 Leyland Drive, Leonia, NJ 07605. A portion of the proceeds go to Lakota educational institutions.

Index